SOUL EATER

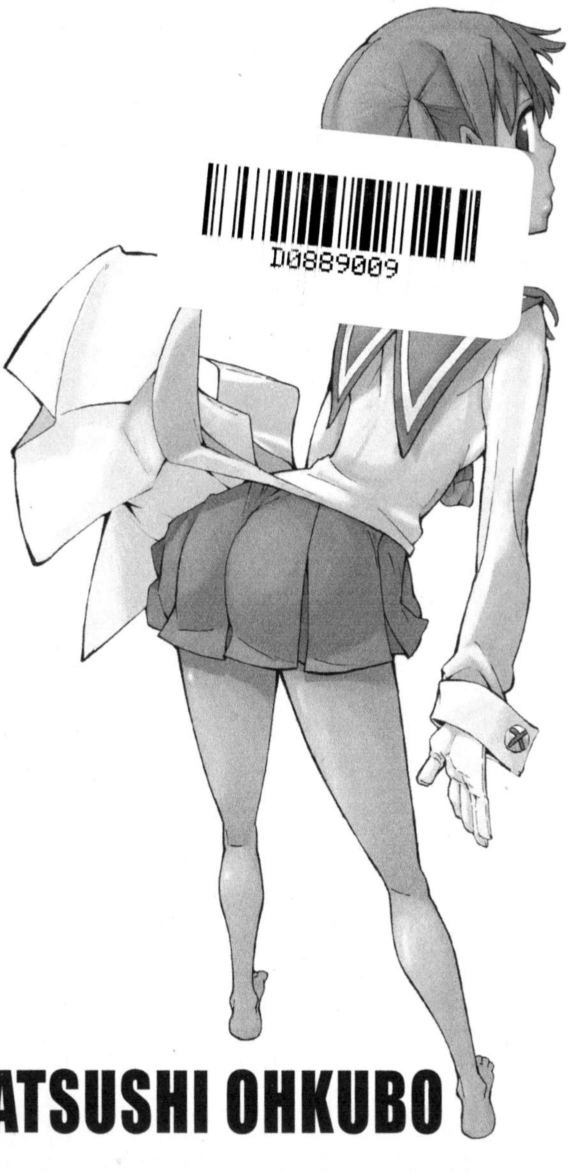

ATSUSHI OHKUBO

19

SOUL EATER

vol. 18
by ATSUSHI OHKUBO

The SOUL does what the SOUL pleases

SOUL EATER 19

CONTENTS

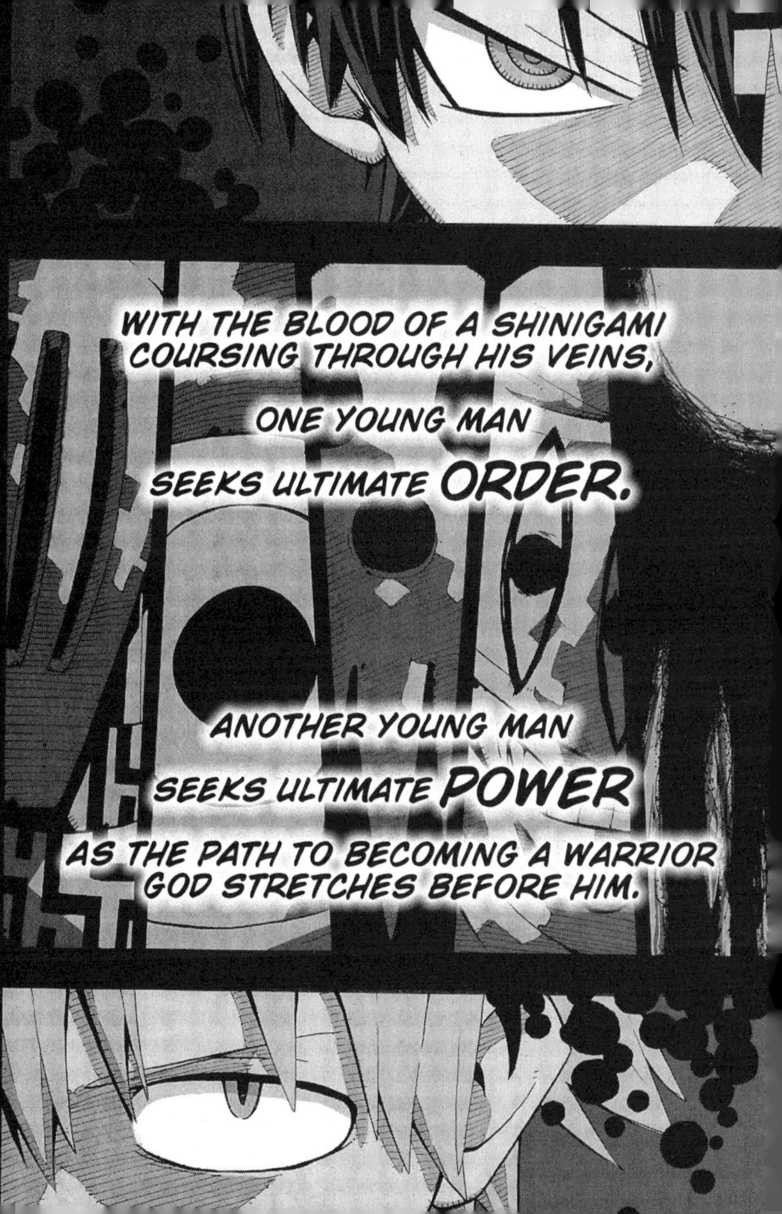
WITH THE BLOOD OF A SHINIGAMI COURSING THROUGH HIS VEINS,
ONE YOUNG MAN
SEEKS ULTIMATE ORDER.
ANOTHER YOUNG MAN
SEEKS ULTIMATE POWER
AS THE PATH TO BECOMING A WARRIOR GOD STRETCHES BEFORE HIM.

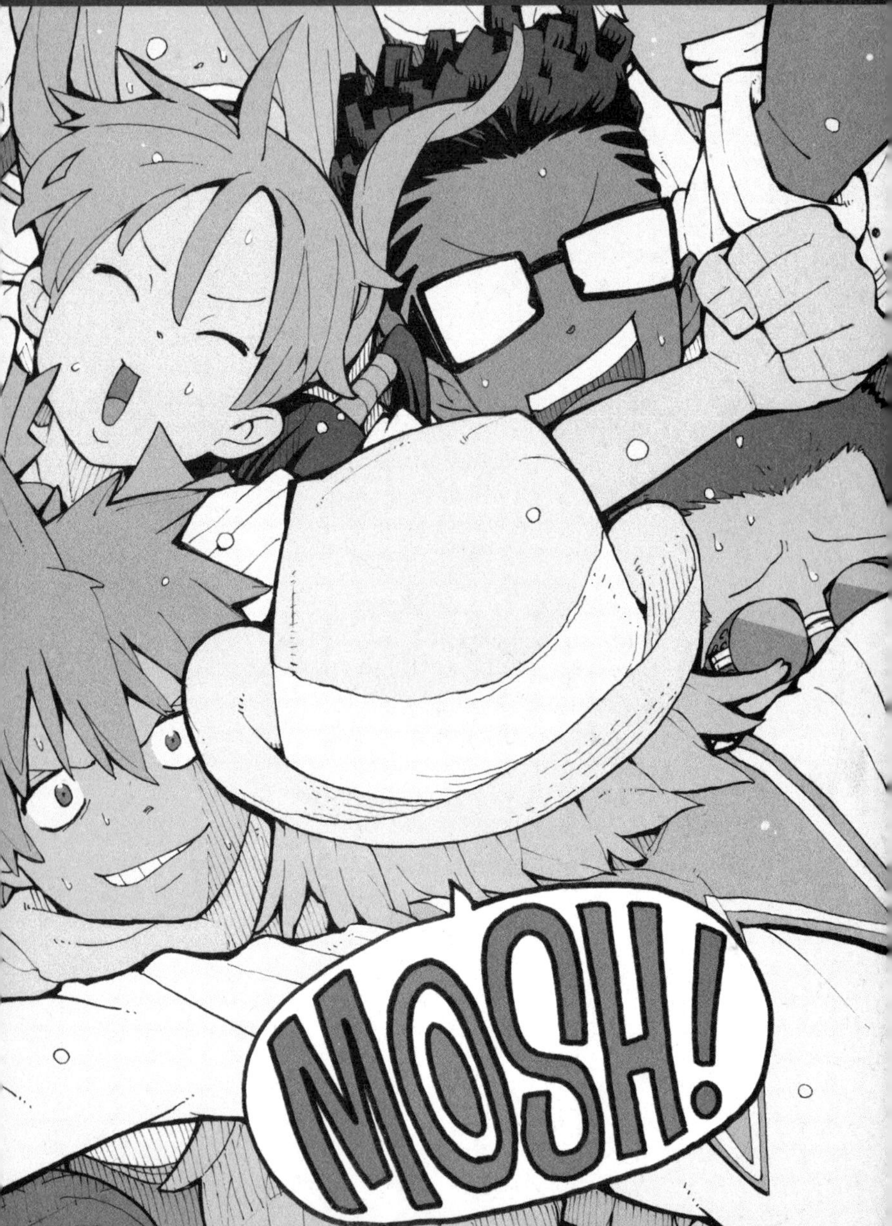
MOSH!

CHAPTER 77: SALVAGE (PART 6)

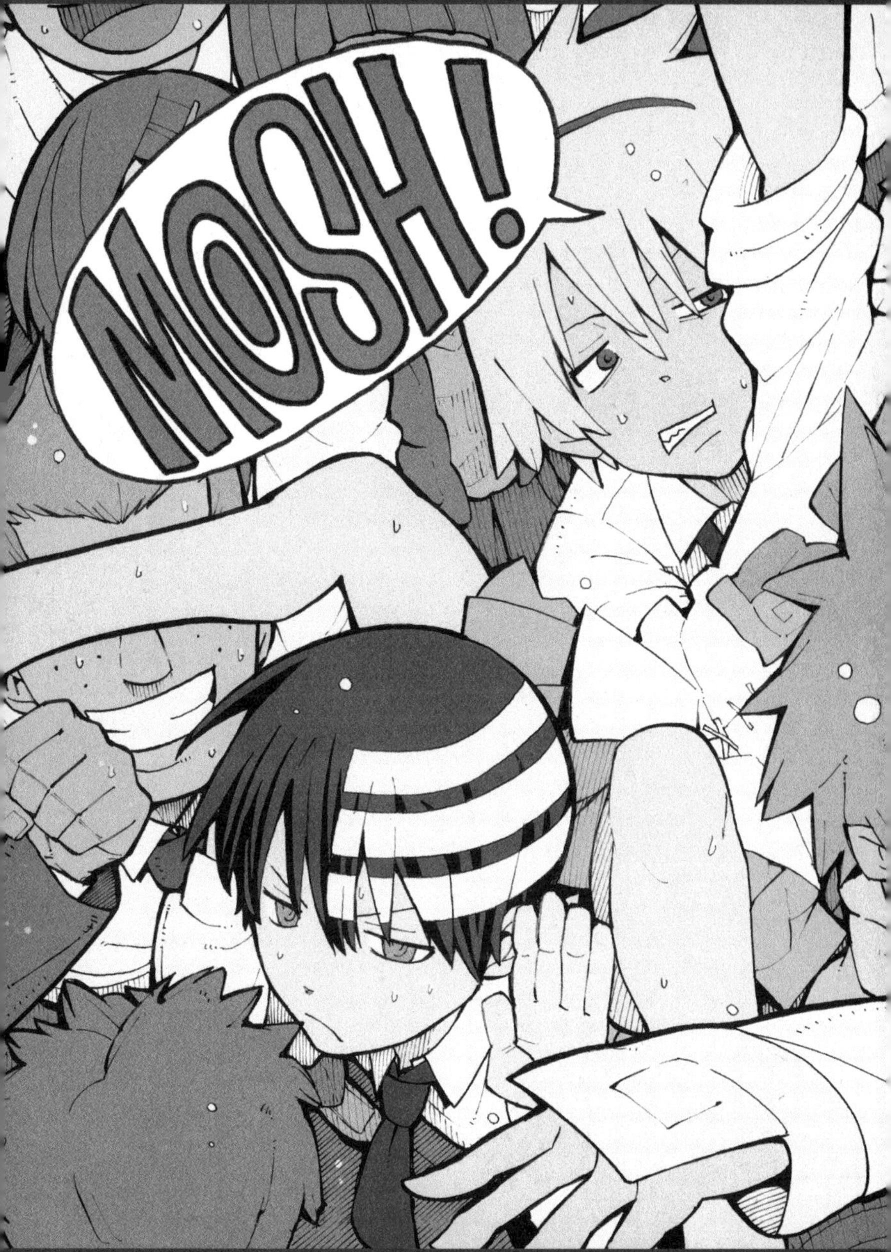
MOSH!

SOUL EATER

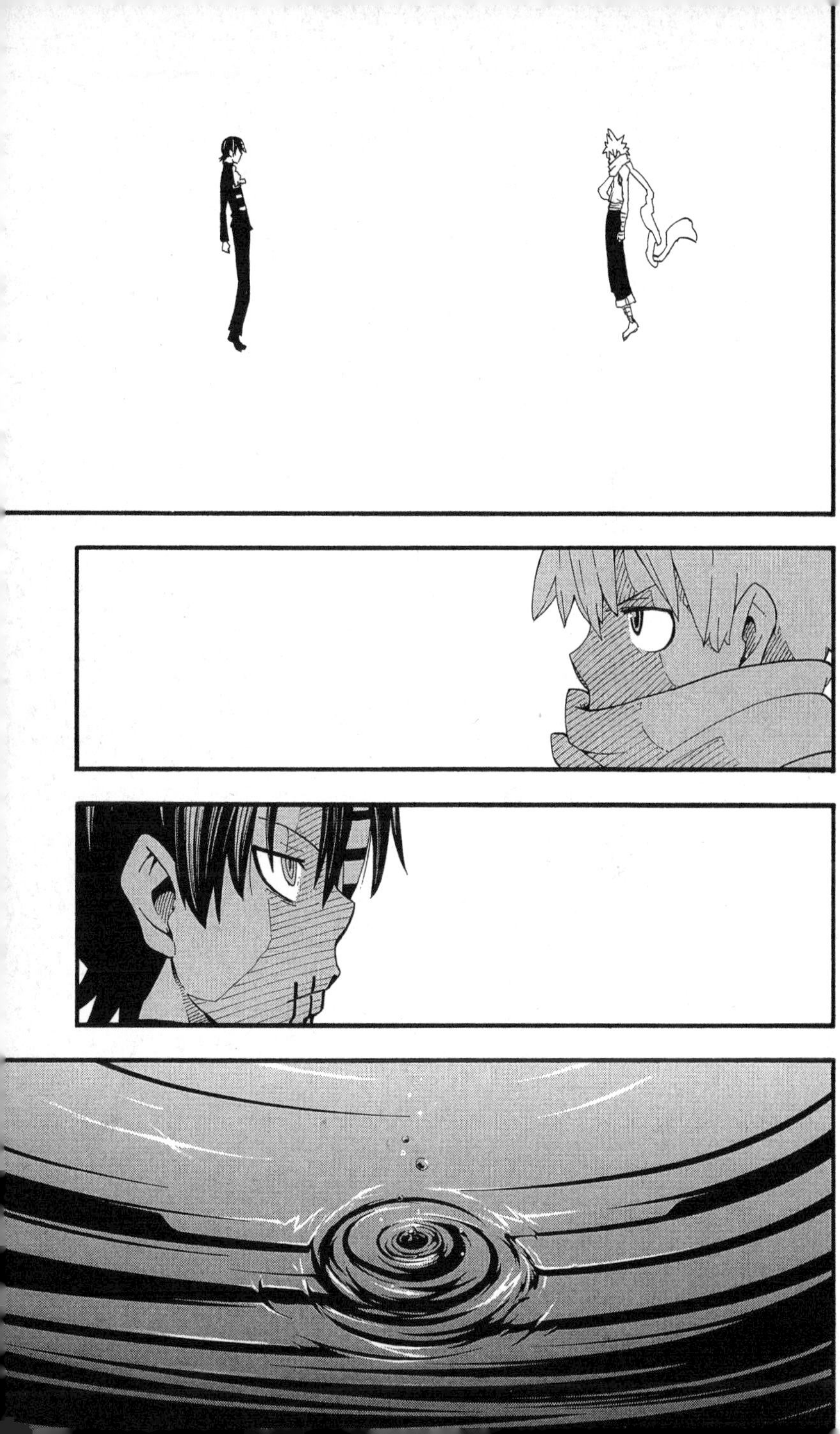

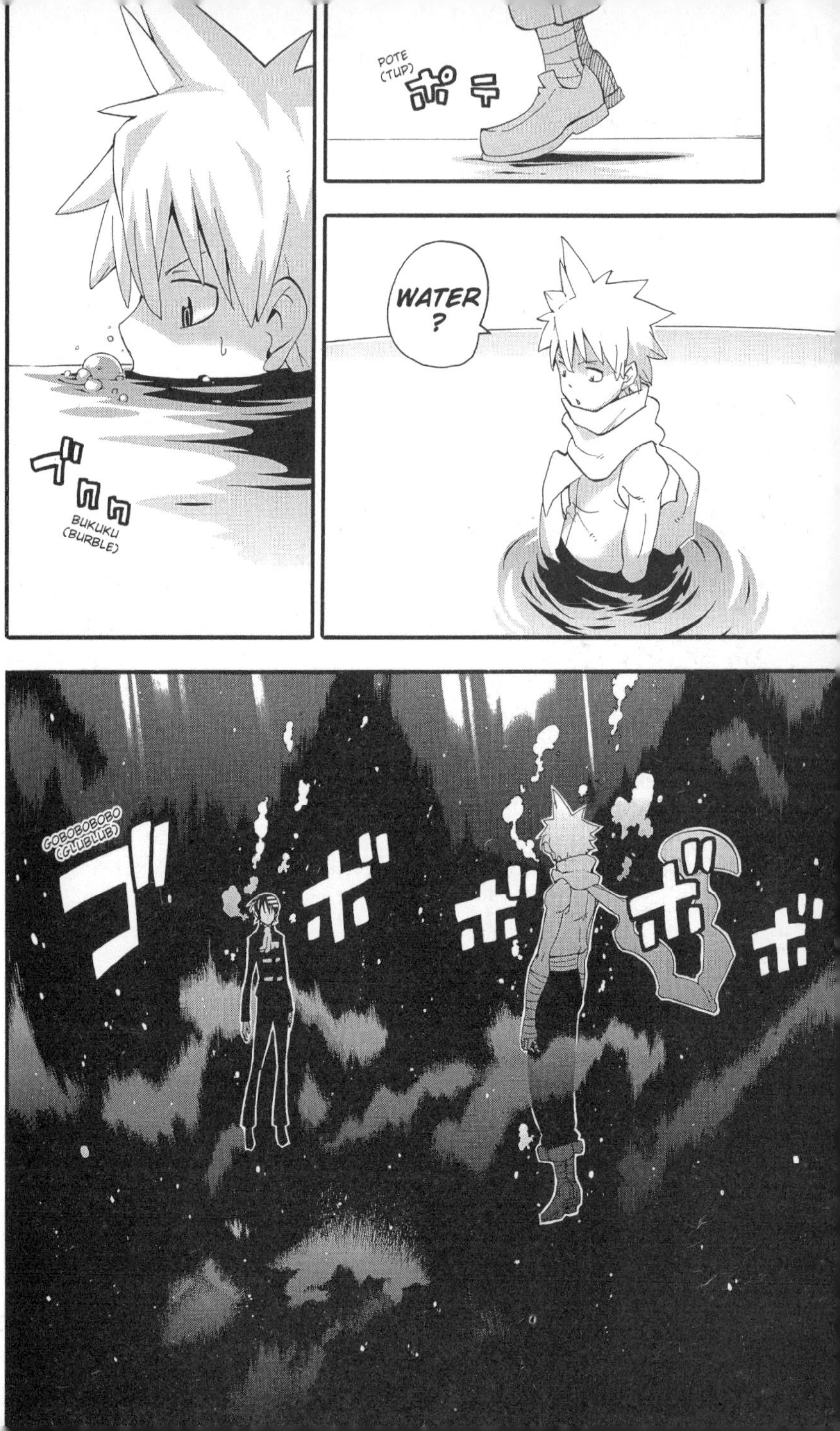
POTE (TUP)
ポテ
WATER ?
ブクク
BUKUKU (BURBLE)
GOBOBOBO (GLUBLUB)
ゴボボボボ

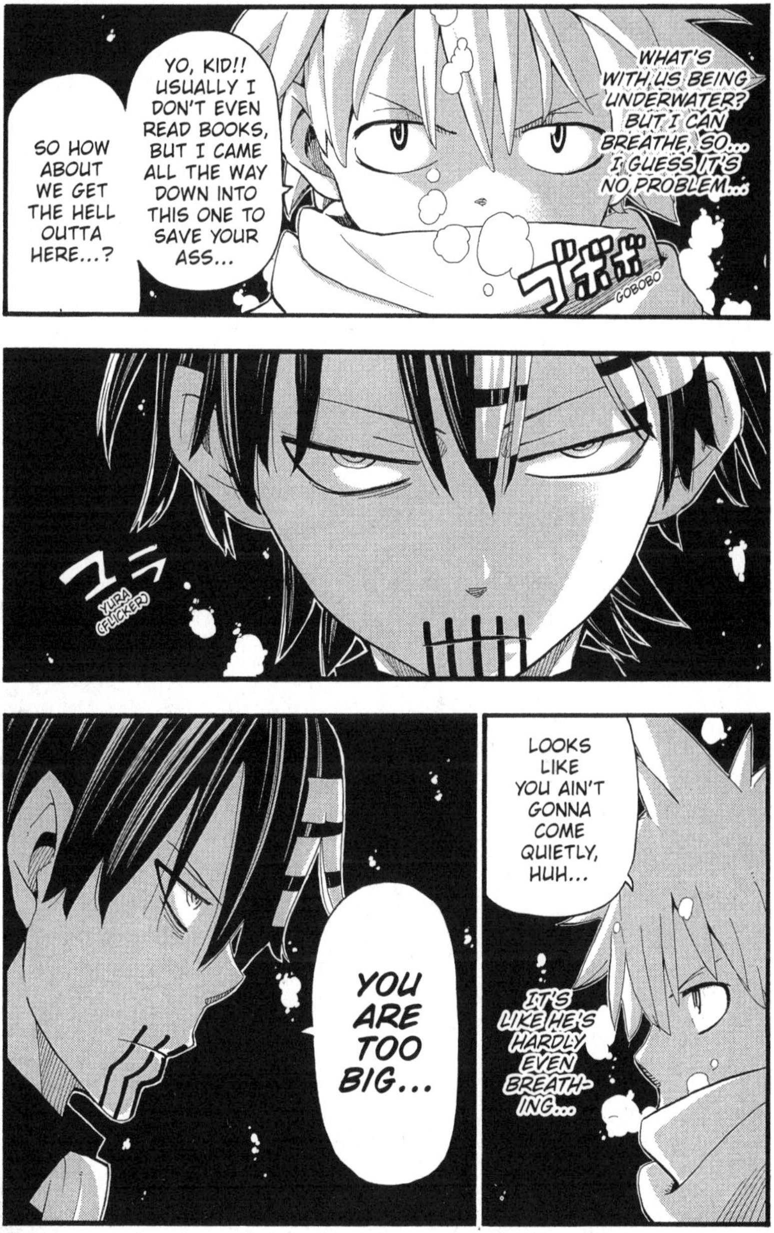
WHAT'S WITH US BEING UNDERWATER? BUT I CAN BREATHE, SO... I GUESS IT'S NO PROBLEM...
ゴボボ
GOBOBO
YO, KID!! USUALLY I DON'T EVEN READ BOOKS, BUT I CAME ALL THE WAY DOWN INTO THIS ONE TO SAVE YOUR ASS...
SO HOW ABOUT WE GET THE HELL OUTTA HERE...?
ユラ
YURA (FLICKER)
LOOKS LIKE YOU AIN'T GONNA COME QUIETLY, HUH...
IT'S LIKE HE'S HARDLY EVEN BREATH-ING...
YOU ARE TOO BIG...

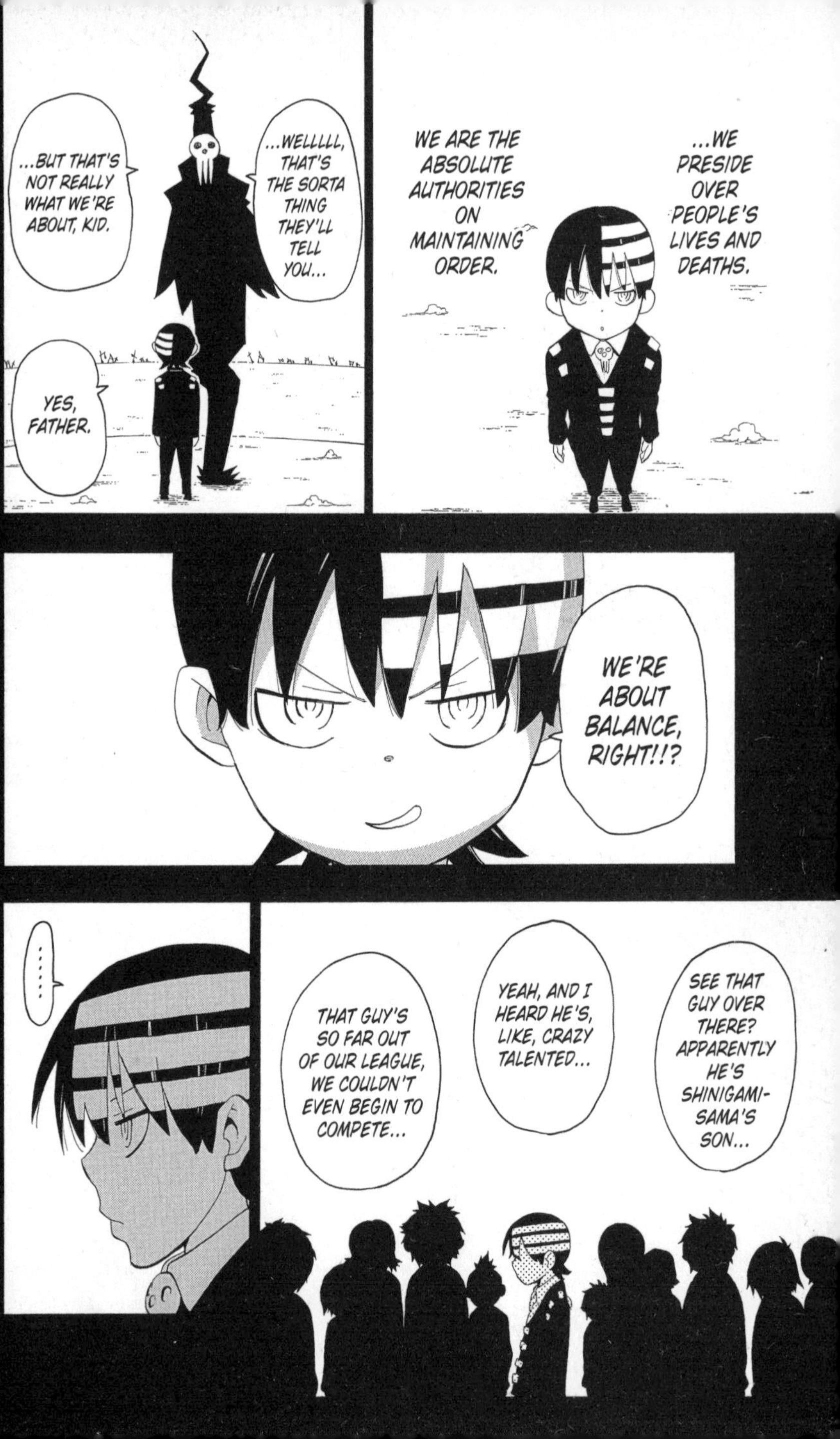
...WE PRESIDE OVER PEOPLE'S LIVES AND DEATHS.
WE ARE THE ABSOLUTE AUTHORITIES ON MAINTAINING ORDER.
...WELLLLL, THAT'S THE SORTA THING THEY'LL TELL YOU...
...BUT THAT'S NOT REALLY WHAT WE'RE ABOUT, KID.
YES, FATHER.
WE'RE ABOUT BALANCE, RIGHT!!?
SEE THAT GUY OVER THERE? APPARENTLY HE'S SHINIGAMI-SAMA'S SON...
YEAH, AND I HEARD HE'S, LIKE, CRAZY TALENTED...
THAT GUY'S SO FAR OUT OF OUR LEAGUE, WE COULDN'T EVEN BEGIN TO COMPETE...
......

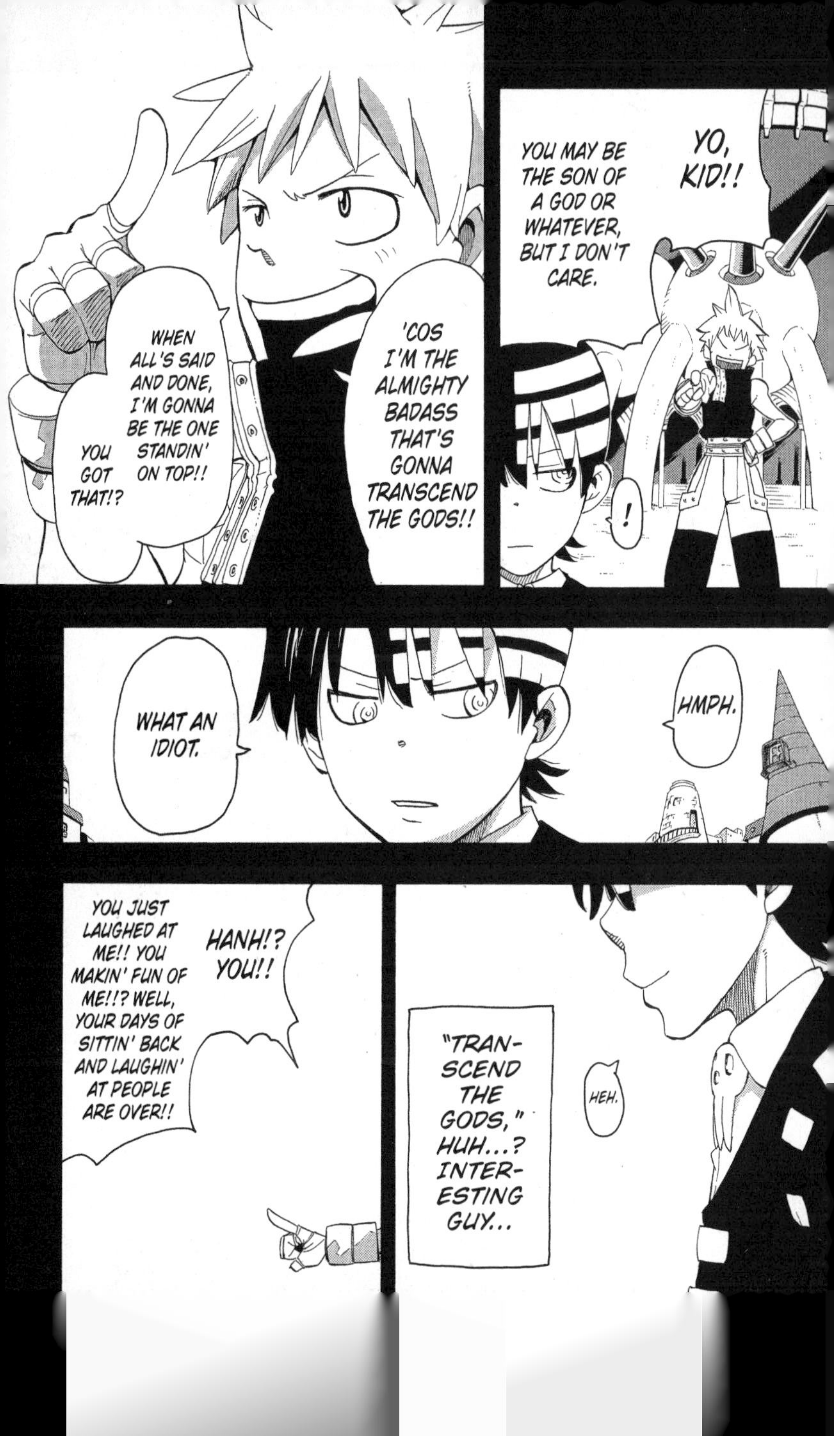
YO, KID!!
YOU MAY BE THE SON OF A GOD OR WHATEVER, BUT I DON'T CARE.
!
'COS I'M THE ALMIGHTY BADASS THAT'S GONNA TRANSCEND THE GODS!!
WHEN ALL'S SAID AND DONE, I'M GONNA BE THE ONE STANDIN' ON TOP!!
YOU GOT THAT!?
HMPH.
WHAT AN IDIOT.
HEH.
"TRAN-SCEND THE GODS," HUH...? INTER-ESTING GUY...
HANH!? YOU!!
YOU JUST LAUGHED AT ME!! YOU MAKIN' FUN OF ME!!? WELL, YOUR DAYS OF SITTIN' BACK AND LAUGHIN' AT PEOPLE ARE OVER!!

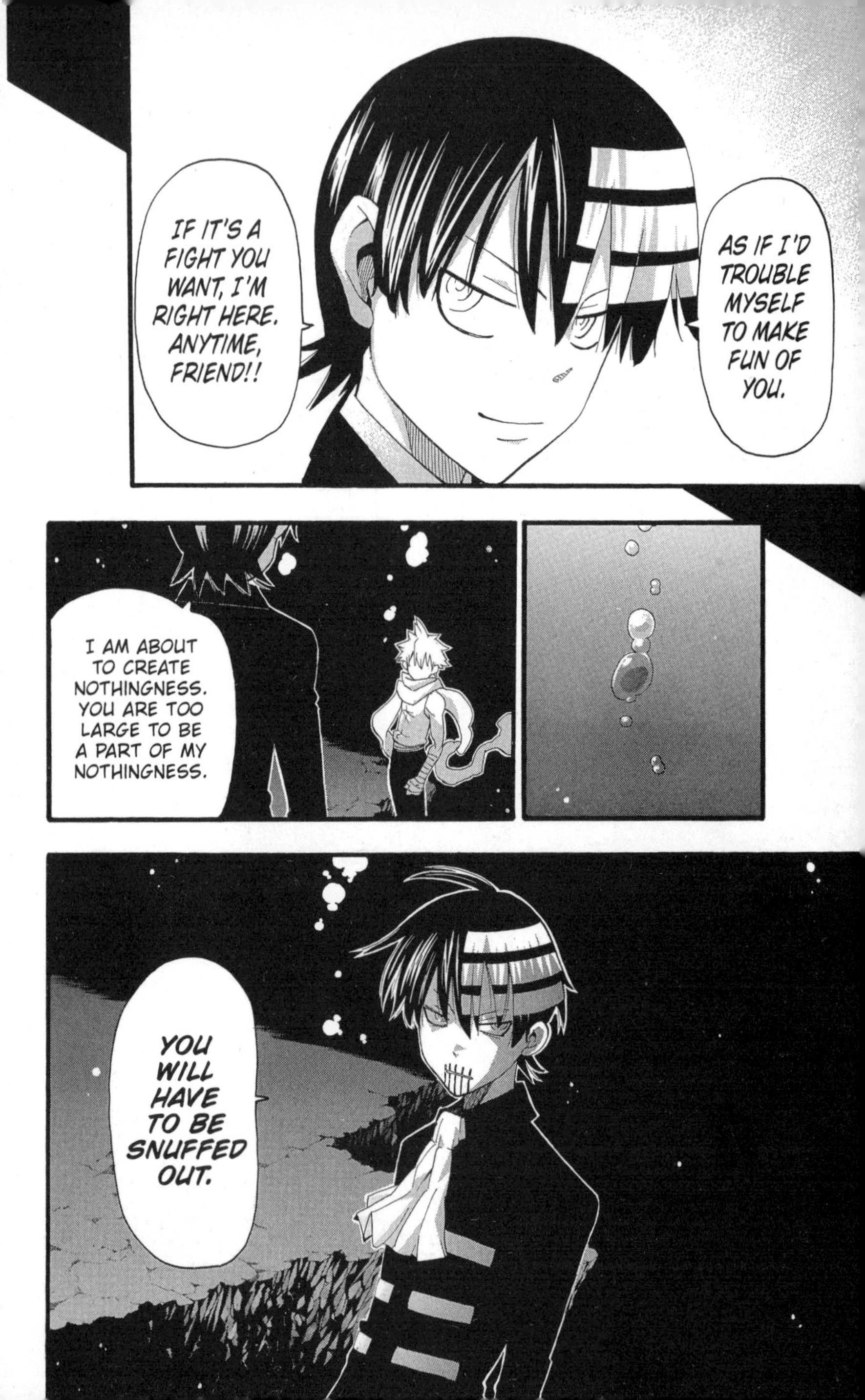
AS IF I'D TROUBLE MYSELF TO MAKE FUN OF YOU.
IF IT'S A FIGHT YOU WANT, I'M RIGHT HERE. ANYTIME, FRIEND!!
I AM ABOUT TO CREATE NOTHINGNESS. YOU ARE TOO LARGE TO BE A PART OF MY NOTHINGNESS.
YOU WILL HAVE TO BE SNUFFED OUT.

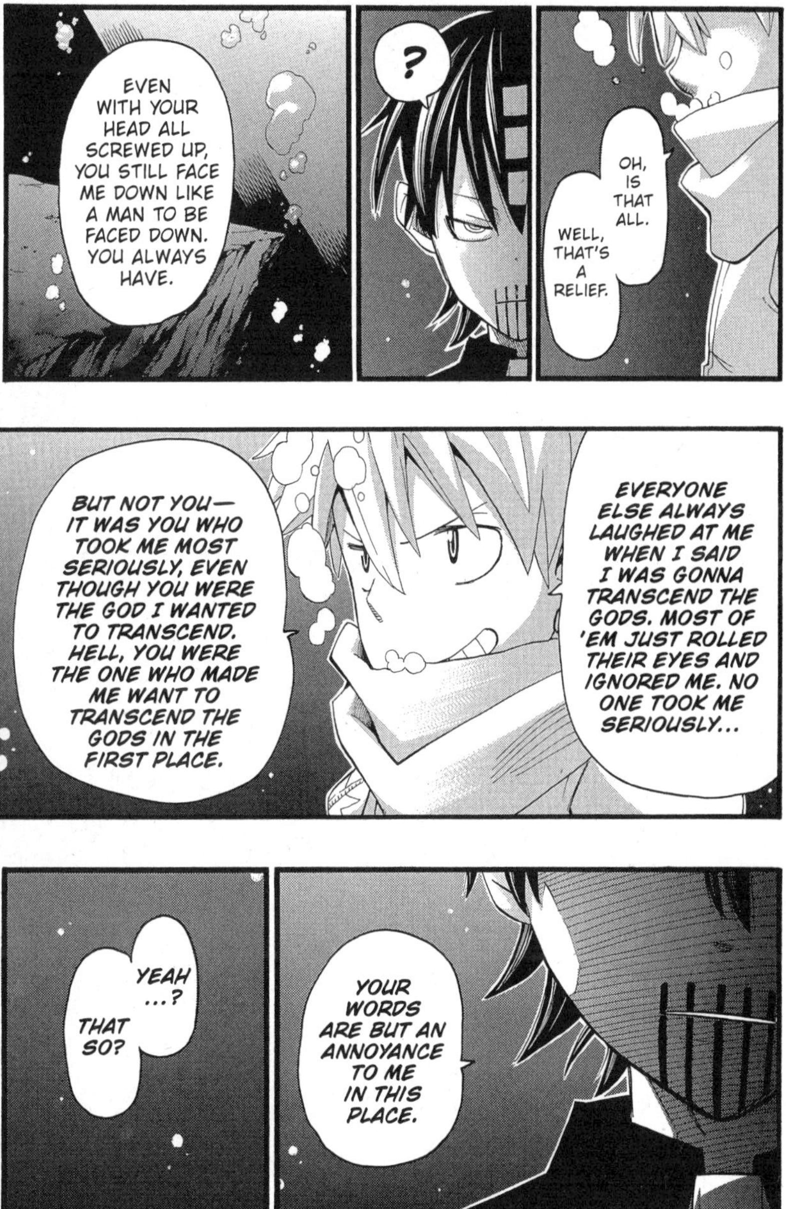
OH, IS THAT ALL.
WELL, THAT'S A RELIEF.
?
EVEN WITH YOUR HEAD ALL SCREWED UP, YOU STILL FACE ME DOWN LIKE A MAN TO BE FACED DOWN. YOU ALWAYS HAVE.
EVERYONE ELSE ALWAYS LAUGHED AT ME WHEN I SAID I WAS GONNA TRANSCEND THE GODS. MOST OF 'EM JUST ROLLED THEIR EYES AND IGNORED ME. NO ONE TOOK ME SERIOUSLY...
BUT NOT YOU— IT WAS YOU WHO TOOK ME MOST SERIOUSLY, EVEN THOUGH YOU WERE THE GOD I WANTED TO TRANSCEND. HELL, YOU WERE THE ONE WHO MADE ME WANT TO TRANSCEND THE GODS IN THE FIRST PLACE.
YOUR WORDS ARE BUT AN ANNOYANCE TO ME IN THIS PLACE.
YEAH ...?
THAT SO?

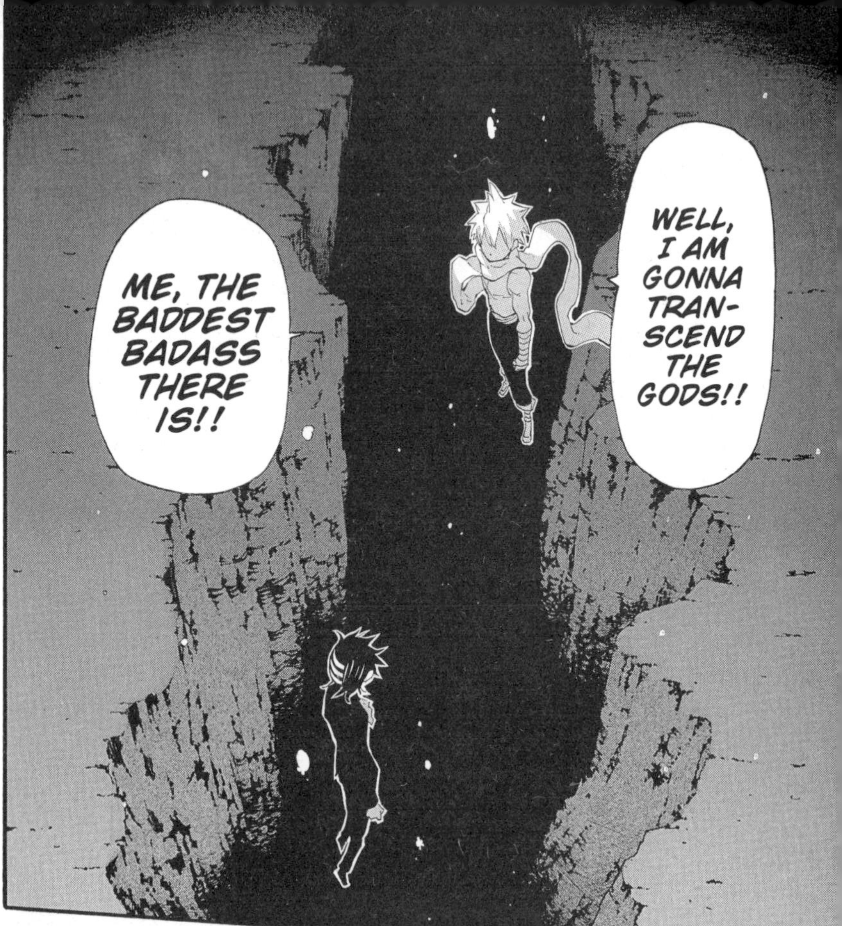
WELL, I AM GONNA TRAN-SCEND THE GODS!!
ME, THE BADDEST BADASS THERE IS!!
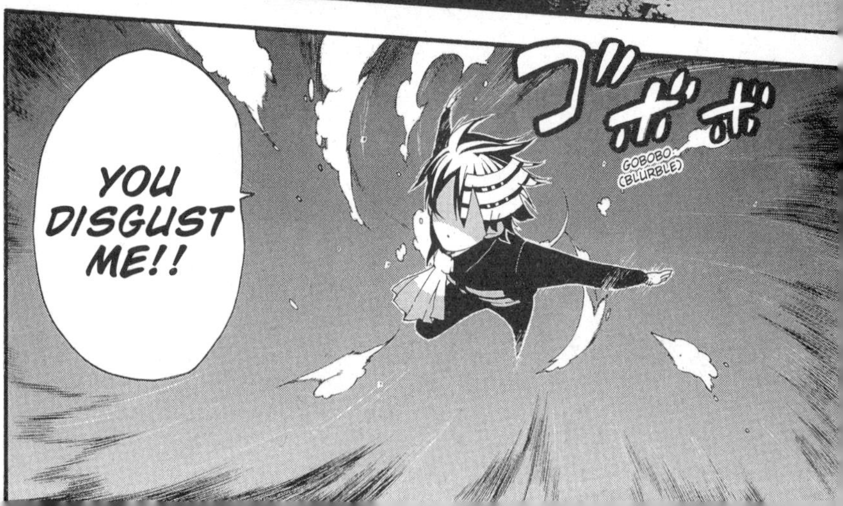
ゴボボ
GOBOBO (BLURBLE)
YOU DISGUST ME!!

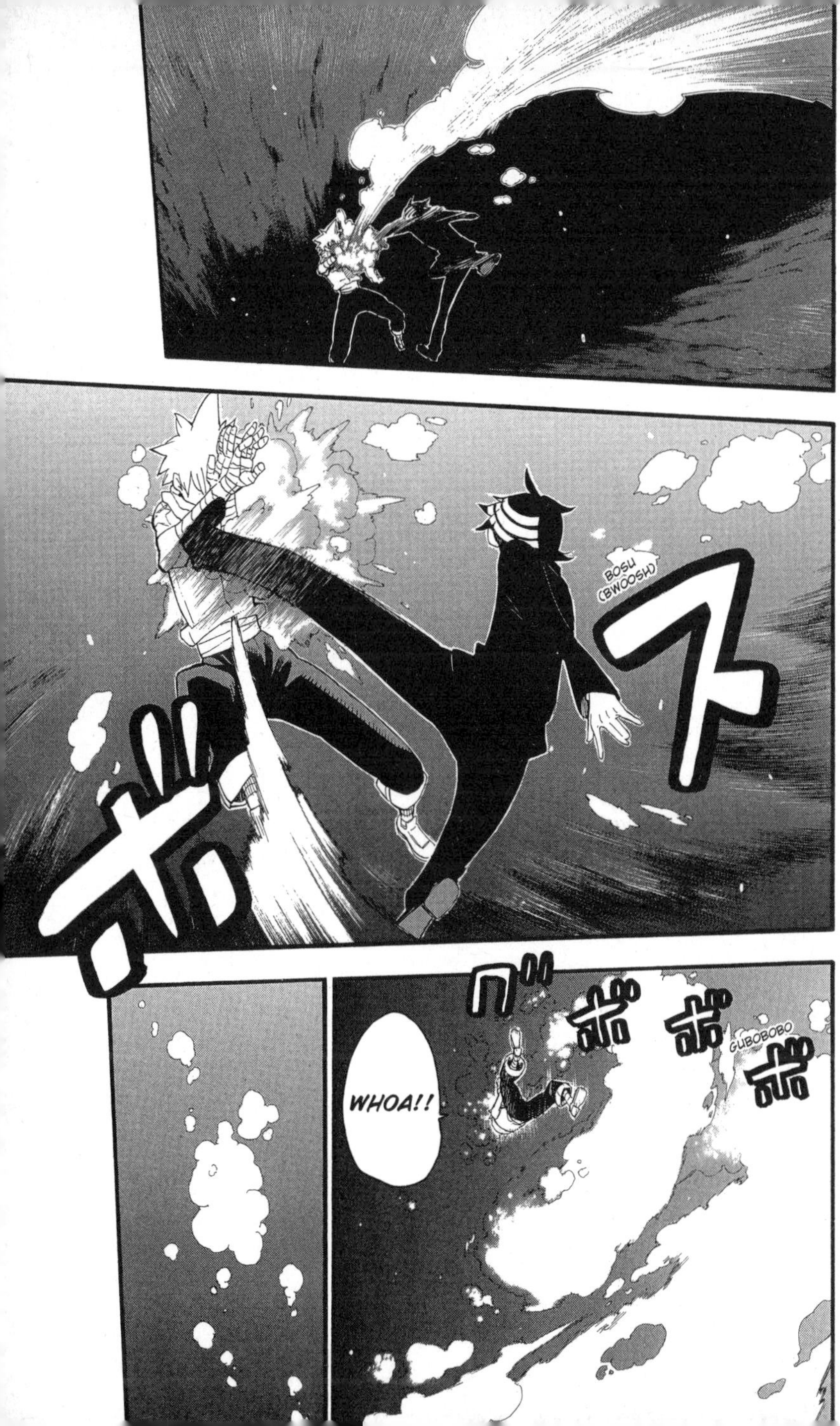
BOSU
(BWOOSH)
GUBOBOBO
WHOA!!

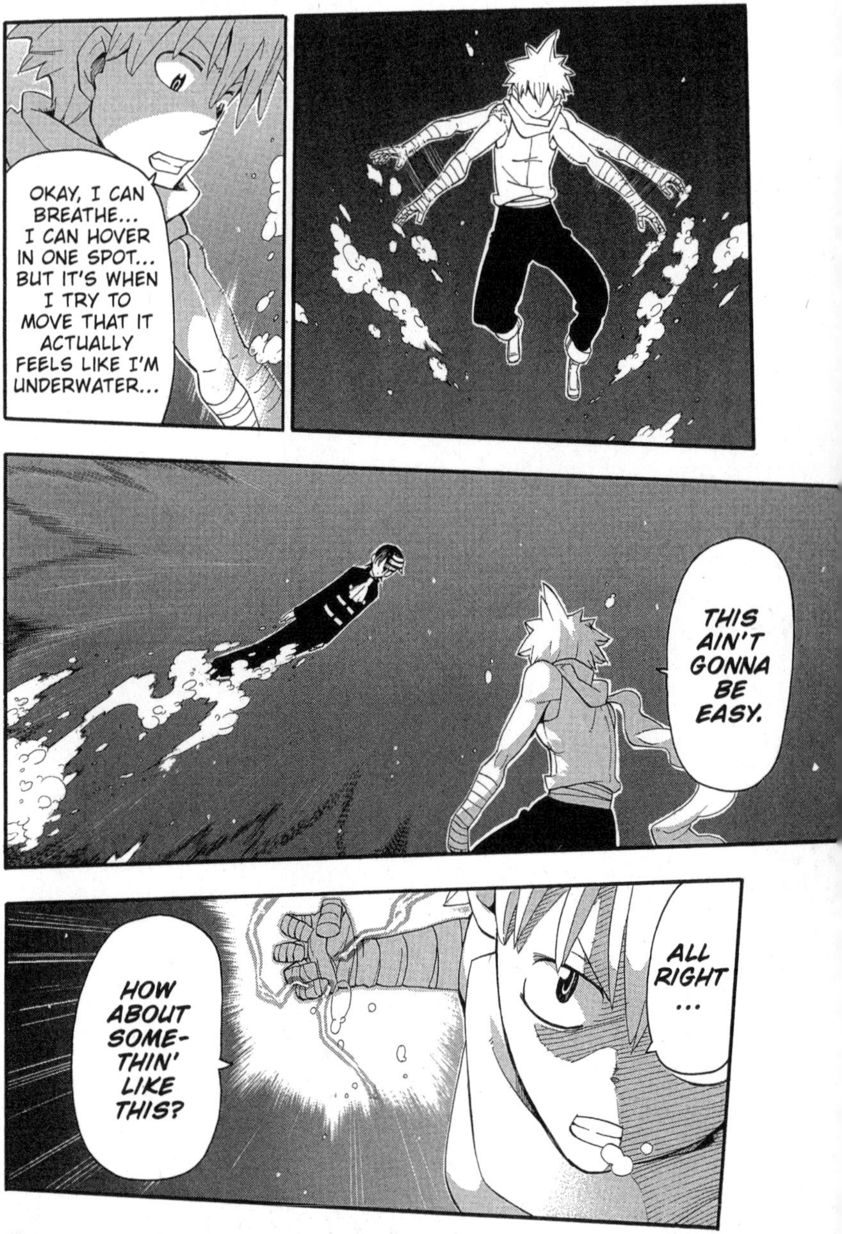
OKAY, I CAN BREATHE... I CAN HOVER IN ONE SPOT... BUT IT'S WHEN I TRY TO MOVE THAT IT ACTUALLY FEELS LIKE I'M UNDERWATER...
THIS AIN'T GONNA BE EASY.
ALL RIGHT...
HOW ABOUT SOMETHIN' LIKE THIS?

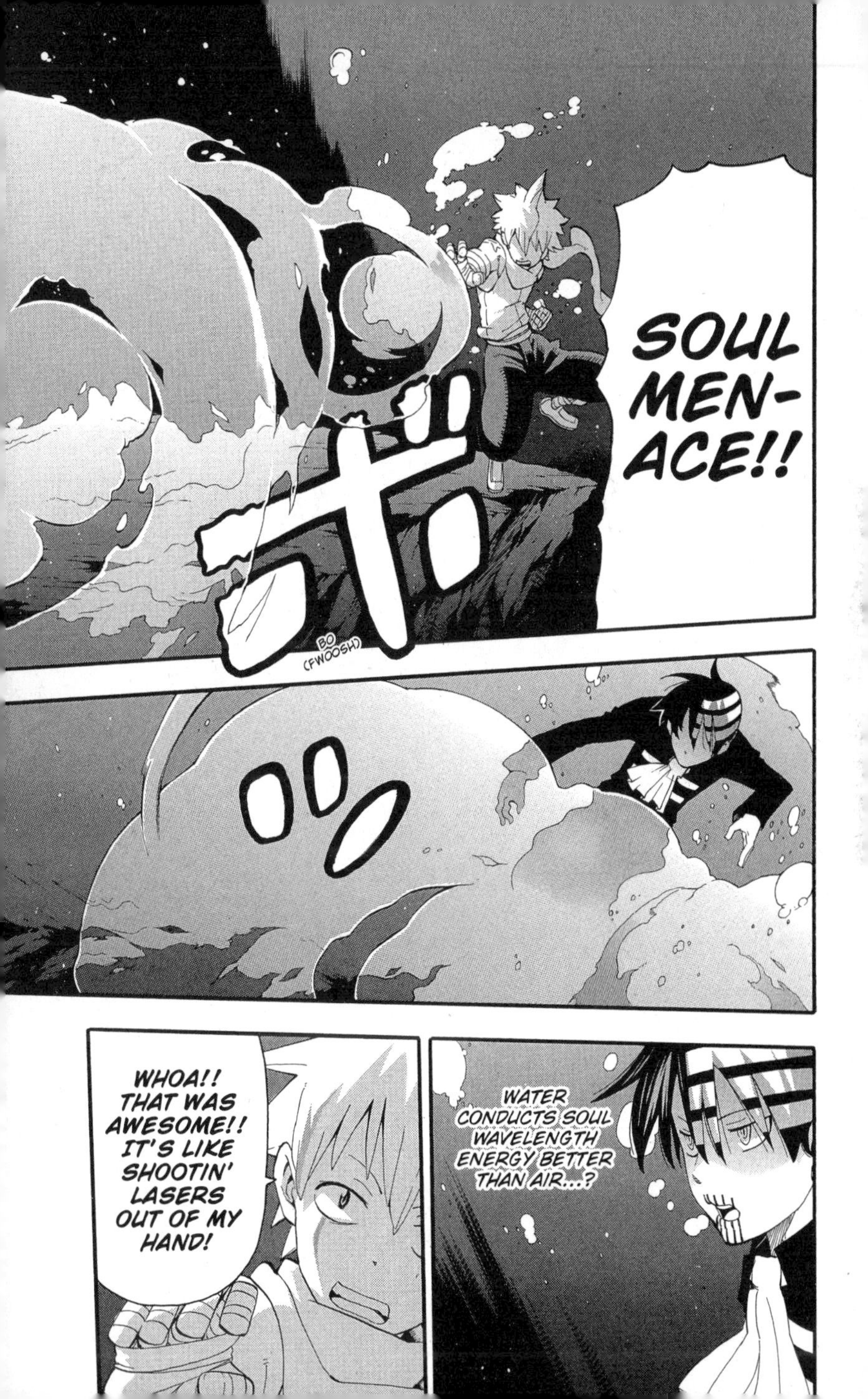
SOUL MEN-ACE!!
BO (FWOOSH)
WATER CONDUCTS SOUL WAVELENGTH ENERGY BETTER THAN AIR...?
WHOA!! THAT WAS AWESOME!! IT'S LIKE SHOOTIN' LASERS OUT OF MY HAND!

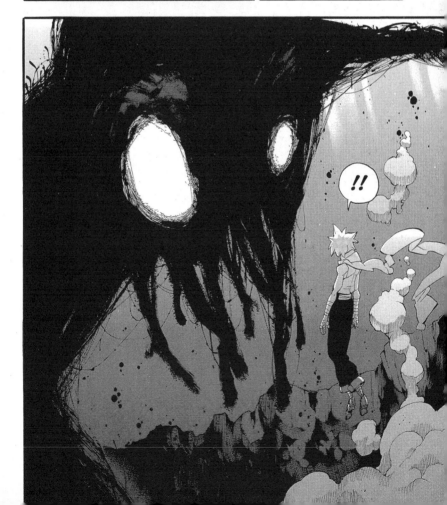

WAIT A SEC... I DIDN'T COME HERE TO FIGHT KID. I CAME HERE TO BRING HIM BACK HOME WITH ME...

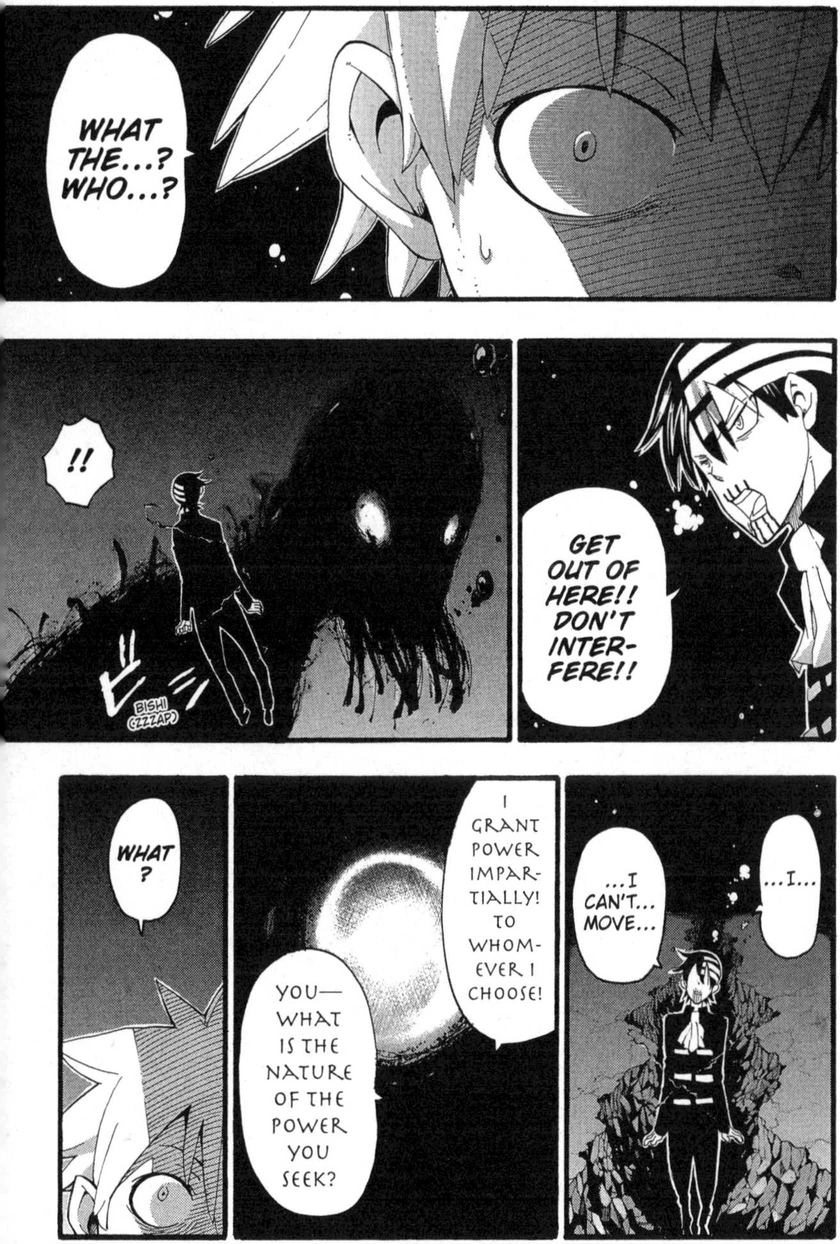
WHAT THE...? WHO...?
GET OUT OF HERE!! DON'T INTER-FERE!!
!!
BISHI (ZZZAP)
...I...
...I CAN'T... MOVE...
I GRANT POWER IMPAR-TIALLY! TO WHOM-EVER I CHOOSE!
YOU—WHAT IS THE NATURE OF THE POWER YOU SEEK?
WHAT?

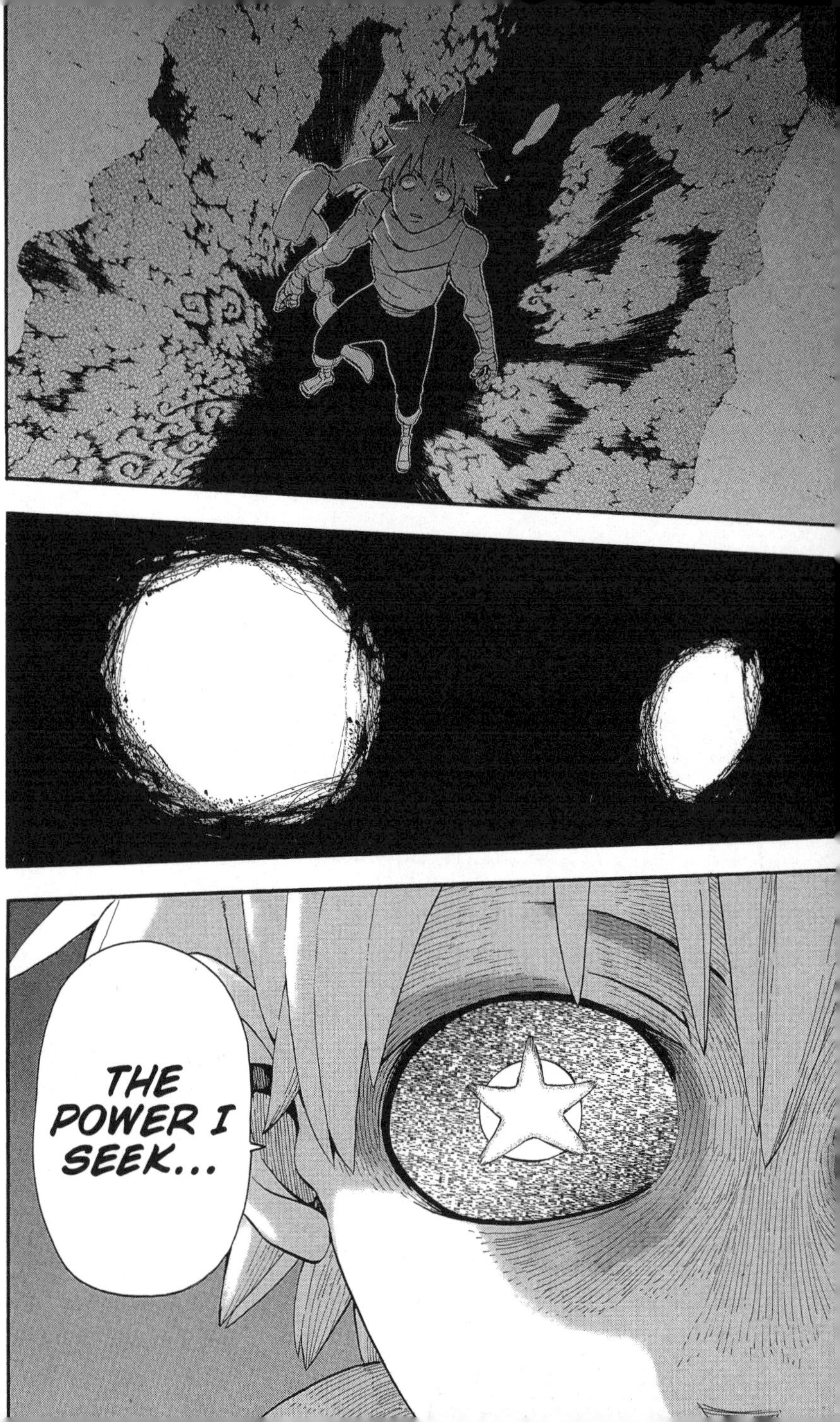
THE POWER I SEEK...

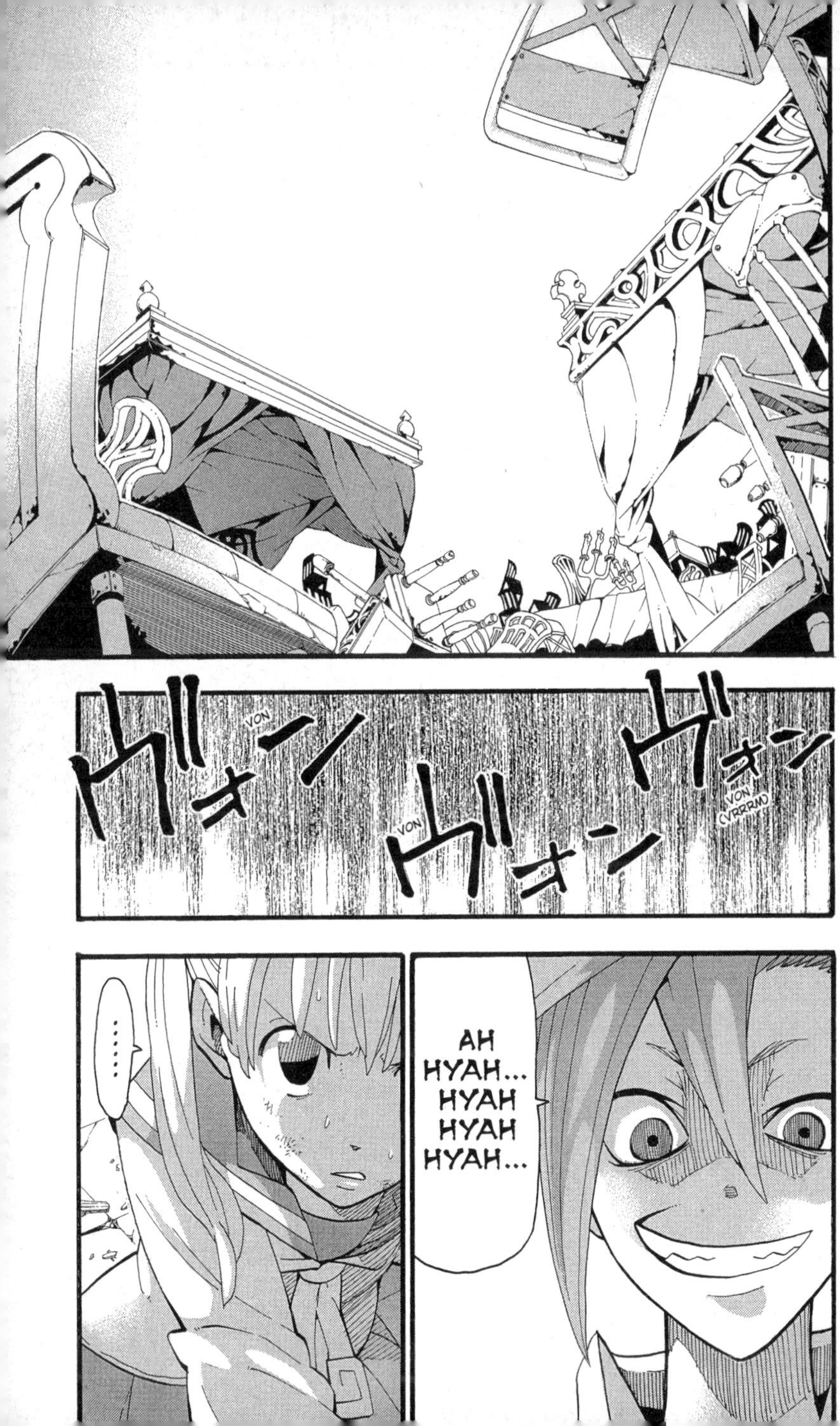
ヴォン
VON (VRRRM)
ヴォーン
VON
ヴォーン
VON
AH HYAH... HYAH HYAH HYAH...
......

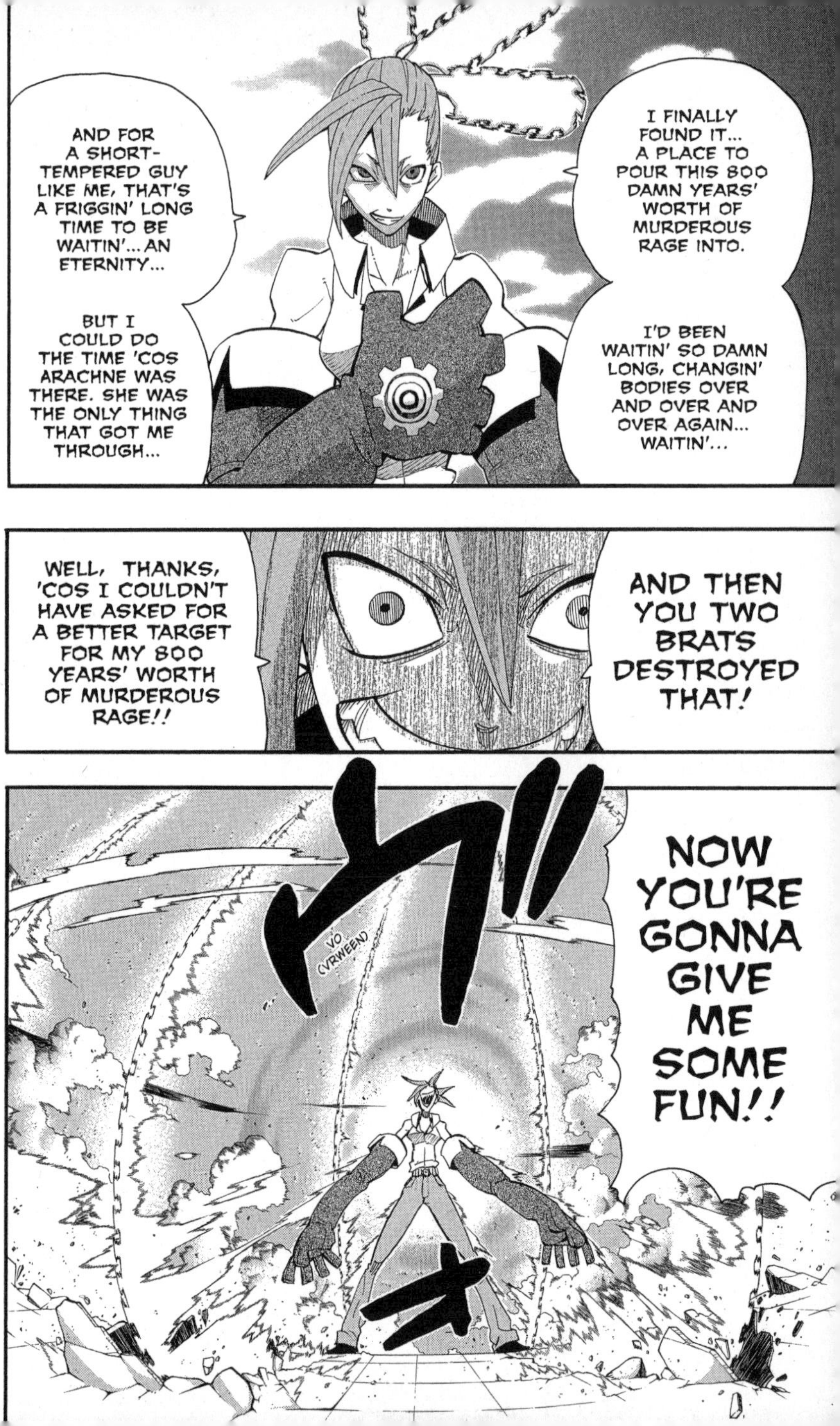
I FINALLY FOUND IT... A PLACE TO POUR THIS 800 DAMN YEARS' WORTH OF MURDEROUS RAGE INTO.
I'D BEEN WAITIN' SO DAMN LONG, CHANGIN' BODIES OVER AND OVER AND OVER AGAIN... WAITIN'...
AND FOR A SHORT-TEMPERED GUY LIKE ME, THAT'S A FRIGGIN' LONG TIME TO BE WAITIN'...AN ETERNITY...
BUT I COULD DO THE TIME 'COS ARACHNE WAS THERE. SHE WAS THE ONLY THING THAT GOT ME THROUGH...
AND THEN YOU TWO BRATS DESTROYED THAT!
WELL, THANKS, 'COS I COULDN'T HAVE ASKED FOR A BETTER TARGET FOR MY 800 YEARS' WORTH OF MURDEROUS RAGE!!
NOW YOU'RE GONNA GIVE ME SOME FUN!!
VO (VRWEEND)

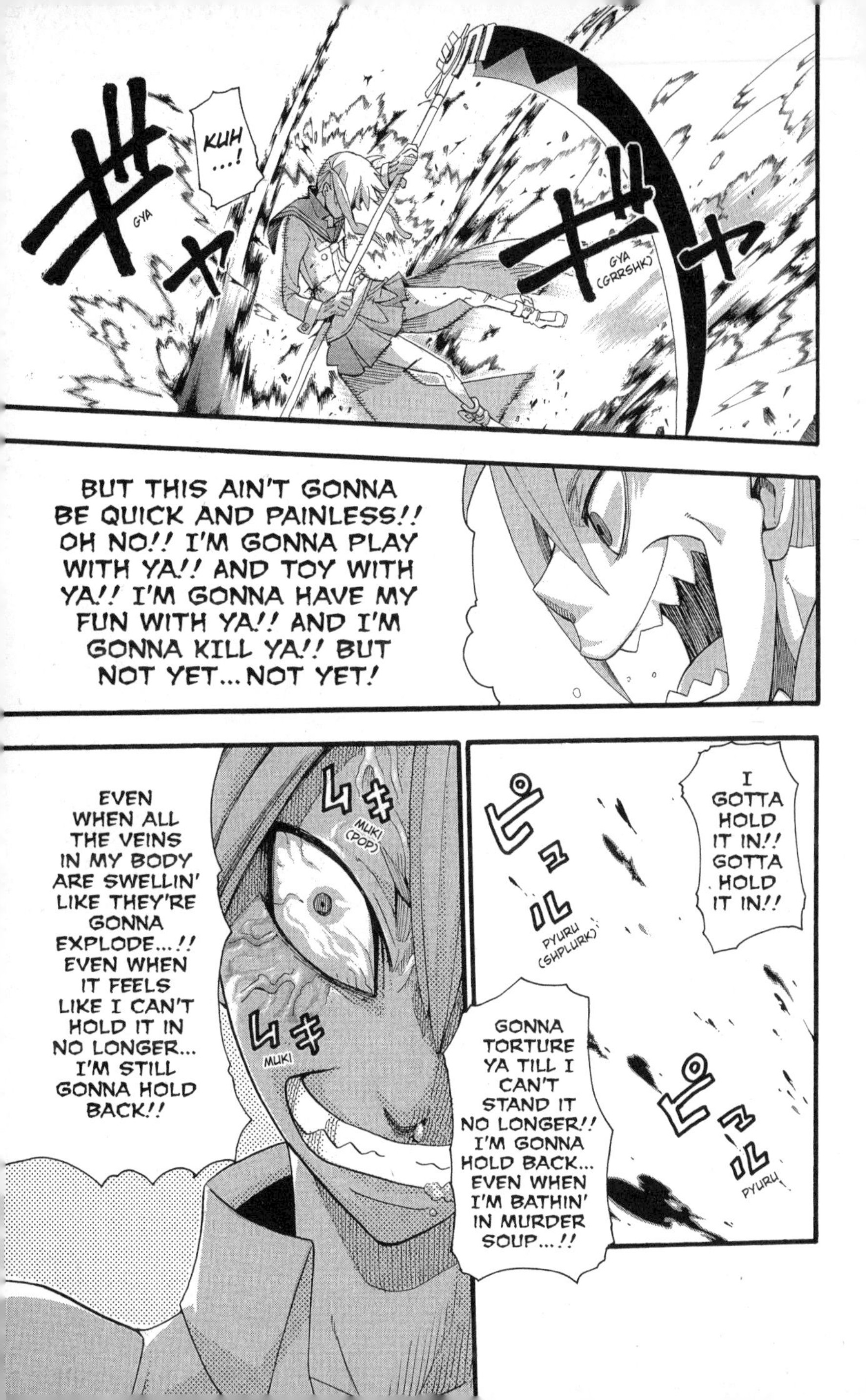
GYA (GRRSHK)
KUH ...!
GYA
BUT THIS AIN'T GONNA BE QUICK AND PAINLESS!! OH NO!! I'M GONNA PLAY WITH YA!! AND TOY WITH YA!! I'M GONNA HAVE MY FUN WITH YA!! AND I'M GONNA KILL YA!! BUT NOT YET...NOT YET!
I GOTTA HOLD IT IN!! GOTTA HOLD IT IN!!
PYURU (SHPLURK)
PYURU
MUKI (POP)
EVEN WHEN ALL THE VEINS IN MY BODY ARE SWELLIN' LIKE THEY'RE GONNA EXPLODE...!! EVEN WHEN IT FEELS LIKE I CAN'T HOLD IT IN NO LONGER... I'M STILL GONNA HOLD BACK!!
MUKI
GONNA TORTURE YA TILL I CAN'T STAND IT NO LONGER!! I'M GONNA HOLD BACK... EVEN WHEN I'M BATHIN' IN MURDER SOUP...!!

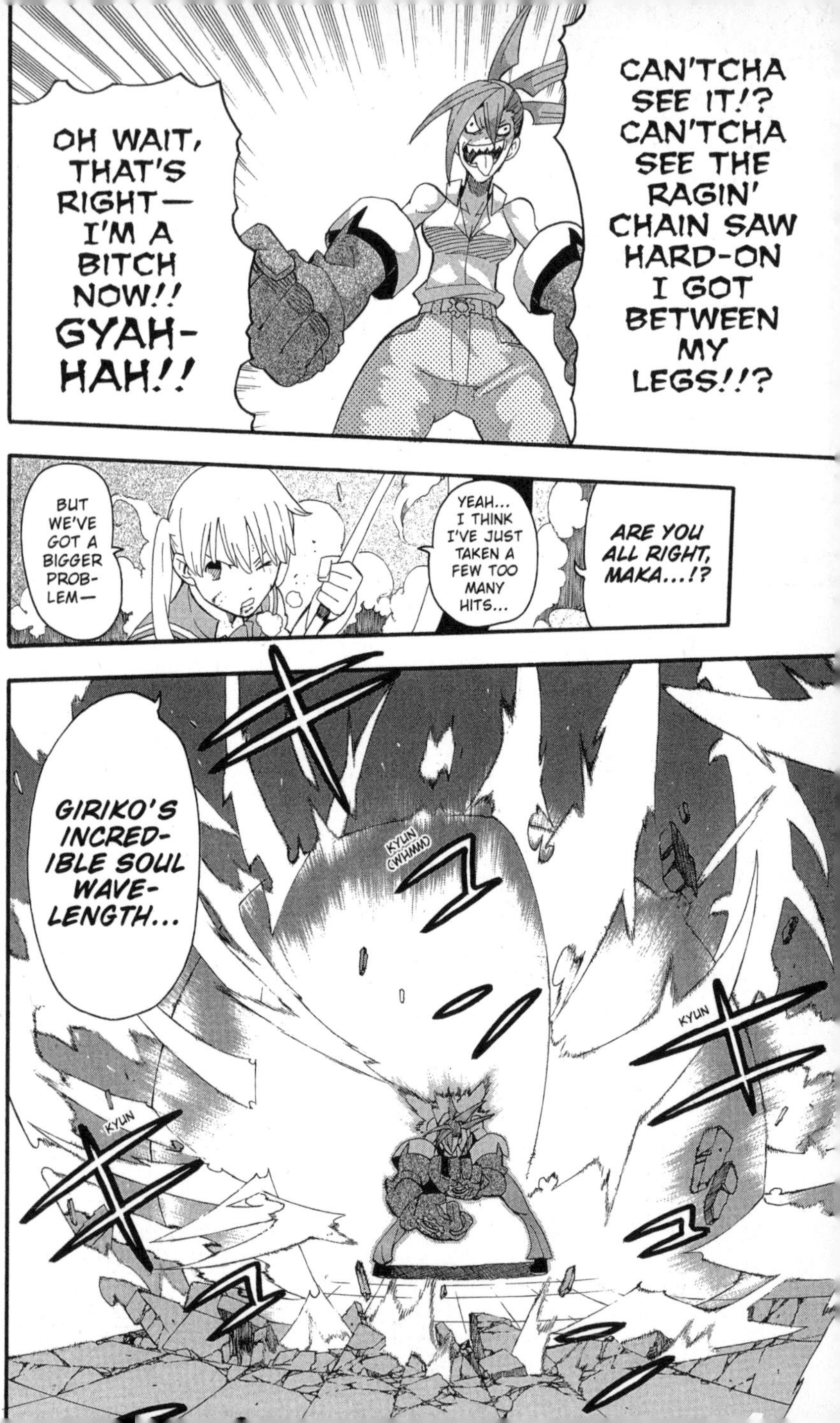
CAN'TCHA SEE IT!? CAN'TCHA SEE THE RAGIN' CHAIN SAW HARD-ON I GOT BETWEEN MY LEGS!!?
OH WAIT, THAT'S RIGHT— I'M A BITCH NOW!! GYAH-HAH!!
ARE YOU ALL RIGHT, MAKA...!?
YEAH... I THINK I'VE JUST TAKEN A FEW TOO MANY HITS...
BUT WE'VE GOT A BIGGER PROB-LEM—
GIRIKO'S INCRED-IBLE SOUL WAVE-LENGTH...
KYUN (WHMM)
KYUN
KYUN

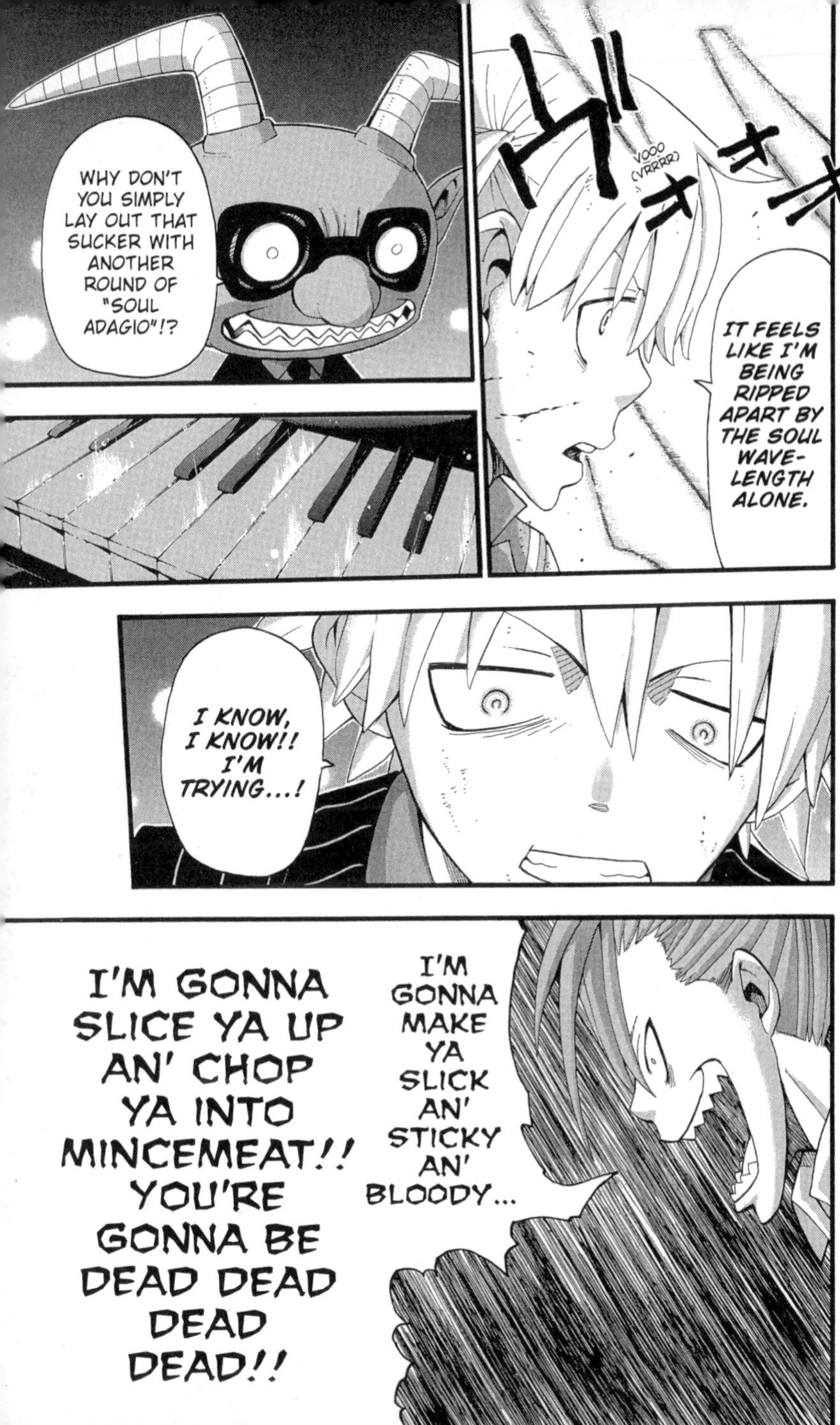
VOOO (VRRRR)
IT FEELS LIKE I'M BEING RIPPED APART BY THE SOUL WAVE-LENGTH ALONE.
WHY DON'T YOU SIMPLY LAY OUT THAT SUCKER WITH ANOTHER ROUND OF "SOUL ADAGIO"!?
I KNOW, I KNOW!! I'M TRYING...!
I'M GONNA MAKE YA SLICK AN' STICKY AN' BLOODY...
I'M GONNA SLICE YA UP AN' CHOP YA INTO MINCEMEAT!! YOU'RE GONNA BE DEAD DEAD DEAD DEAD!!

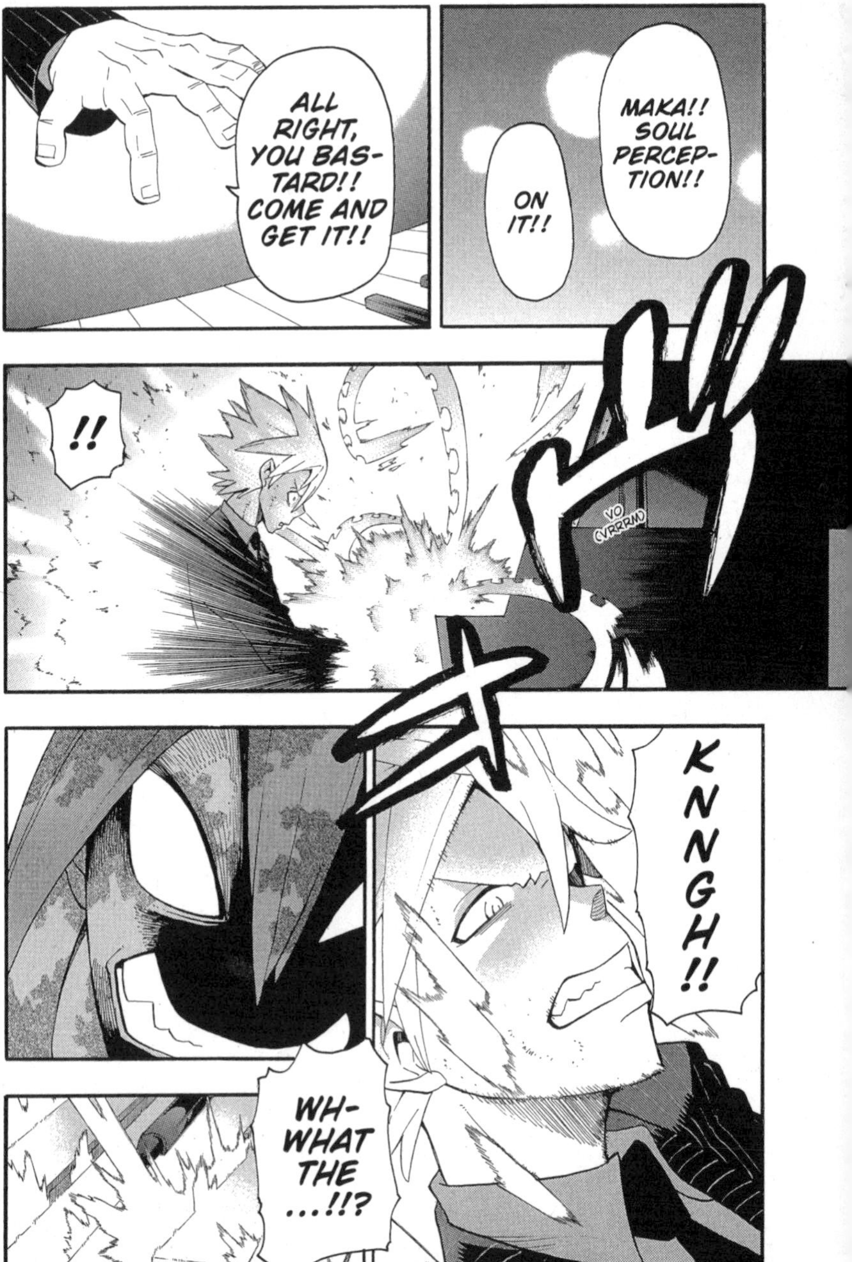
MAKA!! SOUL PERCEPTION!!
ON IT!!
ALL RIGHT, YOU BASTARD!! COME AND GET IT!!
!!
VO (VRRRM)
KNNGH!!
WH-WHAT THE ...!!?

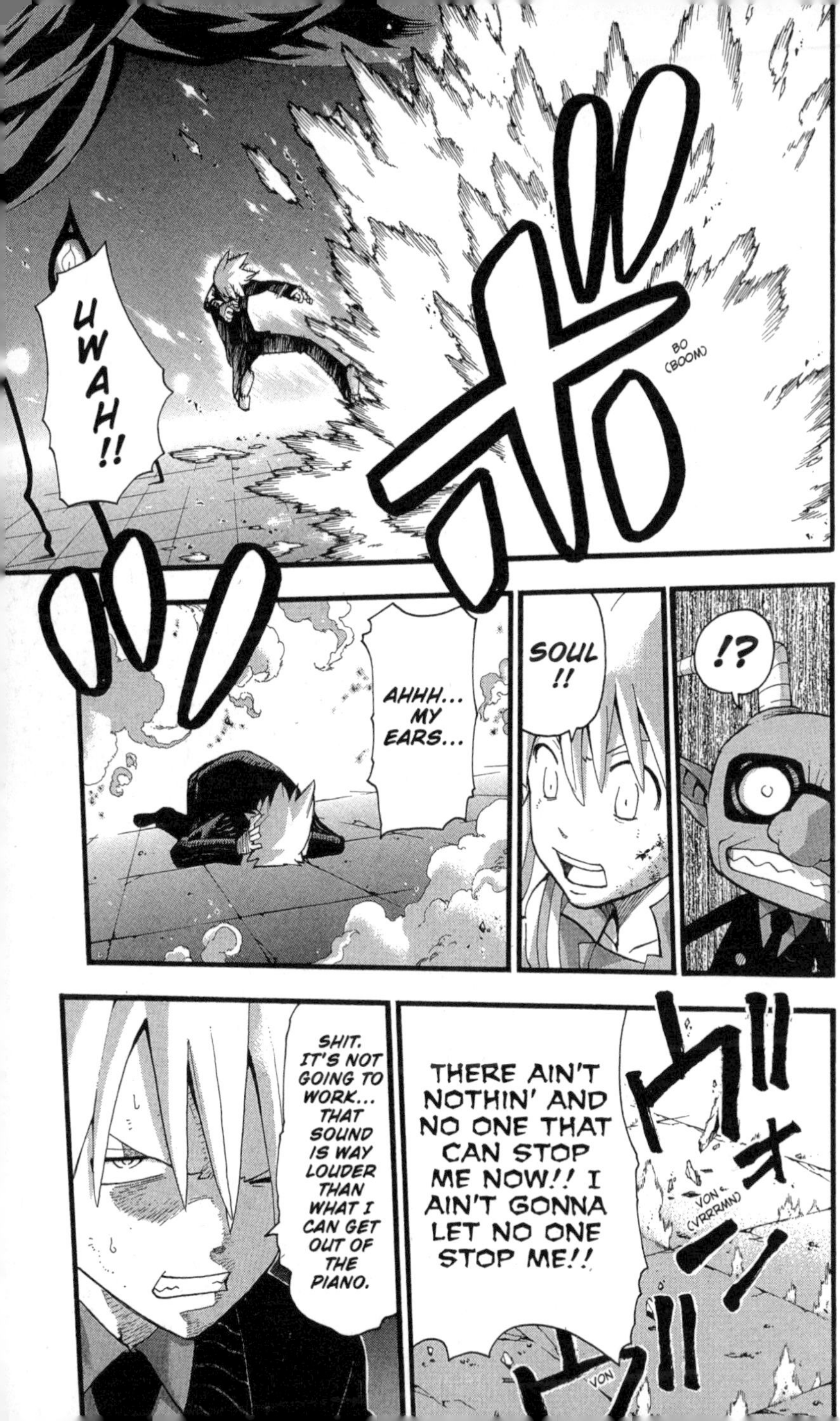
BO
(BOOM)
UWAH!!
!?
SOUL !!
AHHH... MY EARS...
VON
(VRRRMN)
THERE AIN'T NOTHIN' AND NO ONE THAT CAN STOP ME NOW!! I AIN'T GONNA LET NO ONE STOP ME!!
VON
SHIT. IT'S NOT GOING TO WORK... THAT SOUND IS WAY LOUDER THAN WHAT I CAN GET OUT OF THE PIANO.

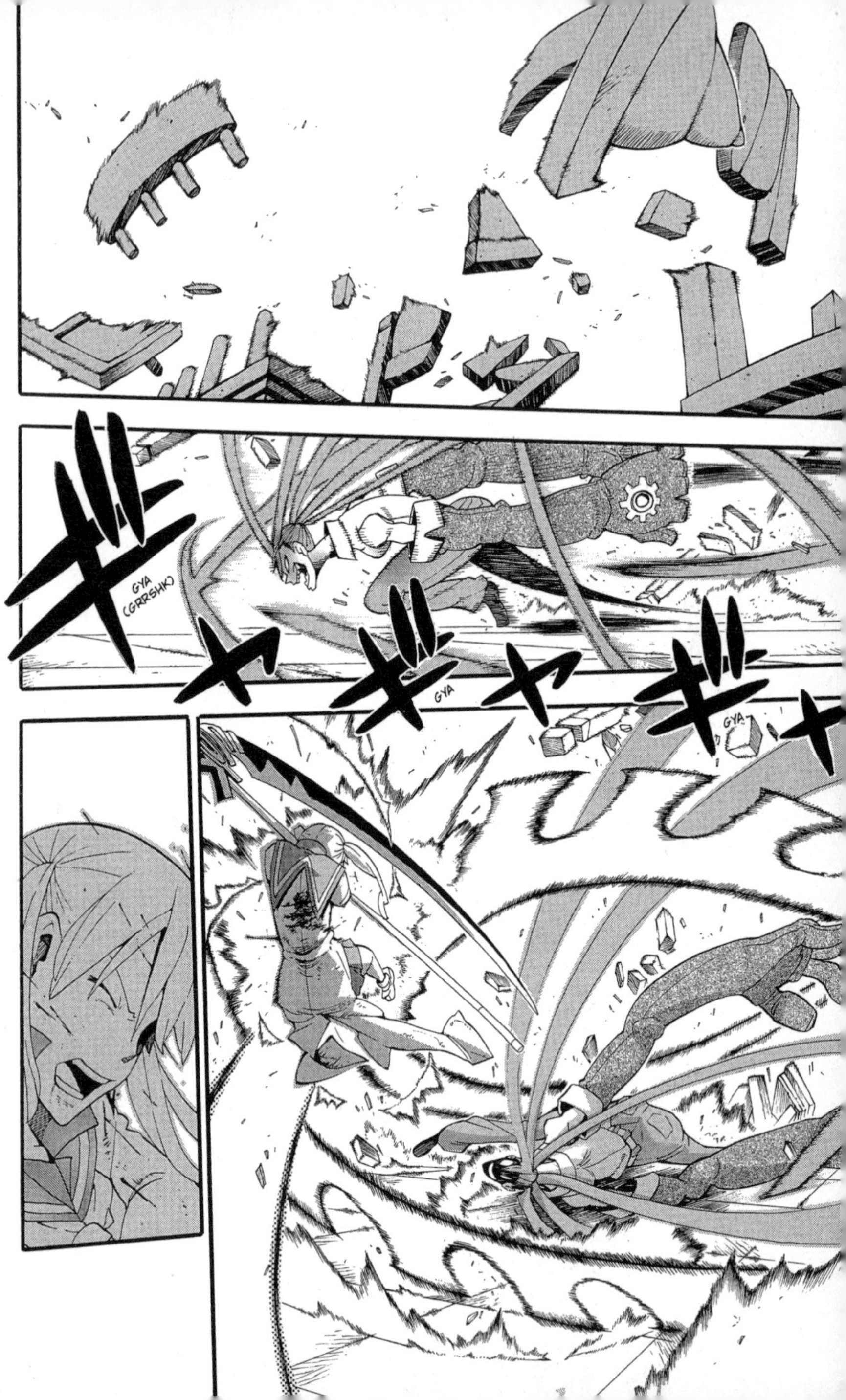
GYA (GRRSHK)
GYA
GYA

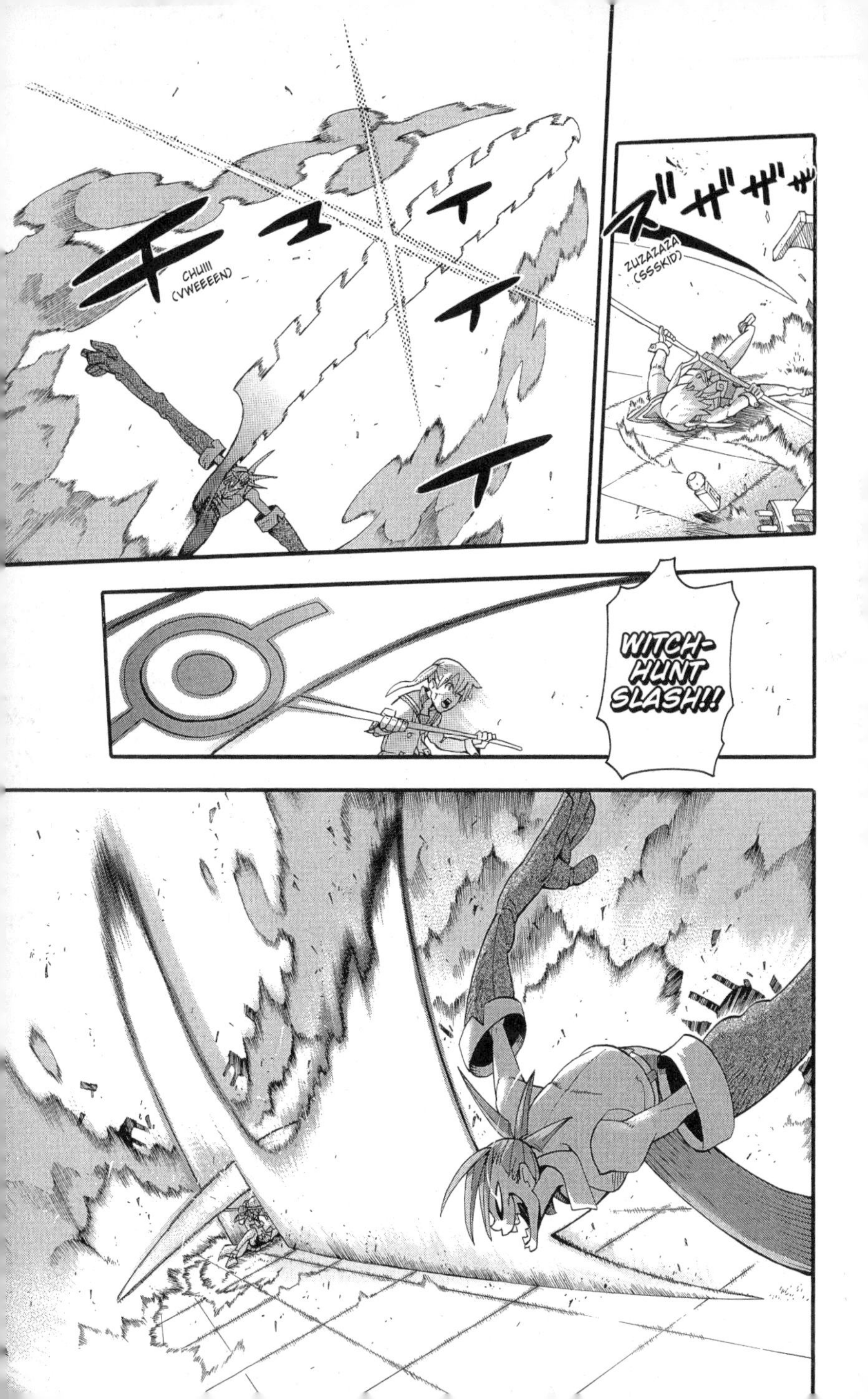
ズザザザ
ZUZAZAZA (SSSKID)
チュイイイ
CHUIII (VWEEEEN)
WITCH-HUNT SLASH!!

YOU DIDN'T THINK YOU COULD STOP 800 YEARS' OF MURDEROUS RAGE WITH THAT PISSY LITTLE MOVE, DID YA...?

DŌ
(THWOOM)

GATA
(SLUMP)

THIS IS BAD...

MAKA!!

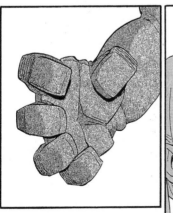

I CAN'T LIFT MY ARMS... I CAN'T STAND... I'M GOING TO BE KILLED...

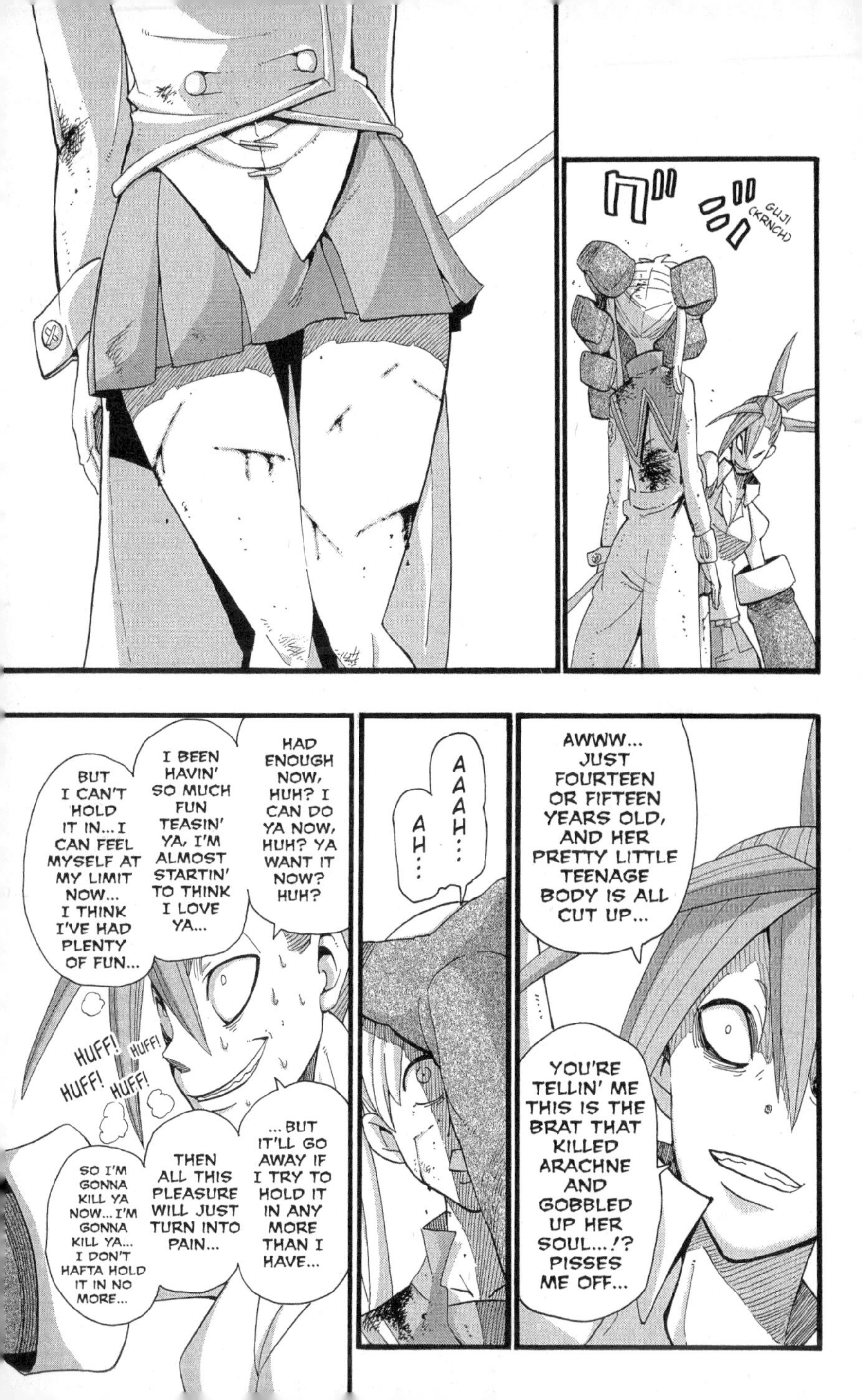
GUJI (KRNCH)
AWWW... JUST FOURTEEN OR FIFTEEN YEARS OLD, AND HER PRETTY LITTLE TEENAGE BODY IS ALL CUT UP...
YOU'RE TELLIN' ME THIS IS THE BRAT THAT KILLED ARACHNE AND GOBBLED UP HER SOUL...!? PISSES ME OFF...
AAAH...
AH...
HAD ENOUGH NOW, HUH? I CAN DO YA NOW, HUH? YA WANT IT NOW? HUH?
I BEEN HAVIN' SO MUCH FUN TEASIN' YA, I'M ALMOST STARTIN' TO THINK I LOVE YA...
BUT I CAN'T HOLD IT IN... I CAN FEEL MYSELF AT MY LIMIT NOW... I THINK I'VE HAD PLENTY OF FUN...
HUFF! HUFF! HUFF! HUFF!
...BUT IT'LL GO AWAY IF I TRY TO HOLD IT IN ANY MORE THAN I HAVE...
THEN ALL THIS PLEASURE WILL JUST TURN INTO PAIN...
SO I'M GONNA KILL YA NOW... I'M GONNA KILL YA... I DON'T HAFTA HOLD IT IN NO MORE...

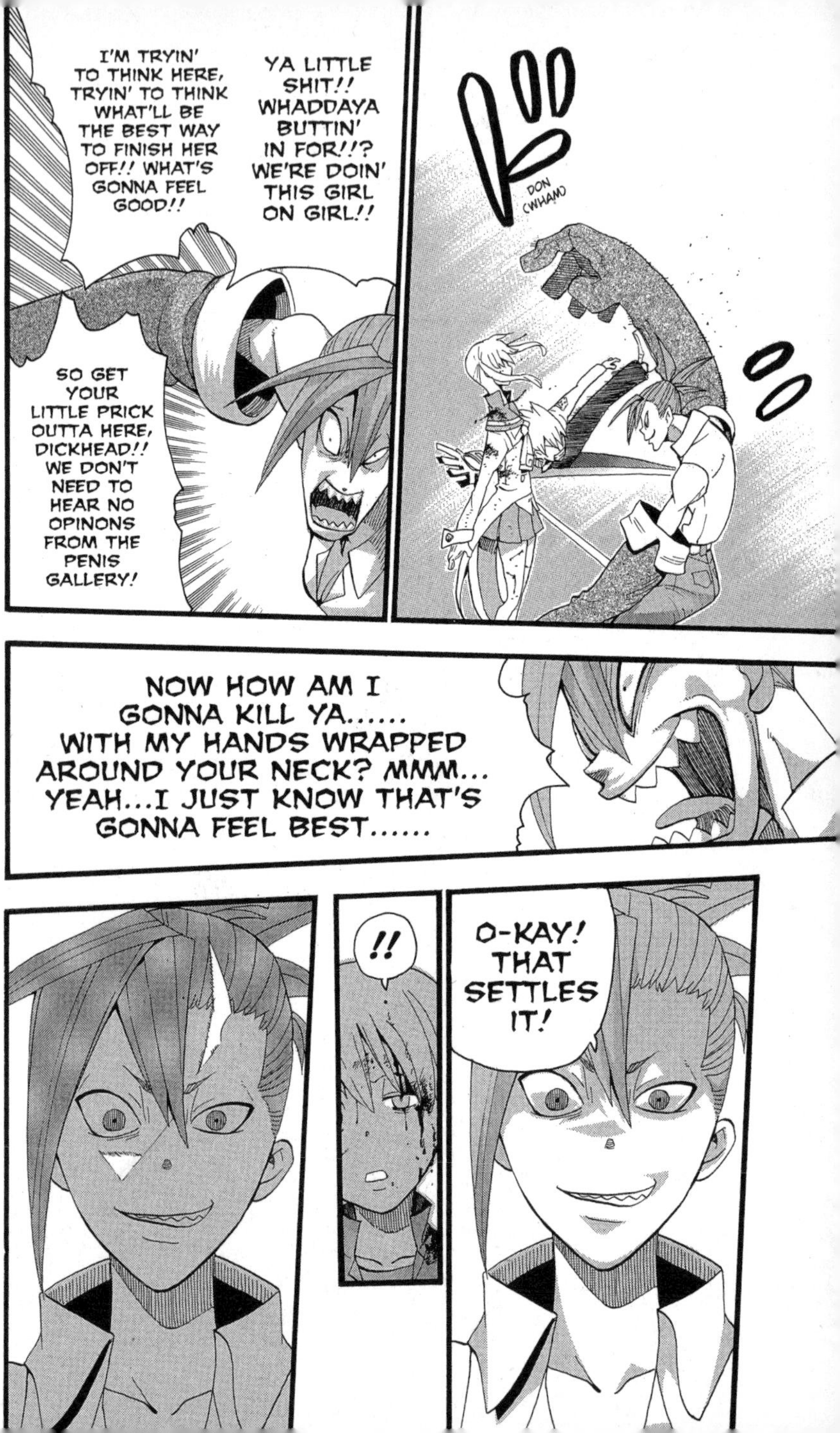
DON (WHAM)
YA LITTLE SHIT!! WHADDAYA BUTTIN' IN FOR!!? WE'RE DOIN' THIS GIRL ON GIRL!!
I'M TRYIN' TO THINK HERE, TRYIN' TO THINK WHAT'LL BE THE BEST WAY TO FINISH HER OFF!! WHAT'S GONNA FEEL GOOD!!
SO GET YOUR LITTLE PRICK OUTTA HERE, DICKHEAD!! WE DON'T NEED TO HEAR NO OPINONS FROM THE PENIS GALLERY!
NOW HOW AM I GONNA KILL YA...... WITH MY HANDS WRAPPED AROUND YOUR NECK? MMM... YEAH...I JUST KNOW THAT'S GONNA FEEL BEST......
O-KAY! THAT SETTLES IT!
!!

WHAT THE ...? IT LOOKS LIKE SOMETHING'S GOING WRONG WITH THAT NEW BODY?

...NNGH...

HIIII (VWEEE)

ヒイイイイイ

IT'S...IT'S ALL THE BLOODLUST... ALL THAT MADNESS... IT'S DOING SOMETHING TO GIRIKO'S SOUL...

SH... SHIT...!

WHA... WHAT'S HAP- PENIN' TO ME...!?

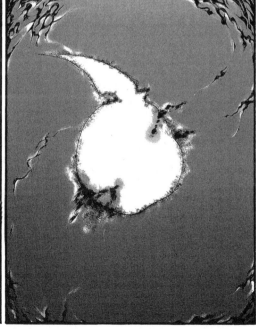

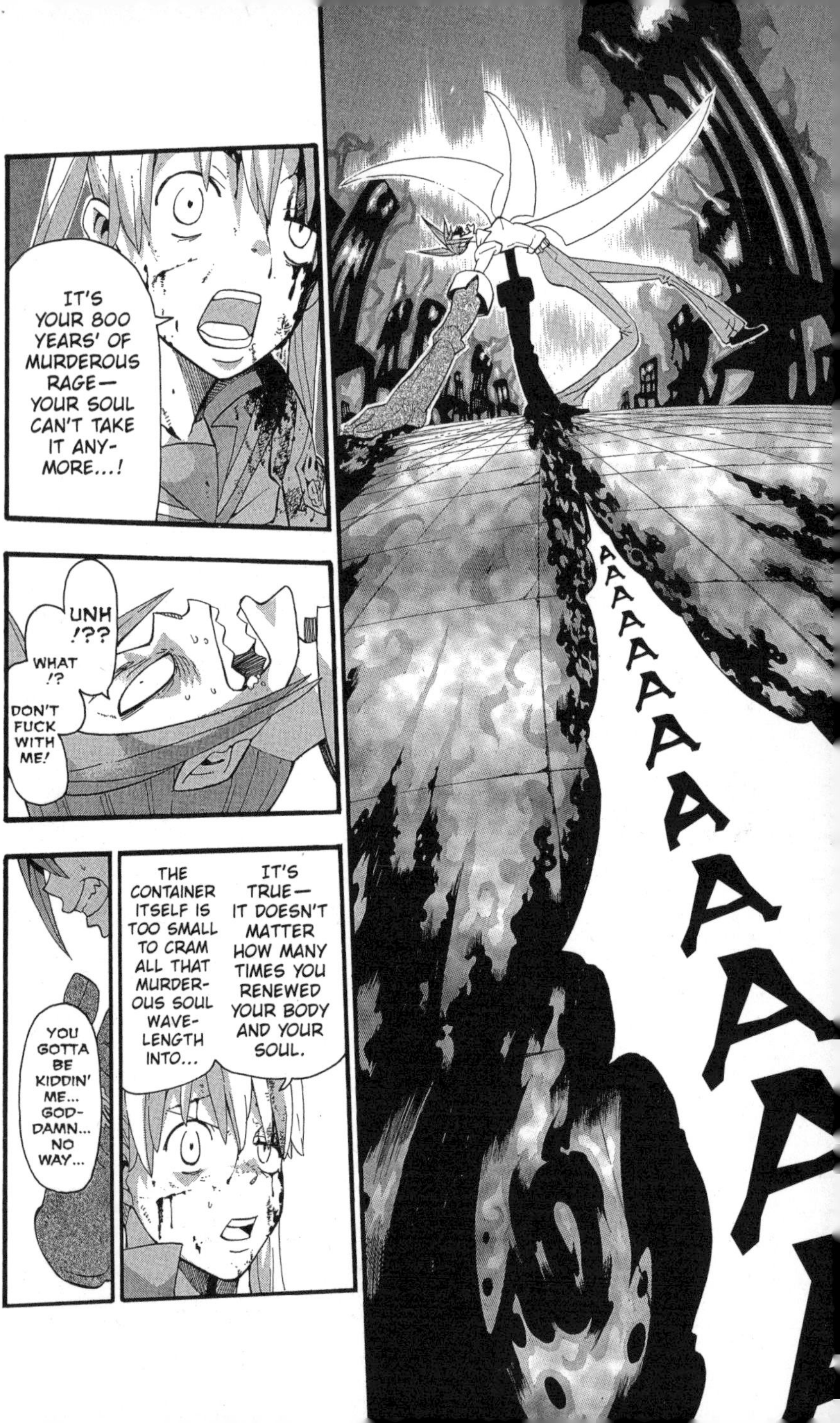
AAAAAAAAAAAAA
IT'S YOUR 800 YEARS' OF MURDEROUS RAGE— YOUR SOUL CAN'T TAKE IT ANY-MORE...!
UNH!?? WHAT!? DON'T FUCK WITH ME!
IT'S TRUE— IT DOESN'T MATTER HOW MANY TIMES YOU RENEWED YOUR BODY AND YOUR SOUL.
THE CONTAINER ITSELF IS TOO SMALL TO CRAM ALL THAT MURDER-OUS SOUL WAVE-LENGTH INTO...
YOU GOTTA BE KIDDIN' ME... GOD-DAMN... NO WAY...

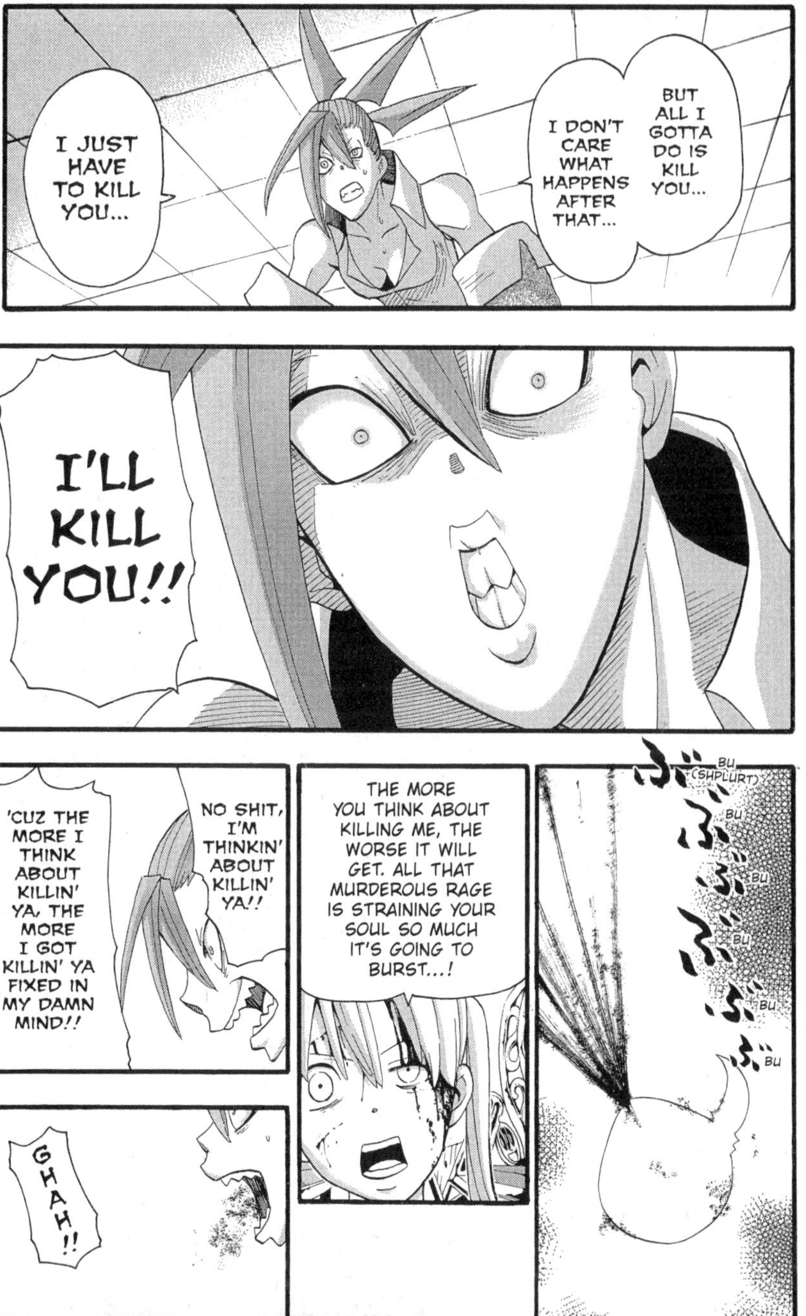
BUT ALL I GOTTA DO IS KILL YOU...
I DON'T CARE WHAT HAPPENS AFTER THAT...
I JUST HAVE TO KILL YOU...
I'LL KILL YOU!!
BU (SHPLURT)
BU
BU
BU
BU
BU
THE MORE YOU THINK ABOUT KILLING ME, THE WORSE IT WILL GET. ALL THAT MURDEROUS RAGE IS STRAINING YOUR SOUL SO MUCH IT'S GOING TO BURST...!
NO SHIT, I'M THINKIN' ABOUT KILLIN' YA!!
'CUZ THE MORE I THINK ABOUT KILLIN' YA, THE MORE I GOT KILLIN' YA FIXED IN MY DAMN MIND!!
GHAH!!

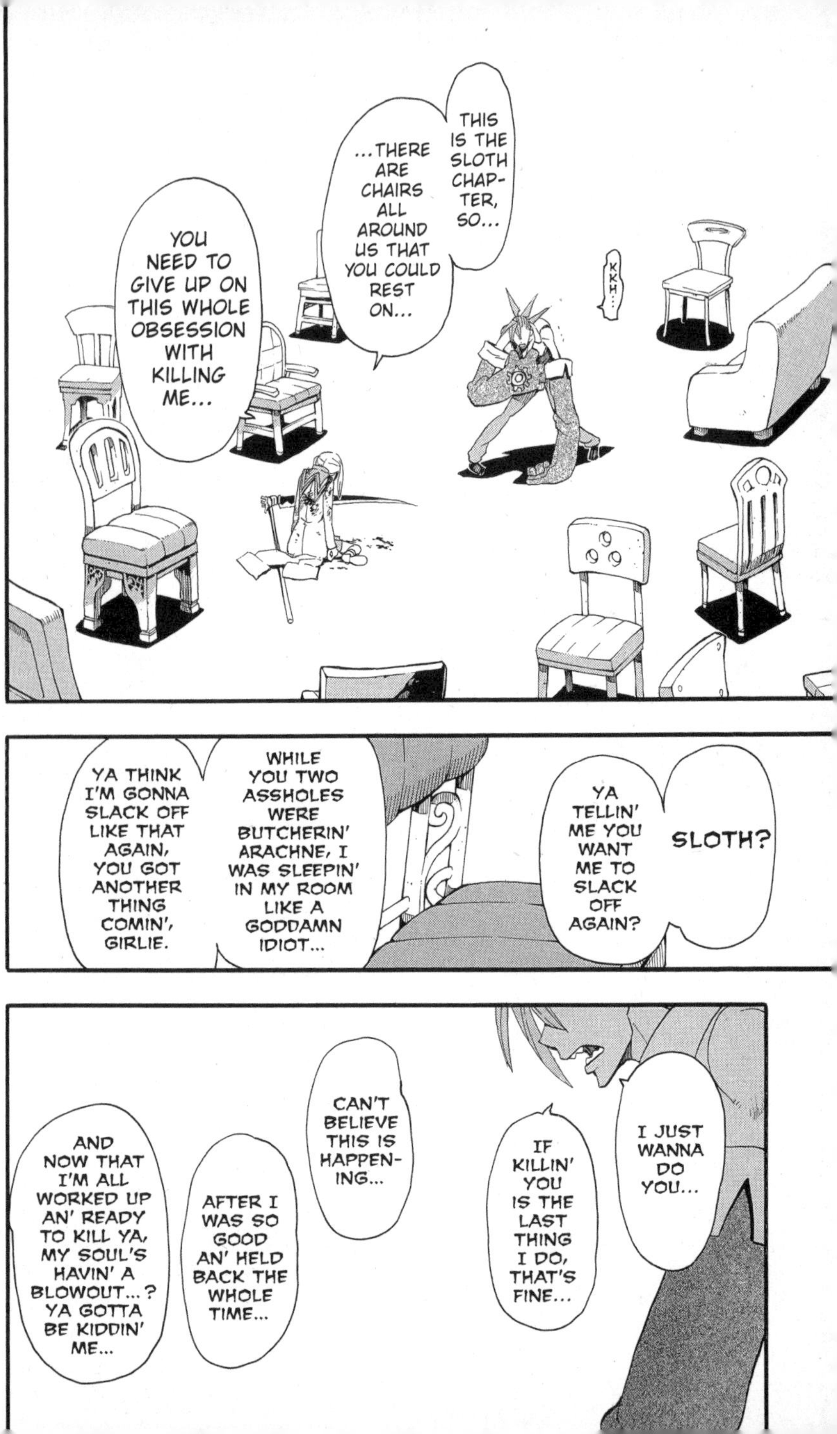
THIS IS THE SLOTH CHAPTER, SO...
...THERE ARE CHAIRS ALL AROUND US THAT YOU COULD REST ON...
KKH...
YOU NEED TO GIVE UP ON THIS WHOLE OBSESSION WITH KILLING ME...
SLOTH?
YA TELLIN' ME YOU WANT ME TO SLACK OFF AGAIN?
WHILE YOU TWO ASSHOLES WERE BUTCHERIN' ARACHNE, I WAS SLEEPIN' IN MY ROOM LIKE A GODDAMN IDIOT...
YA THINK I'M GONNA SLACK OFF LIKE THAT AGAIN, YOU GOT ANOTHER THING COMIN', GIRLIE.
I JUST WANNA DO YOU...
IF KILLIN' YOU IS THE LAST THING I DO, THAT'S FINE...
CAN'T BELIEVE THIS IS HAPPEN-ING...
AFTER I WAS SO GOOD AN' HELD BACK THE WHOLE TIME...
AND NOW THAT I'M ALL WORKED UP AN' READY TO KILL YA, MY SOUL'S HAVIN' A BLOWOUT...? YA GOTTA BE KIDDIN' ME...

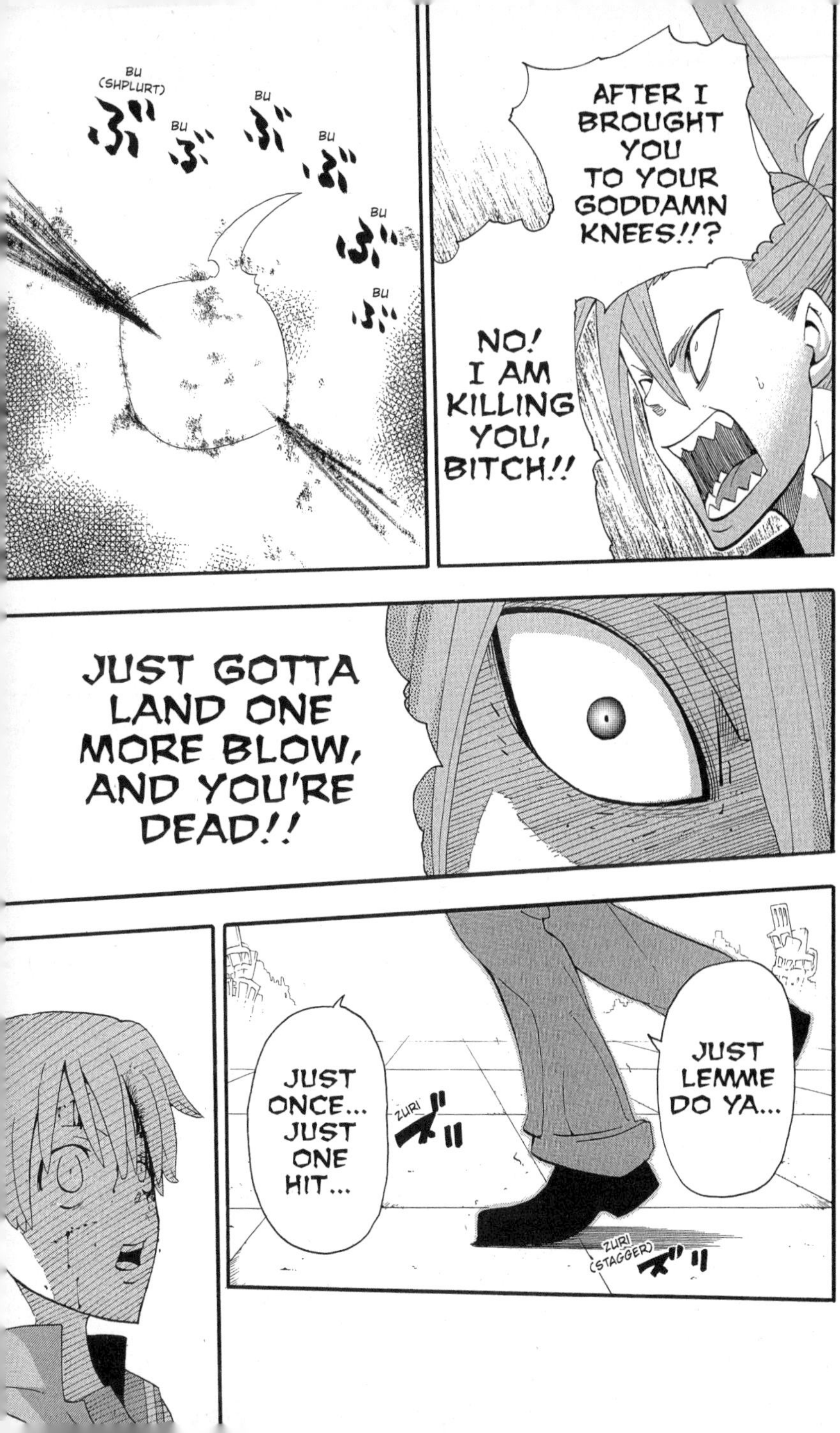
AFTER I BROUGHT YOU TO YOUR GODDAMN KNEES!!?
NO! I AM KILLING YOU, BITCH!!
ぶ BU (SHPLURT)
ぶ BU
ぶ BU
ぶ BU
ぶ BU
ぶ BU
JUST GOTTA LAND ONE MORE BLOW, AND YOU'RE DEAD!!
JUST LEMME DO YA...
ZURI
JUST ONCE... JUST ONE HIT...
ZURI (STAGGER)

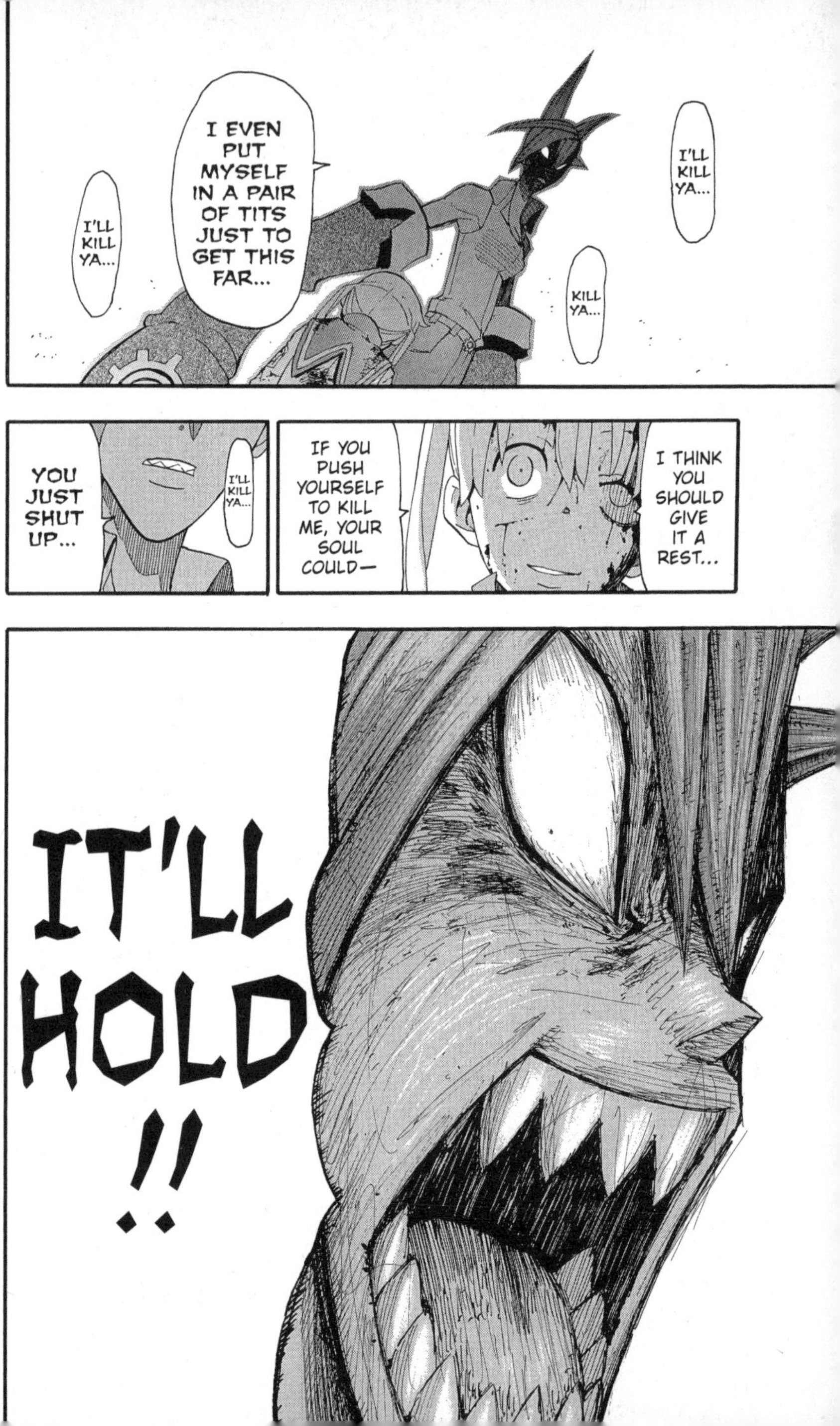
I'LL KILL YA...
KILL YA...
I EVEN PUT MYSELF IN A PAIR OF TITS JUST TO GET THIS FAR...
I'LL KILL YA...
I THINK YOU SHOULD GIVE IT A REST...
IF YOU PUSH YOURSELF TO KILL ME, YOUR SOUL COULD—
I'LL KILL YA...
YOU JUST SHUT UP...
IT'LL HOLD!!

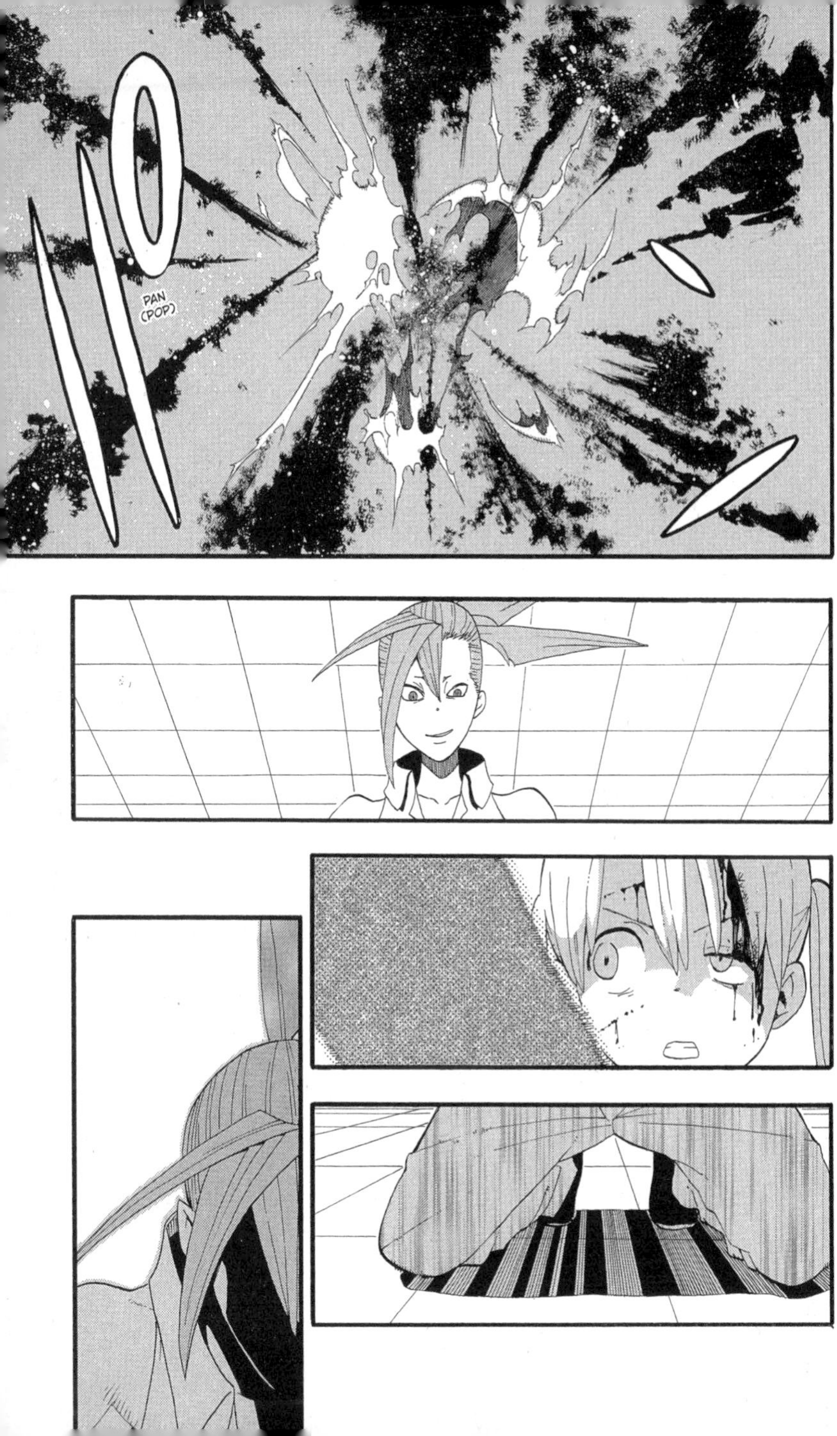
PAN
(POP)

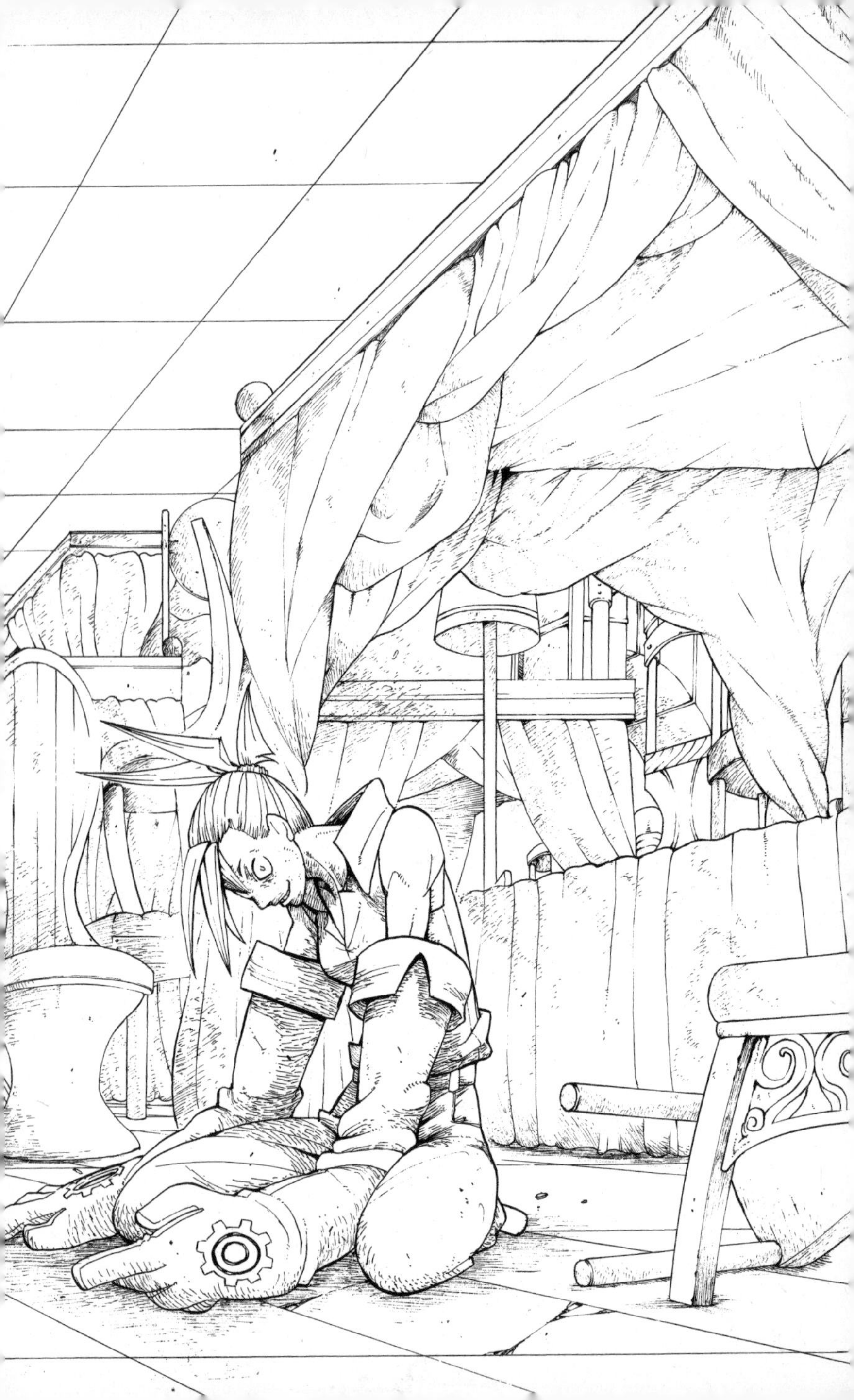

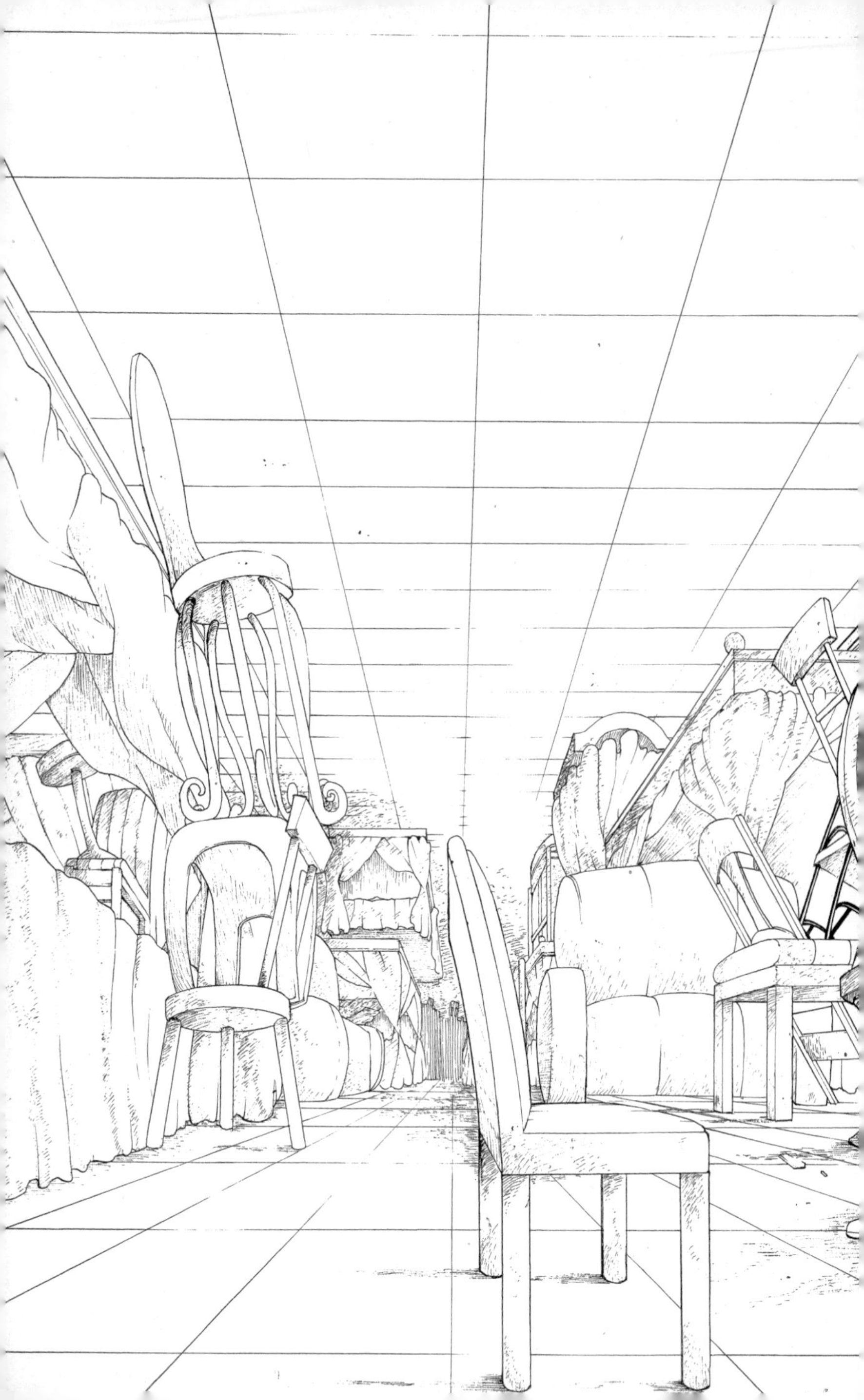

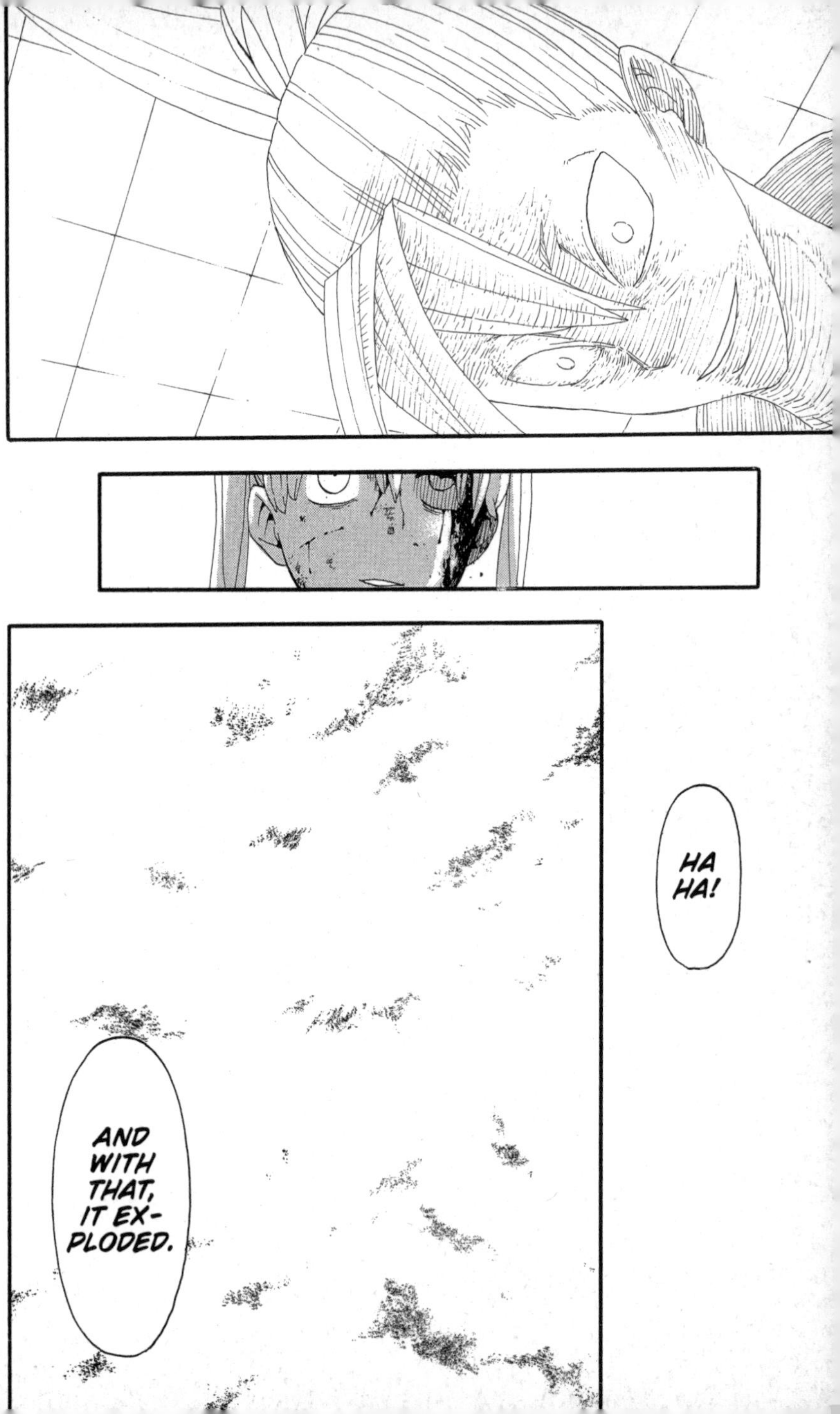
HA HA!
AND WITH THAT, IT EX- PLODED.

SOUL EATER

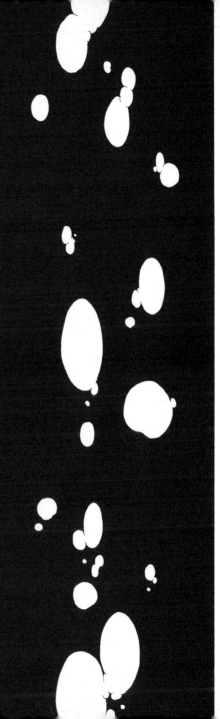

WHAT IS THE NATURE OF THE POWER YOU SEEK?

WHY, YOU...SO YOU'RE TRYING TO DRAW BLACK☆STAR INTO THE MADNESS TOO...?

THE POWER...

...I SEEK...

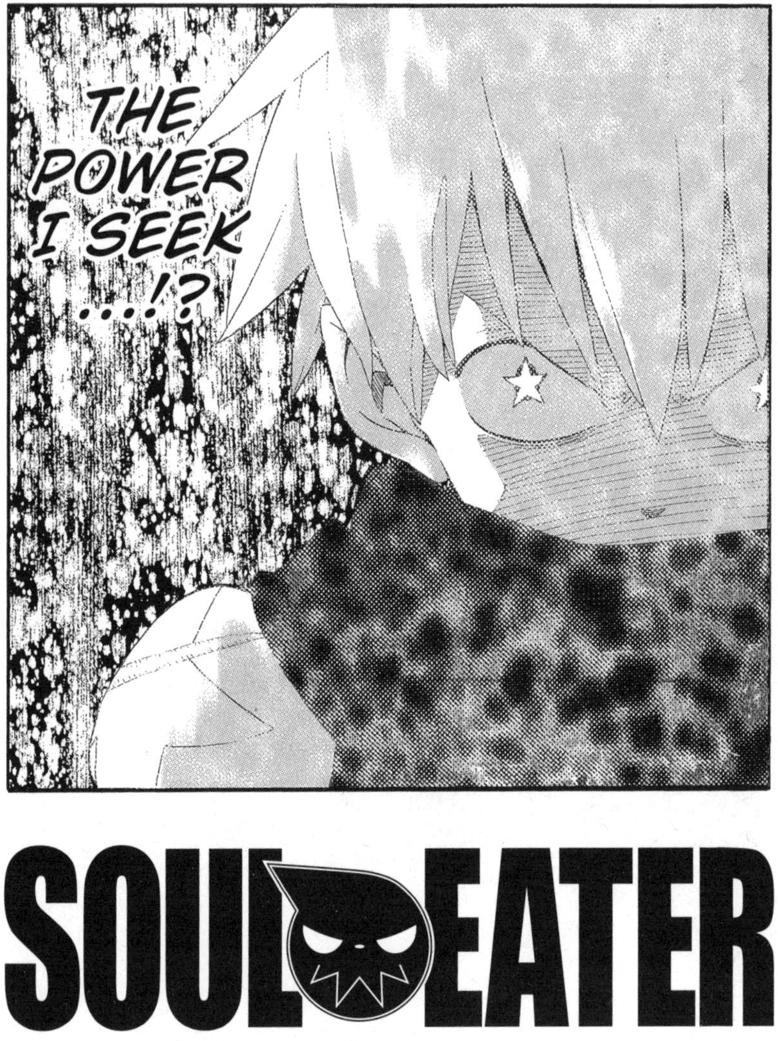
THE POWER I SEEK ...!?

SOUL EATER

CHAPTER 78: SALVAGE (PART 7)

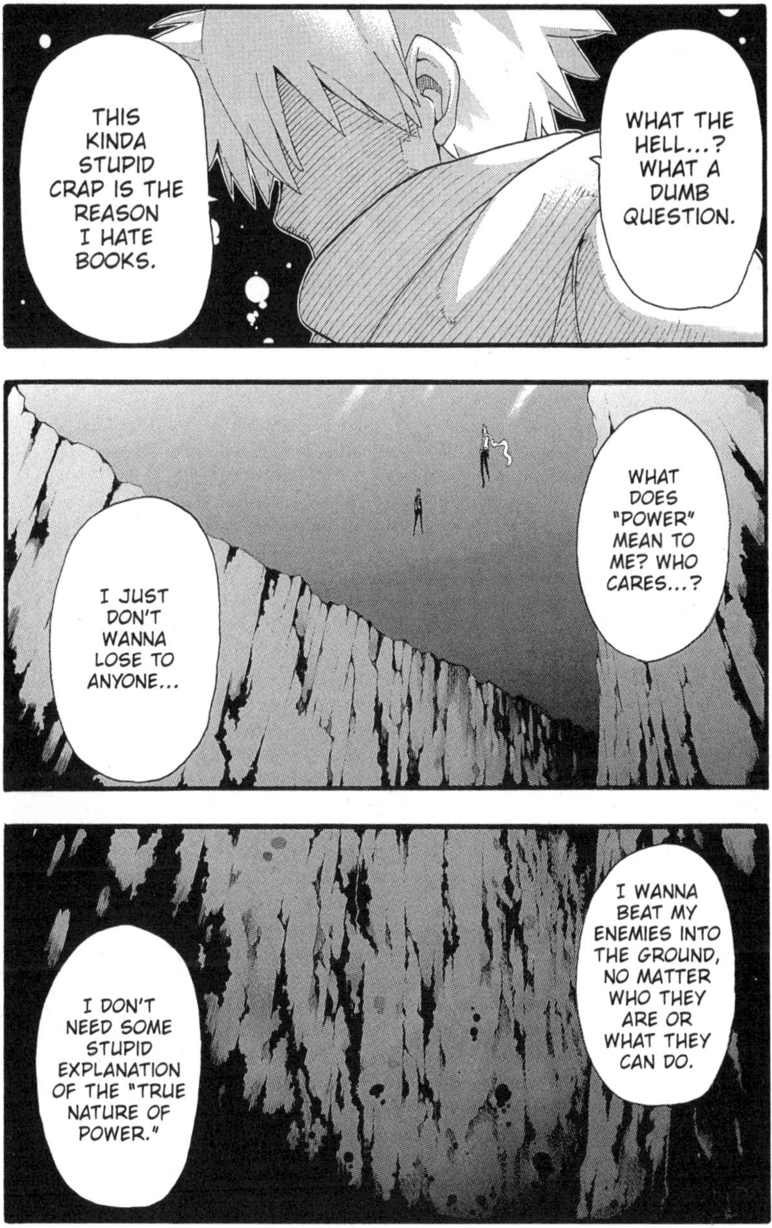
WHAT THE HELL...? WHAT A DUMB QUESTION.
THIS KINDA STUPID CRAP IS THE REASON I HATE BOOKS.
WHAT DOES "POWER" MEAN TO ME? WHO CARES...?
I JUST DON'T WANNA LOSE TO ANYONE...
I WANNA BEAT MY ENEMIES INTO THE GROUND, NO MATTER WHO THEY ARE OR WHAT THEY CAN DO.
I DON'T NEED SOME STUPID EXPLANATION OF THE "TRUE NATURE OF POWER."

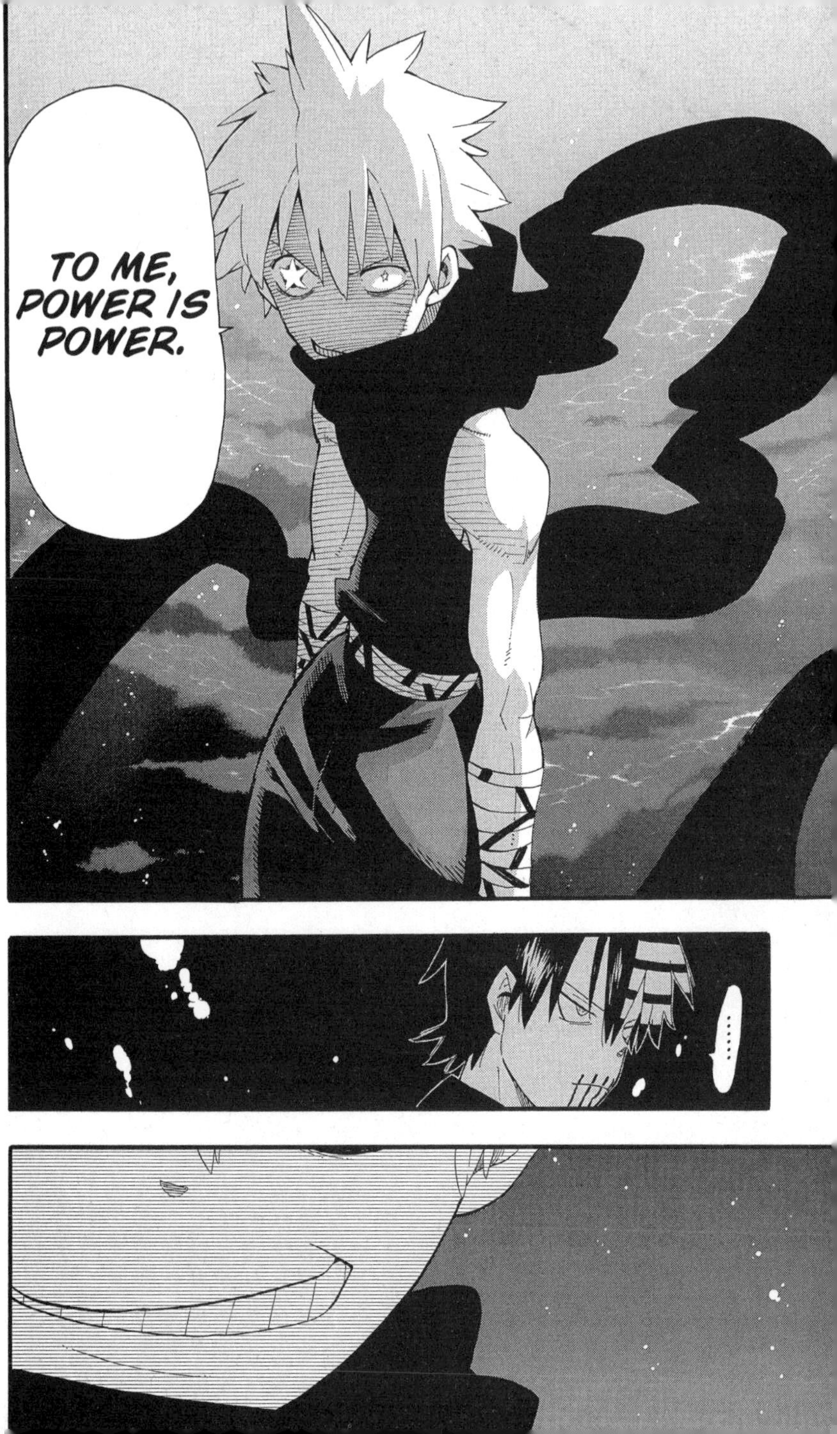
TO ME, POWER IS POWER.
......

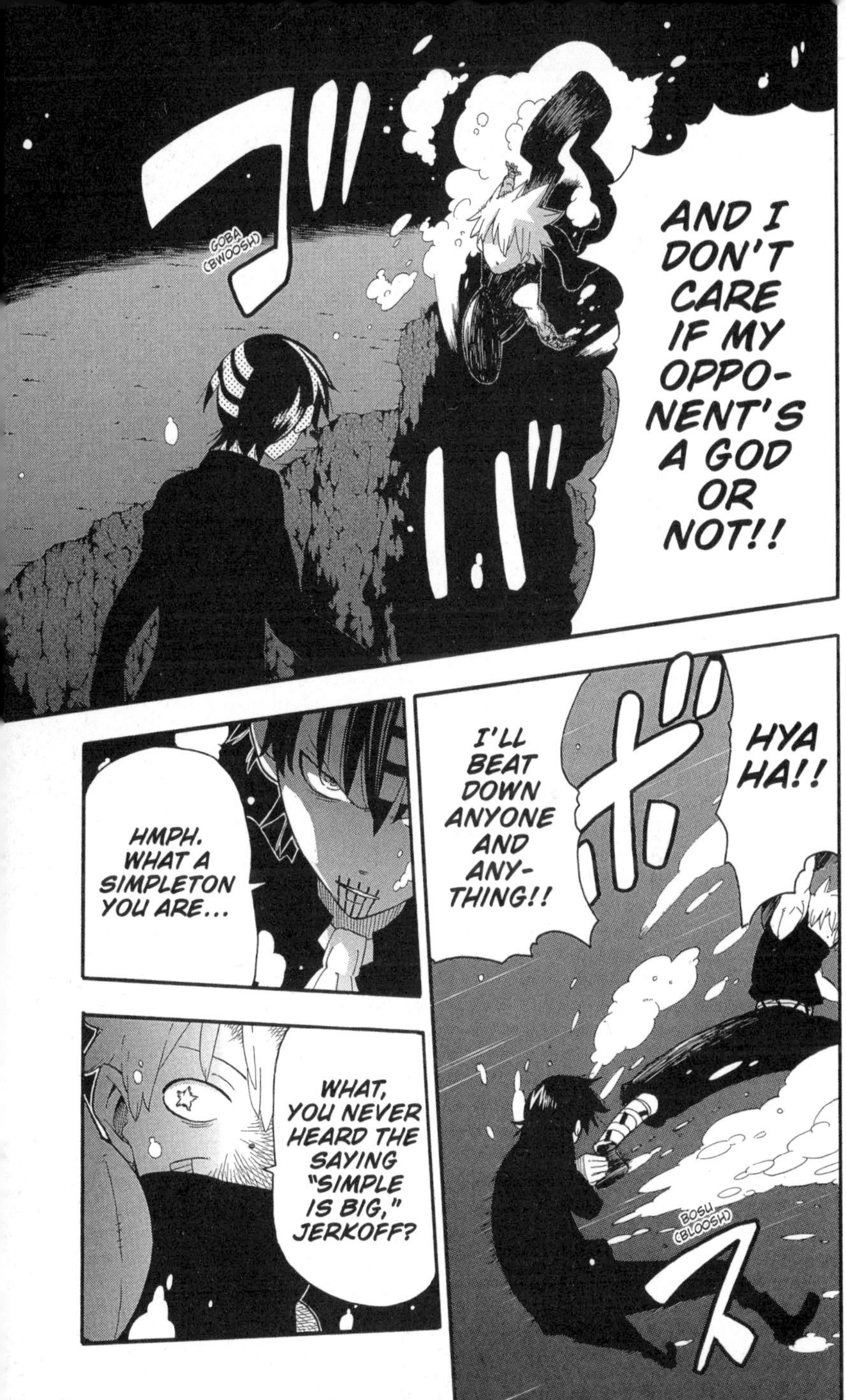
AND I DON'T CARE IF MY OPPONENT'S A GOD OR NOT!!
GOBA (BWOOSH)
HYA HA!!
I'LL BEAT DOWN ANYONE AND ANYTHING!!
BOSU (BLOOSH)
HMPH. WHAT A SIMPLETON YOU ARE...
WHAT, YOU NEVER HEARD THE SAYING "SIMPLE IS BIG," JERKOFF?

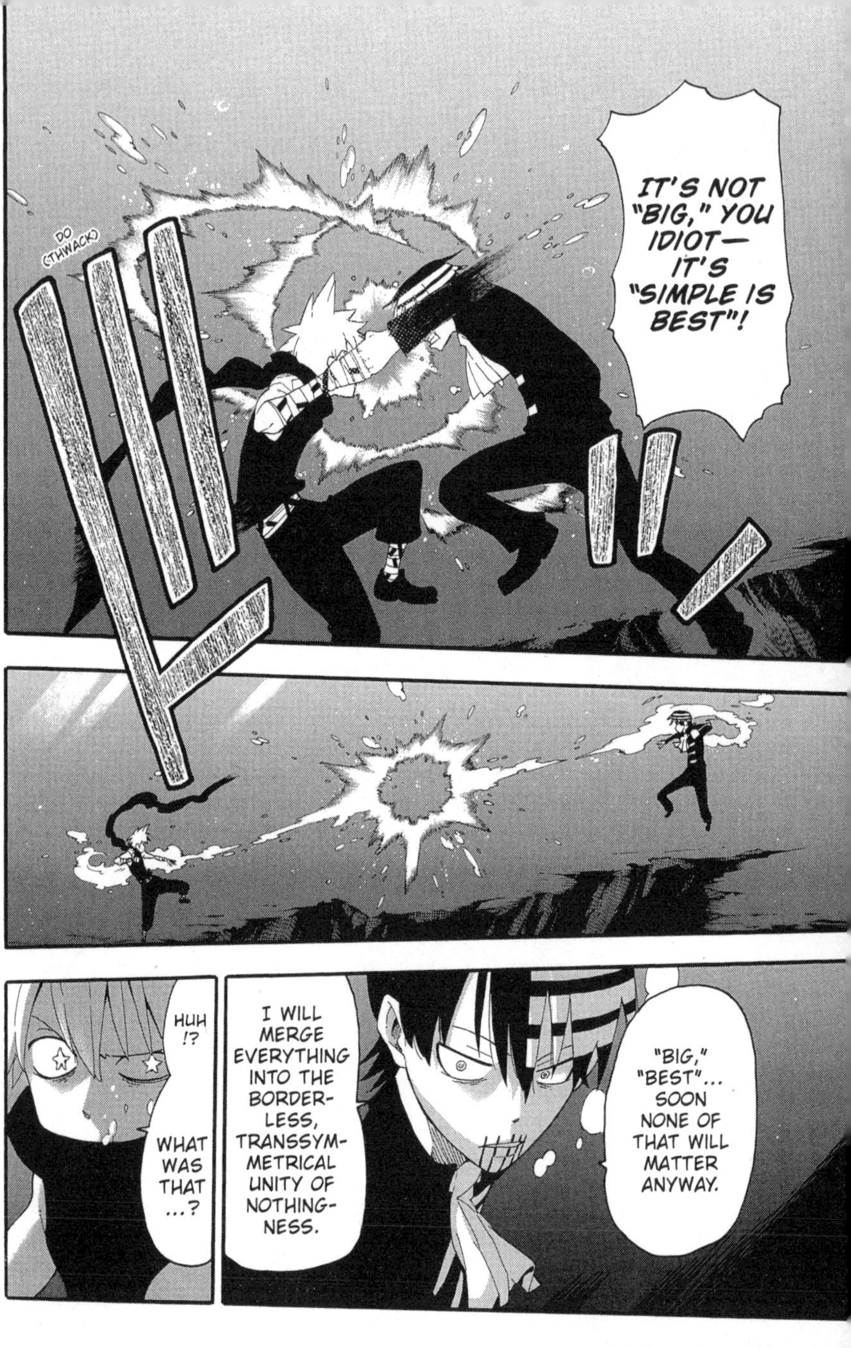
IT'S NOT "BIG," YOU IDIOT— IT'S "SIMPLE IS BEST"!
DO (THWACK)
"BIG," "BEST"... SOON NONE OF THAT WILL MATTER ANYWAY.
I WILL MERGE EVERYTHING INTO THE BORDERLESS, TRANSSYMMETRICAL UNITY OF NOTHINGNESS.
HUH!?
WHAT WAS THAT...?

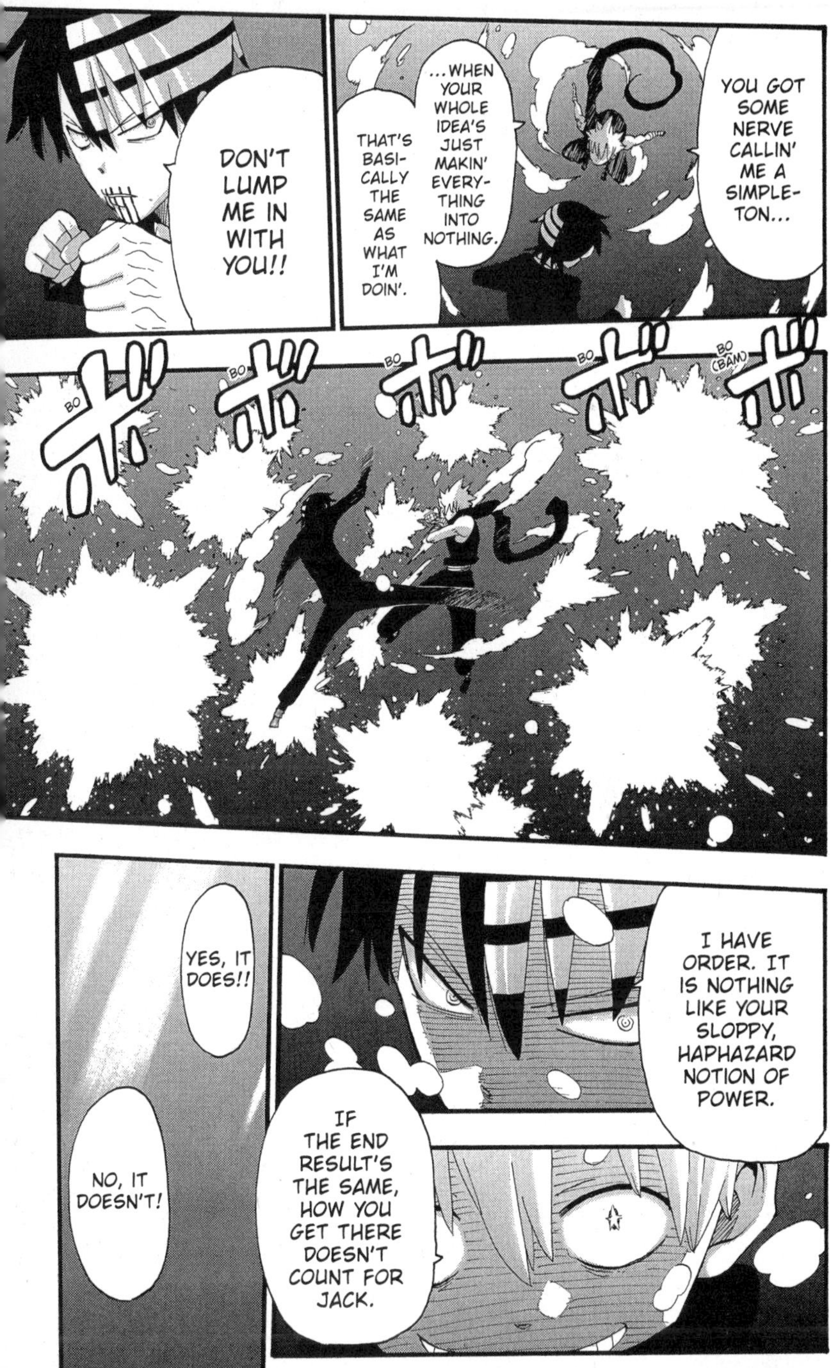
YOU GOT SOME NERVE CALLIN' ME A SIMPLETON...
...WHEN YOUR WHOLE IDEA'S JUST MAKIN' EVERYTHING INTO NOTHING.
THAT'S BASICALLY THE SAME AS WHAT I'M DOIN'.
DON'T LUMP ME IN WITH YOU!!
BO (BAM)
BO
BO
BO
BO
I HAVE ORDER. IT IS NOTHING LIKE YOUR SLOPPY, HAPHAZARD NOTION OF POWER.
IF THE END RESULT'S THE SAME, HOW YOU GET THERE DOESN'T COUNT FOR JACK.
YES, IT DOES!!
NO, IT DOESN'T!

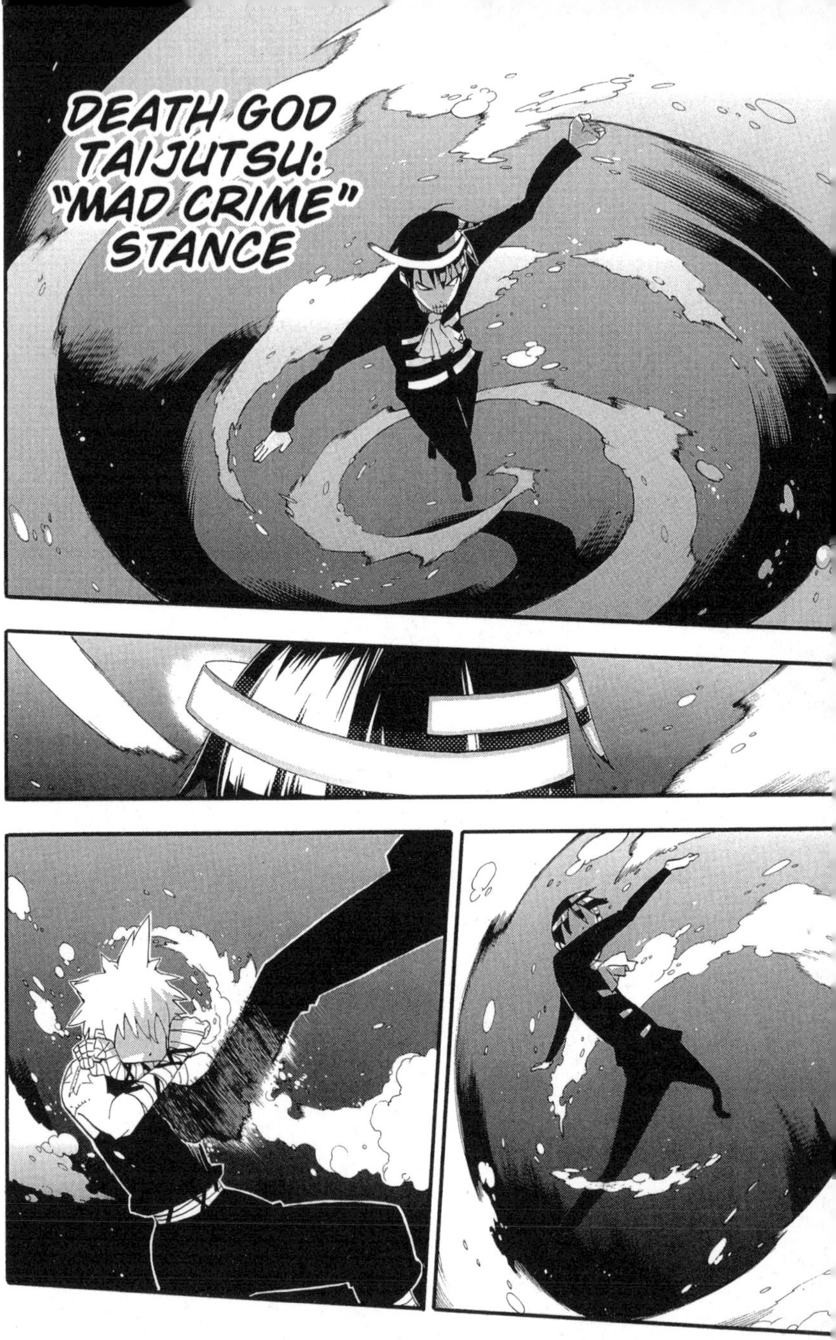
DEATH GOD TAIJUTSU: "MAD CRIME" STANCE

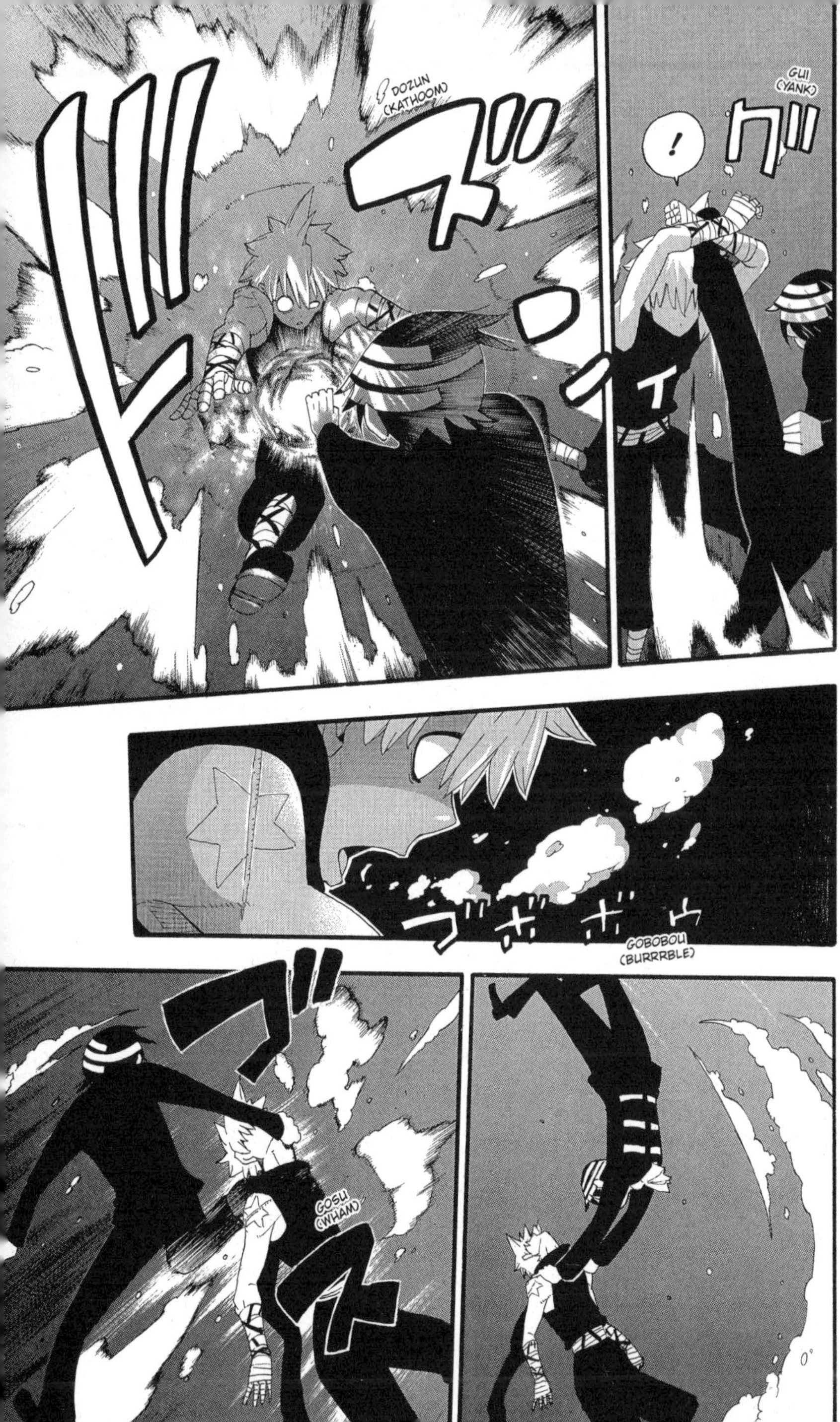
!
GUI (YANK)
DOZUN (KATHOOM)
GOBOBOU (BURRRBLE)
GOSU (WHAM)

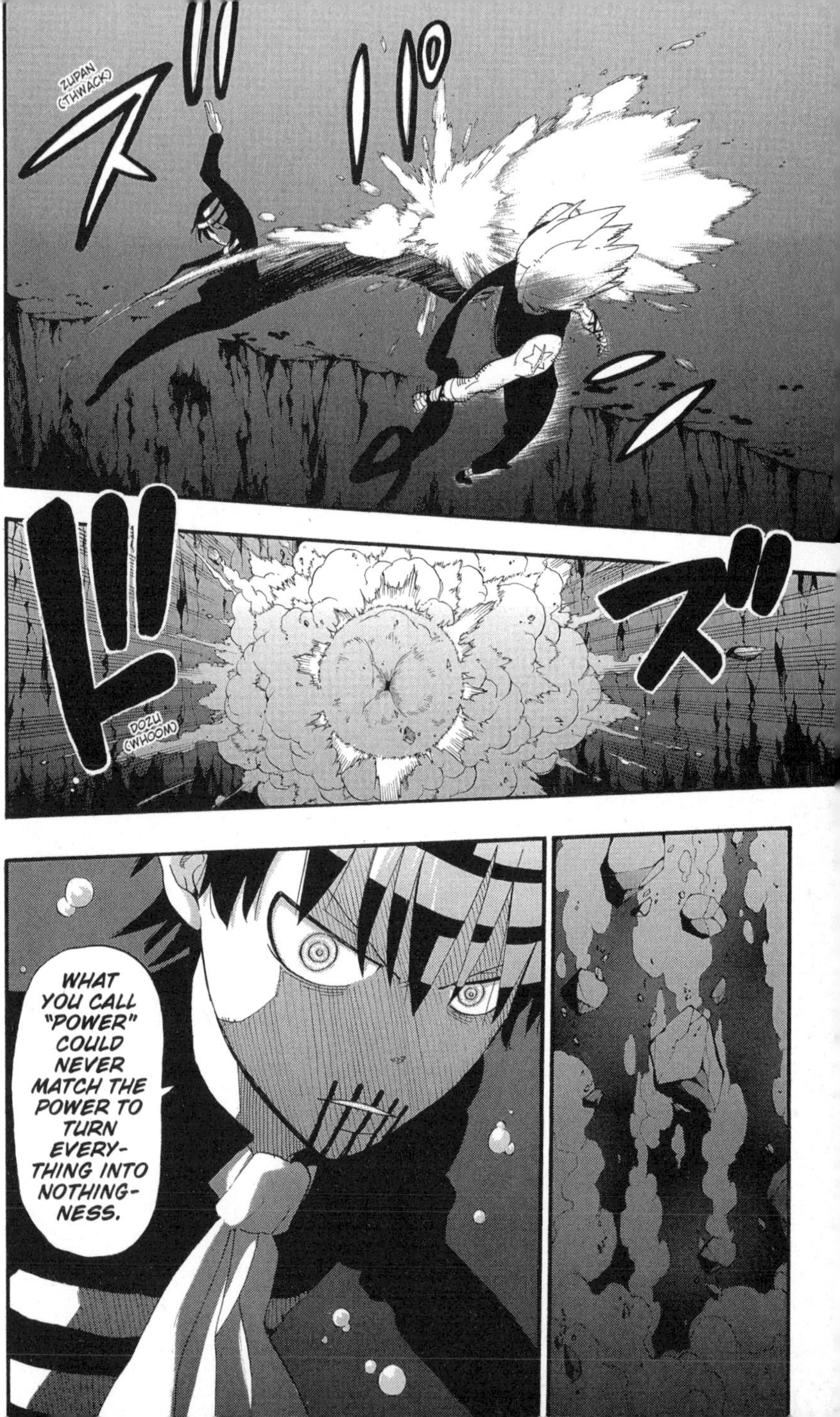
ZUPAN (THWACK)
DOZU (WHOOM)
WHAT YOU CALL "POWER" COULD NEVER MATCH THE POWER TO TURN EVERY-THING INTO NOTHING-NESS.

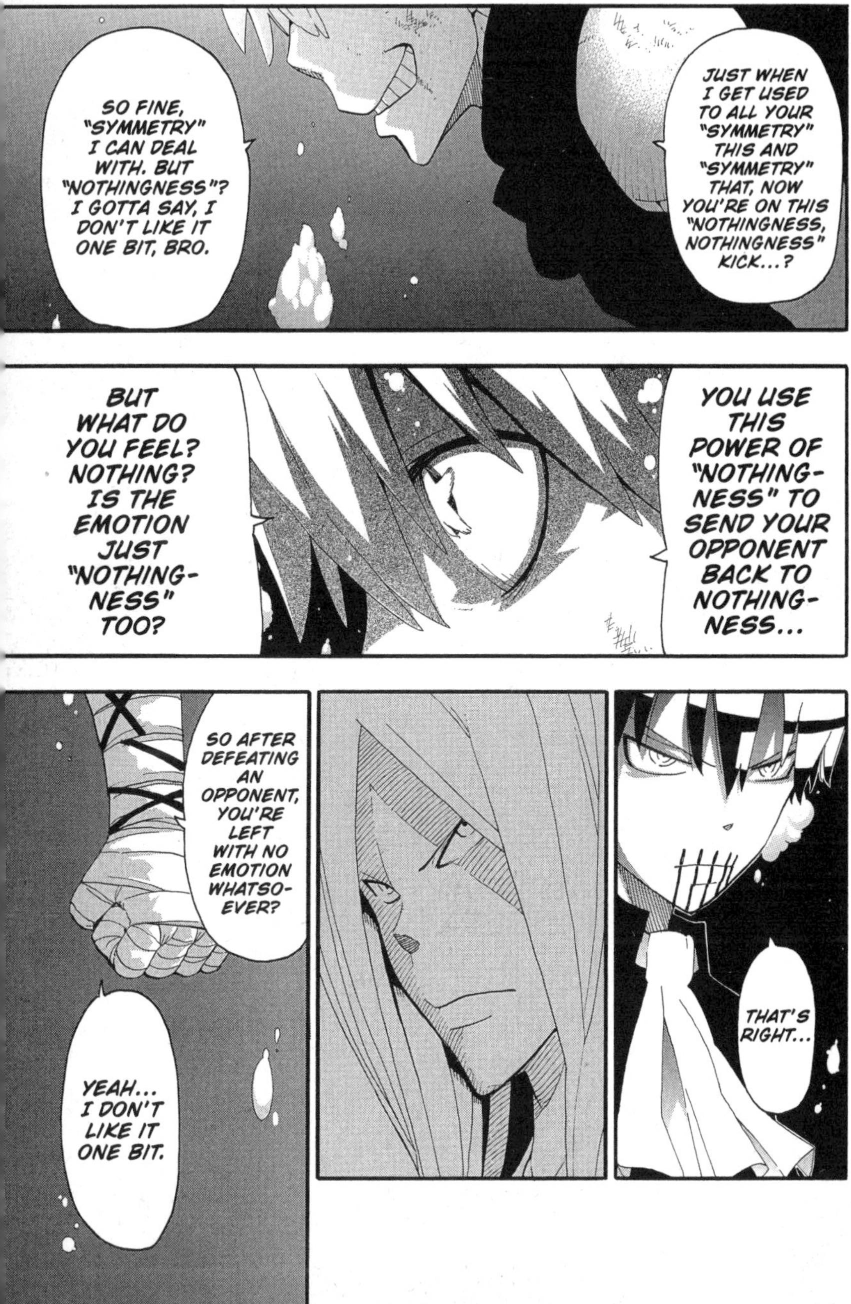
JUST WHEN I GET USED TO ALL YOUR "SYMMETRY" THIS AND "SYMMETRY" THAT, NOW YOU'RE ON THIS "NOTHINGNESS, NOTHINGNESS" KICK...?
SO FINE, "SYMMETRY" I CAN DEAL WITH. BUT "NOTHINGNESS"? I GOTTA SAY, I DON'T LIKE IT ONE BIT, BRO.
YOU USE THIS POWER OF "NOTHING-NESS" TO SEND YOUR OPPONENT BACK TO NOTHING-NESS...
BUT WHAT DO YOU FEEL? NOTHING? IS THE EMOTION JUST "NOTHING-NESS" TOO?
THAT'S RIGHT...
SO AFTER DEFEATING AN OPPONENT, YOU'RE LEFT WITH NO EMOTION WHATSO-EVER?
YEAH... I DON'T LIKE IT ONE BIT.

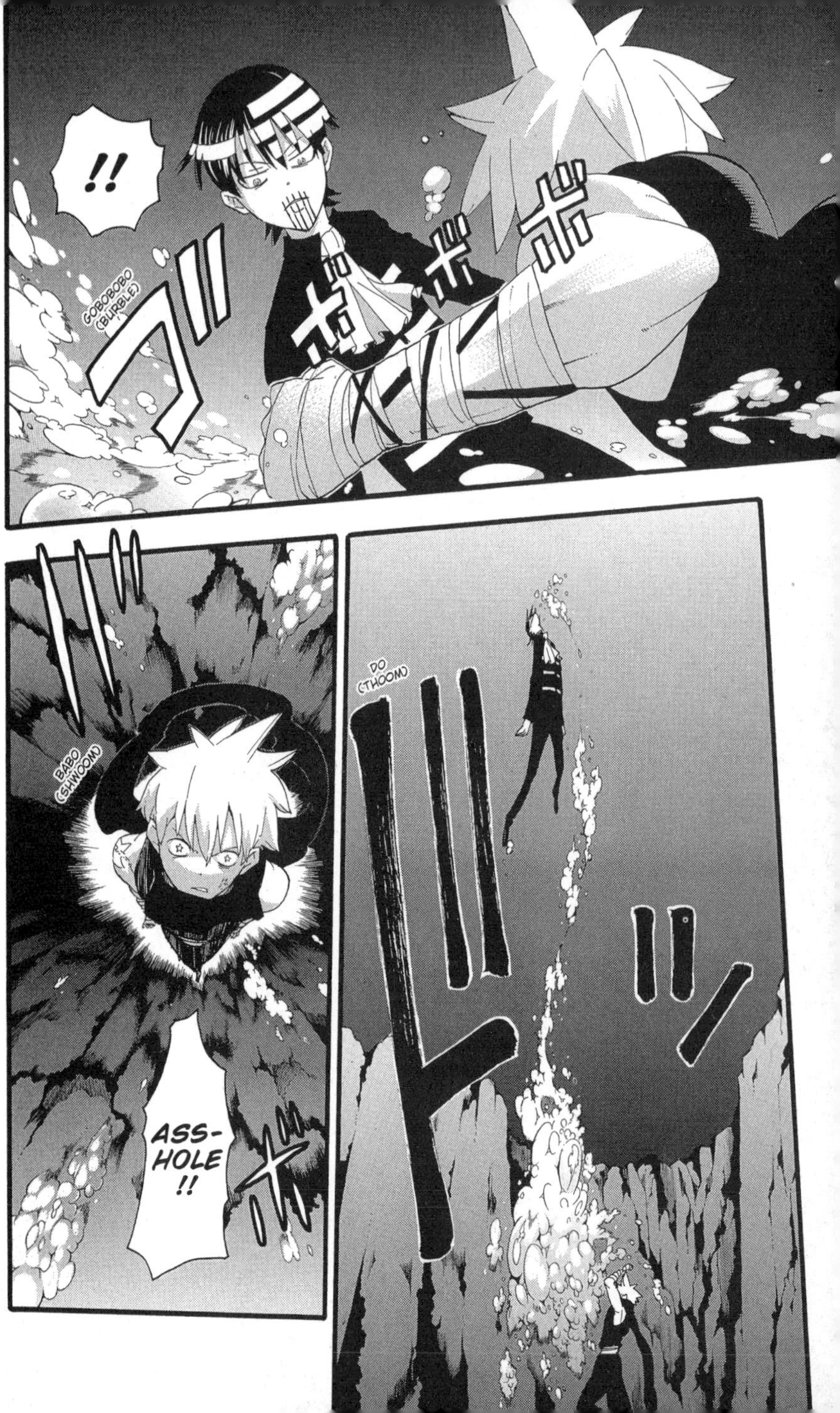
!!
GOBOBOBO (BURBLE)
DO (THOOM)
BABO (SHWOOM)
ASS-HOLE !!

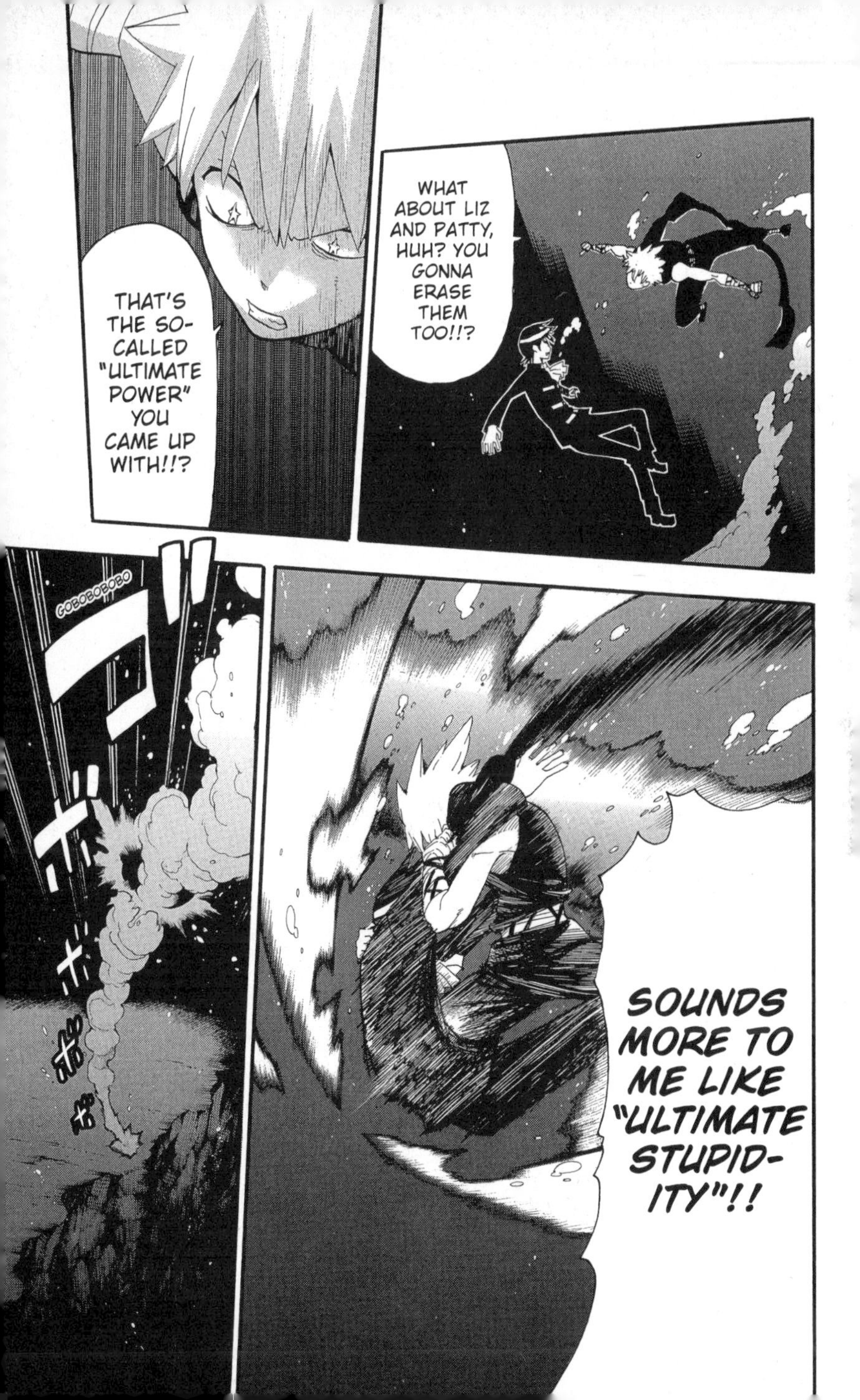

WHAT ABOUT LIZ AND PATTY, HUH? YOU GONNA ERASE THEM TOO!!?
THAT'S THE SO-CALLED "ULTIMATE POWER" YOU CAME UP WITH!!?
SOUNDS MORE TO ME LIKE "ULTIMATE STUPID-ITY"!!
GOBOBOBO

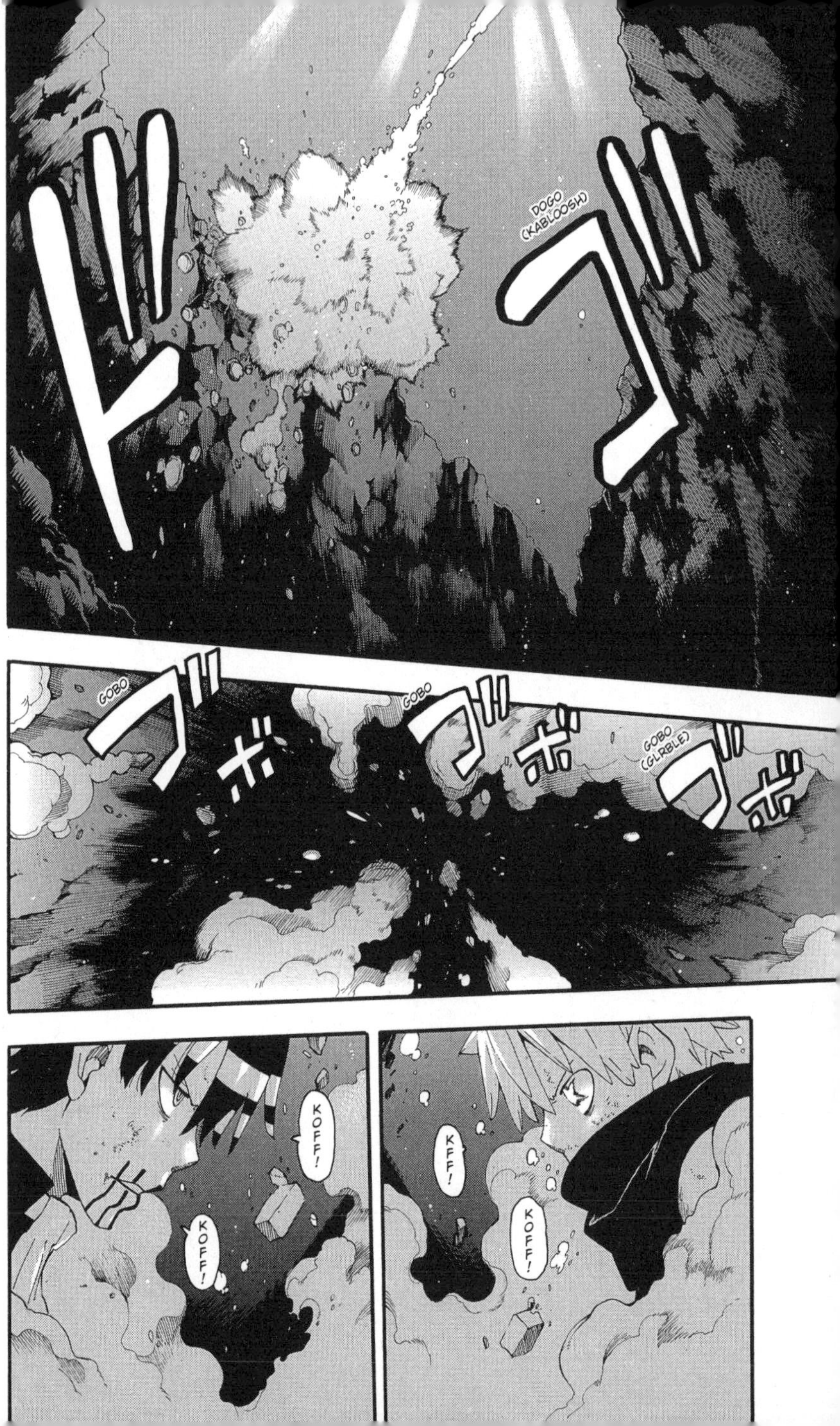

ドゴ
DOGO (KABLOOSH)
ゴボ
GOBO (GLRBLE)
ゴボ
GOBO
ゴボ
GOBO
KFF!
KOFF!
KOFF!
KOFF!

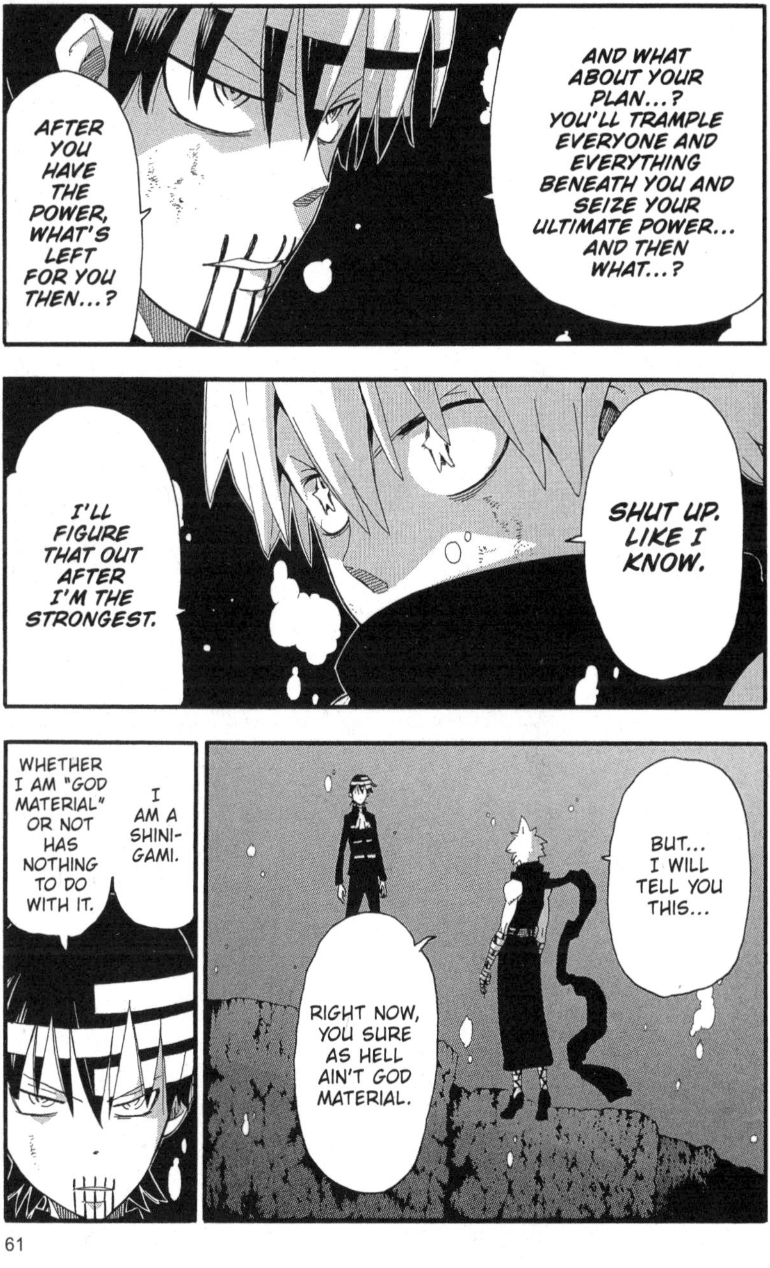
AND WHAT ABOUT YOUR PLAN...? YOU'LL TRAMPLE EVERYONE AND EVERYTHING BENEATH YOU AND SEIZE YOUR ULTIMATE POWER... AND THEN WHAT...?
AFTER YOU HAVE THE POWER, WHAT'S LEFT FOR YOU THEN...?
SHUT UP. LIKE I KNOW.
I'LL FIGURE THAT OUT AFTER I'M THE STRONGEST.
BUT... I WILL TELL YOU THIS...
RIGHT NOW, YOU SURE AS HELL AIN'T GOD MATERIAL.
I AM A SHINI-GAMI.
WHETHER I AM "GOD MATERIAL" OR NOT HAS NOTHING TO DO WITH IT.

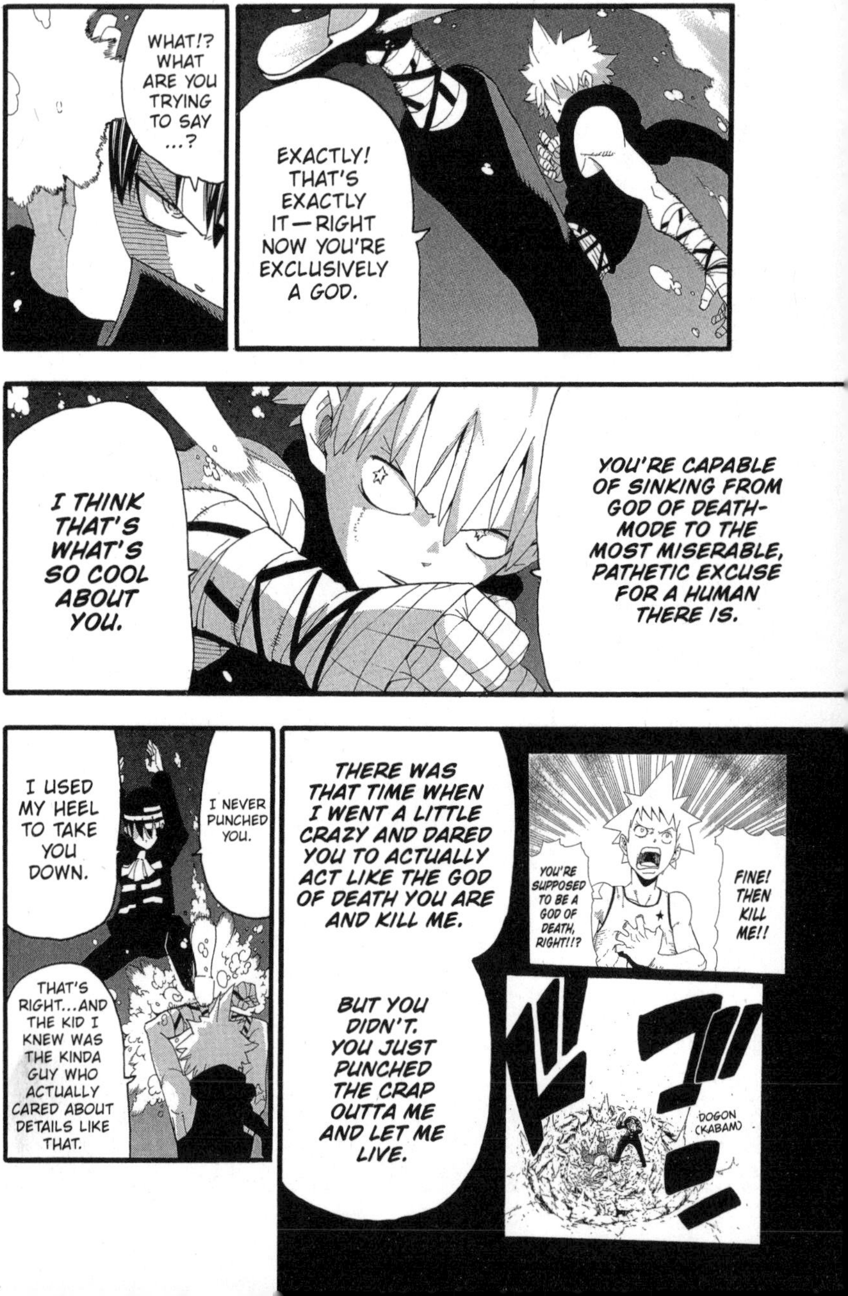
EXACTLY! THAT'S EXACTLY IT—RIGHT NOW YOU'RE EXCLUSIVELY A GOD.
WHAT!? WHAT ARE YOU TRYING TO SAY ...?
YOU'RE CAPABLE OF SINKING FROM GOD OF DEATH-MODE TO THE MOST MISERABLE, PATHETIC EXCUSE FOR A HUMAN THERE IS.
I THINK THAT'S WHAT'S SO COOL ABOUT YOU.
THERE WAS THAT TIME WHEN I WENT A LITTLE CRAZY AND DARED YOU TO ACTUALLY ACT LIKE THE GOD OF DEATH YOU ARE AND KILL ME.
FINE! THEN KILL ME!!
YOU'RE SUPPOSED TO BE A GOD OF DEATH, RIGHT!!?
DOGON (KABAM)
BUT YOU DIDN'T. YOU JUST PUNCHED THE CRAP OUTTA ME AND LET ME LIVE.
I NEVER PUNCHED YOU.
I USED MY HEEL TO TAKE YOU DOWN.
THAT'S RIGHT...AND THE KID I KNEW WAS THE KINDA GUY WHO ACTUALLY CARED ABOUT DETAILS LIKE THAT.

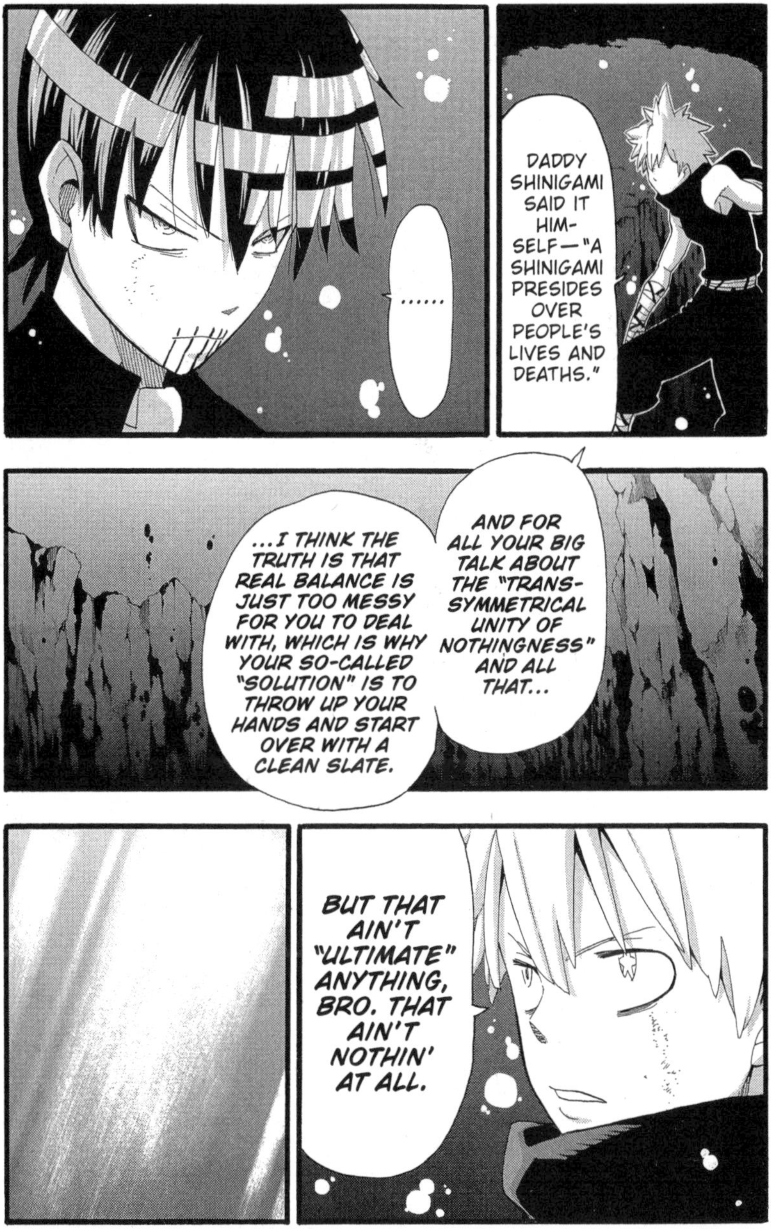
DADDY SHINIGAMI SAID IT HIM-SELF—"A SHINIGAMI PRESIDES OVER PEOPLE'S LIVES AND DEATHS."
......
AND FOR ALL YOUR BIG TALK ABOUT THE "TRANS-SYMMETRICAL UNITY OF NOTHINGNESS" AND ALL THAT...
...I THINK THE TRUTH IS THAT REAL BALANCE IS JUST TOO MESSY FOR YOU TO DEAL WITH, WHICH IS WHY YOUR SO-CALLED "SOLUTION" IS TO THROW UP YOUR HANDS AND START OVER WITH A CLEAN SLATE.
BUT THAT AIN'T "ULTIMATE" ANYTHING, BRO. THAT AIN'T NOTHIN' AT ALL.

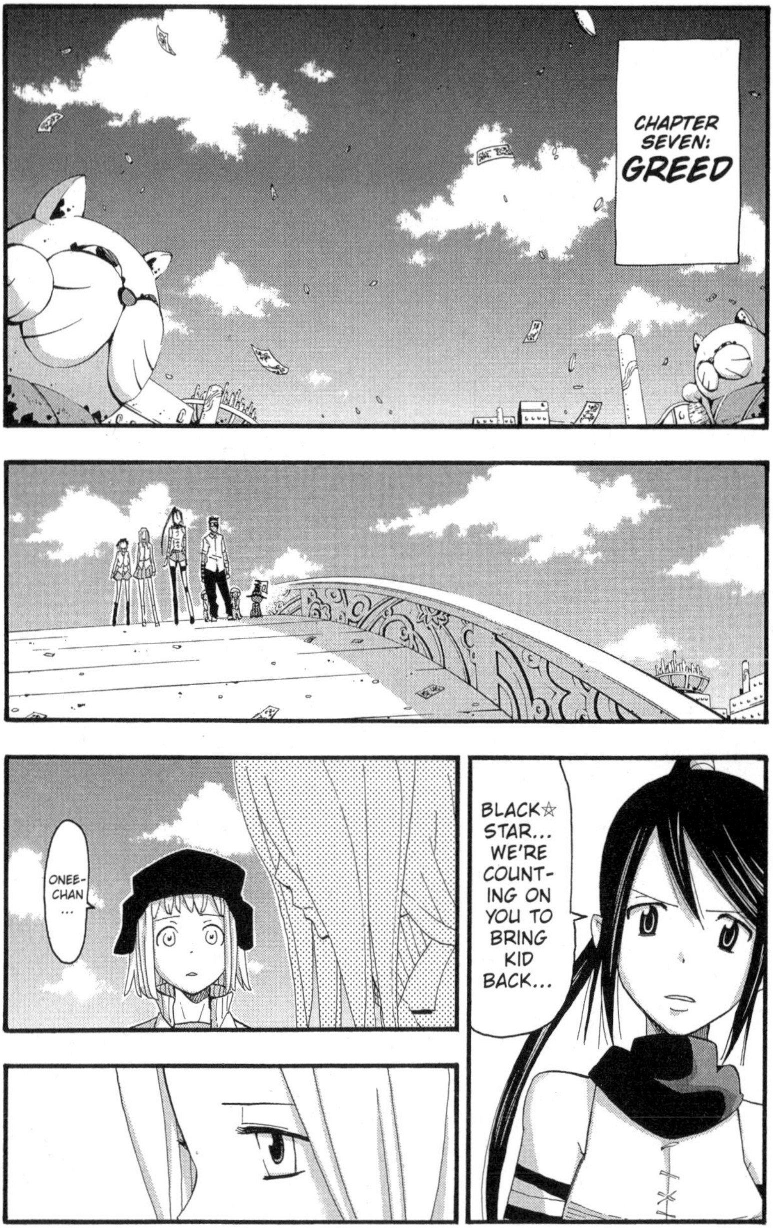
CHAPTER SEVEN: GREED
BLACK☆STAR... WE'RE COUNTING ON YOU TO BRING KID BACK...
ONEE-CHAN...

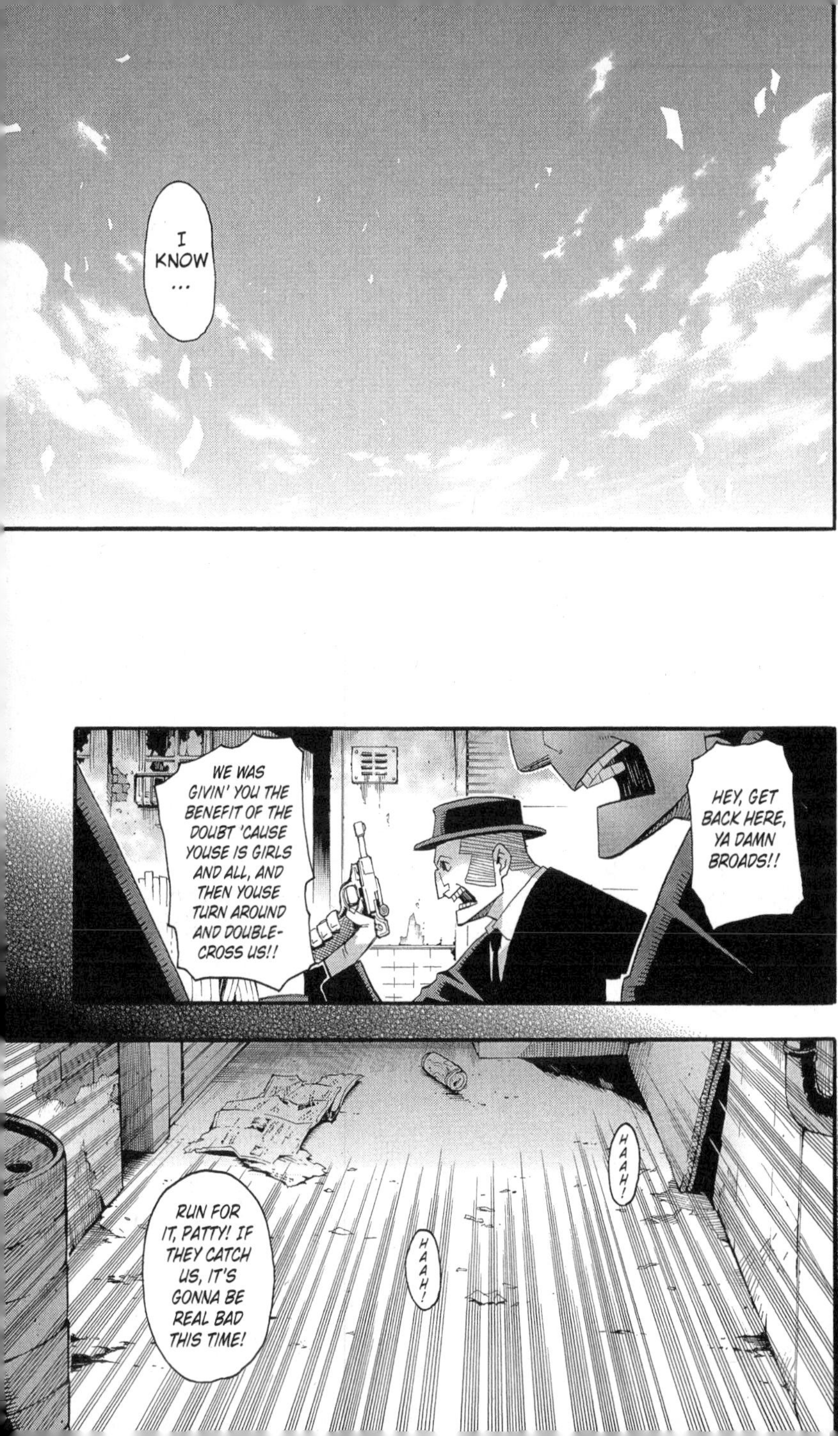
I KNOW...
HEY, GET BACK HERE, YA DAMN BROADS!!
WE WAS GIVIN' YOU THE BENEFIT OF THE DOUBT 'CAUSE YOUSE IS GIRLS AND ALL, AND THEN YOUSE TURN AROUND AND DOUBLE-CROSS US!!
HAAAH!
HAAAH!
RUN FOR IT, PATTY! IF THEY CATCH US, IT'S GONNA BE REAL BAD THIS TIME!

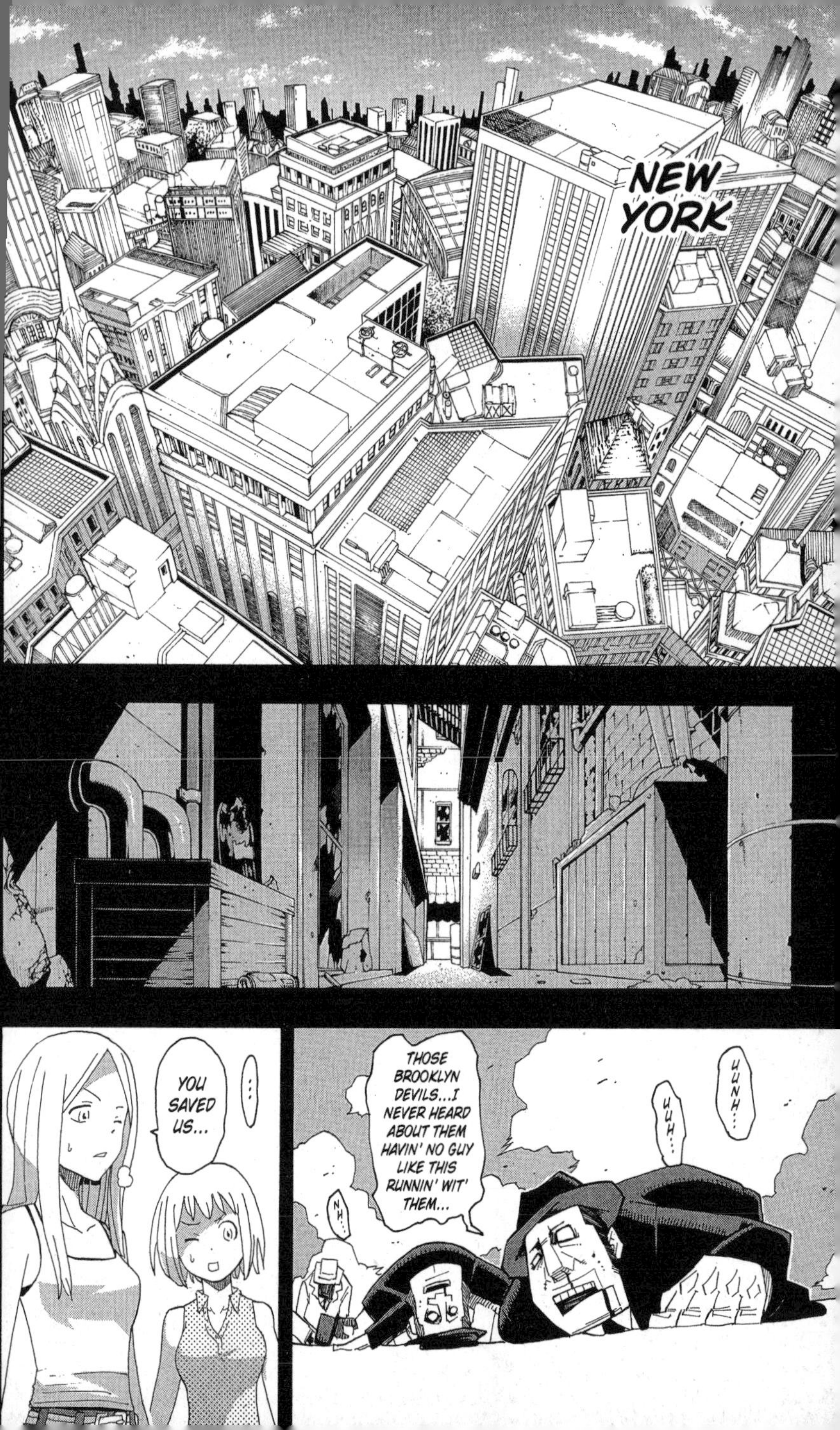
NEW YORK
UUNH...
UUH...
THOSE BROOKLYN DEVILS...I NEVER HEARD ABOUT THEM HAVIN' NO GUY LIKE THIS RUNNIN' WIT' THEM...
NH...
...
YOU SAVED US...

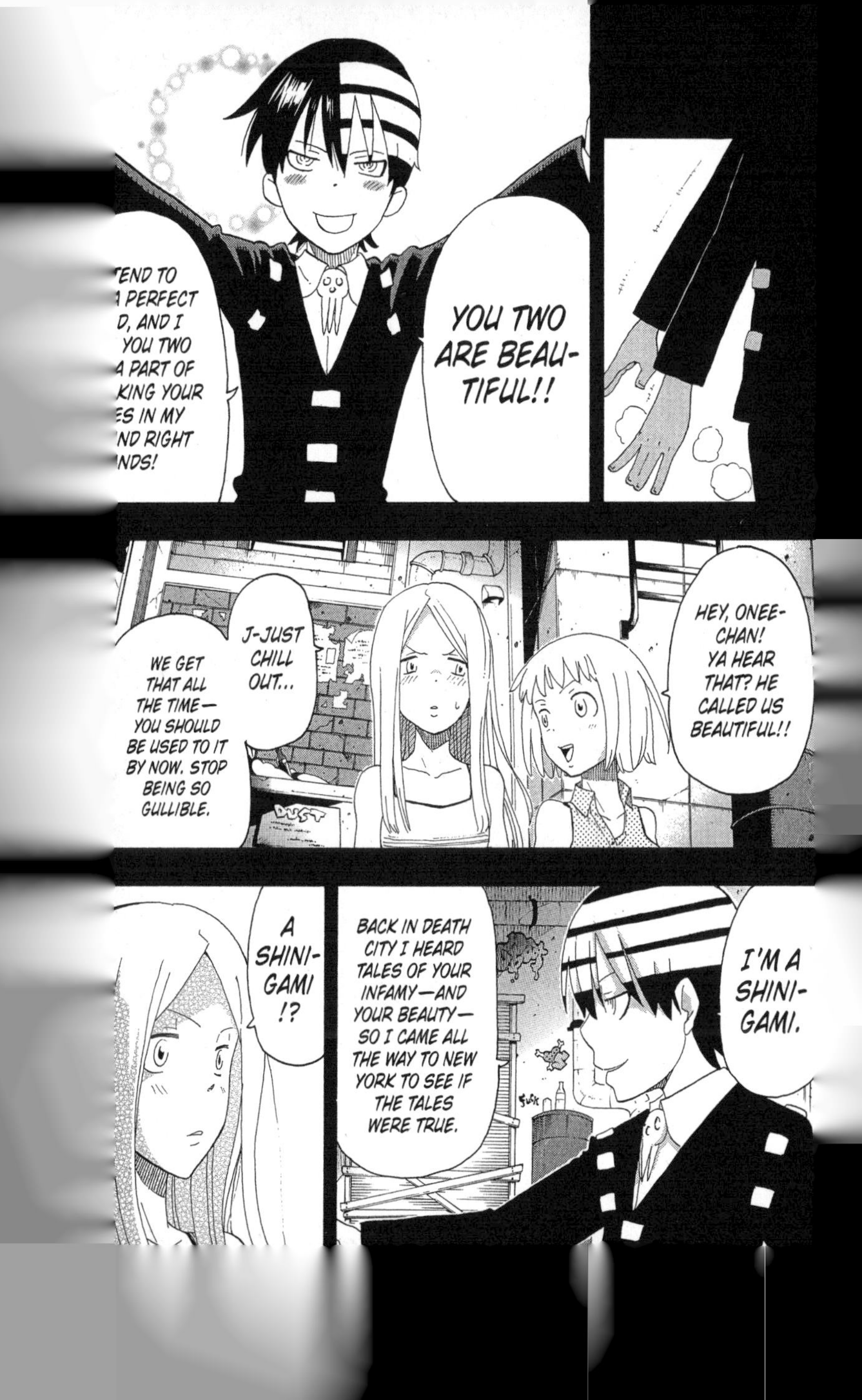
YOU TWO ARE BEAUTIFUL!!
TEND TO A PERFECT D, AND I YOU TWO A PART OF KING YOUR ES IN MY ND RIGHT NDS!
HEY, ONEE-CHAN! YA HEAR THAT? HE CALLED US BEAUTIFUL!!
J-JUST CHILL OUT...
WE GET THAT ALL THE TIME—YOU SHOULD BE USED TO IT BY NOW. STOP BEING SO GULLIBLE.
DUST
I'M A SHINIGAMI.
BACK IN DEATH CITY I HEARD TALES OF YOUR INFAMY—AND YOUR BEAUTY—SO I CAME ALL THE WAY TO NEW YORK TO SEE IF THE TALES WERE TRUE.
A SHINIGAMI!?

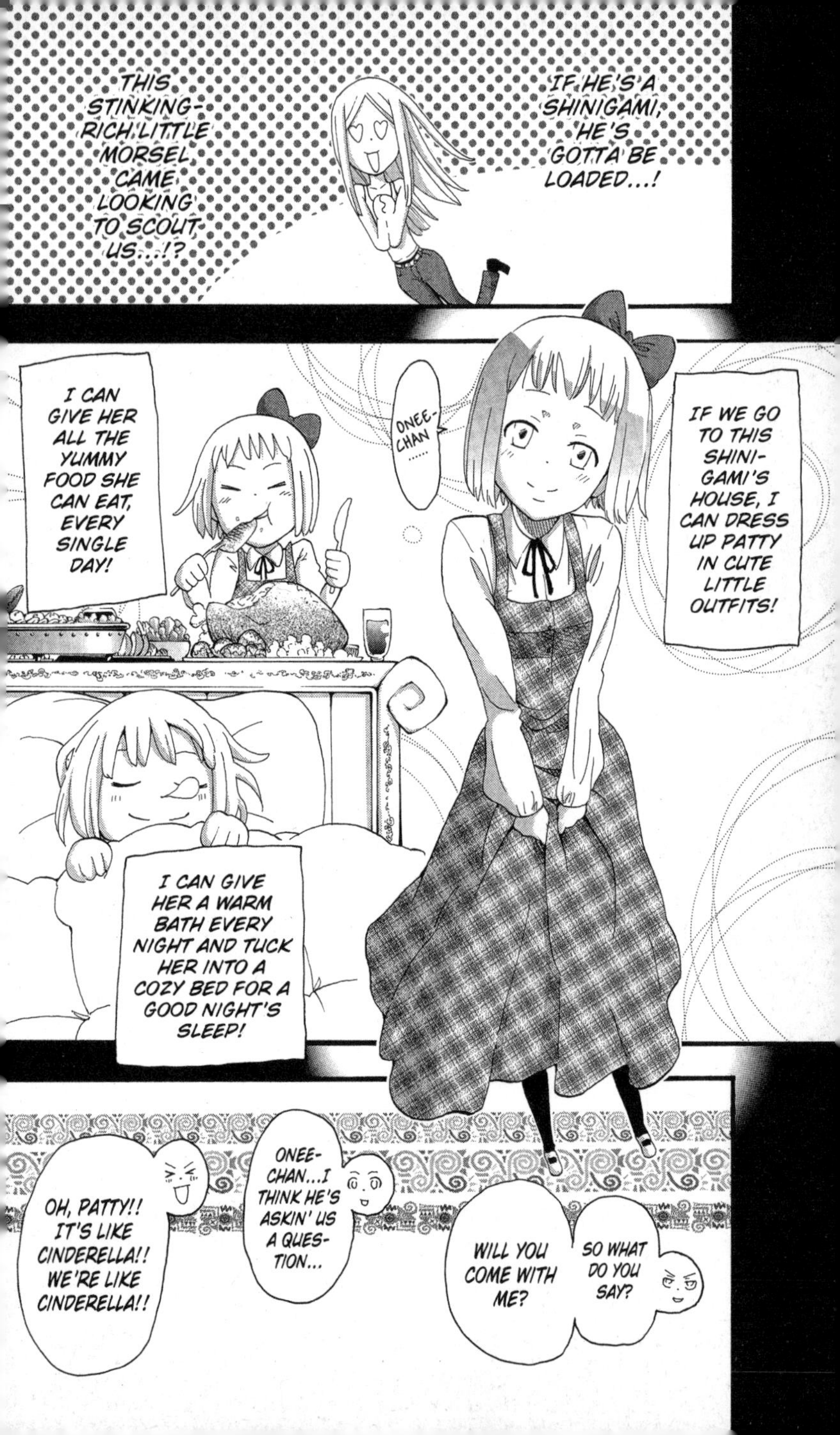
IF HE'S A SHINIGAMI, HE'S GOTTA BE LOADED...!
THIS STINKING-RICH LITTLE MORSEL CAME LOOKING TO SCOUT US...!?
IF WE GO TO THIS SHINIGAMI'S HOUSE, I CAN DRESS UP PATTY IN CUTE LITTLE OUTFITS!
ONEE-CHAN ......
I CAN GIVE HER ALL THE YUMMY FOOD SHE CAN EAT, EVERY SINGLE DAY!
I CAN GIVE HER A WARM BATH EVERY NIGHT AND TUCK HER INTO A COZY BED FOR A GOOD NIGHT'S SLEEP!
SO WHAT DO YOU SAY?
WILL YOU COME WITH ME?
ONEE-CHAN...I THINK HE'S ASKIN' US A QUESTION...
OH, PATTY!! IT'S LIKE CINDERELLA!! WE'RE LIKE CINDERELLA!!

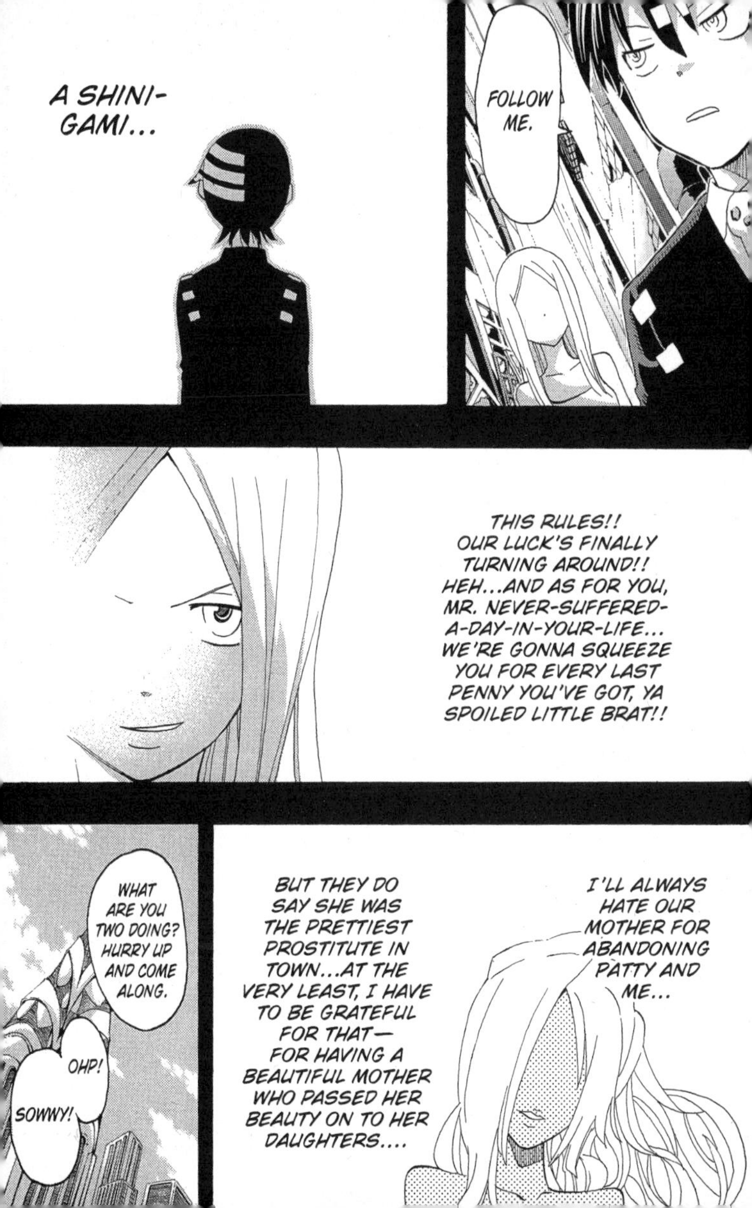
FOLLOW ME.
A SHINI-GAMI...
THIS RULES!! OUR LUCK'S FINALLY TURNING AROUND!! HEH...AND AS FOR YOU, MR. NEVER-SUFFERED-A-DAY-IN-YOUR-LIFE... WE'RE GONNA SQUEEZE YOU FOR EVERY LAST PENNY YOU'VE GOT, YA SPOILED LITTLE BRAT!!
I'LL ALWAYS HATE OUR MOTHER FOR ABANDONING PATTY AND ME...
BUT THEY DO SAY SHE WAS THE PRETTIEST PROSTITUTE IN TOWN...AT THE VERY LEAST, I HAVE TO BE GRATEFUL FOR THAT— FOR HAVING A BEAUTIFUL MOTHER WHO PASSED HER BEAUTY ON TO HER DAUGHTERS....
WHAT ARE YOU TWO DOING? HURRY UP AND COME ALONG.
OHP!
SOWWY!

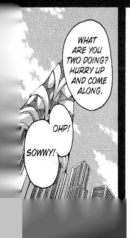

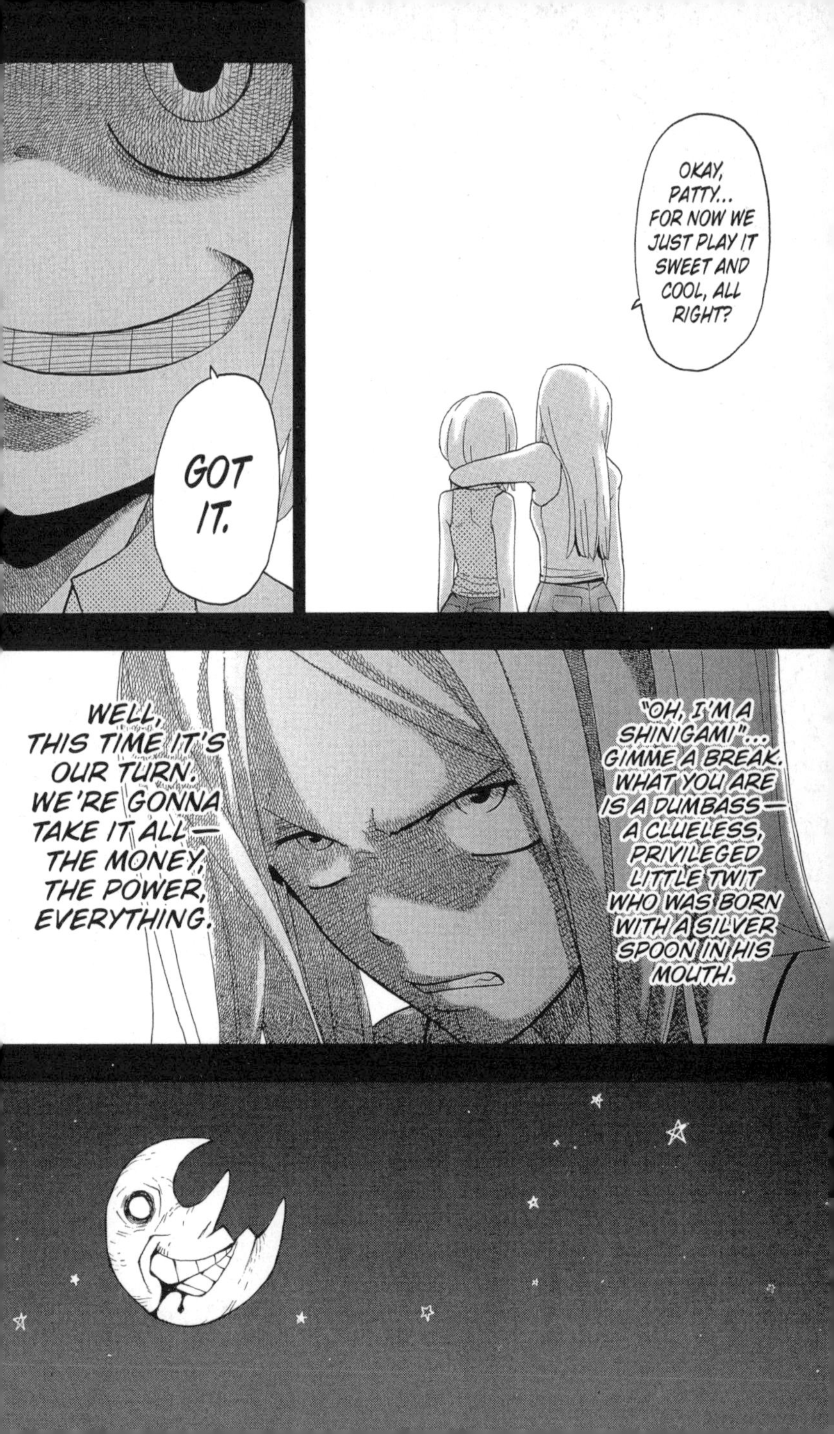
OKAY, PATTY... FOR NOW WE JUST PLAY IT SWEET AND COOL, ALL RIGHT?
GOT IT.
"OH, I'M A SHINIGAMI"... GIMME A BREAK. WHAT YOU ARE IS A DUMBASS—A CLUELESS, PRIVILEGED LITTLE TWIT WHO WAS BORN WITH A SILVER SPOON IN HIS MOUTH.
WELL, THIS TIME IT'S OUR TURN. WE'RE GONNA TAKE IT ALL—THE MONEY, THE POWER, EVERYTHING.

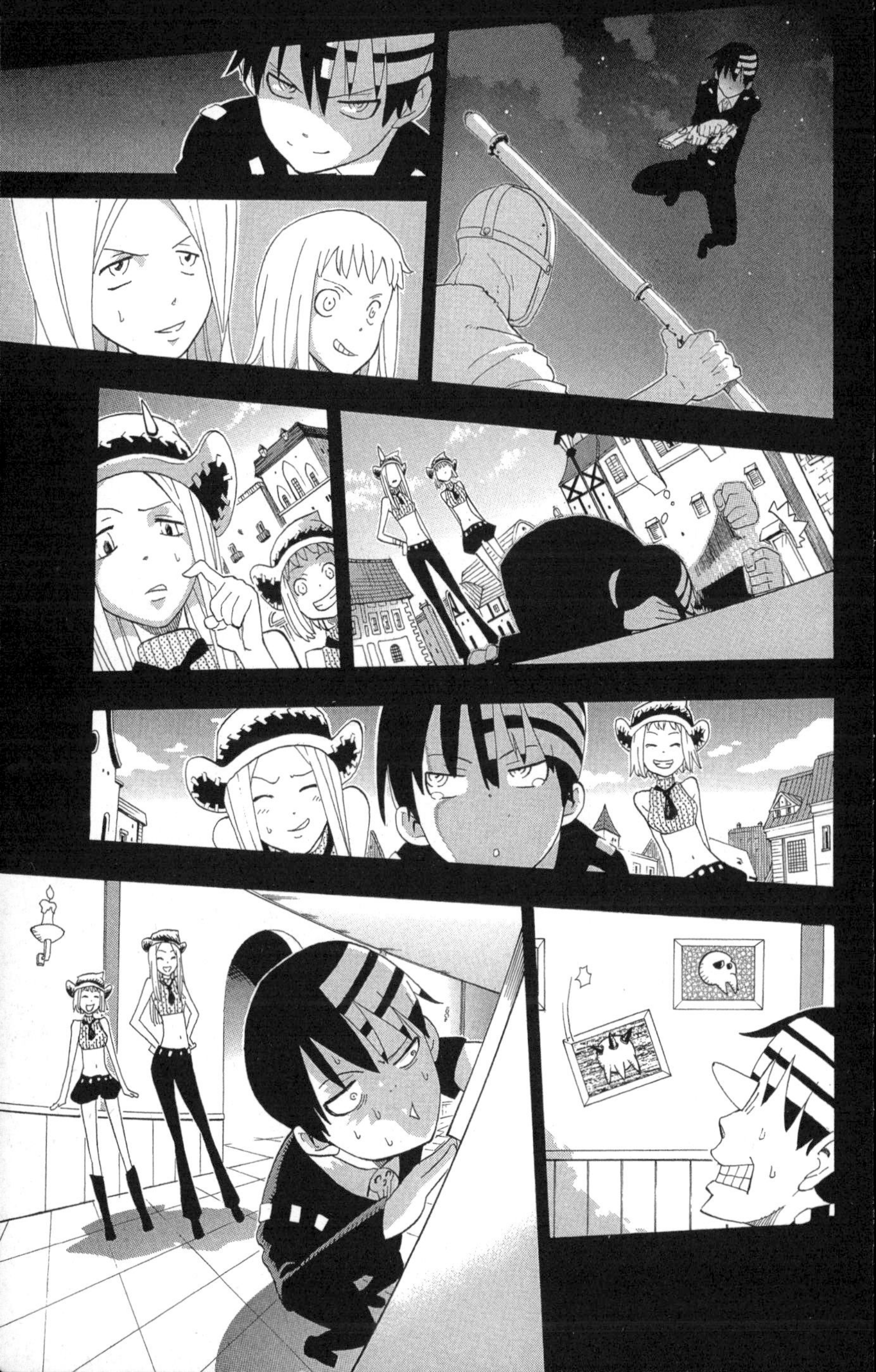

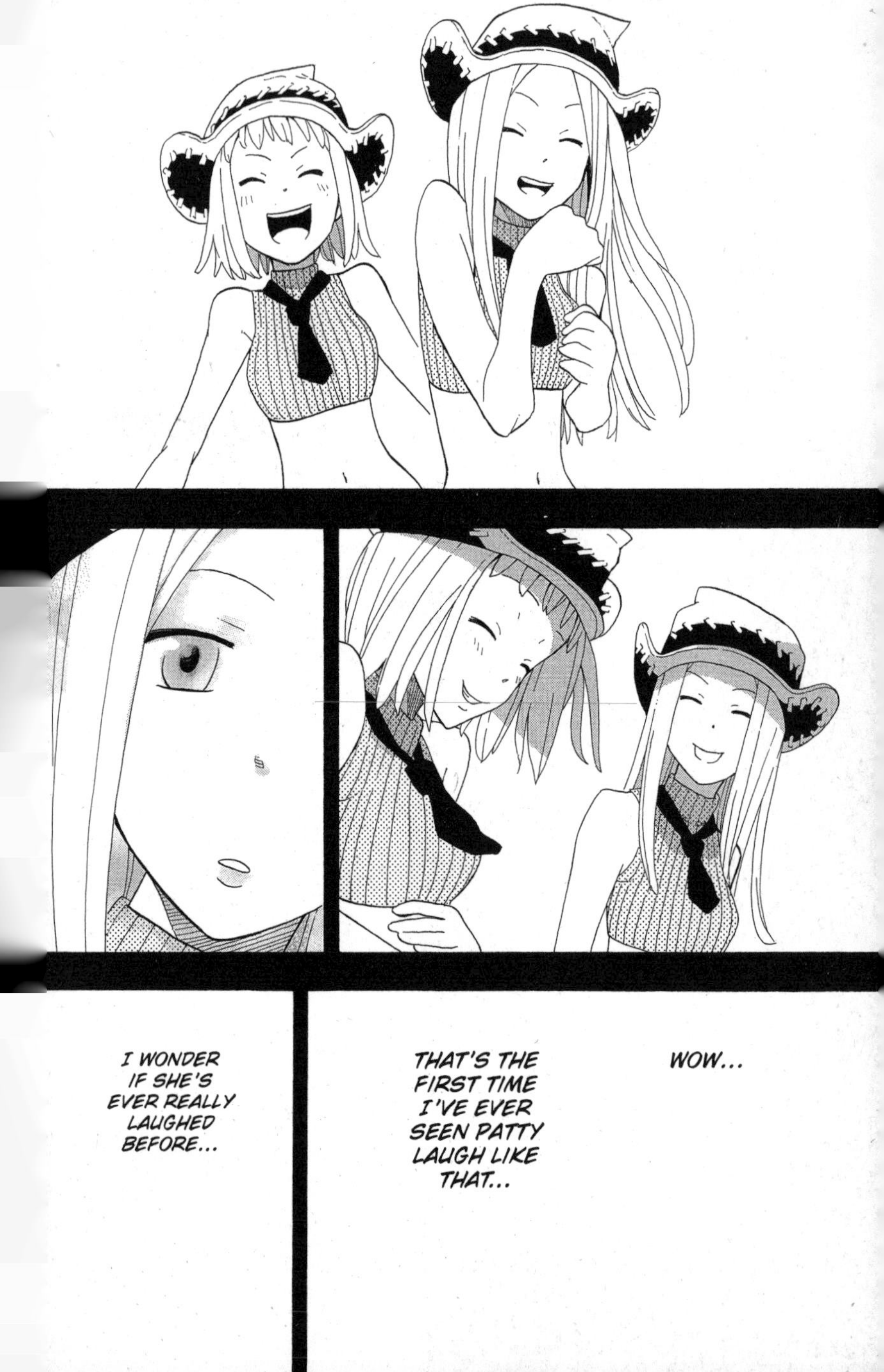
WOW…
THAT'S THE FIRST TIME I'VE EVER SEEN PATTY LAUGH LIKE THAT…
I WONDER IF SHE'S EVER REALLY LAUGHED BEFORE…

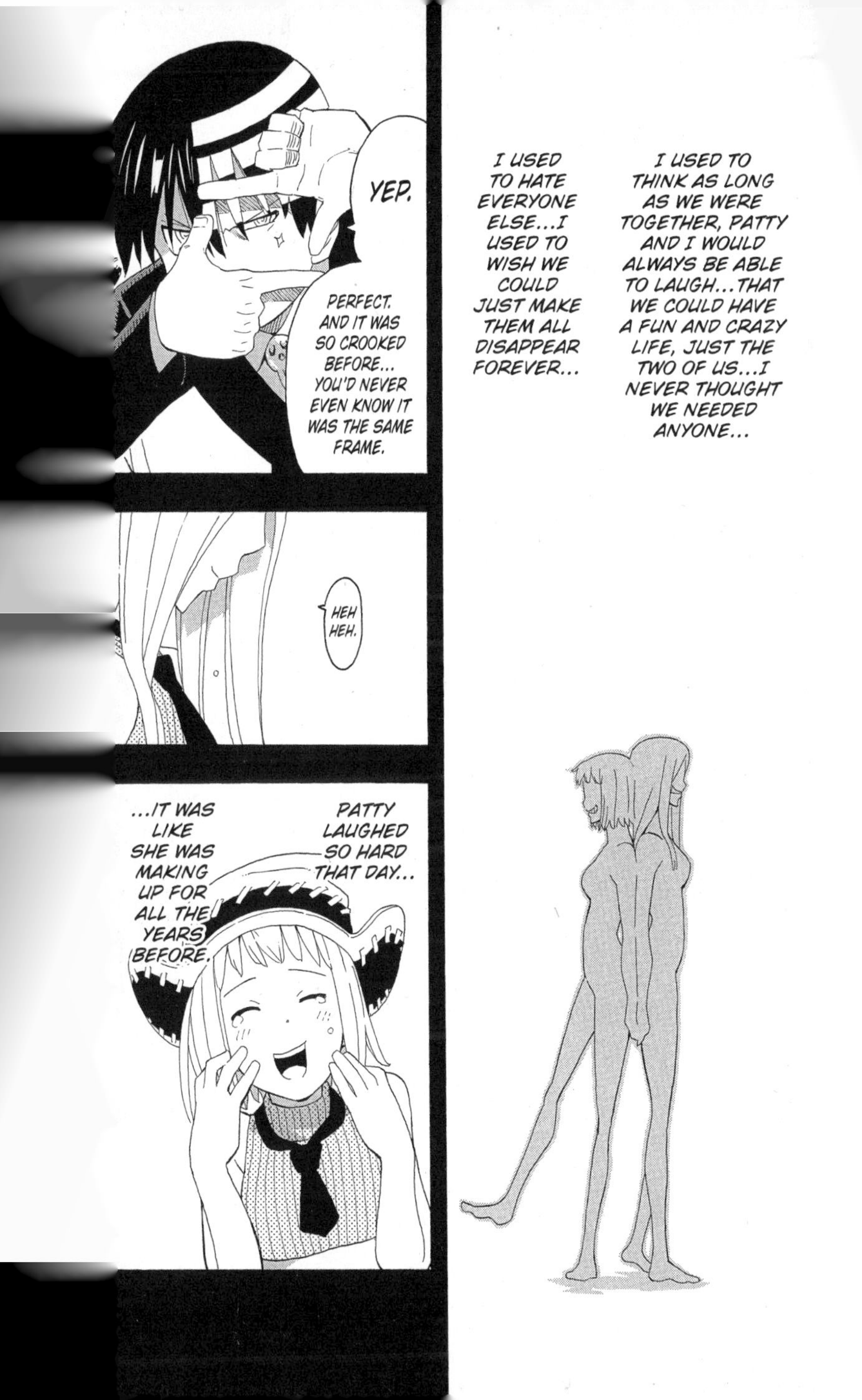
I USED TO THINK AS LONG AS WE WERE TOGETHER, PATTY AND I WOULD ALWAYS BE ABLE TO LAUGH...THAT WE COULD HAVE A FUN AND CRAZY LIFE, JUST THE TWO OF US...I NEVER THOUGHT WE NEEDED ANYONE...
I USED TO HATE EVERYONE ELSE...I USED TO WISH WE COULD JUST MAKE THEM ALL DISAPPEAR FOREVER...
YEP.
PERFECT. AND IT WAS SO CROOKED BEFORE... YOU'D NEVER EVEN KNOW IT WAS THE SAME FRAME.
HEH HEH.
PATTY LAUGHED SO HARD THAT DAY...
...IT WAS LIKE SHE WAS MAKING UP FOR ALL THE YEARS BEFORE.

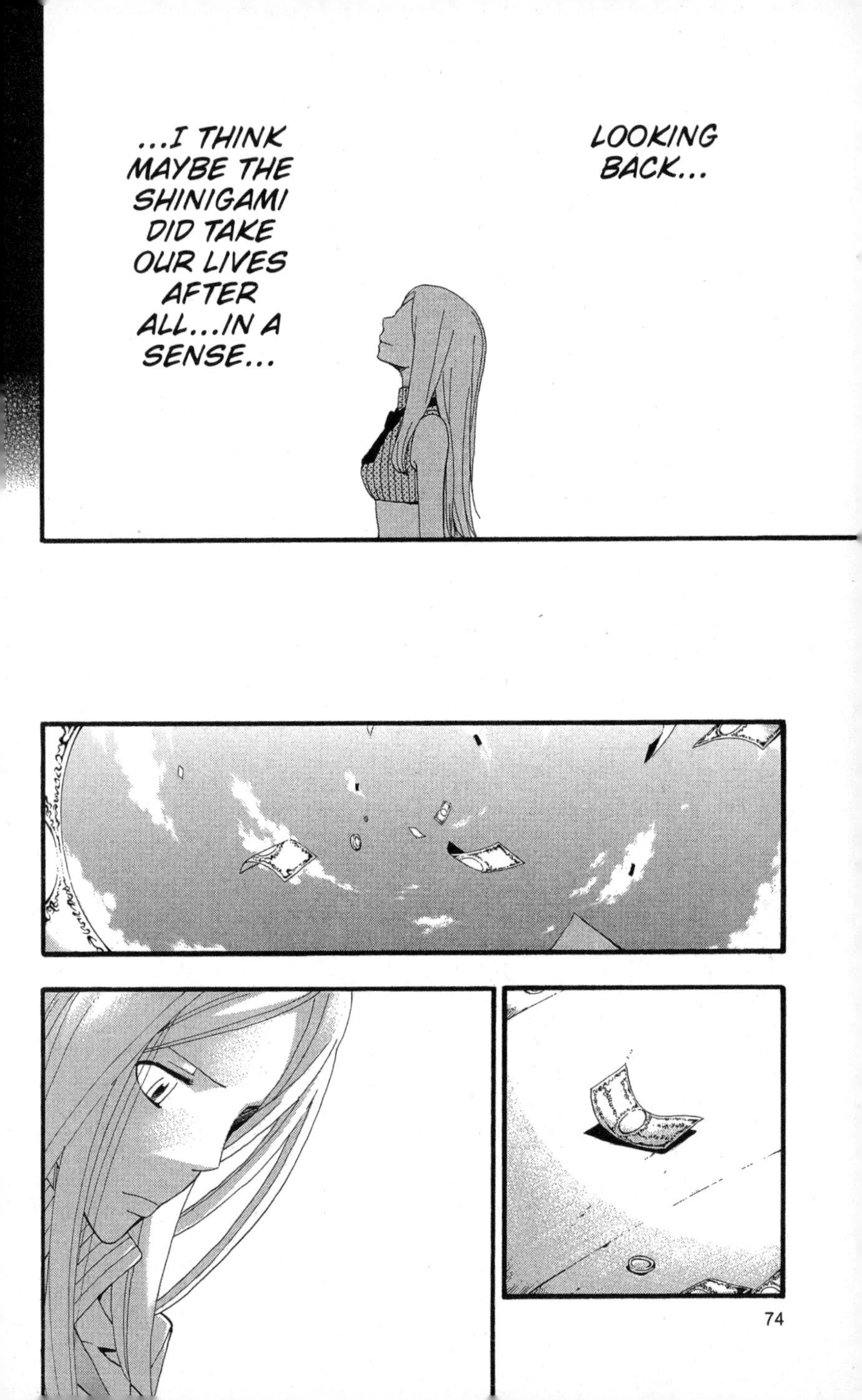
LOOKING BACK...
...I THINK MAYBE THE SHINIGAMI DID TAKE OUR LIVES AFTER ALL...IN A SENSE...

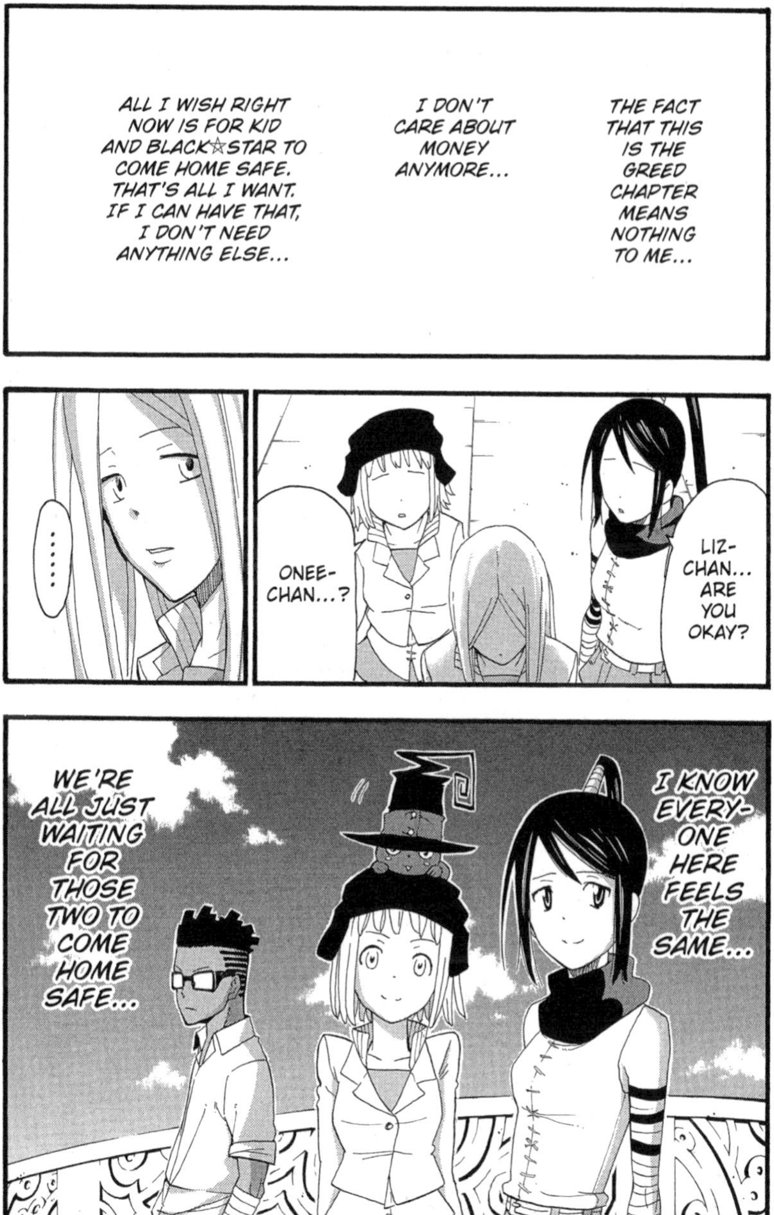
THE FACT THAT THIS IS THE GREED CHAPTER MEANS NOTHING TO ME...
I DON'T CARE ABOUT MONEY ANYMORE...
ALL I WISH RIGHT NOW IS FOR KID AND BLACK☆STAR TO COME HOME SAFE. THAT'S ALL I WANT. IF I CAN HAVE THAT, I DON'T NEED ANYTHING ELSE...
LIZ-CHAN... ARE YOU OKAY?
ONEE-CHAN...?
......
I KNOW EVERYONE HERE FEELS THE SAME...
WE'RE ALL JUST WAITING FOR THOSE TWO TO COME HOME SAFE...

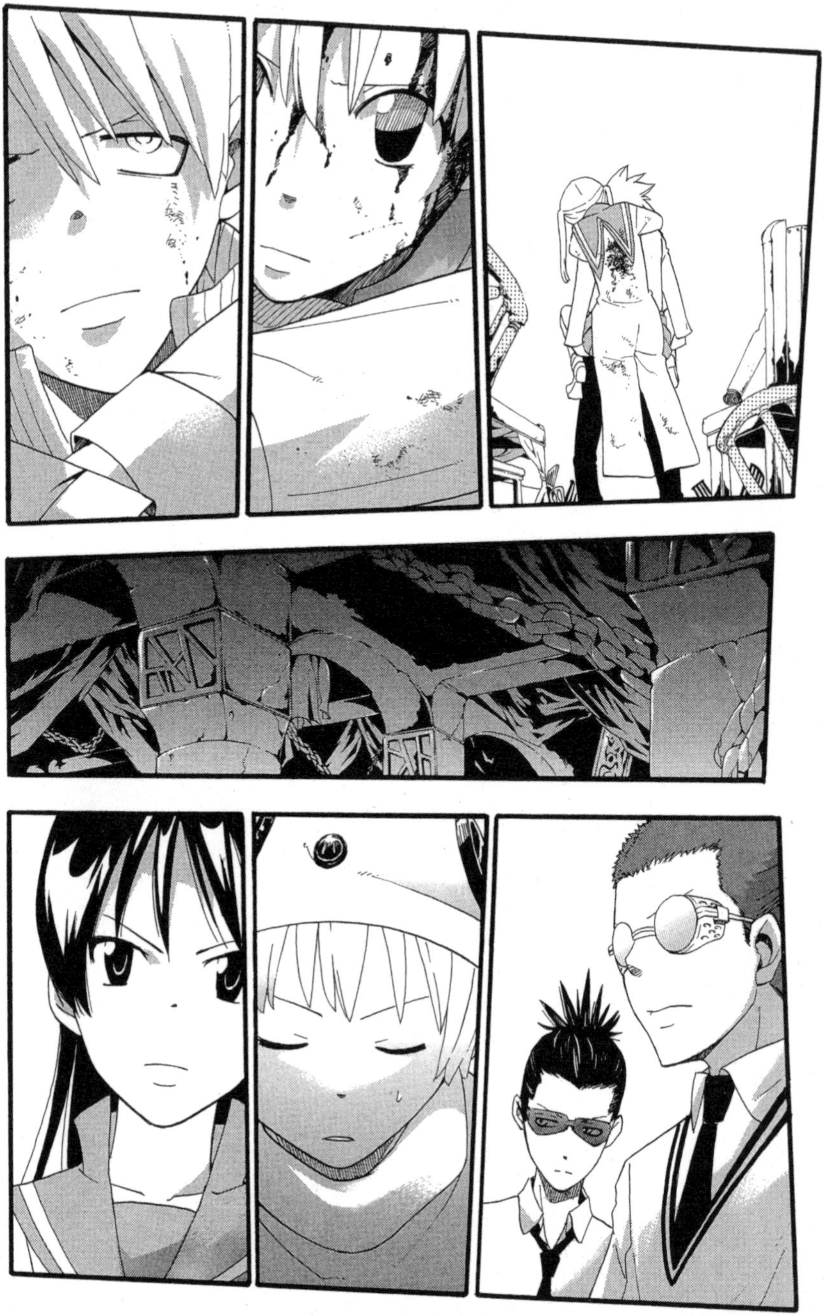

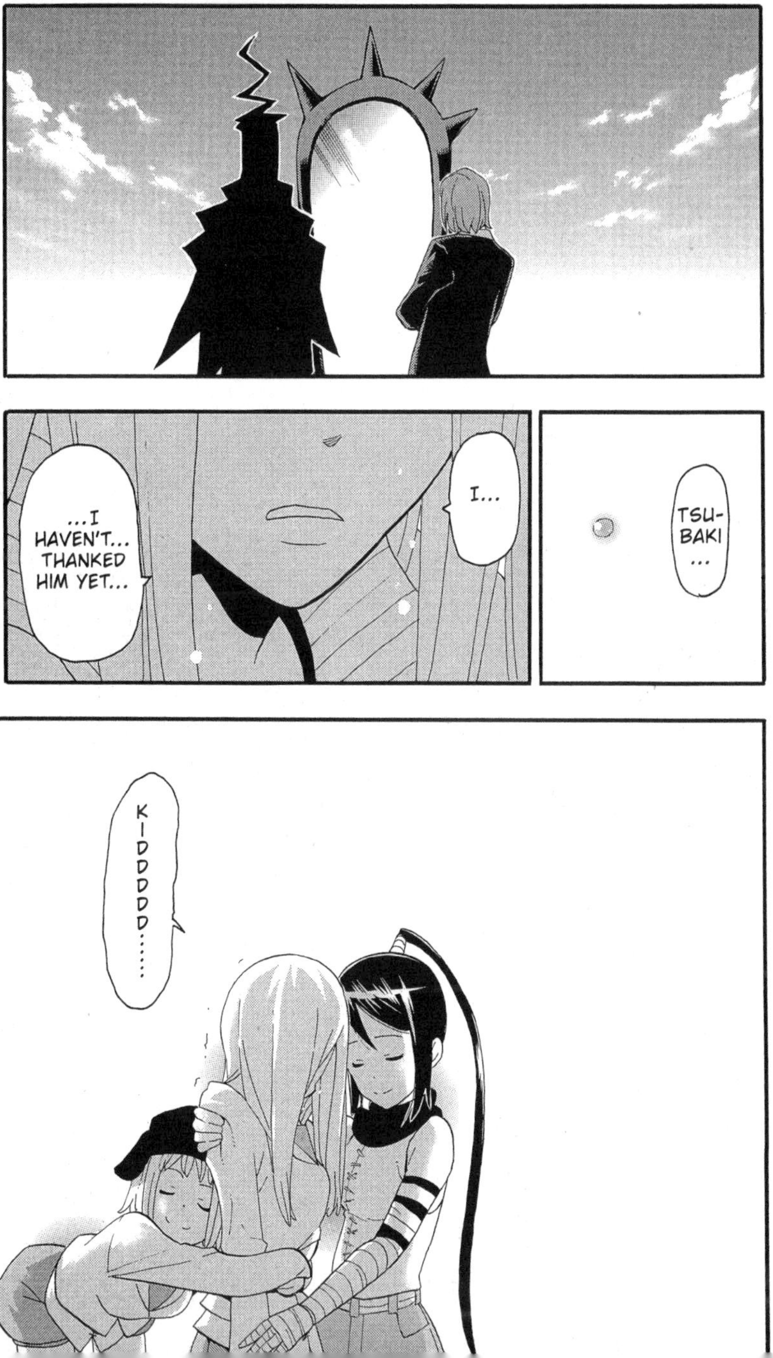
TSU-BAKI...
I...
...I HAVEN'T... THANKED HIM YET...
KIDDDDDD......

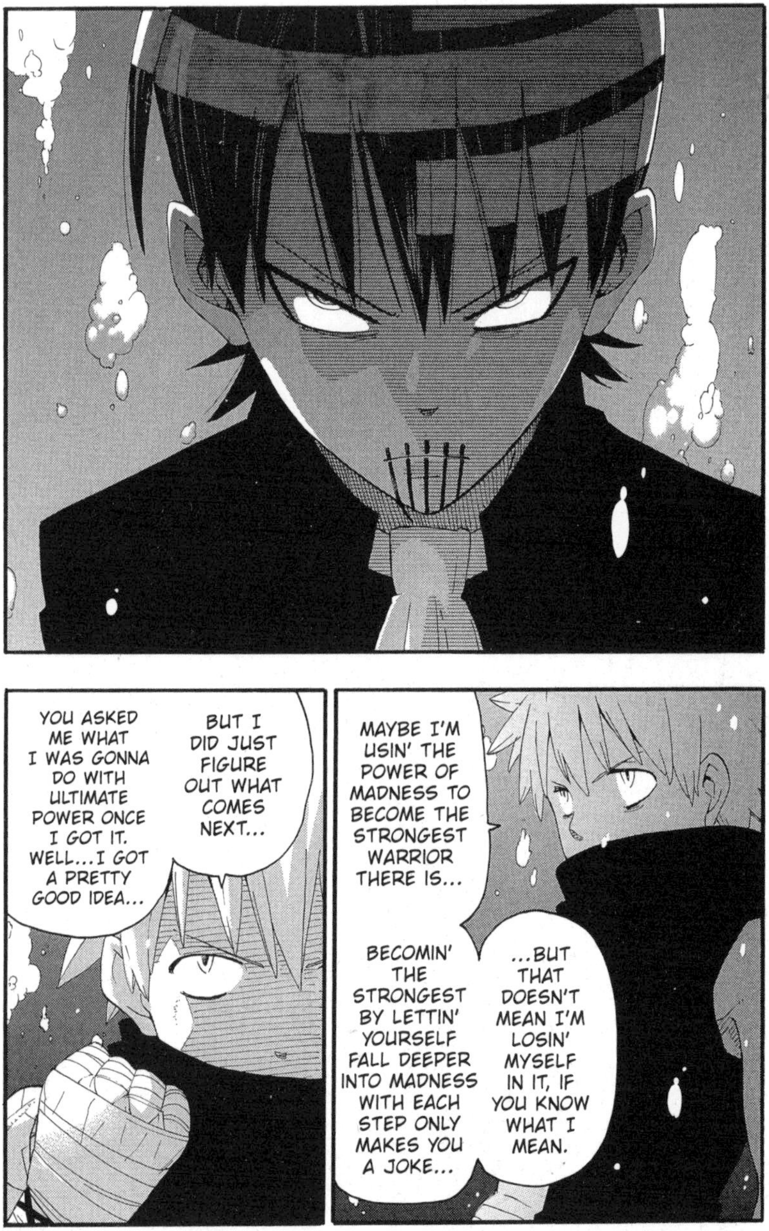
YOU ASKED ME WHAT I WAS GONNA DO WITH ULTIMATE POWER ONCE I GOT IT. WELL...I GOT A PRETTY GOOD IDEA...
BUT I DID JUST FIGURE OUT WHAT COMES NEXT...
MAYBE I'M USIN' THE POWER OF MADNESS TO BECOME THE STRONGEST WARRIOR THERE IS...
BECOMIN' THE STRONGEST BY LETTIN' YOURSELF FALL DEEPER INTO MADNESS WITH EACH STEP ONLY MAKES YOU A JOKE...
...BUT THAT DOESN'T MEAN I'M LOSIN' MYSELF IN IT, IF YOU KNOW WHAT I MEAN.

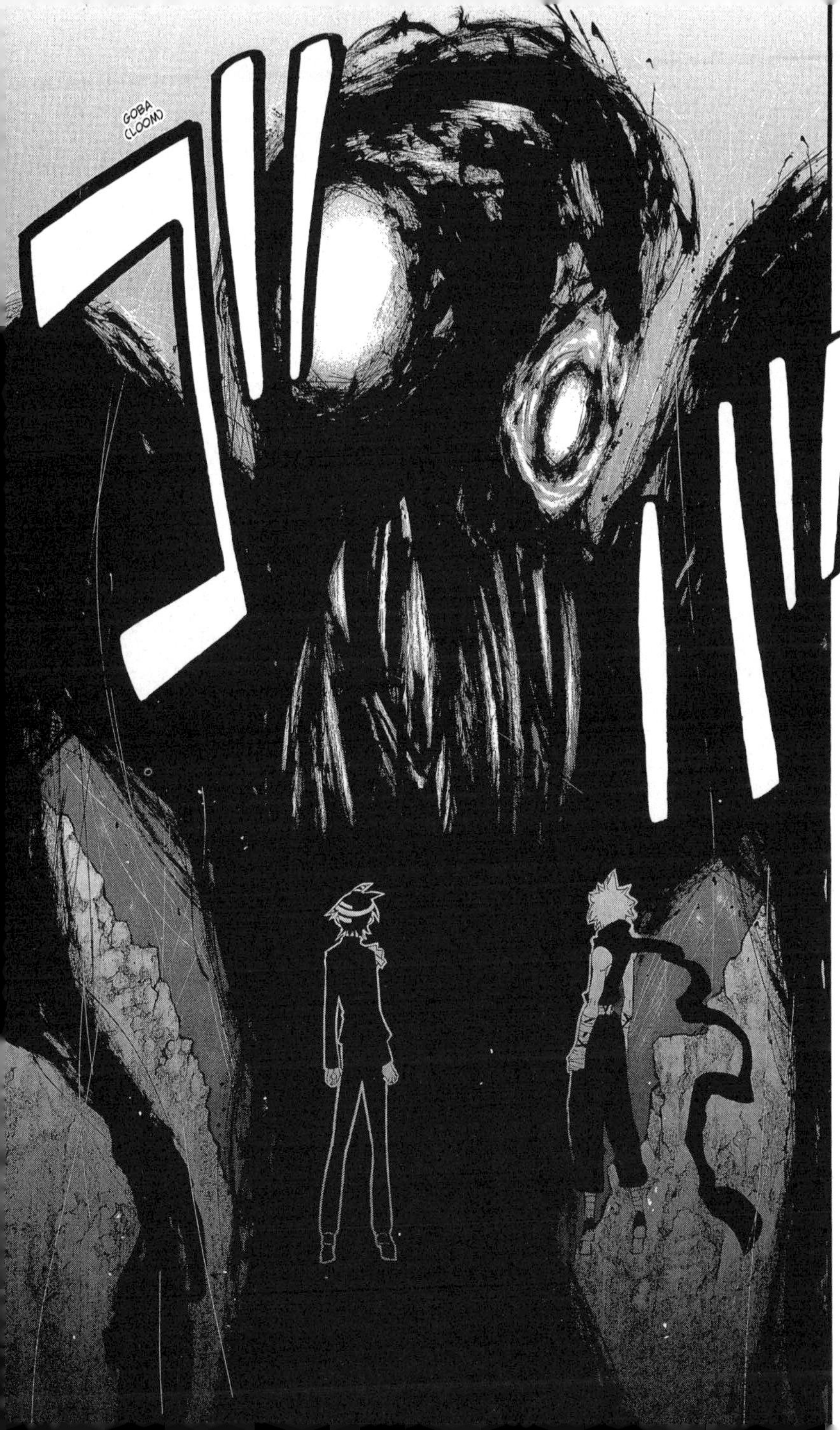
GOBA
(LOOM)

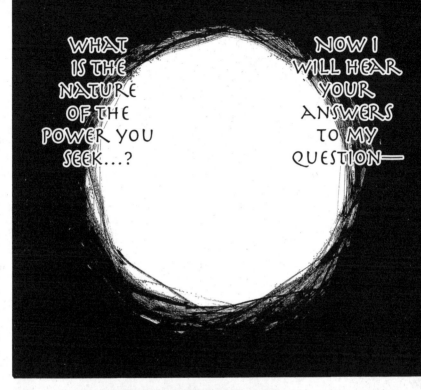

NOW I WILL HEAR YOUR ANSWERS TO MY QUESTION—

WHAT IS THE NATURE OF THE POWER YOU SEEK...?

CHAPTER 79: SALVAGE (PART 8)

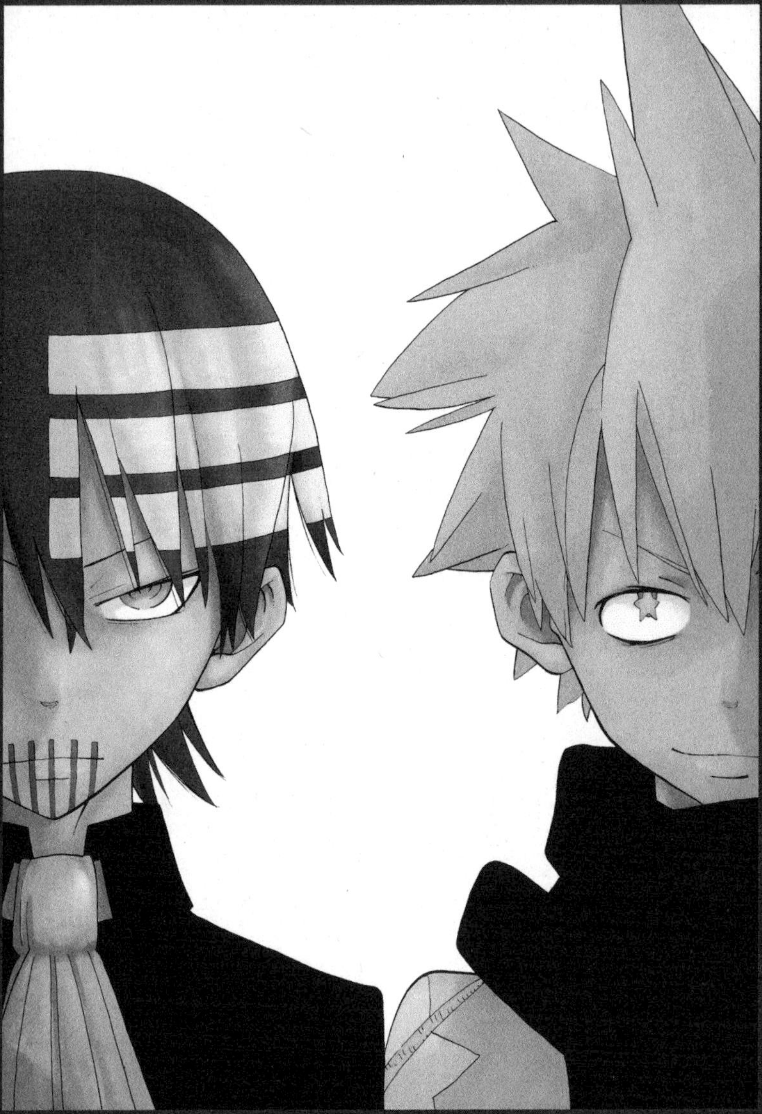

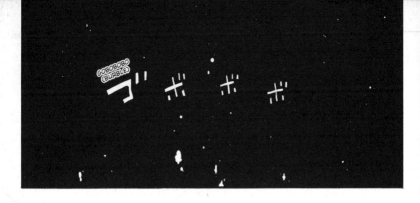

POWER...

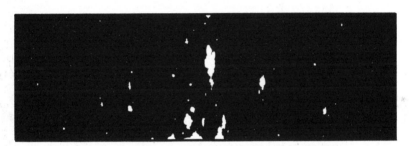

MY ANSWER TO THE
QUESTION OF "POWER"...?

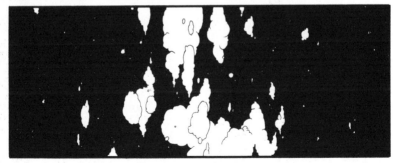

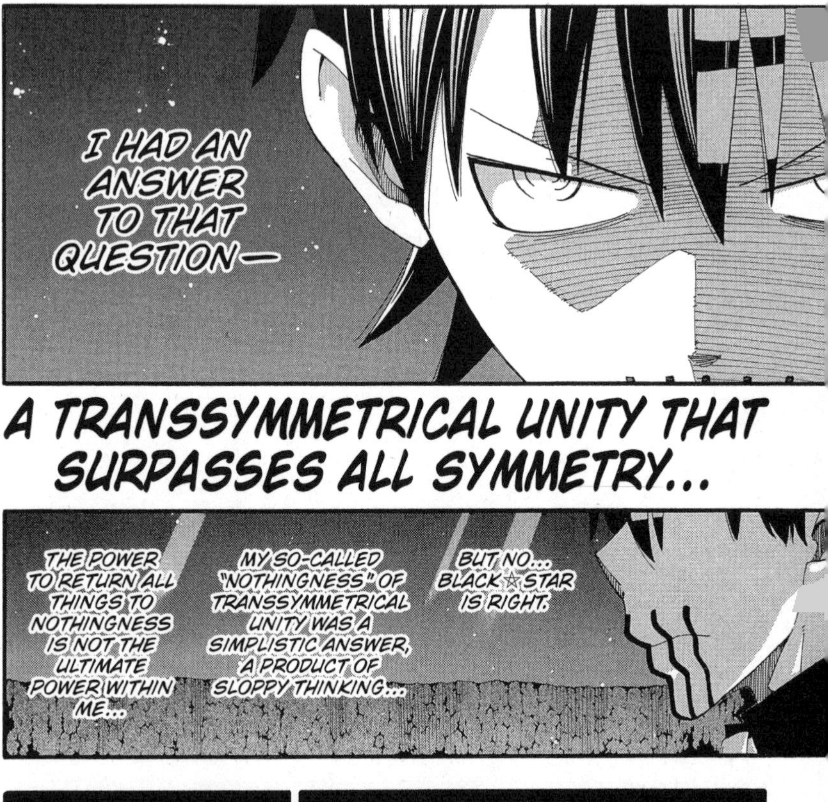

I HAD AN ANSWER TO THAT QUESTION—
A TRANSSYMMETRICAL UNITY THAT SURPASSES ALL SYMMETRY...
BUT NO... BLACK☆STAR IS RIGHT.
MY SO-CALLED "NOTHINGNESS" OF TRANSSYMMETRICAL UNITY WAS A SIMPLISTIC ANSWER, A PRODUCT OF SLOPPY THINKING...
THE POWER TO RETURN ALL THINGS TO NOTHINGNESS IS NOT THE ULTIMATE POWER WITHIN ME...
I AM A SHINIGAMI, AND I SHOULD KNOW— NOTHINGNESS IS NOT THE SAME THING AS DEATH!! NOT AT ALL!!
"NOTHINGNESS" MEANS NEGATING EVEN THE POSSIBILITY OF LIFE...! IT'S THE SAME AS DENYING LIFE ITSELF!
THAT IS NOT ME... THAT IS NOT THE THINKING OF A SHINIGAMI!!

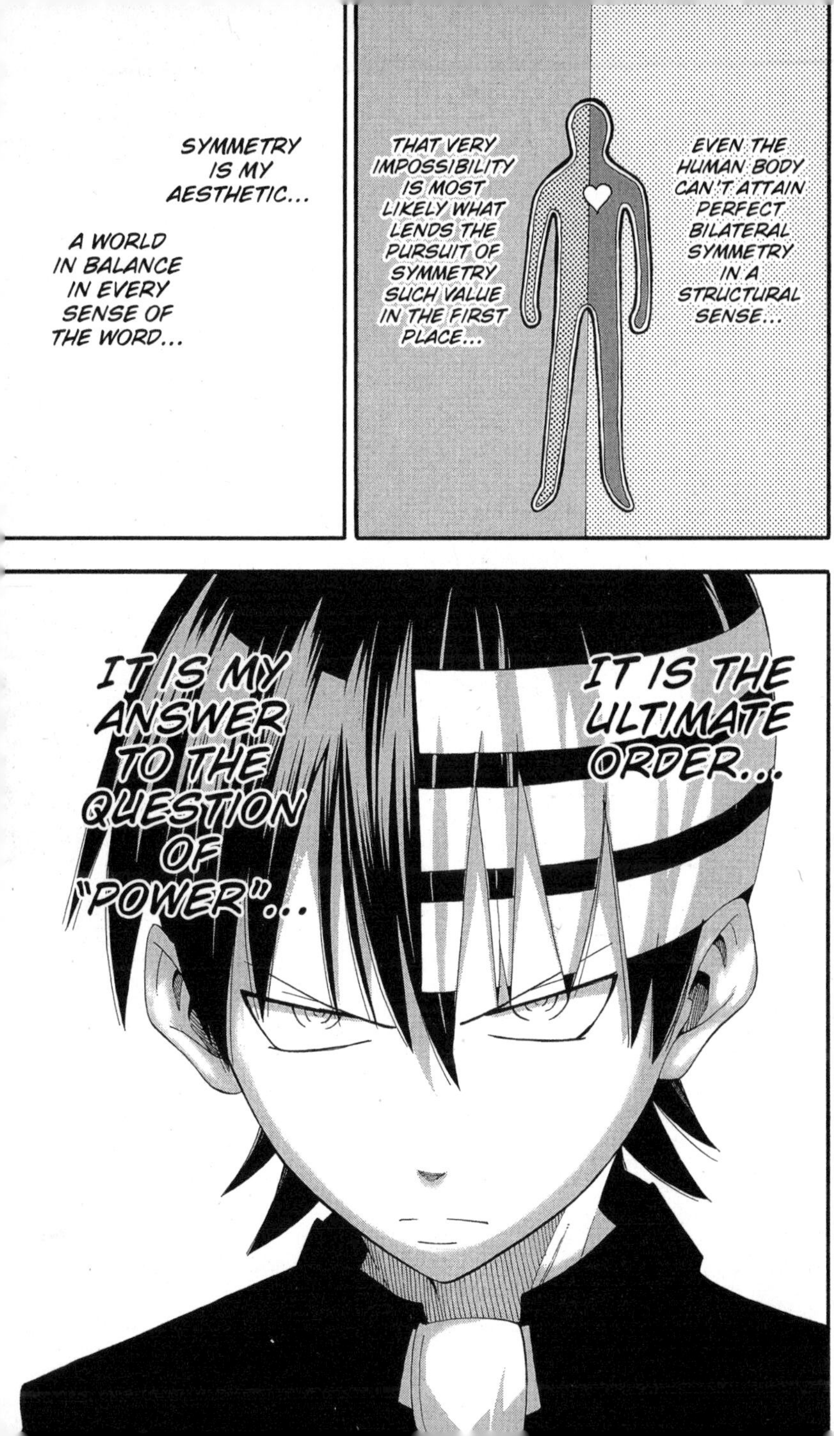
EVEN THE HUMAN BODY CAN'T ATTAIN PERFECT BILATERAL SYMMETRY IN A STRUCTURAL SENSE...
THAT VERY IMPOSSIBILITY IS MOST LIKELY WHAT LENDS THE PURSUIT OF SYMMETRY SUCH VALUE IN THE FIRST PLACE...
SYMMETRY IS MY AESTHETIC...
A WORLD IN BALANCE IN EVERY SENSE OF THE WORD...
IT IS THE ULTIMATE ORDER...
IT IS MY ANSWER TO THE QUESTION OF "POWER"...

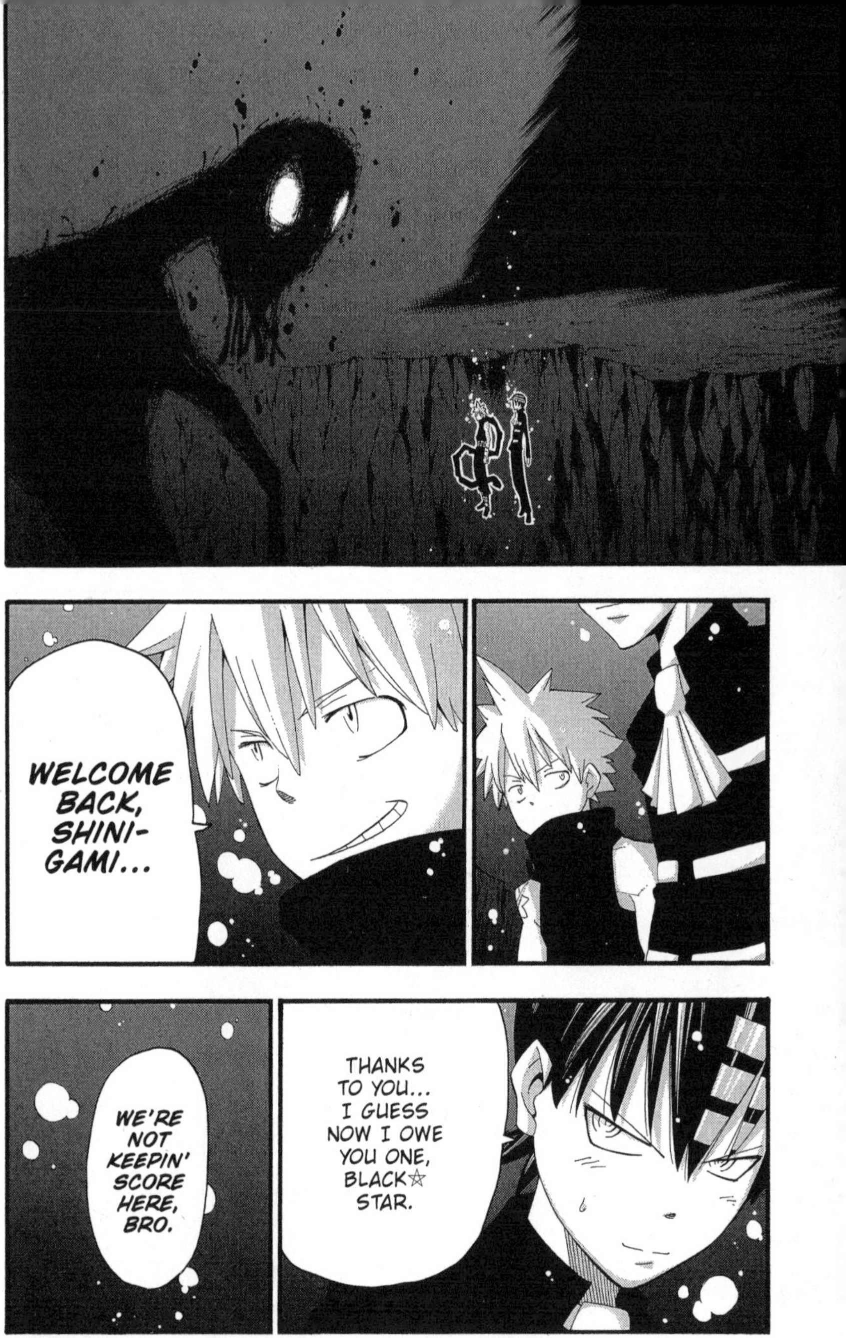
WELCOME BACK, SHINI-GAMI...
THANKS TO YOU... I GUESS NOW I OWE YOU ONE, BLACK☆STAR.
WE'RE NOT KEEPIN' SCORE HERE, BRO.

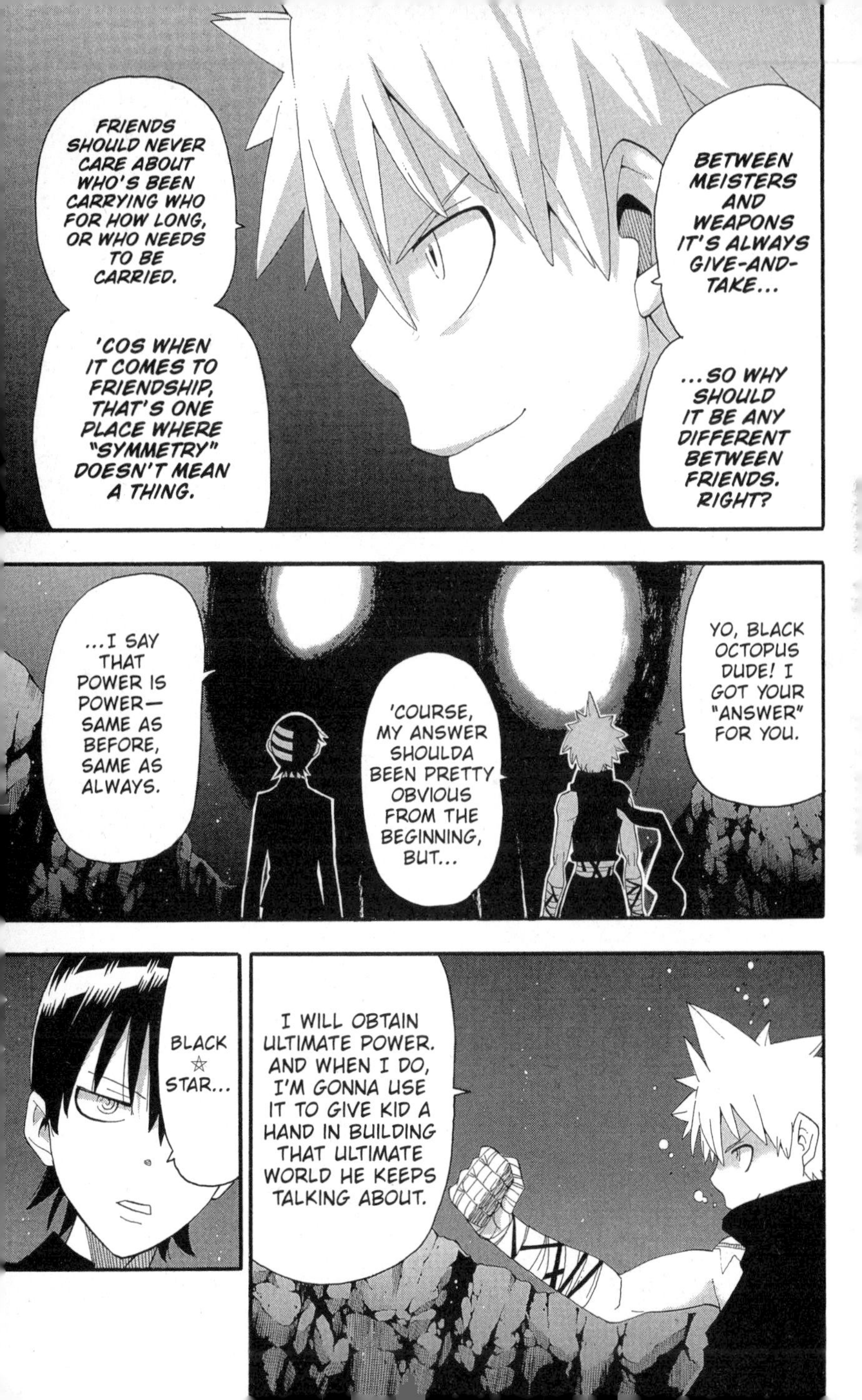
BETWEEN MEISTERS AND WEAPONS IT'S ALWAYS GIVE-AND-TAKE...
...SO WHY SHOULD IT BE ANY DIFFERENT BETWEEN FRIENDS. RIGHT?
FRIENDS SHOULD NEVER CARE ABOUT WHO'S BEEN CARRYING WHO FOR HOW LONG, OR WHO NEEDS TO BE CARRIED.
'COS WHEN IT COMES TO FRIENDSHIP, THAT'S ONE PLACE WHERE "SYMMETRY" DOESN'T MEAN A THING.
YO, BLACK OCTOPUS DUDE! I GOT YOUR "ANSWER" FOR YOU.
'COURSE, MY ANSWER SHOULDA BEEN PRETTY OBVIOUS FROM THE BEGINNING, BUT...
...I SAY THAT POWER IS POWER—SAME AS BEFORE, SAME AS ALWAYS.
I WILL OBTAIN ULTIMATE POWER. AND WHEN I DO, I'M GONNA USE IT TO GIVE KID A HAND IN BUILDING THAT ULTIMATE WORLD HE KEEPS TALKING ABOUT.
BLACK ☆ STAR...

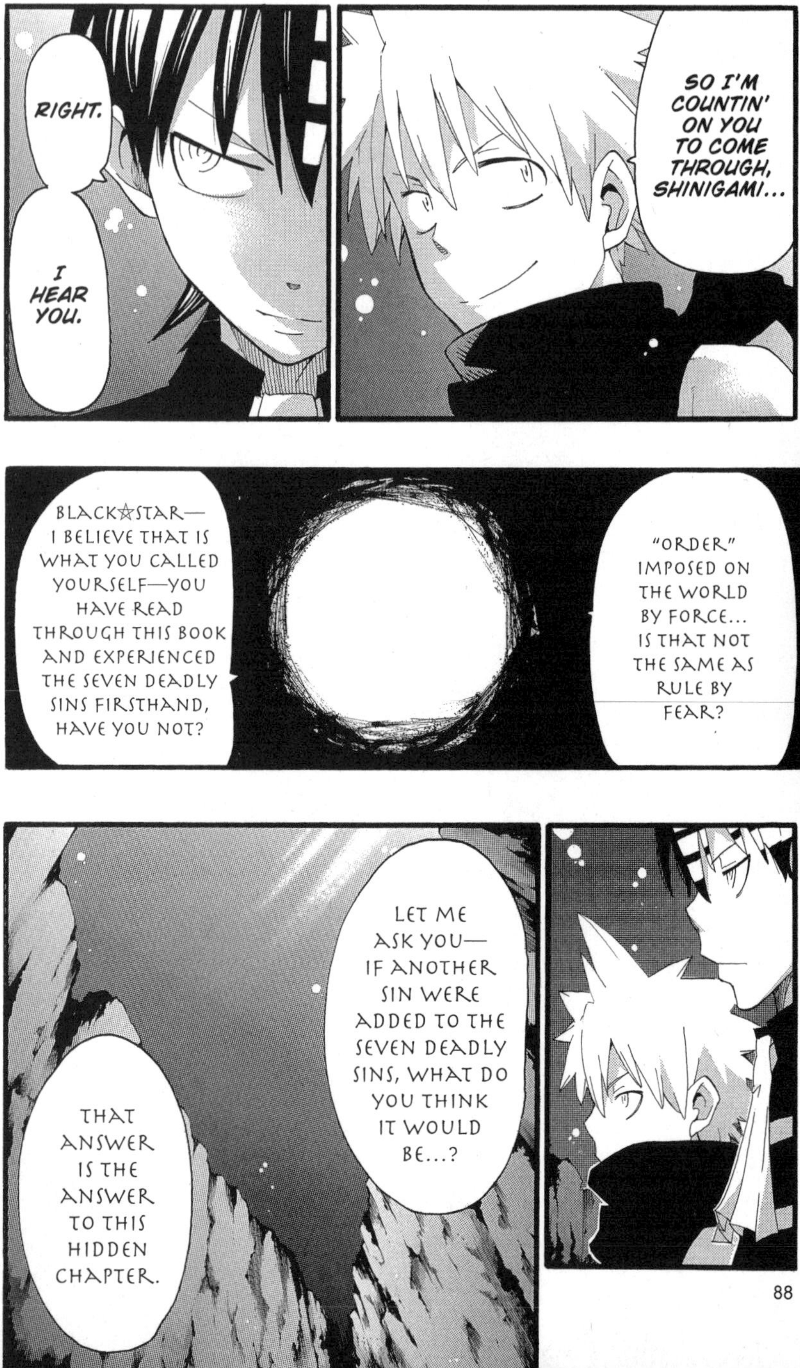
SO I'M COUNTIN' ON YOU TO COME THROUGH, SHINIGAMI...
RIGHT.
I HEAR YOU.
BLACK☆STAR—I BELIEVE THAT IS WHAT YOU CALLED YOURSELF—YOU HAVE READ THROUGH THIS BOOK AND EXPERIENCED THE SEVEN DEADLY SINS FIRSTHAND, HAVE YOU NOT?
"ORDER" IMPOSED ON THE WORLD BY FORCE... IS THAT NOT THE SAME AS RULE BY FEAR?
LET ME ASK YOU—IF ANOTHER SIN WERE ADDED TO THE SEVEN DEADLY SINS, WHAT DO YOU THINK IT WOULD BE...?
THAT ANSWER IS THE ANSWER TO THIS HIDDEN CHAPTER.

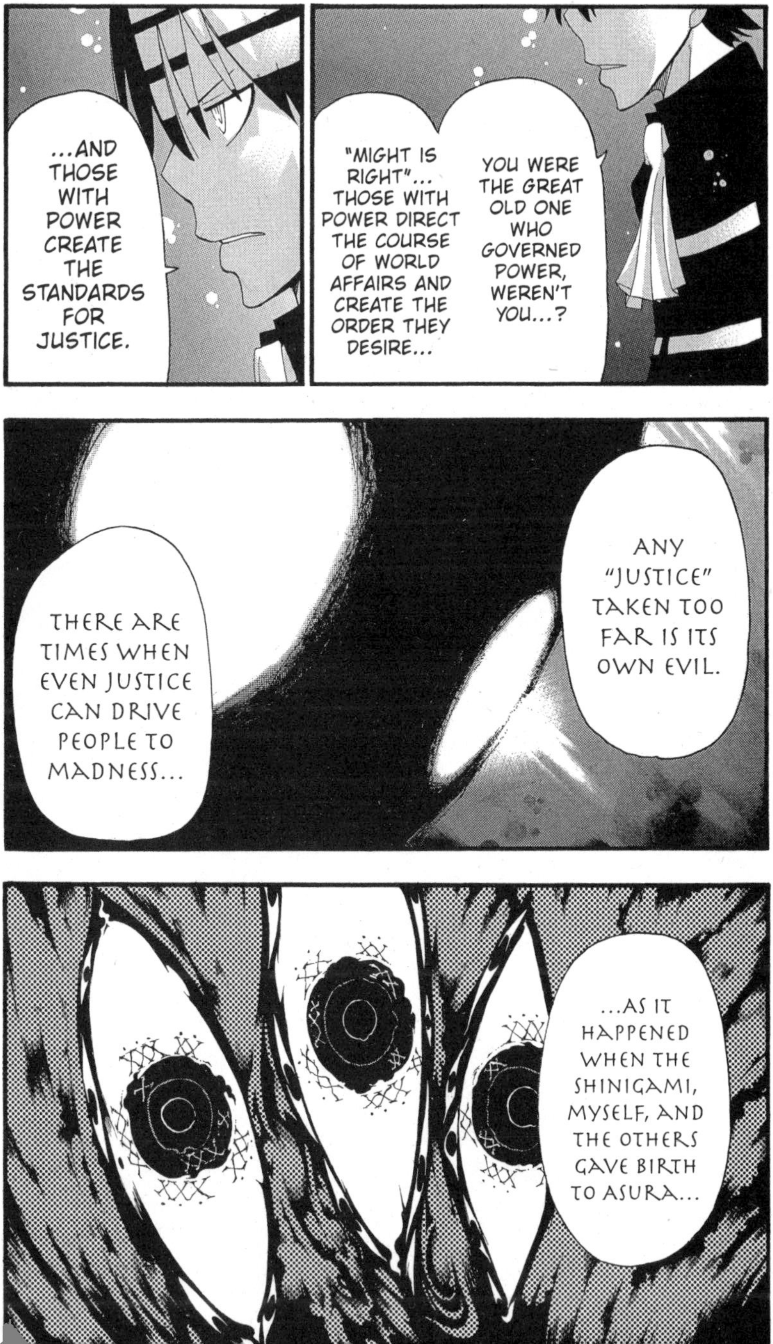
YOU WERE THE GREAT OLD ONE WHO GOVERNED POWER, WEREN'T YOU...?
"MIGHT IS RIGHT"... THOSE WITH POWER DIRECT THE COURSE OF WORLD AFFAIRS AND CREATE THE ORDER THEY DESIRE...
...AND THOSE WITH POWER CREATE THE STANDARDS FOR JUSTICE.
ANY "JUSTICE" TAKEN TOO FAR IS ITS OWN EVIL.
THERE ARE TIMES WHEN EVEN JUSTICE CAN DRIVE PEOPLE TO MADNESS...
...AS IT HAPPENED WHEN THE SHINIGAMI, MYSELF, AND THE OTHERS GAVE BIRTH TO ASURA...

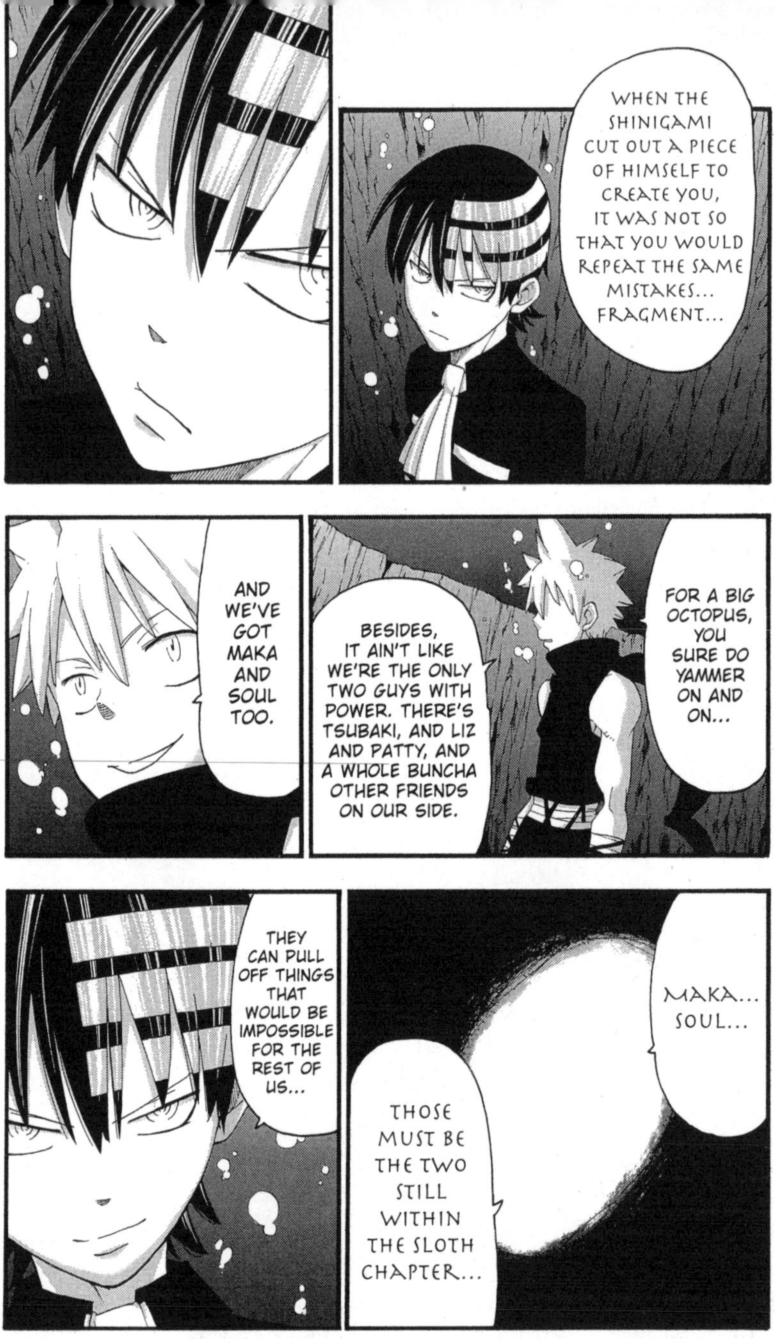
WHEN THE SHINIGAMI CUT OUT A PIECE OF HIMSELF TO CREATE YOU, IT WAS NOT SO THAT YOU WOULD REPEAT THE SAME MISTAKES... FRAGMENT...
FOR A BIG OCTOPUS, YOU SURE DO YAMMER ON AND ON...
BESIDES, IT AIN'T LIKE WE'RE THE ONLY TWO GUYS WITH POWER. THERE'S TSUBAKI, AND LIZ AND PATTY, AND A WHOLE BUNCHA OTHER FRIENDS ON OUR SIDE.
AND WE'VE GOT MAKA AND SOUL TOO.
MAKA... SOUL...
THOSE MUST BE THE TWO STILL WITHIN THE SLOTH CHAPTER...
THEY CAN PULL OFF THINGS THAT WOULD BE IMPOSSIBLE FOR THE REST OF US...

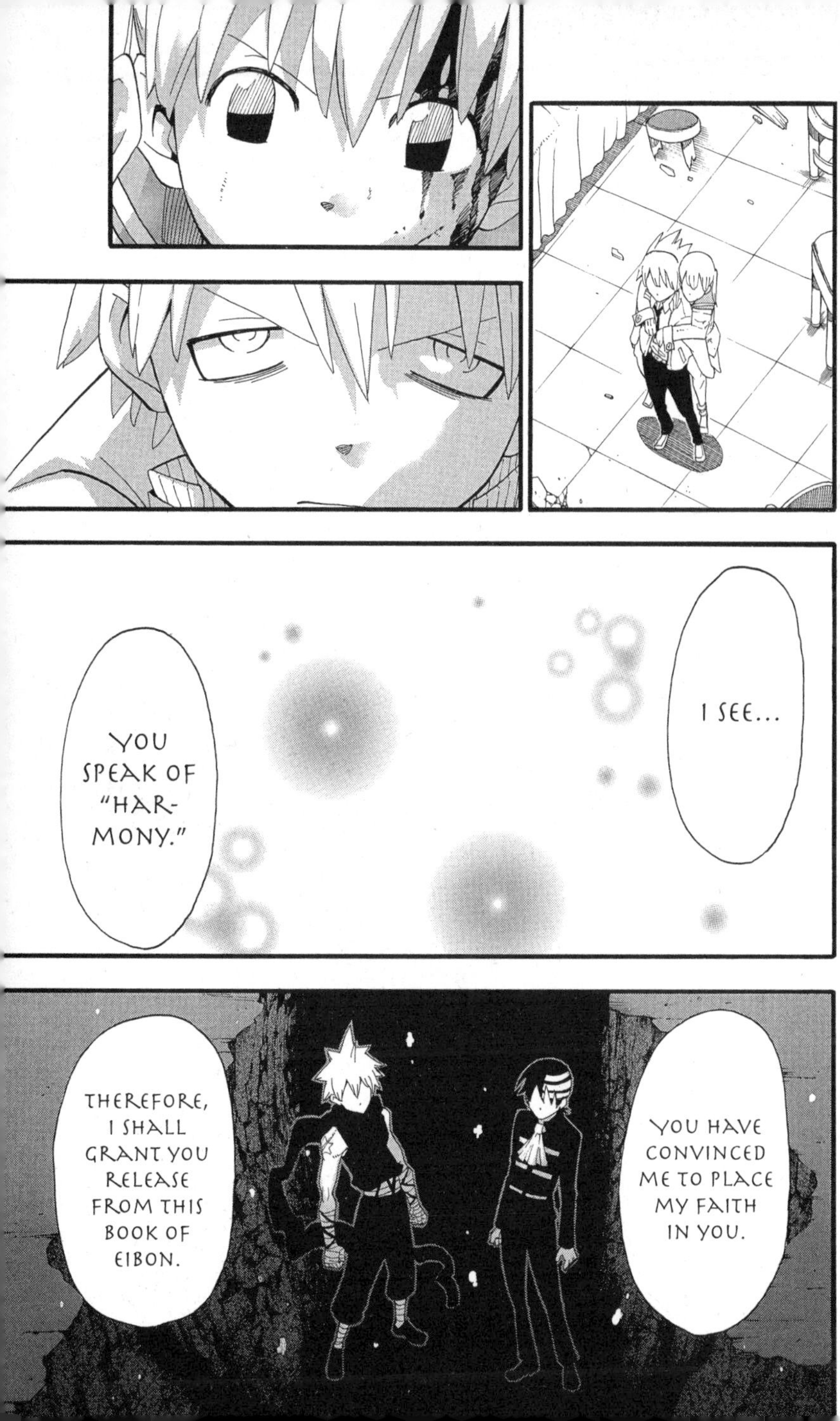
I SEE...
YOU SPEAK OF "HARMONY."
YOU HAVE CONVINCED ME TO PLACE MY FAITH IN YOU.
THEREFORE, I SHALL GRANT YOU RELEASE FROM THIS BOOK OF EIBON.

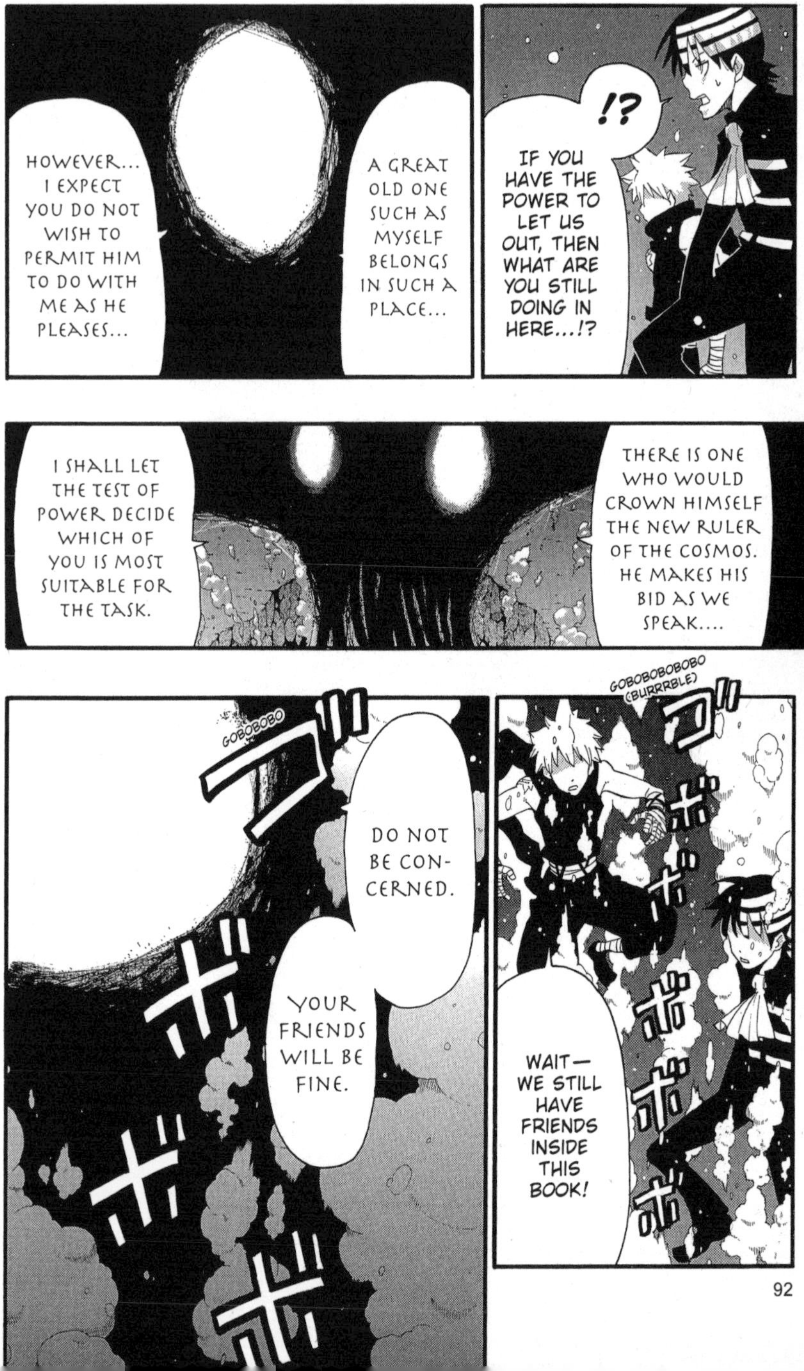
!?
IF YOU HAVE THE POWER TO LET US OUT, THEN WHAT ARE YOU STILL DOING IN HERE...!?
A GREAT OLD ONE SUCH AS MYSELF BELONGS IN SUCH A PLACE...
HOWEVER... I EXPECT YOU DO NOT WISH TO PERMIT HIM TO DO WITH ME AS HE PLEASES...
THERE IS ONE WHO WOULD CROWN HIMSELF THE NEW RULER OF THE COSMOS. HE MAKES HIS BID AS WE SPEAK....
I SHALL LET THE TEST OF POWER DECIDE WHICH OF YOU IS MOST SUITABLE FOR THE TASK.
GOBOBOBOBOBO (BURRRBLE)
WAIT—WE STILL HAVE FRIENDS INSIDE THIS BOOK!
GOBOBOBO
DO NOT BE CONCERNED.
YOUR FRIENDS WILL BE FINE.

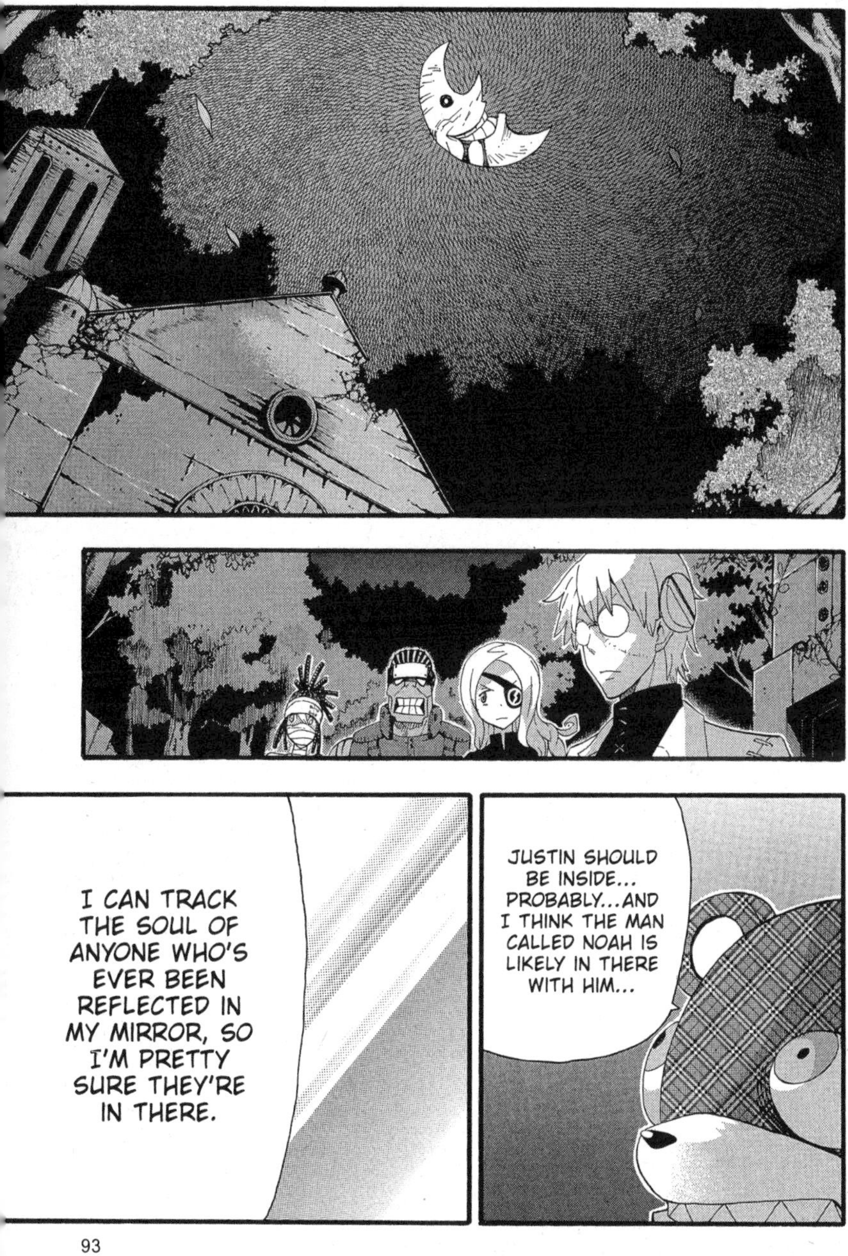
JUSTIN SHOULD BE INSIDE... PROBABLY...AND I THINK THE MAN CALLED NOAH IS LIKELY IN THERE WITH HIM...
I CAN TRACK THE SOUL OF ANYONE WHO'S EVER BEEN REFLECTED IN MY MIRROR, SO I'M PRETTY SURE THEY'RE IN THERE.

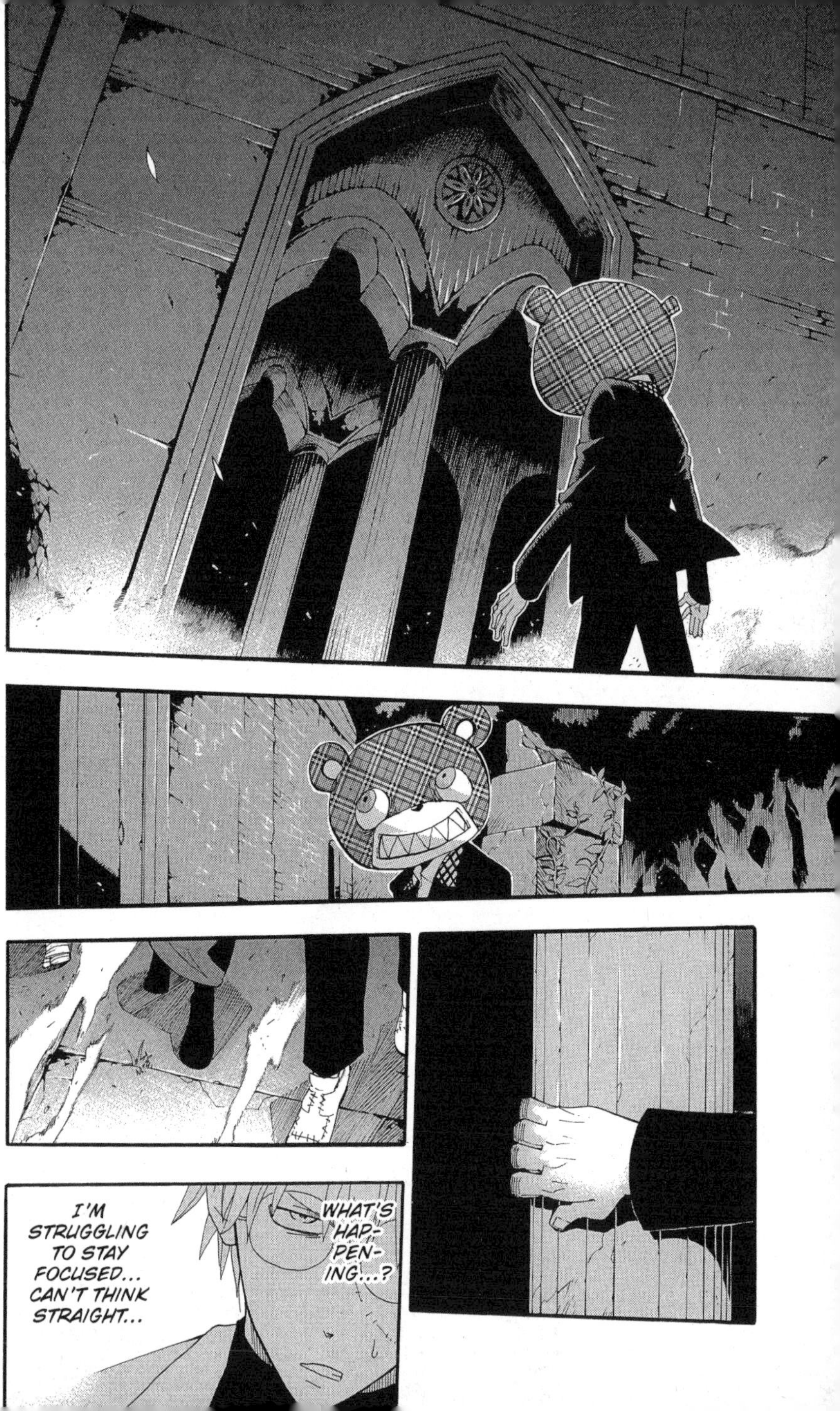
WHAT'S HAP-PEN-ING...?
I'M STRUGGLING TO STAY FOCUSED... CAN'T THINK STRAIGHT...

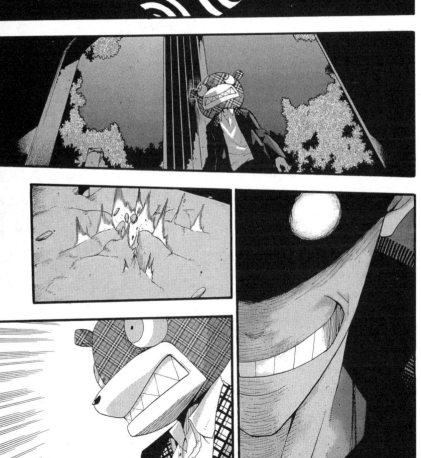

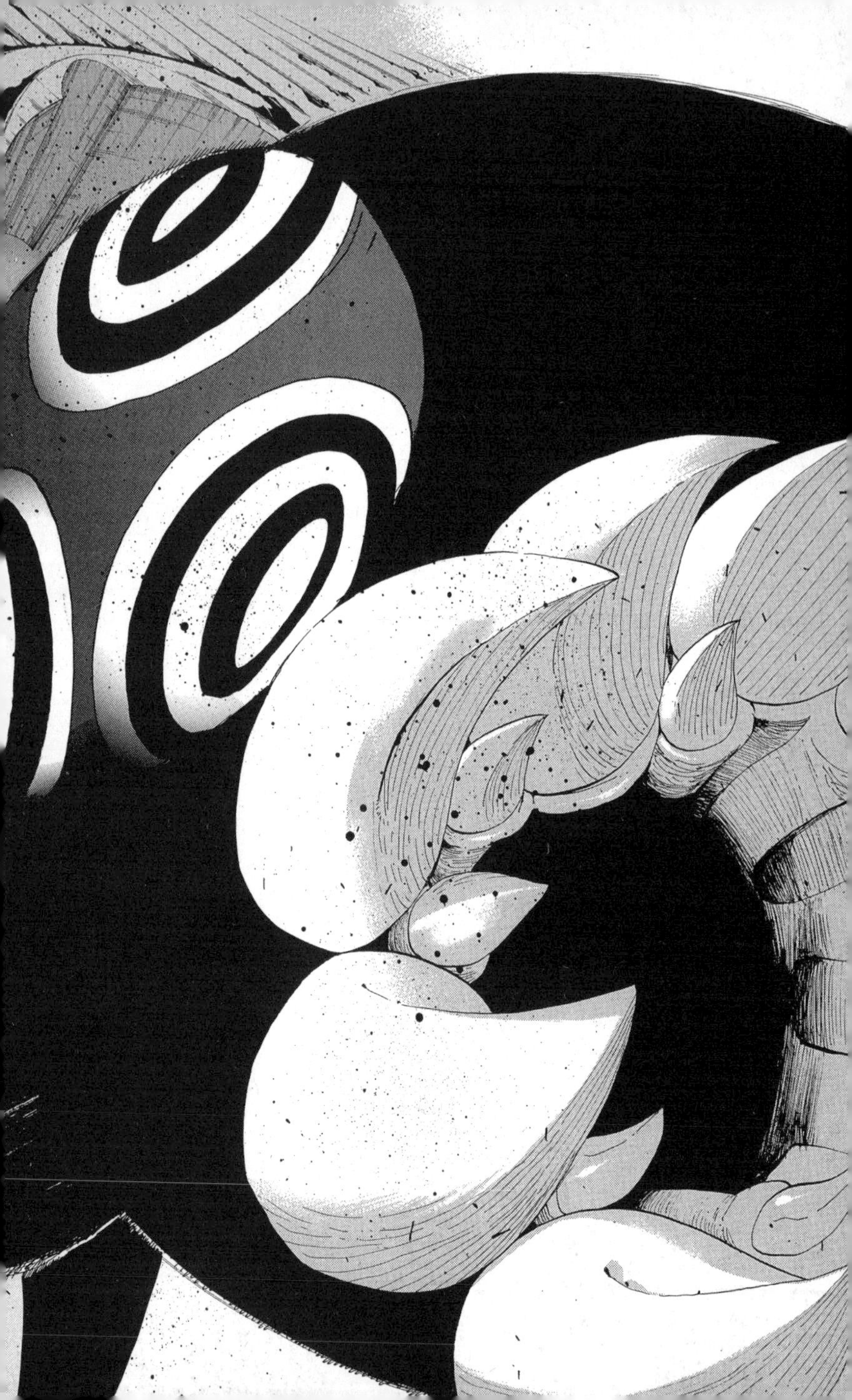

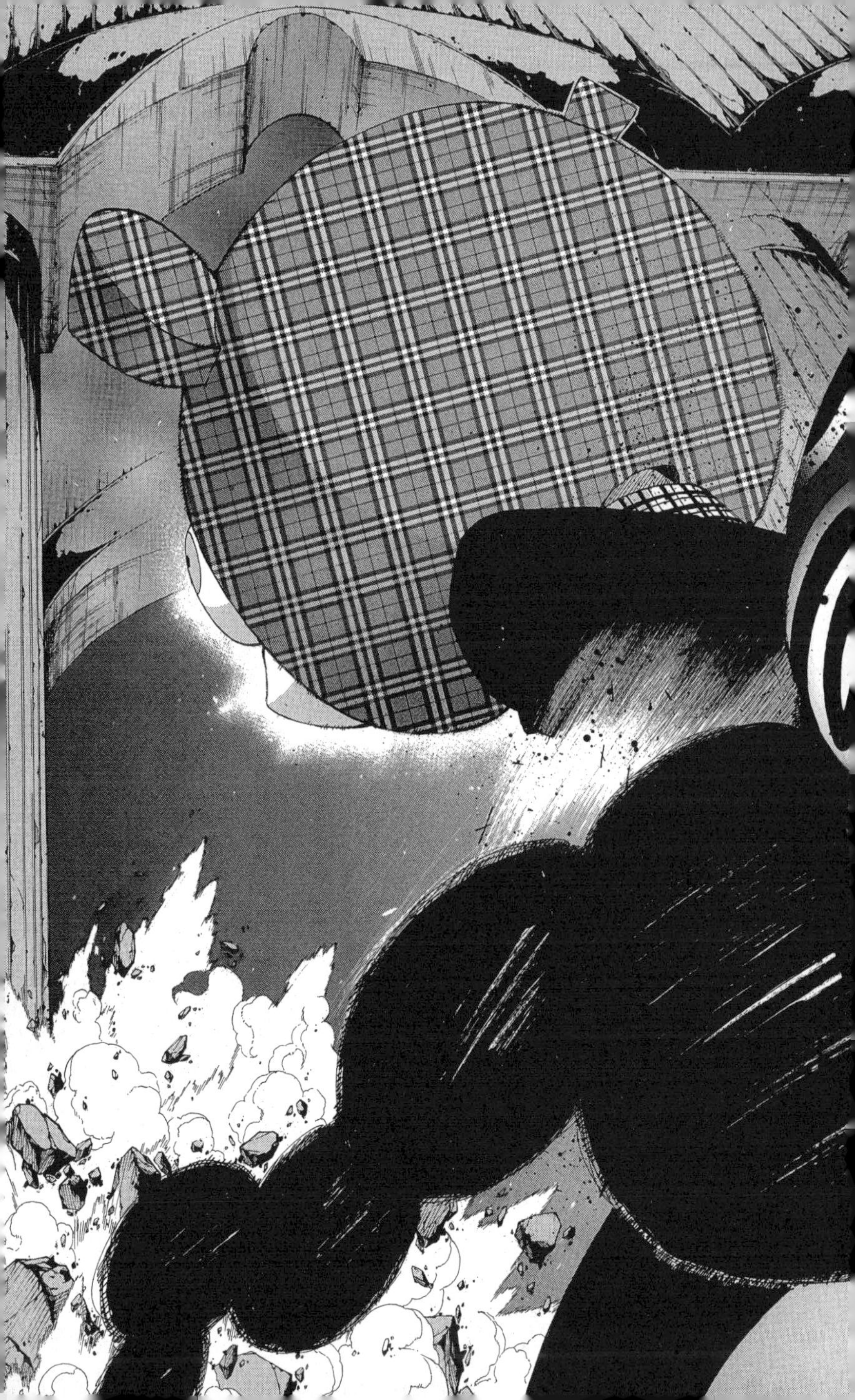

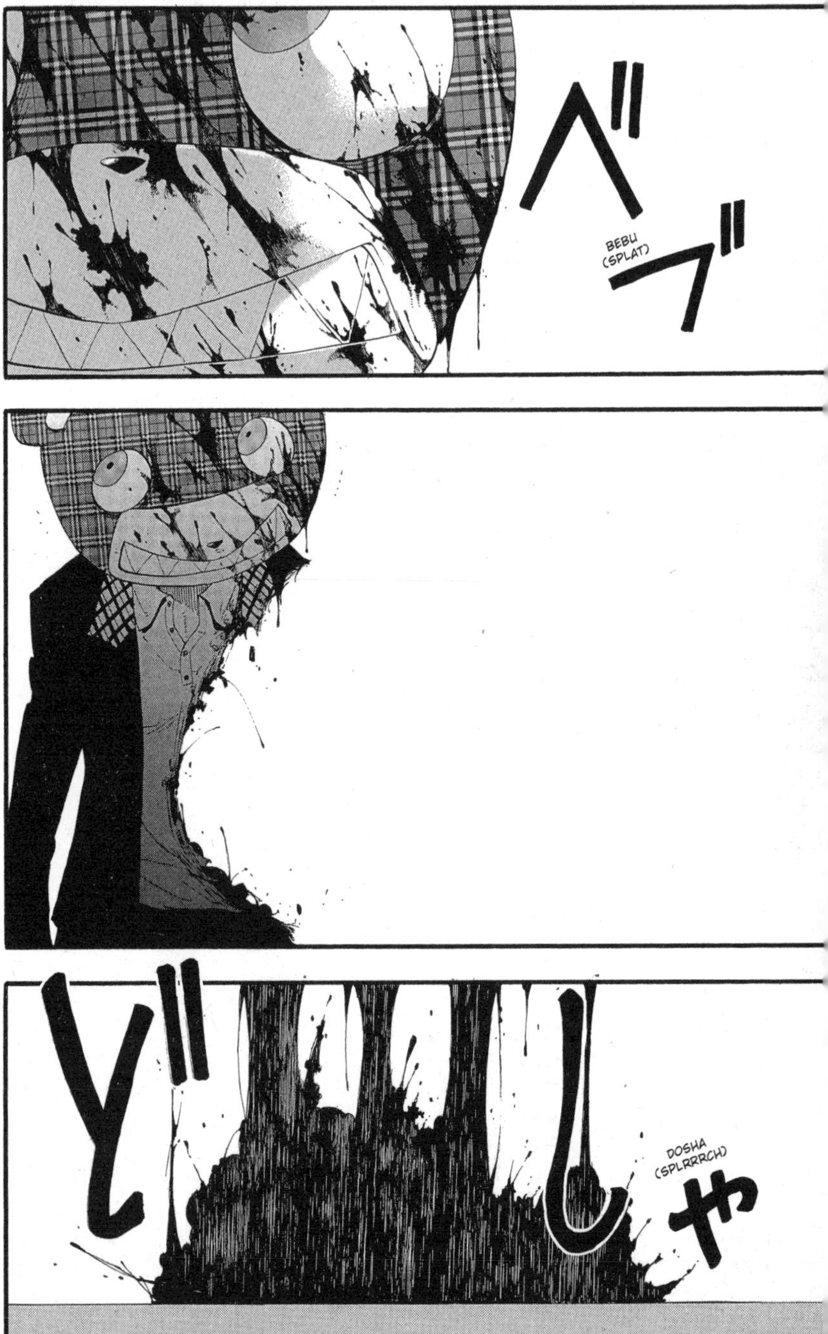
ベブ
BEBU
(SPLAT)
どしゃ
DOSHA
(SPLRRRCH)

TEZCA TLIPOCA!!

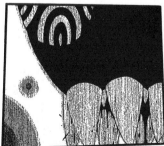

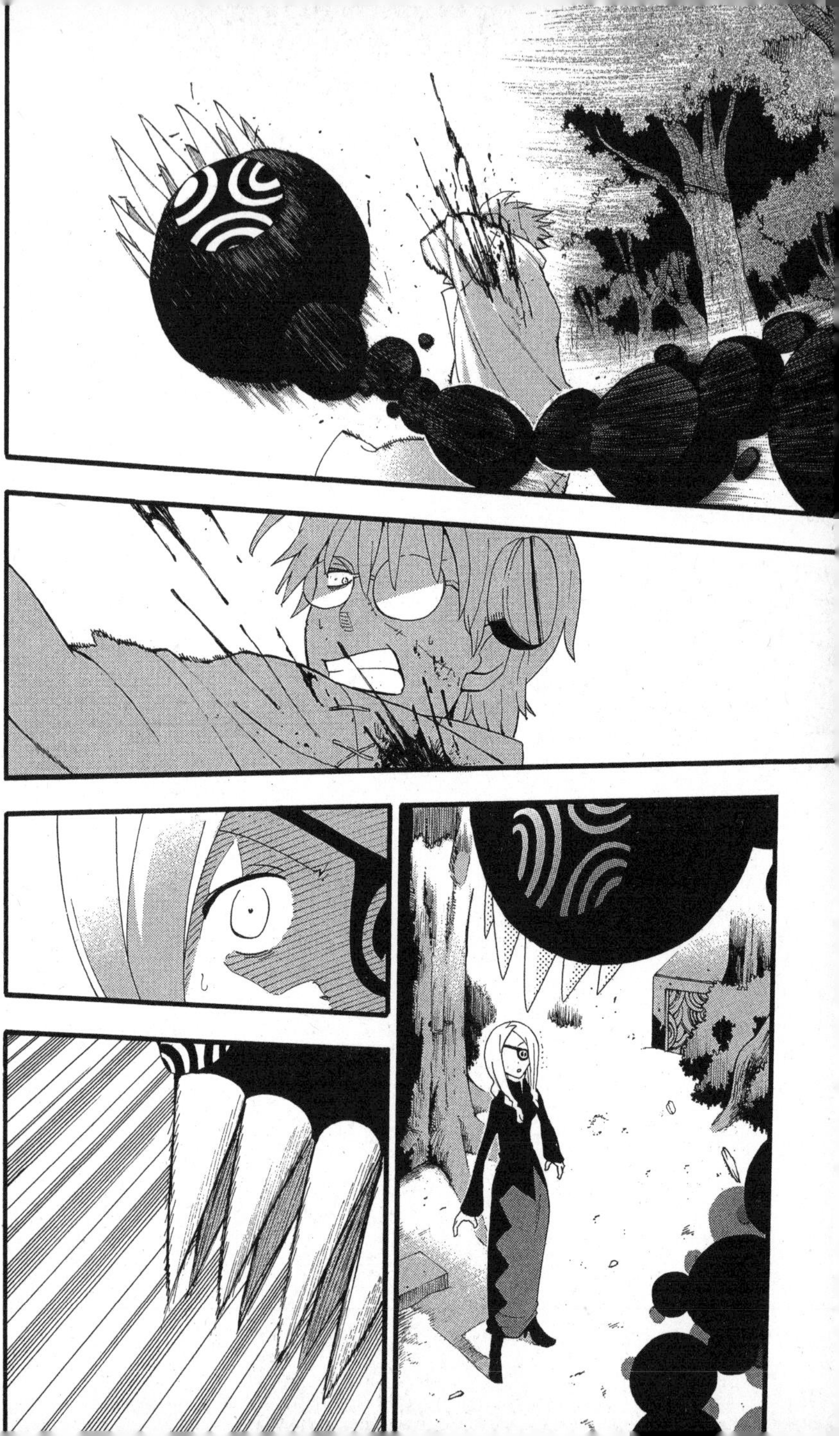

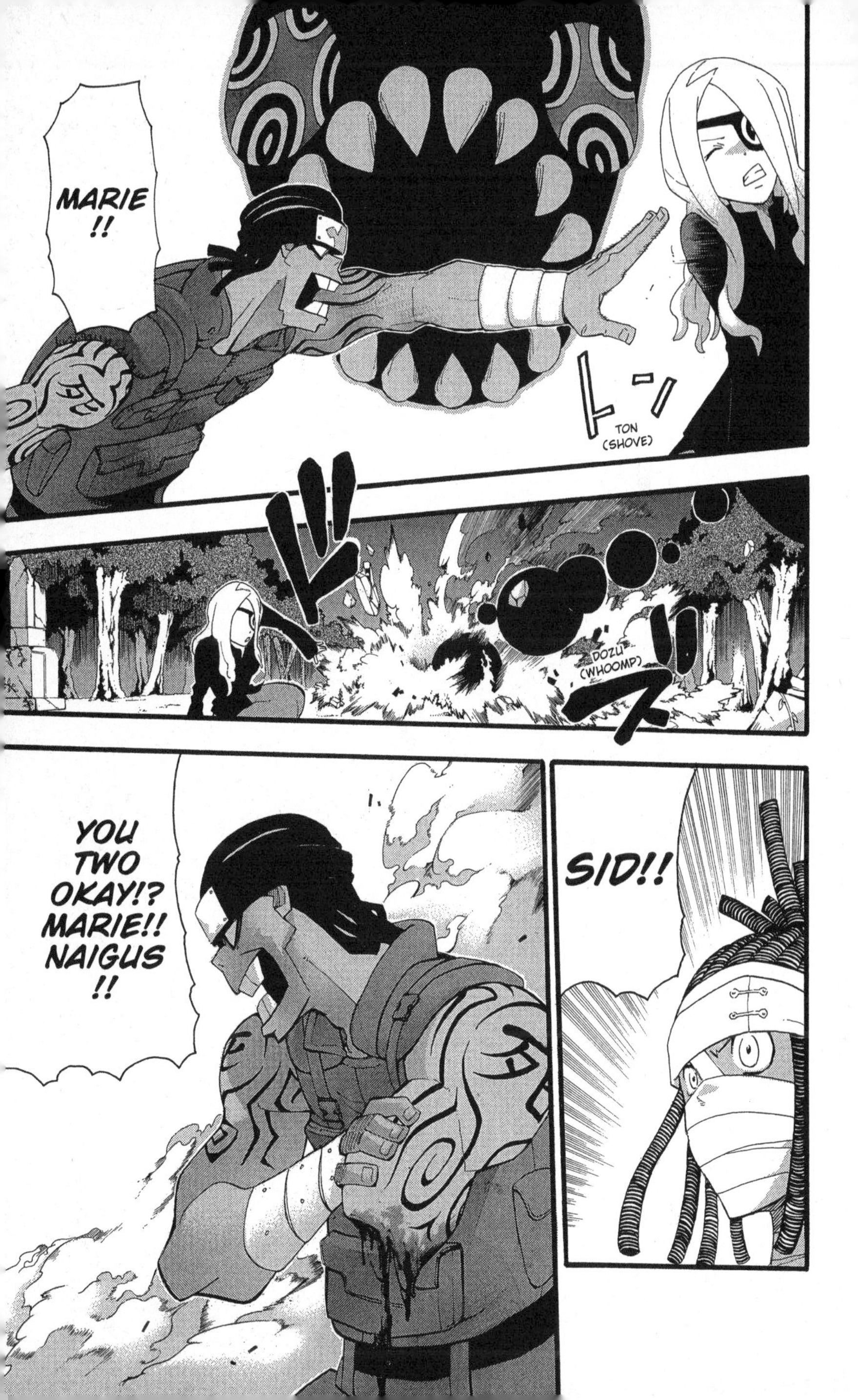
TON
(SHOVE)
MARIE !!
DOZU
(WHOOMP)
SID!!
YOU TWO OKAY!? MARIE!! NAIGUS !!

SO IS THIS THE BEST WE CAN EXPECT FROM THE DWMA ELITE...?

MIMIN

MIN
(VWEE)

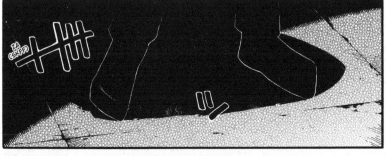

ZA
(SKFF)

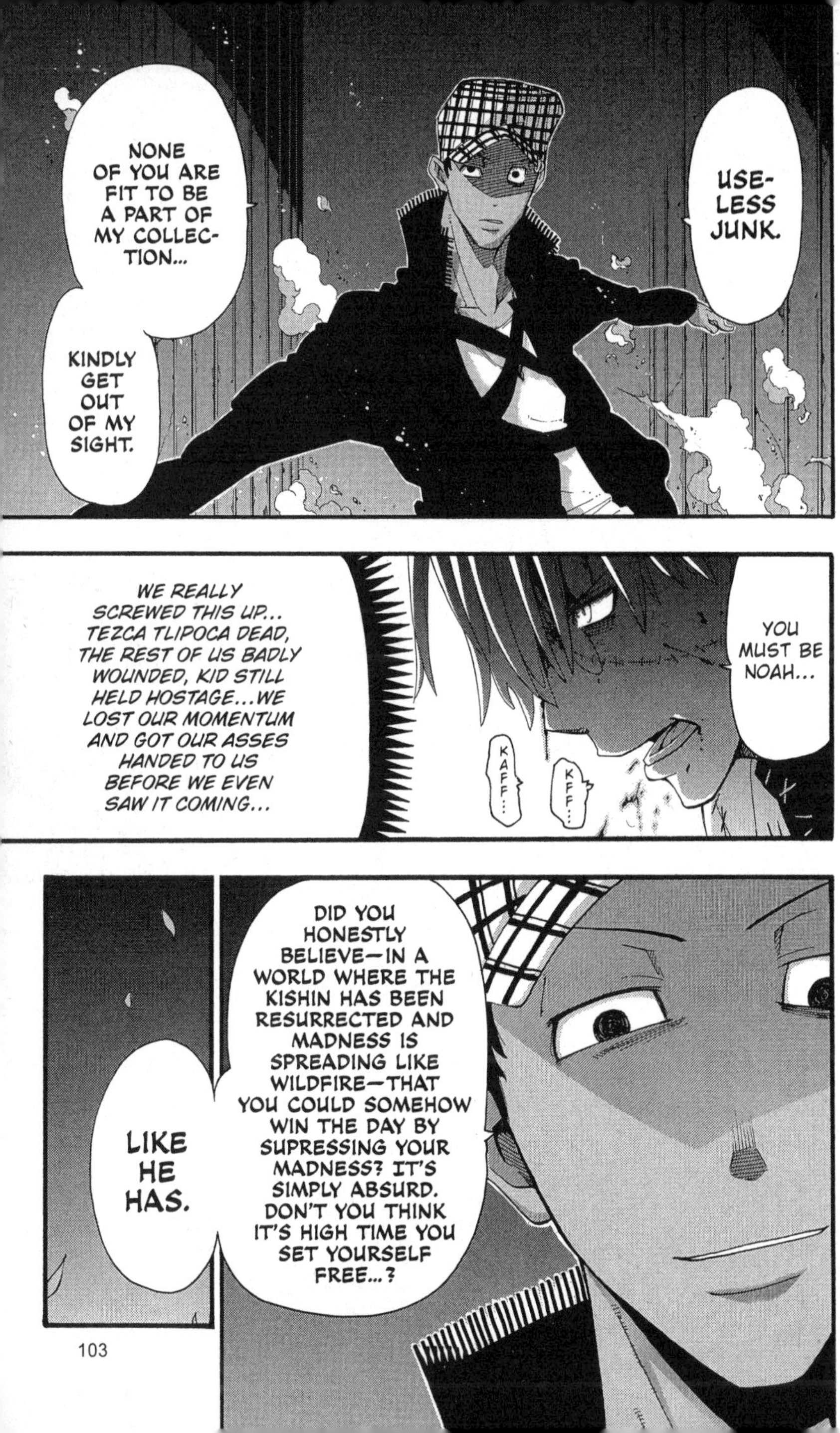
USE-LESS JUNK.
NONE OF YOU ARE FIT TO BE A PART OF MY COLLEC-TION...
KINDLY GET OUT OF MY SIGHT.
YOU MUST BE NOAH...
KFF...
KAFF...
WE REALLY SCREWED THIS UP... TEZCA TLIPOCA DEAD, THE REST OF US BADLY WOUNDED, KID STILL HELD HOSTAGE...WE LOST OUR MOMENTUM AND GOT OUR ASSES HANDED TO US BEFORE WE EVEN SAW IT COMING...
DID YOU HONESTLY BELIEVE—IN A WORLD WHERE THE KISHIN HAS BEEN RESURRECTED AND MADNESS IS SPREADING LIKE WILDFIRE—THAT YOU COULD SOMEHOW WIN THE DAY BY SUPRESSING YOUR MADNESS? IT'S SIMPLY ABSURD. DON'T YOU THINK IT'S HIGH TIME YOU SET YOURSELF FREE...?
LIKE HE HAS.

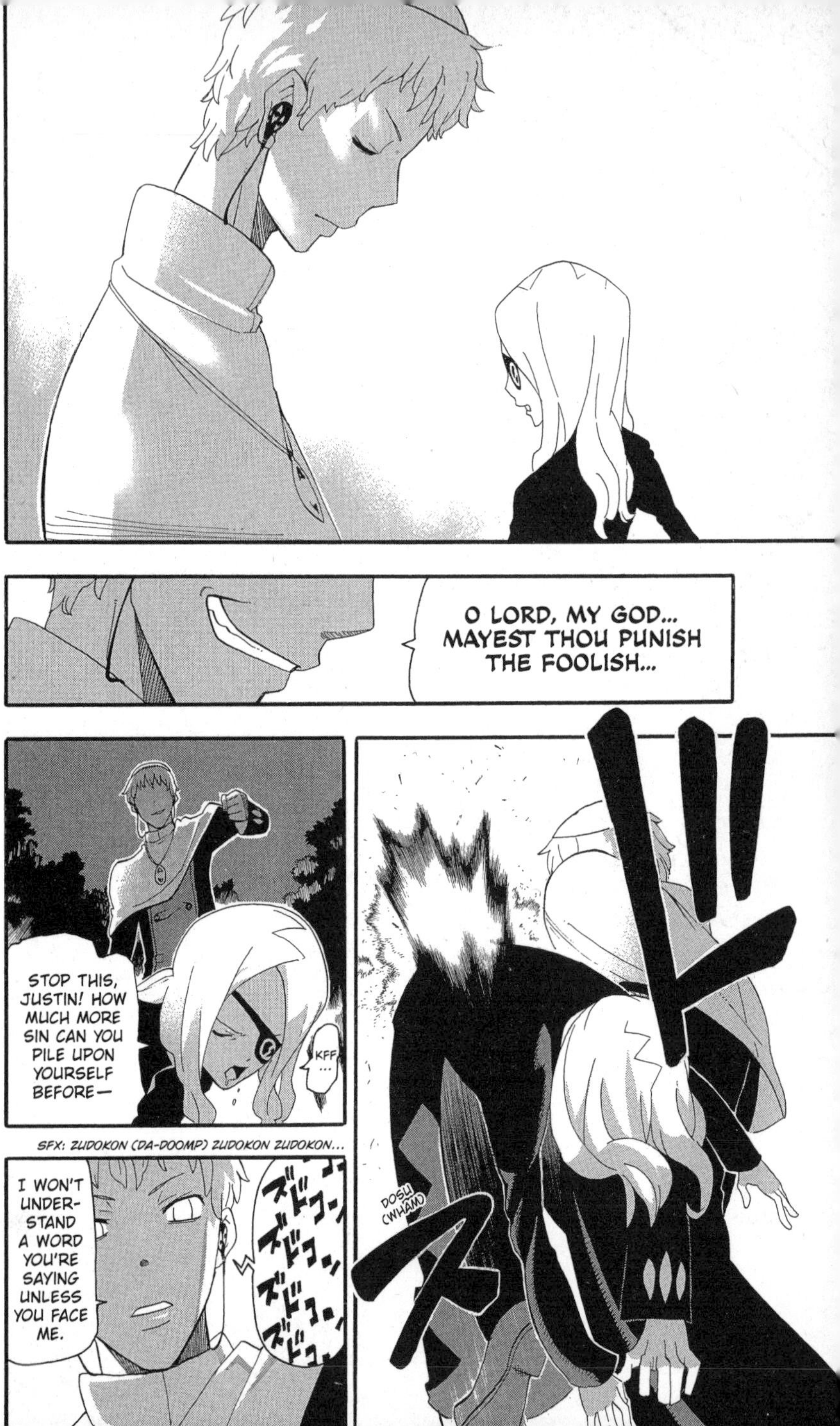
O LORD, MY GOD... MAYEST THOU PUNISH THE FOOLISH...
DOSU (WHAM)
STOP THIS, JUSTIN! HOW MUCH MORE SIN CAN YOU PILE UPON YOURSELF BEFORE—
KFF...
SFX: ZUDOKON (DA-DOOMP) ZUDOKON ZUDOKON...
I WON'T UNDER-STAND A WORD YOU'RE SAYING UNLESS YOU FACE ME.

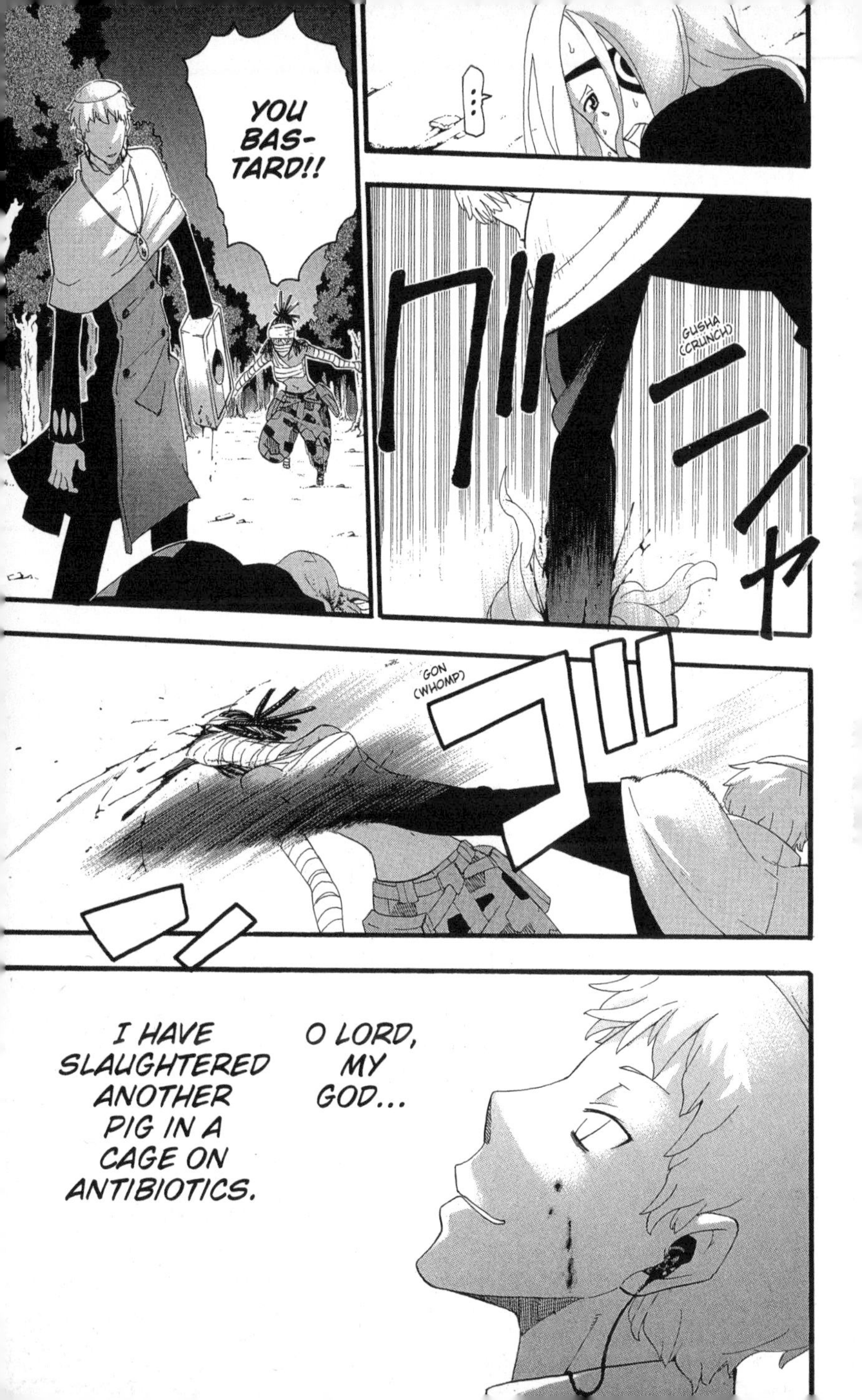
...
GUSHA (CRUNCH)
YOU BASTARD!!
GON (WHOMP)
O LORD, MY GOD...
I HAVE SLAUGHTERED ANOTHER PIG IN A CAGE ON ANTIBIOTICS.

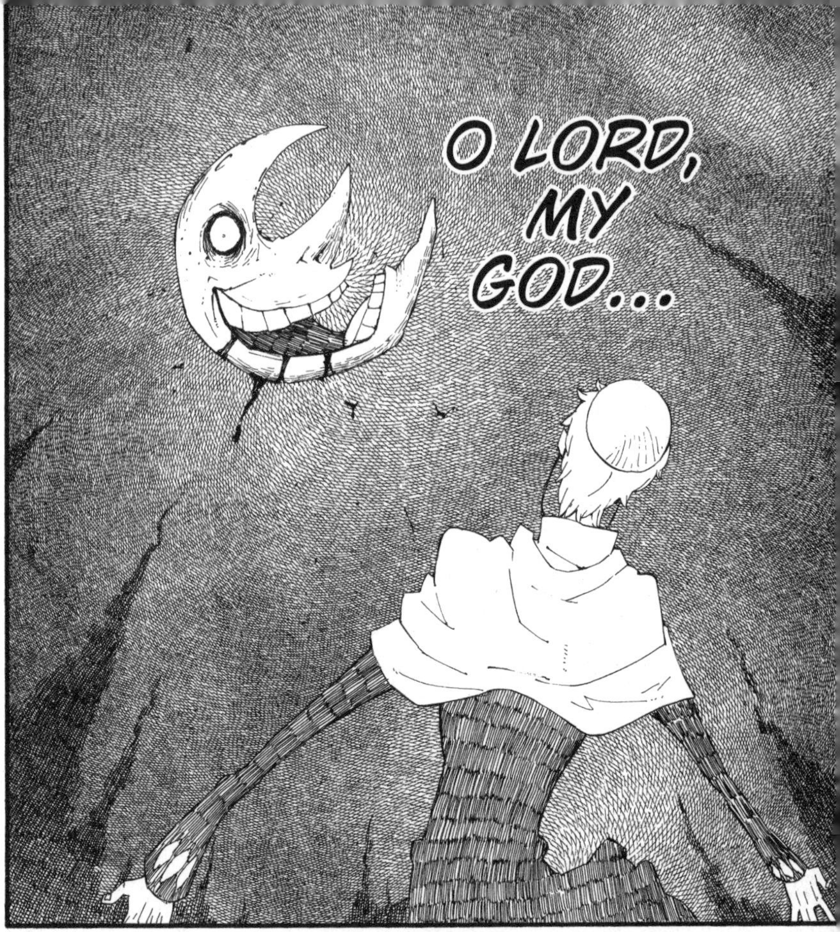
O LORD, MY GOD...
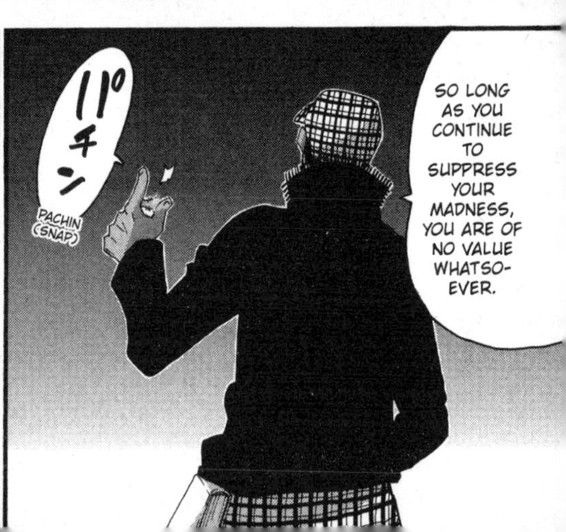
SO LONG AS YOU CONTINUE TO SUPPRESS YOUR MADNESS, YOU ARE OF NO VALUE WHATSO-EVER.
パチン
PACHIN (SNAP)
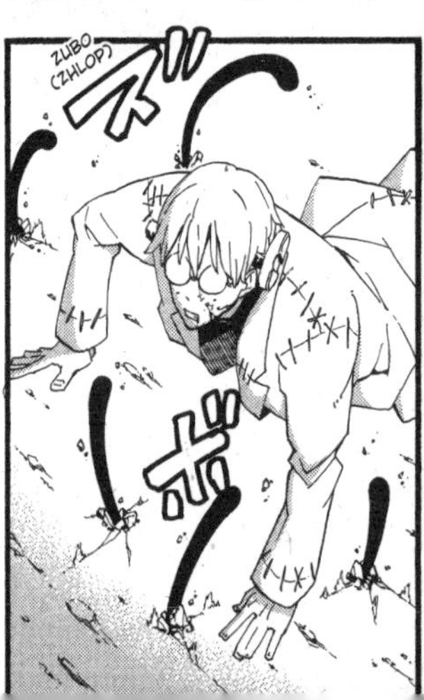
ズボ
ZUBO (ZHLOP)

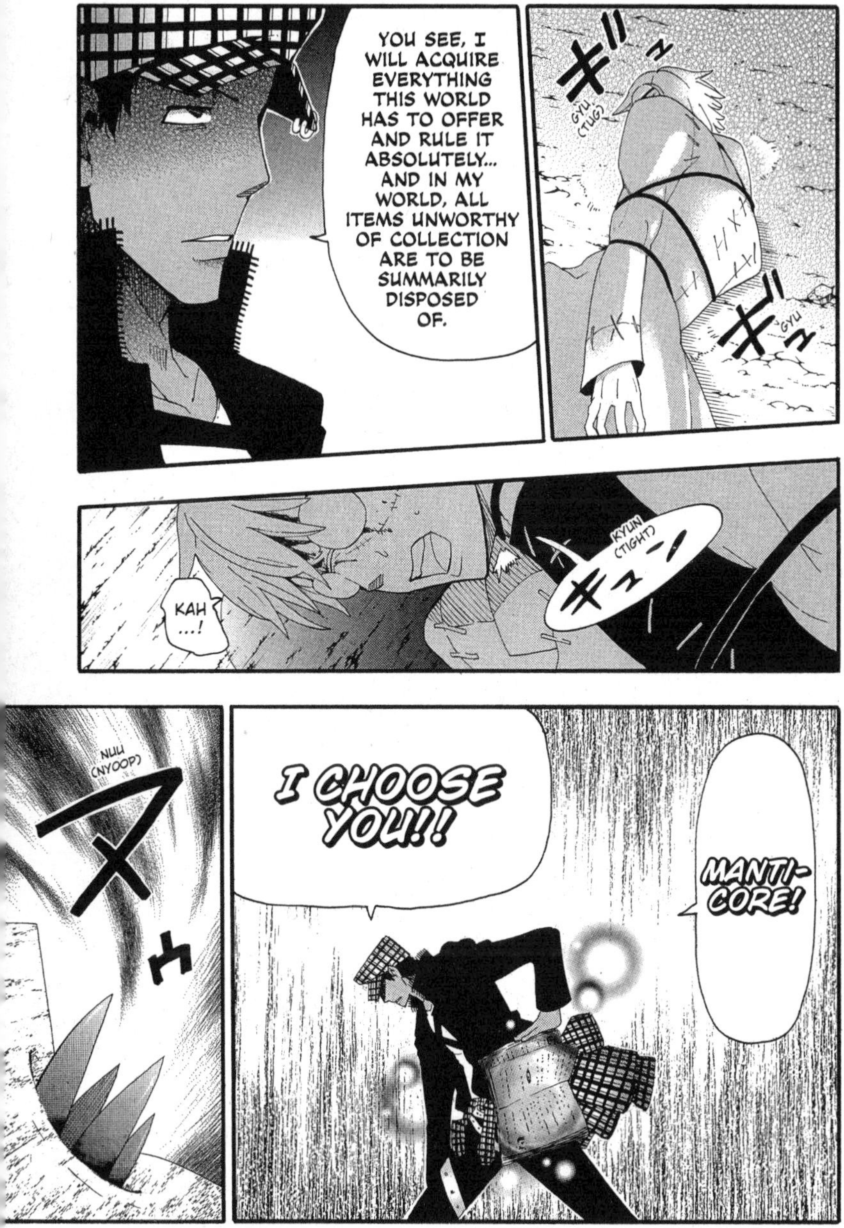
GYU (TUG)
GYU
YOU SEE, I WILL ACQUIRE EVERYTHING THIS WORLD HAS TO OFFER AND RULE IT ABSOLUTELY... AND IN MY WORLD, ALL ITEMS UNWORTHY OF COLLECTION ARE TO BE SUMMARILY DISPOSED OF.
KYUN (TIGHT)
KAH ...!
MANTI-CORE!
I CHOOSE YOU!!
NUU (NYOOP)

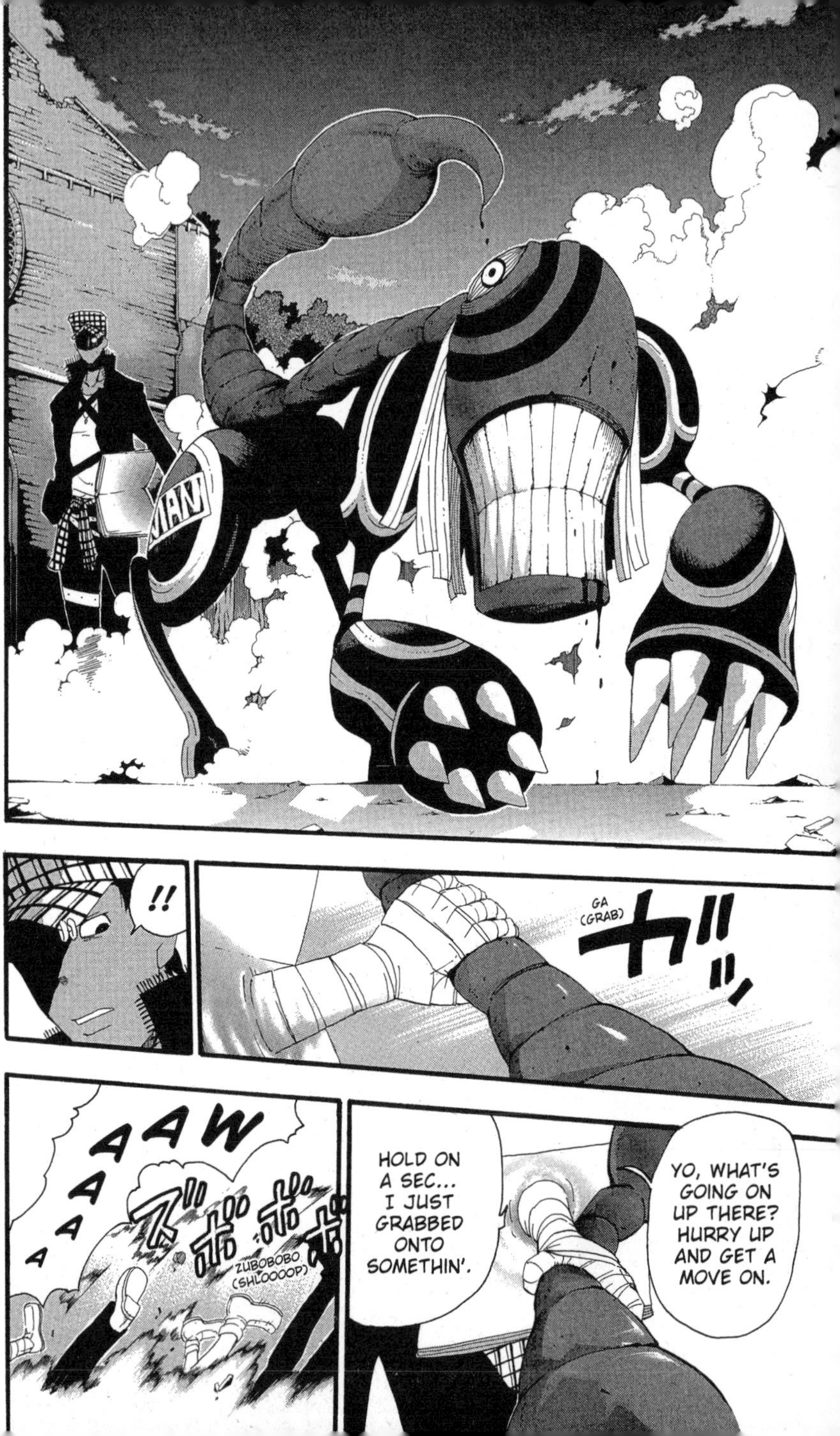
GA
(GRAB)
!!
YO, WHAT'S GOING ON UP THERE? HURRY UP AND GET A MOVE ON.
HOLD ON A SEC... I JUST GRABBED ONTO SOMETHIN'.
AAAAAAAW
ZUBOBOBO
(SHLOOOOP)

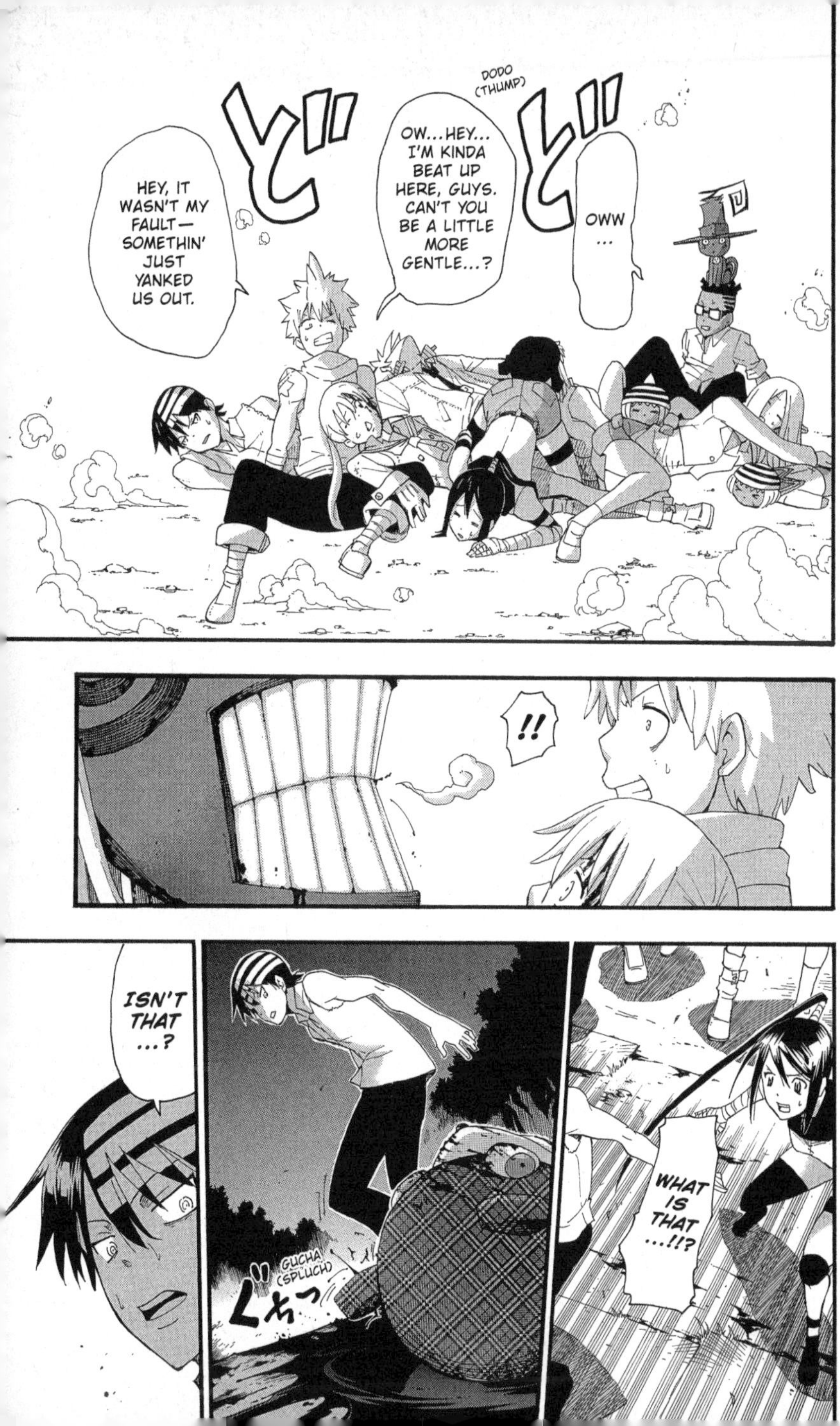
DODO (THUMP)
OWW...
OW...HEY... I'M KINDA BEAT UP HERE, GUYS. CAN'T YOU BE A LITTLE MORE GENTLE...?
HEY, IT WASN'T MY FAULT—SOMETHIN' JUST YANKED US OUT.
!!
WHAT IS THAT...!!?
GUCHA (SPLUCH)
ISN'T THAT...?

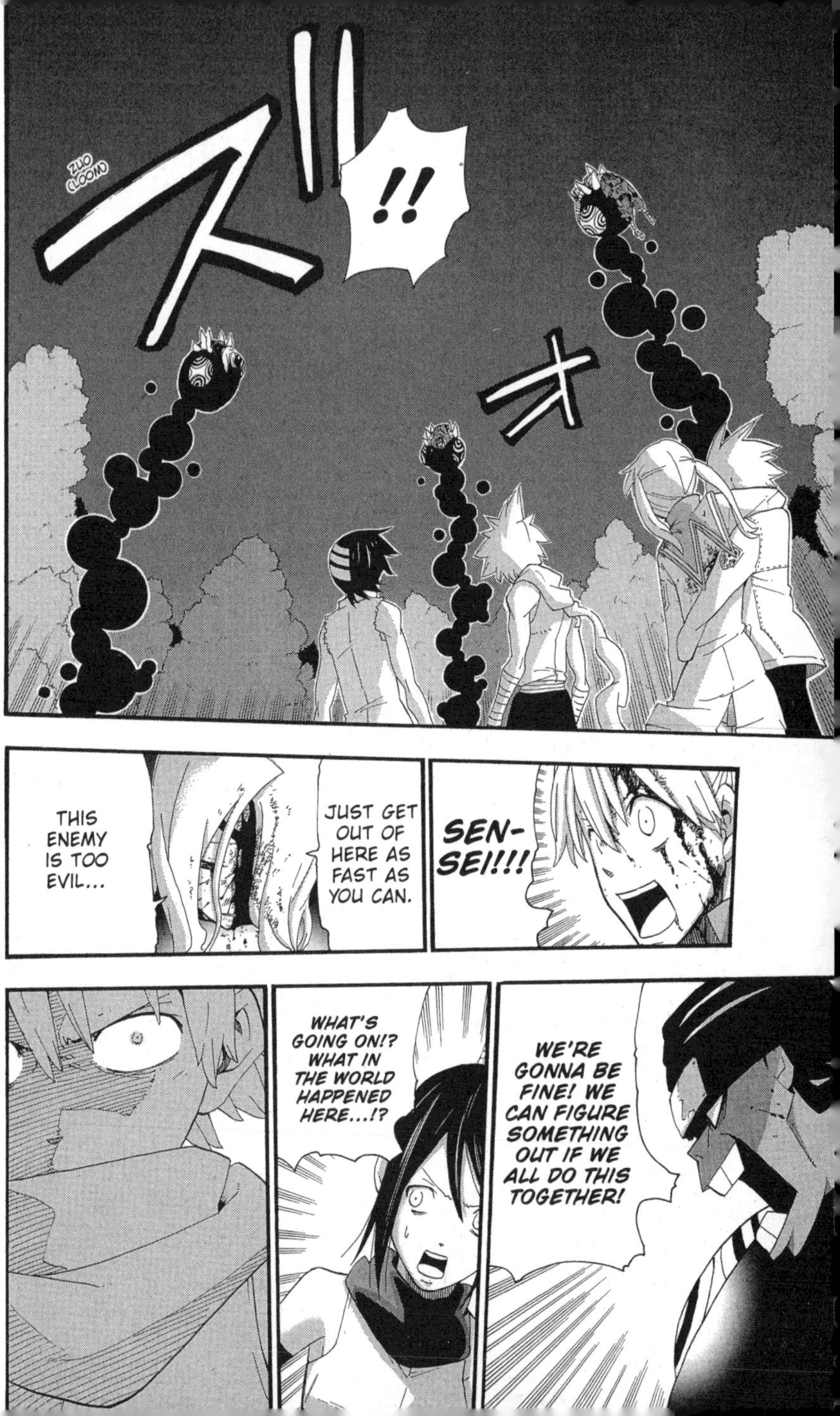
ZUO (LOOM)
!!
SEN-SEI!!!
JUST GET OUT OF HERE AS FAST AS YOU CAN.
THIS ENEMY IS TOO EVIL...
WE'RE GONNA BE FINE! WE CAN FIGURE SOMETHING OUT IF WE ALL DO THIS TOGETHER!
WHAT'S GOING ON!? WHAT IN THE WORLD HAPPENED HERE...!?

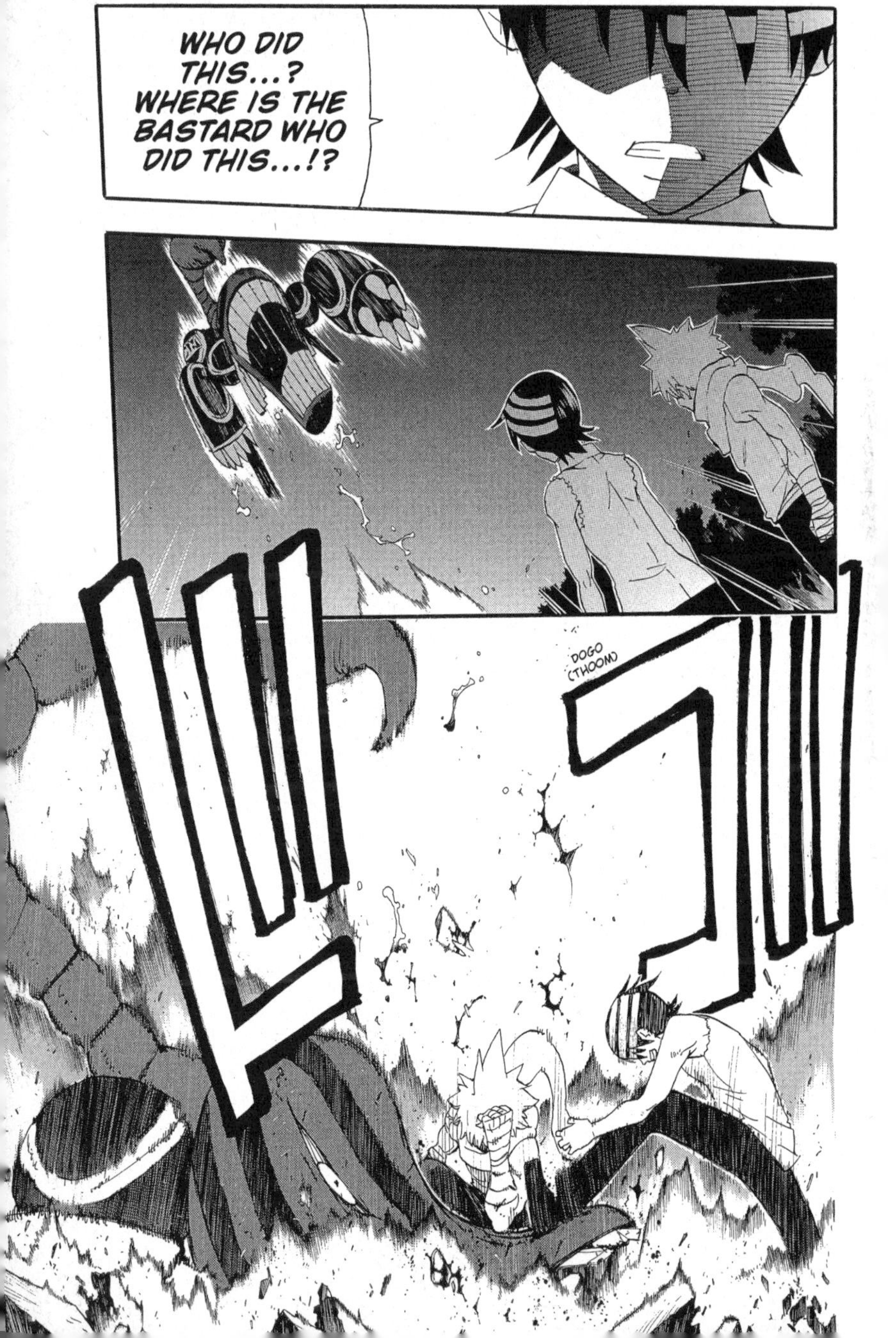
WHO DID THIS...? WHERE IS THE BASTARD WHO DID THIS...!?
DOGO (THOOM)

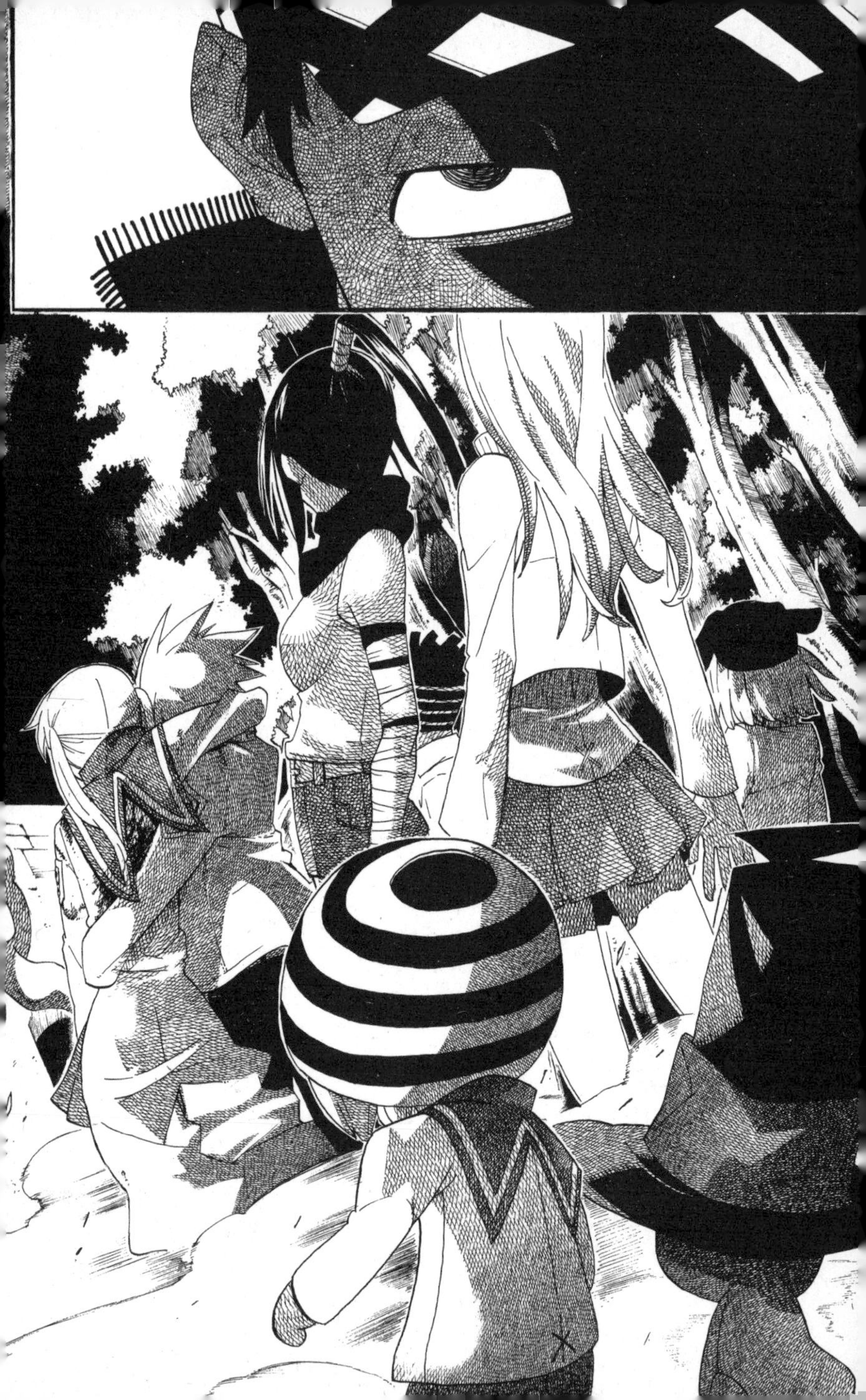

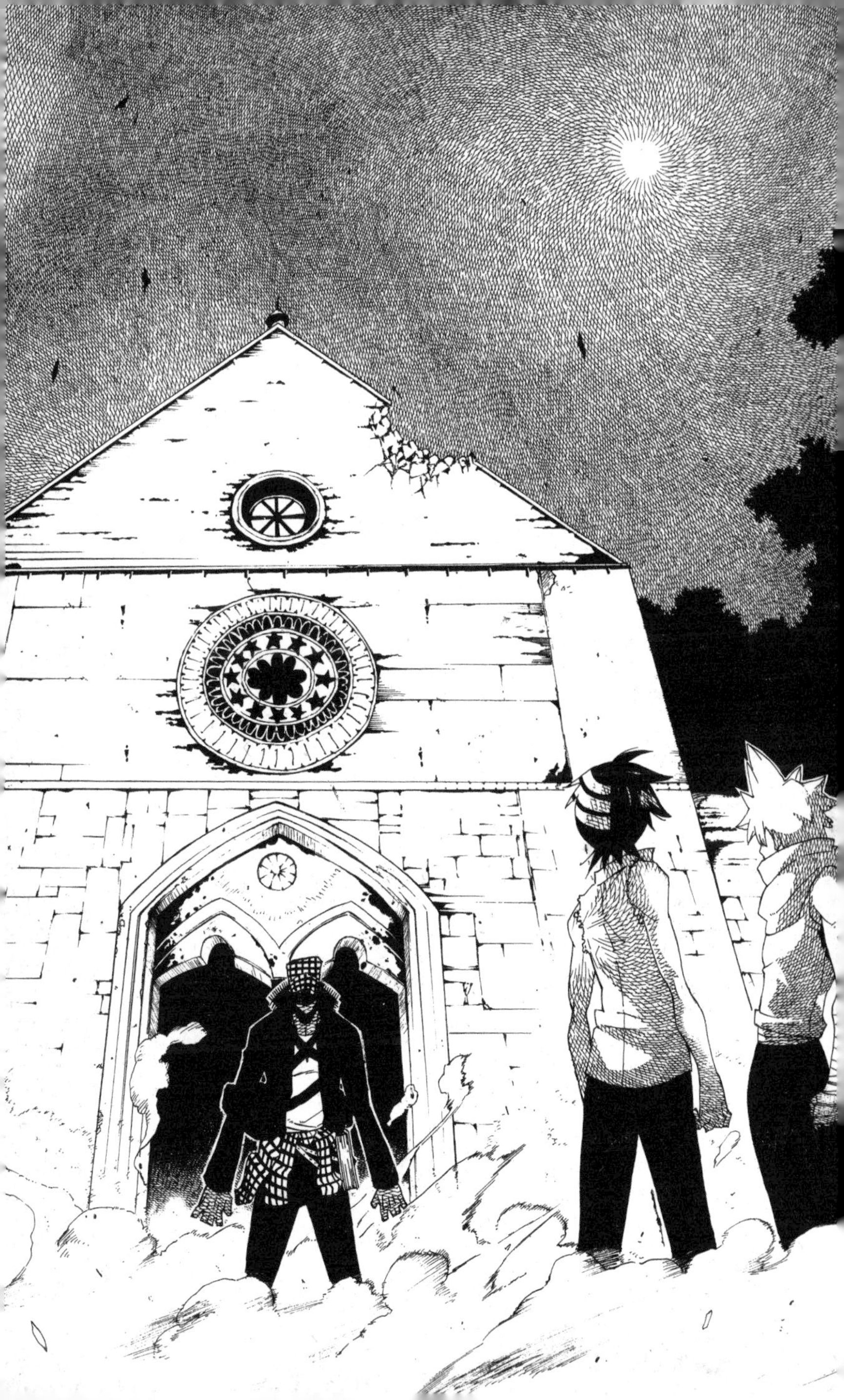

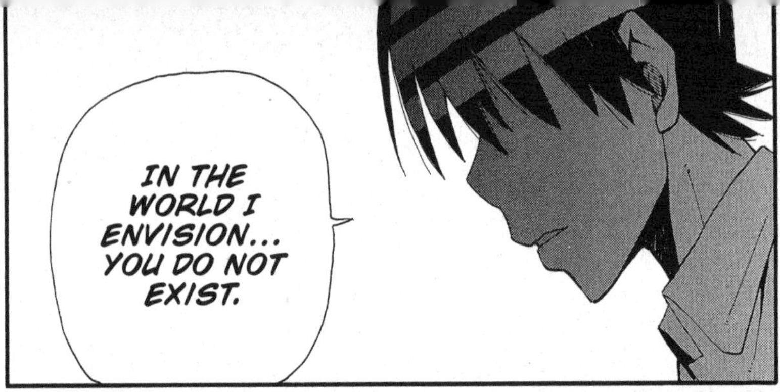
IN THE WORLD I ENVISION... YOU DO NOT EXIST.
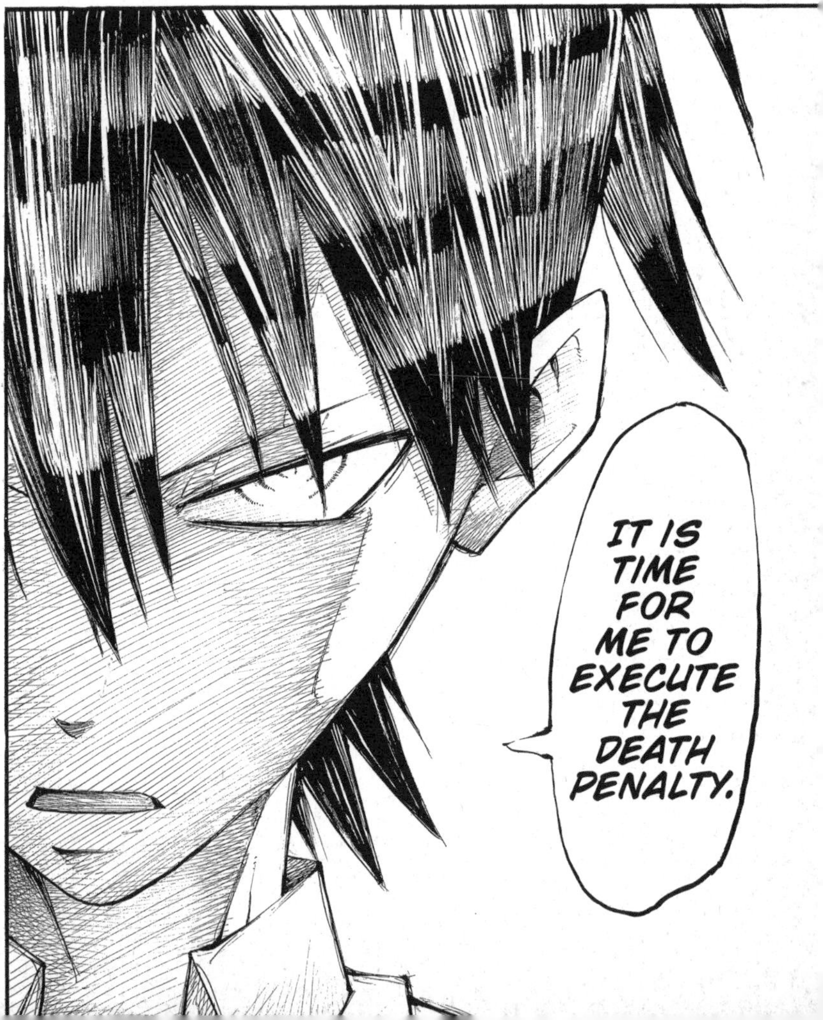
IT IS TIME FOR ME TO EXECUTE THE DEATH PENALTY.

SOUL EATER

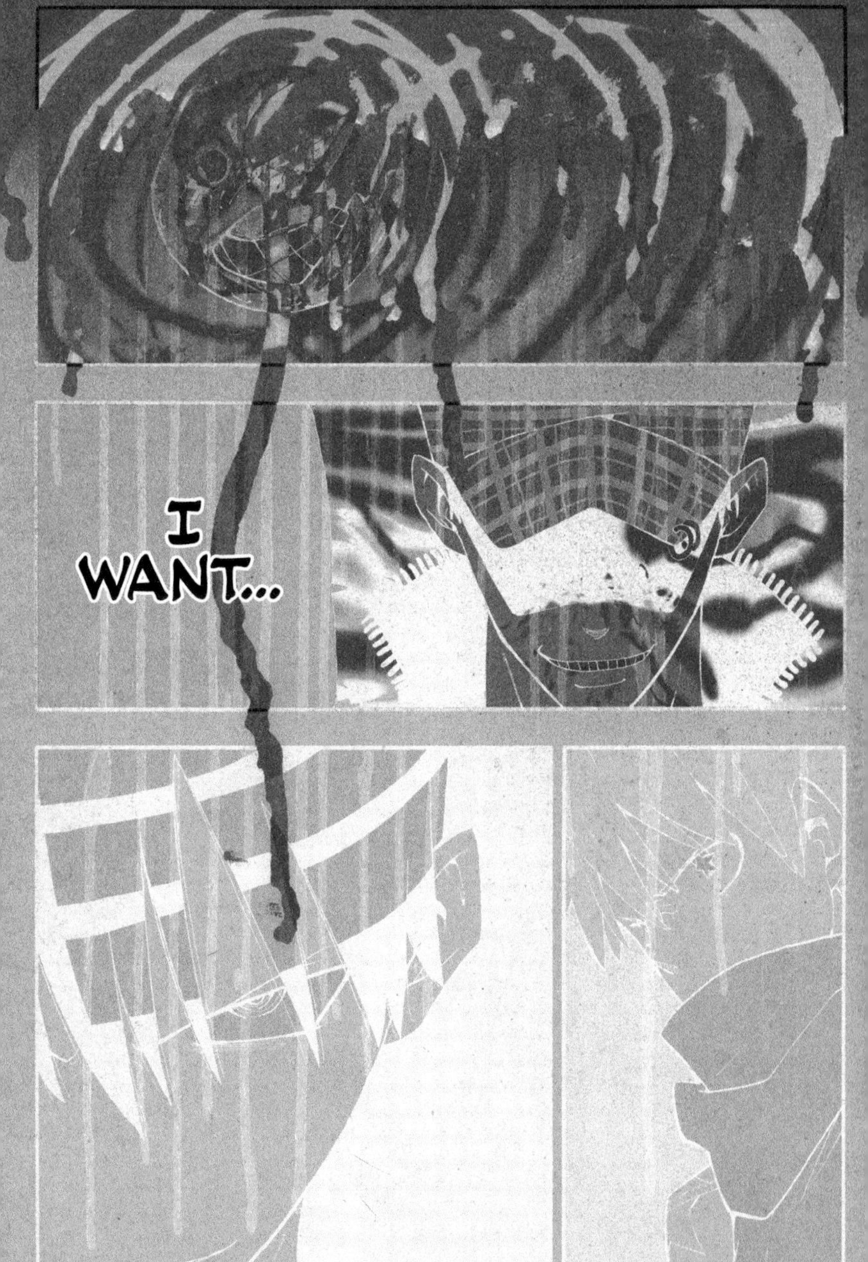
I WANT...

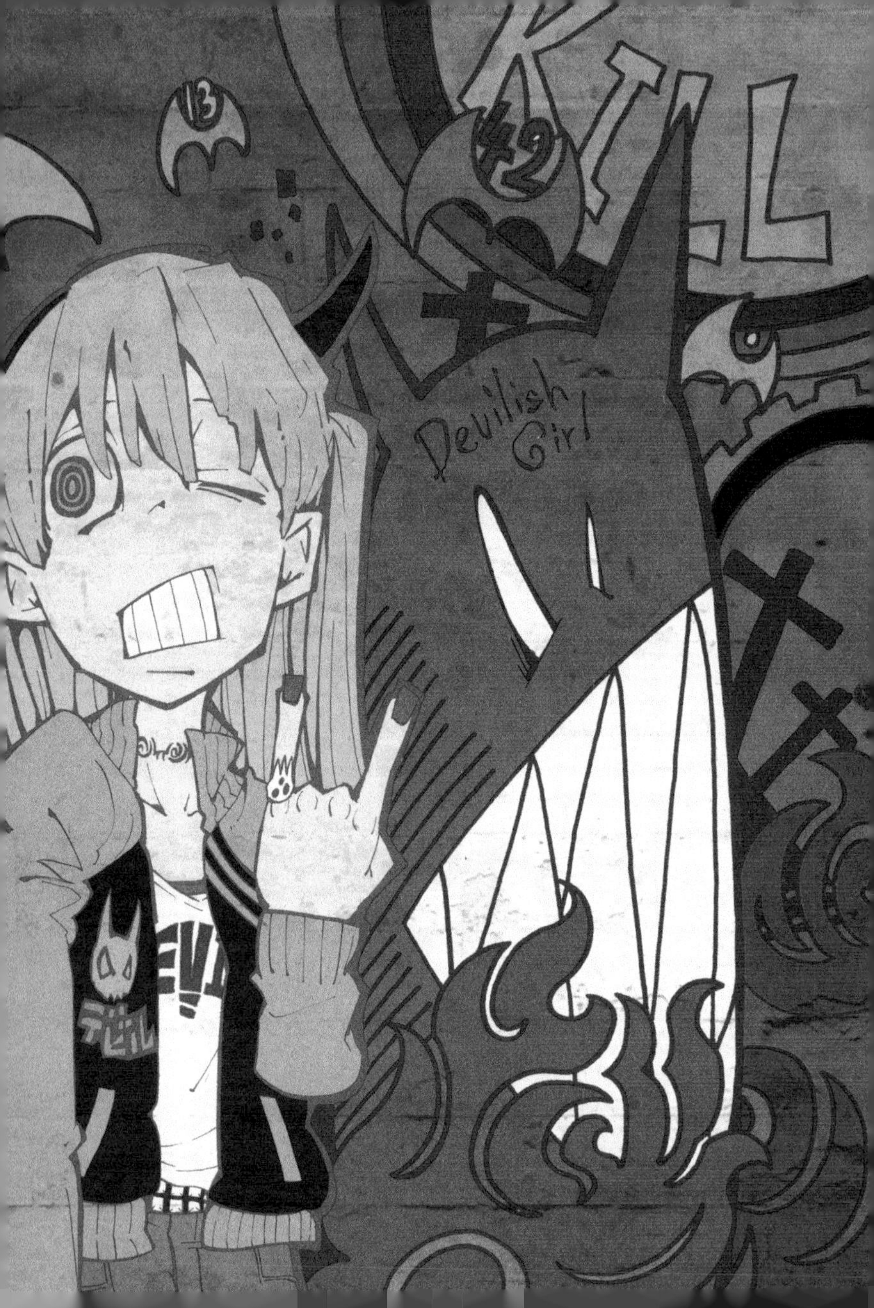
13
42
Devilish Girl

CHAPTER 80: SALVAGE (PART 9)

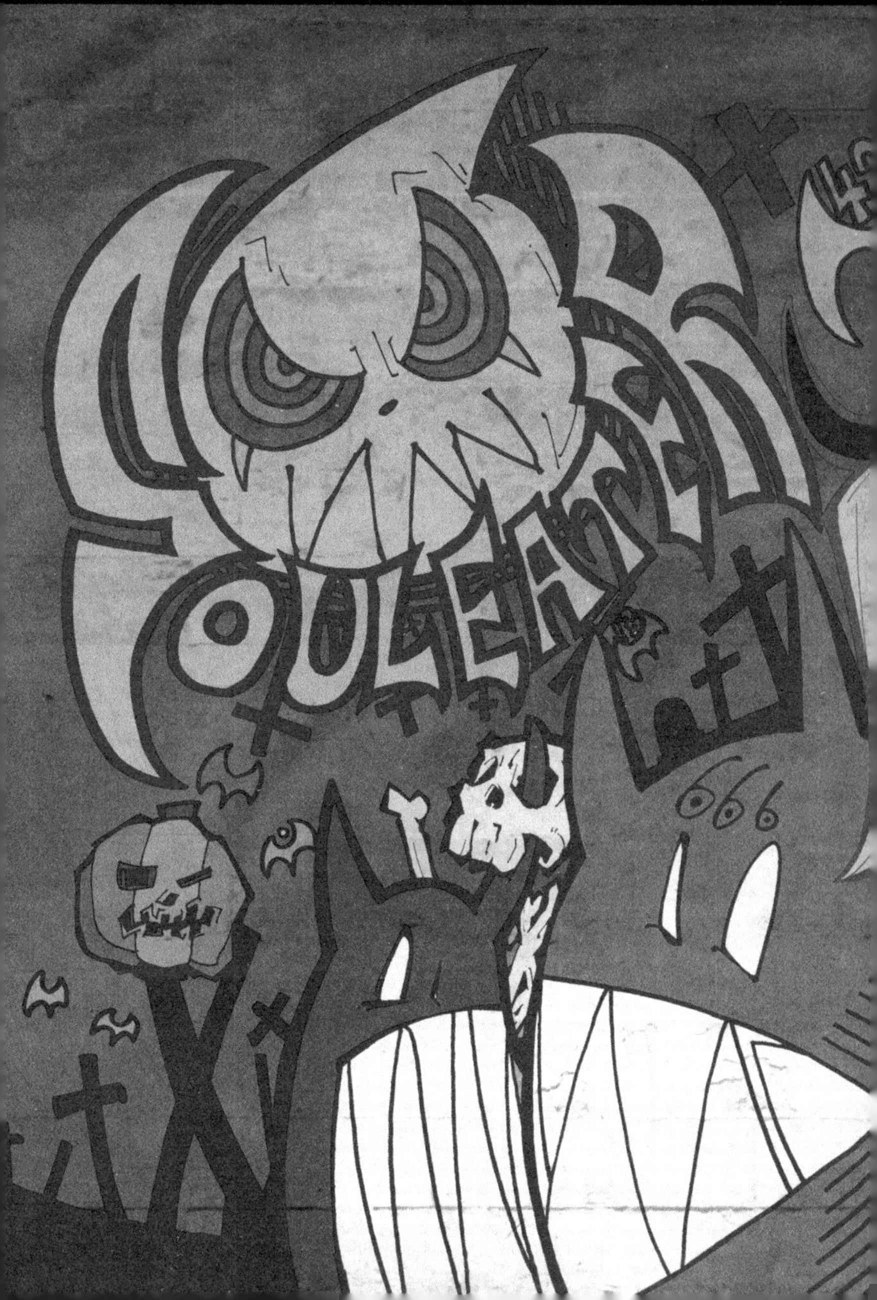
666

SOUL EATER

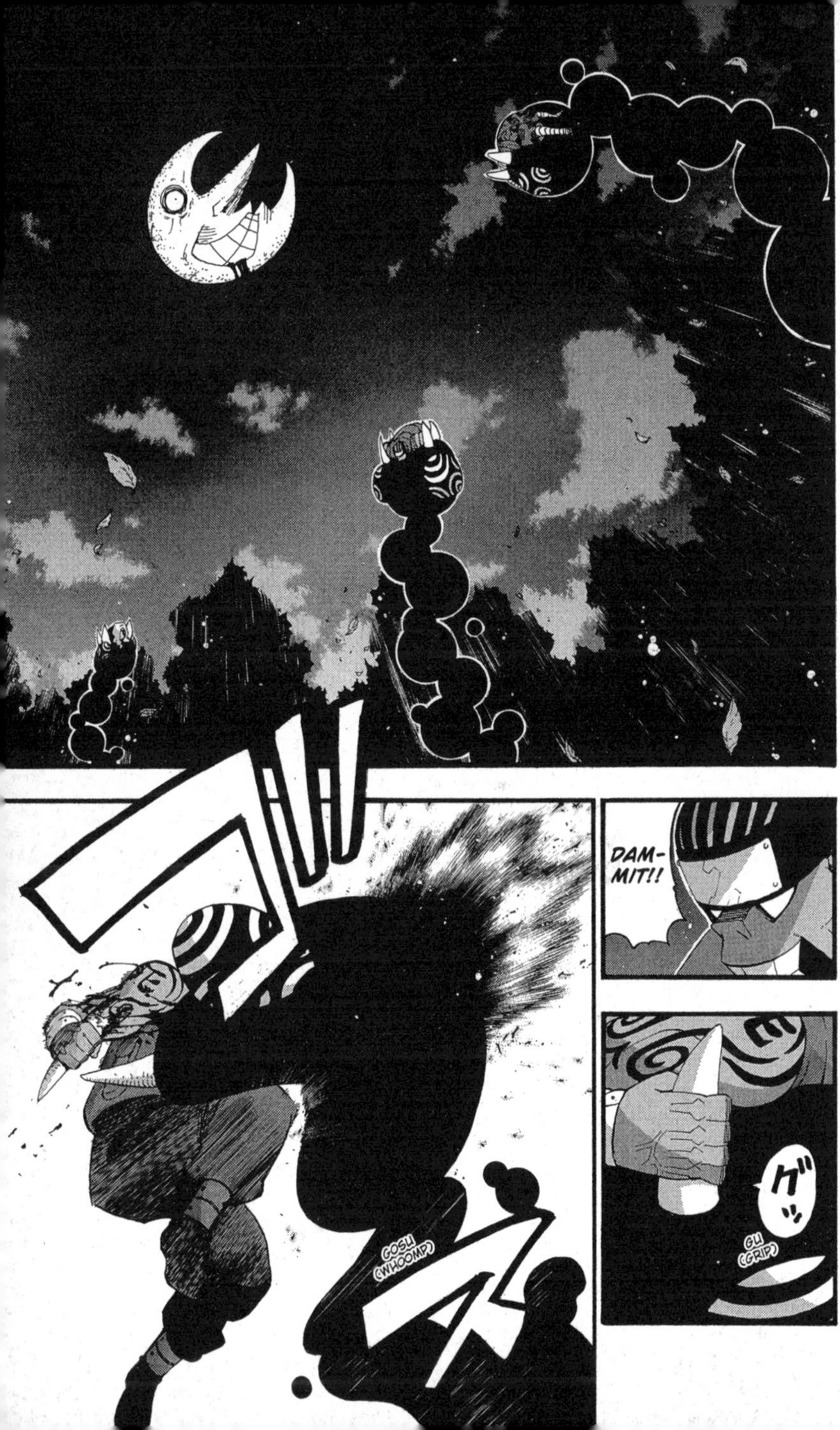
DAM-MIT!!
グッ
GU (GRIP)
GOSU (WHOOMP)

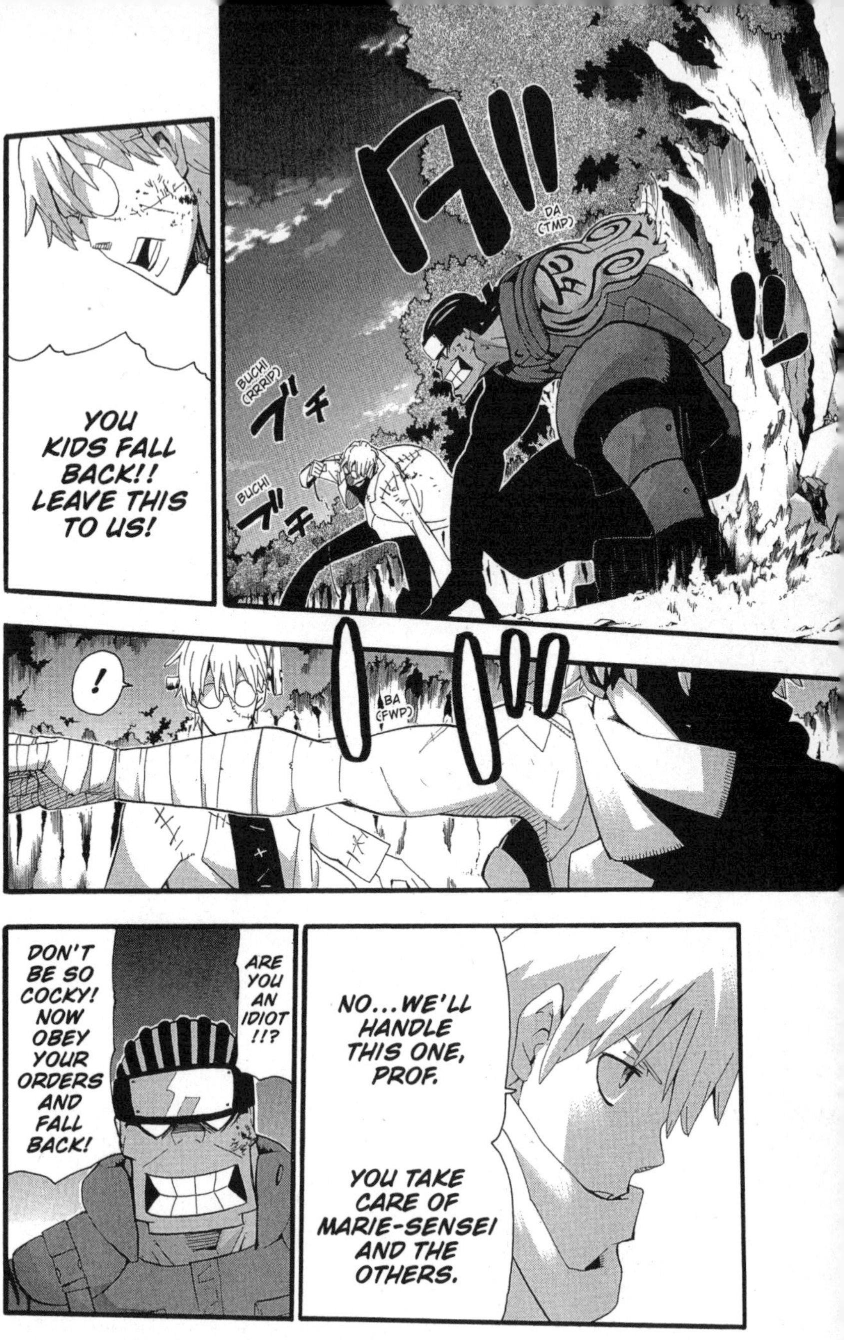
DA (TMP)
BUCHI (RRRIP)
BUCHI
YOU KIDS FALL BACK!! LEAVE THIS TO US!
!
BA (FWP)
NO...WE'LL HANDLE THIS ONE, PROF.
YOU TAKE CARE OF MARIE-SENSEI AND THE OTHERS.
ARE YOU AN IDIOT!!?
DON'T BE SO COCKY! NOW OBEY YOUR ORDERS AND FALL BACK!

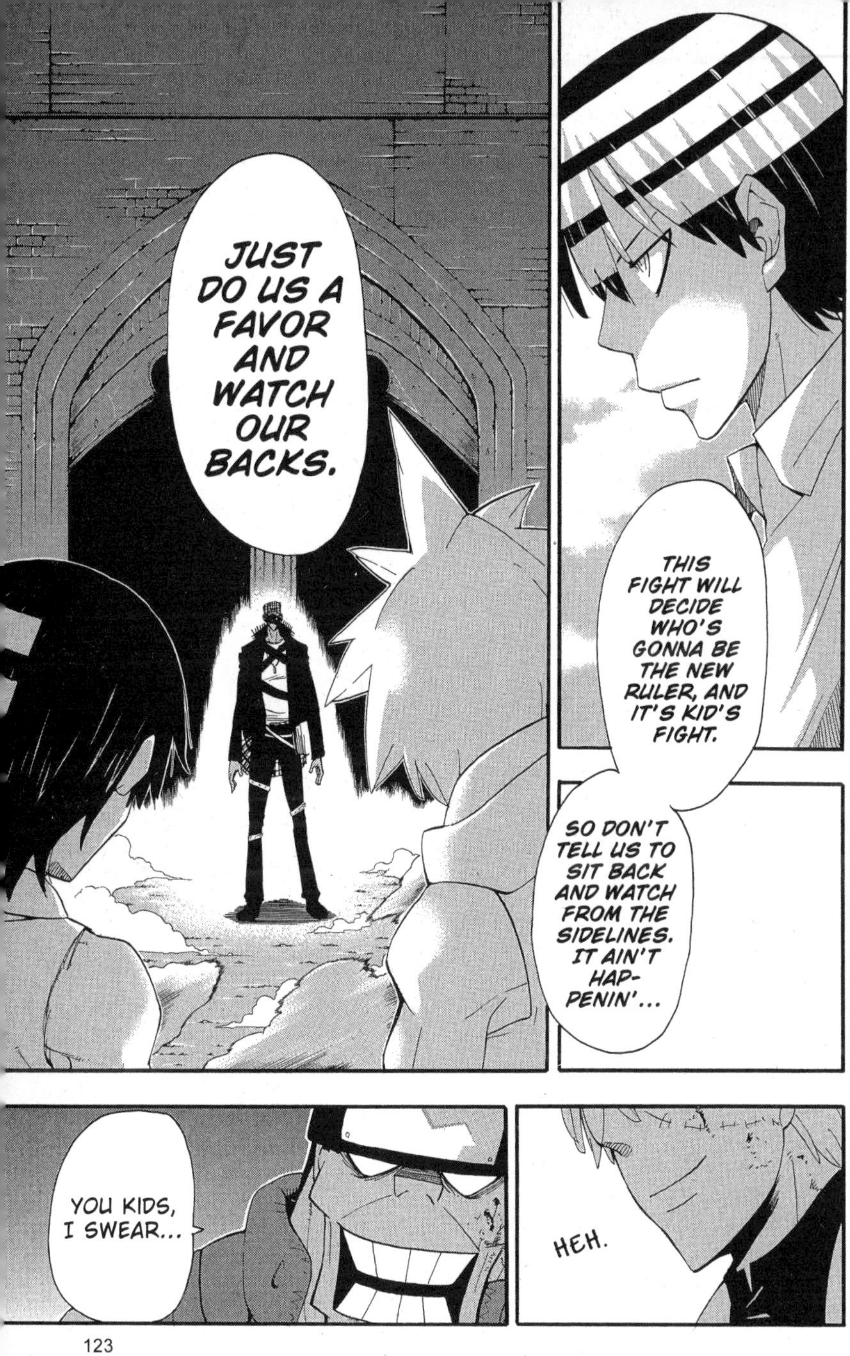
THIS FIGHT WILL DECIDE WHO'S GONNA BE THE NEW RULER, AND IT'S KID'S FIGHT.
SO DON'T TELL US TO SIT BACK AND WATCH FROM THE SIDELINES. IT AIN'T HAP-PENIN'...
JUST DO US A FAVOR AND WATCH OUR BACKS.
HEH.
YOU KIDS, I SWEAR...

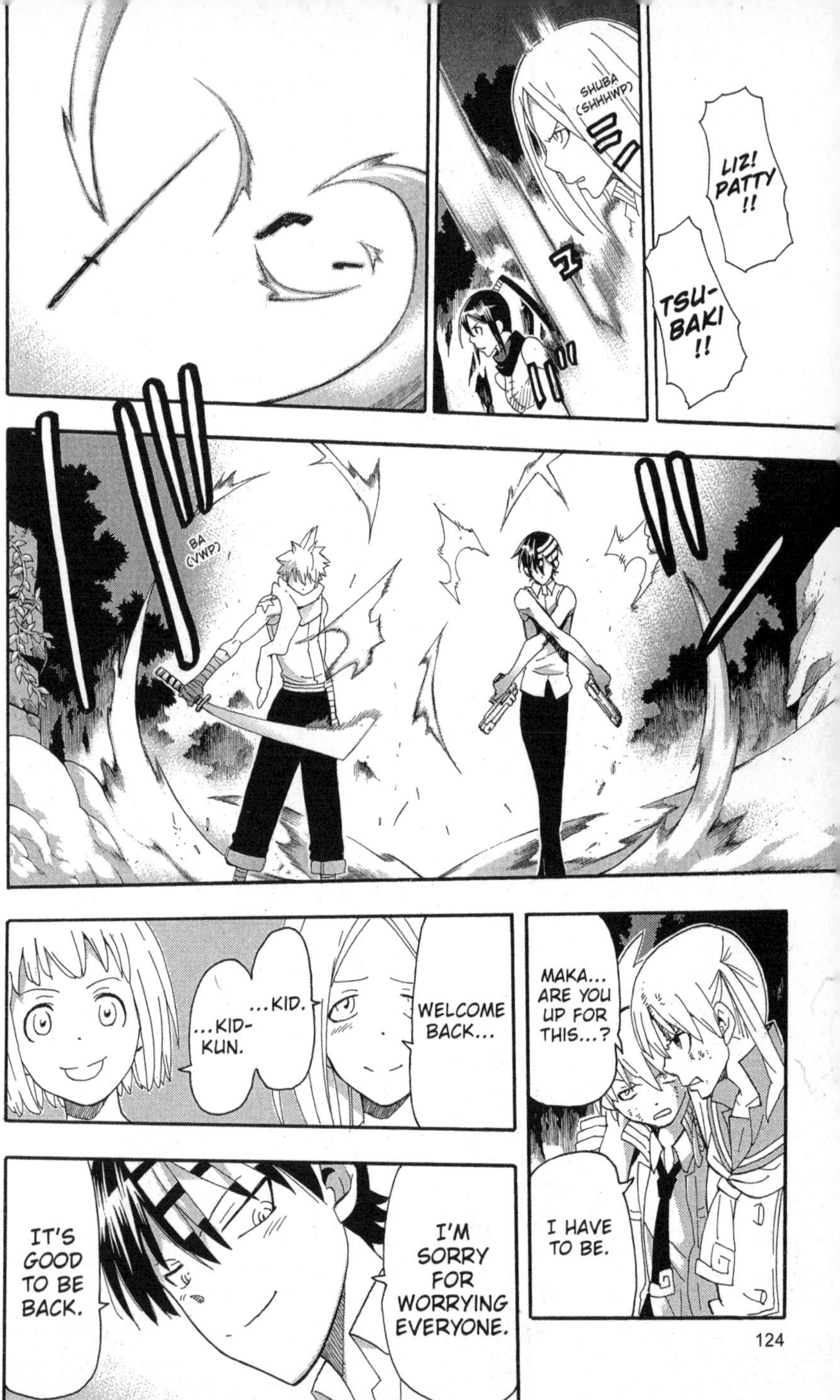
LIZ! PATTY!!
TSU-BAKI!!
SHUBA (SHHHWP)
BA (VWP)
MAKA... ARE YOU UP FOR THIS...?
I HAVE TO BE.
WELCOME BACK...
...KID.
...KID-KUN.
I'M SORRY FOR WORRYING EVERYONE.
IT'S GOOD TO BE BACK.

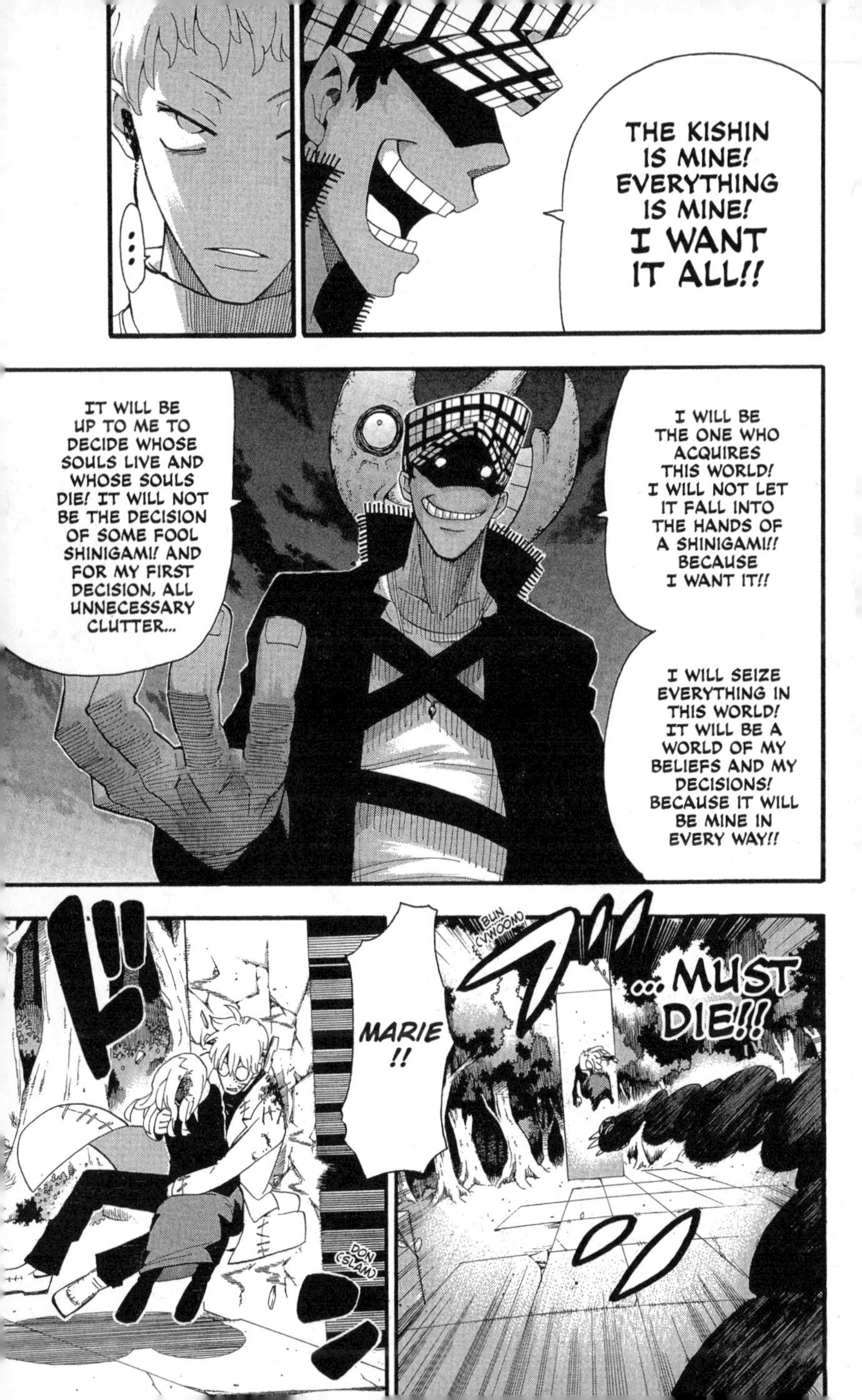
THE KISHIN IS MINE! EVERYTHING IS MINE! I WANT IT ALL!!
...
I WILL BE THE ONE WHO ACQUIRES THIS WORLD! I WILL NOT LET IT FALL INTO THE HANDS OF A SHINIGAMI!! BECAUSE I WANT IT!!
I WILL SEIZE EVERYTHING IN THIS WORLD! IT WILL BE A WORLD OF MY BELIEFS AND MY DECISIONS! BECAUSE IT WILL BE MINE IN EVERY WAY!!
IT WILL BE UP TO ME TO DECIDE WHOSE SOULS LIVE AND WHOSE SOULS DIE! IT WILL NOT BE THE DECISION OF SOME FOOL SHINIGAMI! AND FOR MY FIRST DECISION, ALL UNNECESSARY CLUTTER...
BUN (VWOOM)
...MUST DIE!!
MARIE !!
DON (SLAM)

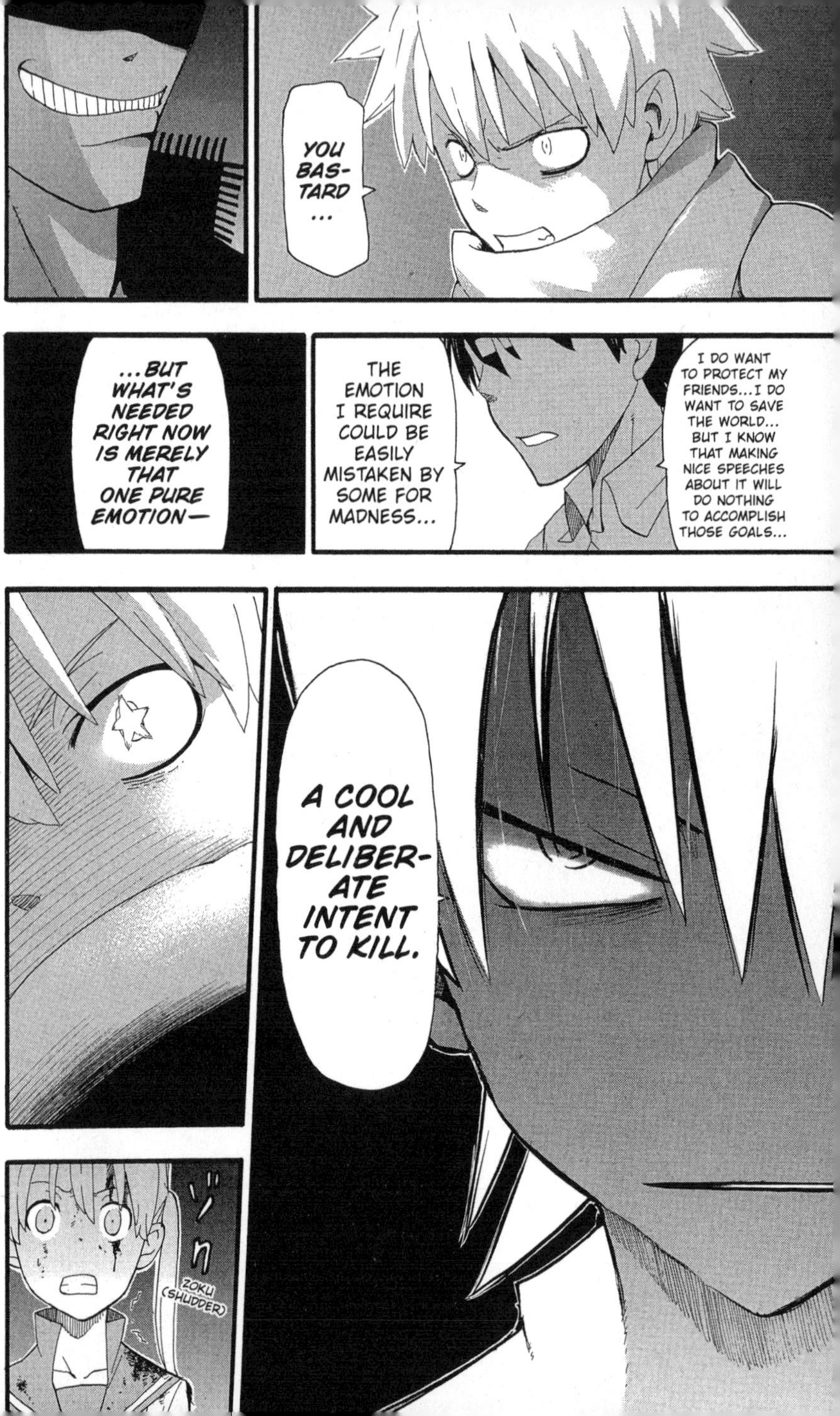
YOU BAS-TARD ...
I DO WANT TO PROTECT MY FRIENDS...I DO WANT TO SAVE THE WORLD... BUT I KNOW THAT MAKING NICE SPEECHES ABOUT IT WILL DO NOTHING TO ACCOMPLISH THOSE GOALS...
THE EMOTION I REQUIRE COULD BE EASILY MISTAKEN BY SOME FOR MADNESS...
...BUT WHAT'S NEEDED RIGHT NOW IS MERELY THAT ONE PURE EMOTION—
A COOL AND DELIBER-ATE INTENT TO KILL.
ZOKU (SHUDDER)

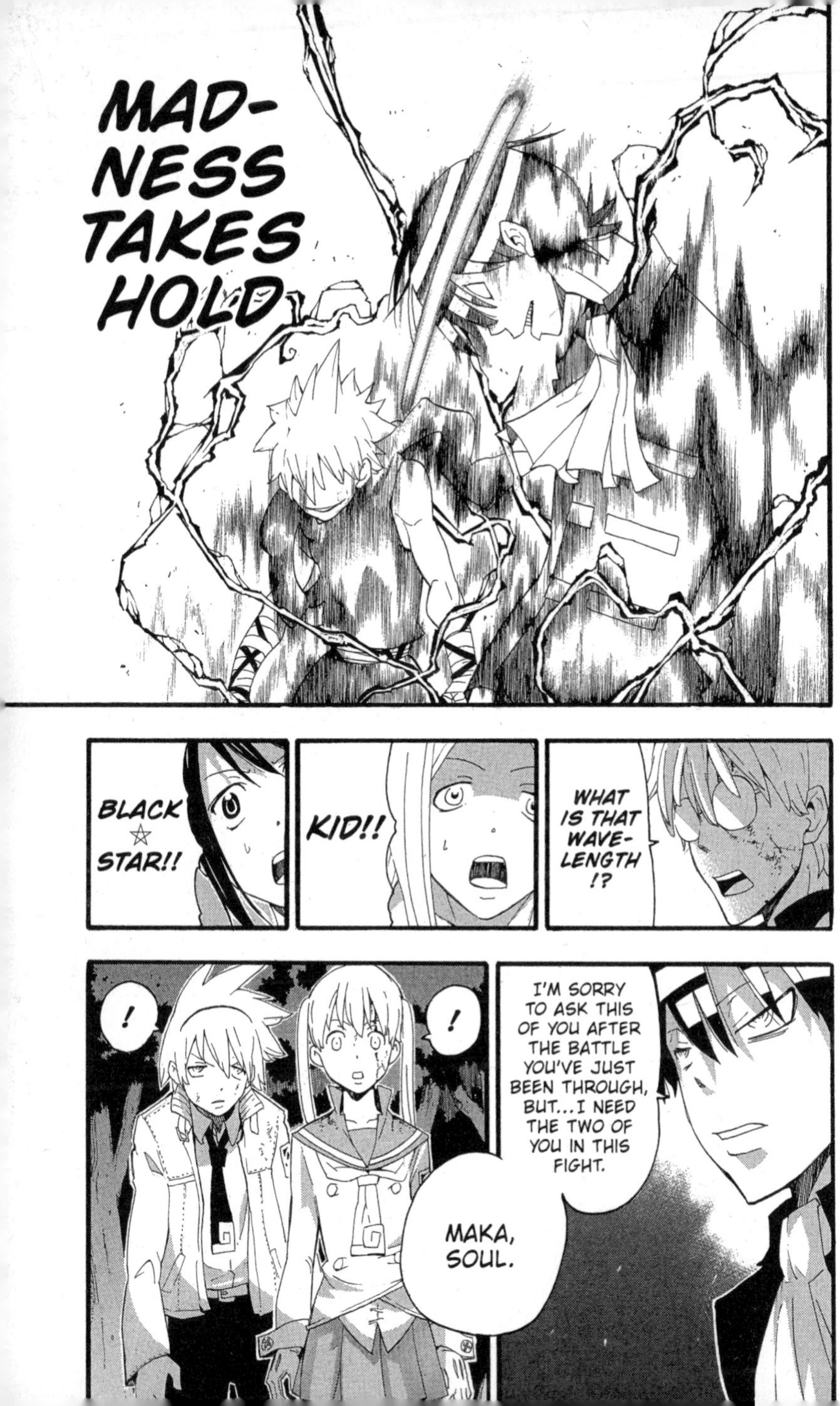
MADNESS TAKES HOLD
WHAT IS THAT WAVELENGTH!?
KID!!
BLACK☆STAR!!
I'M SORRY TO ASK THIS OF YOU AFTER THE BATTLE YOU'VE JUST BEEN THROUGH, BUT...I NEED THE TWO OF YOU IN THIS FIGHT.
MAKA, SOUL.
!
!

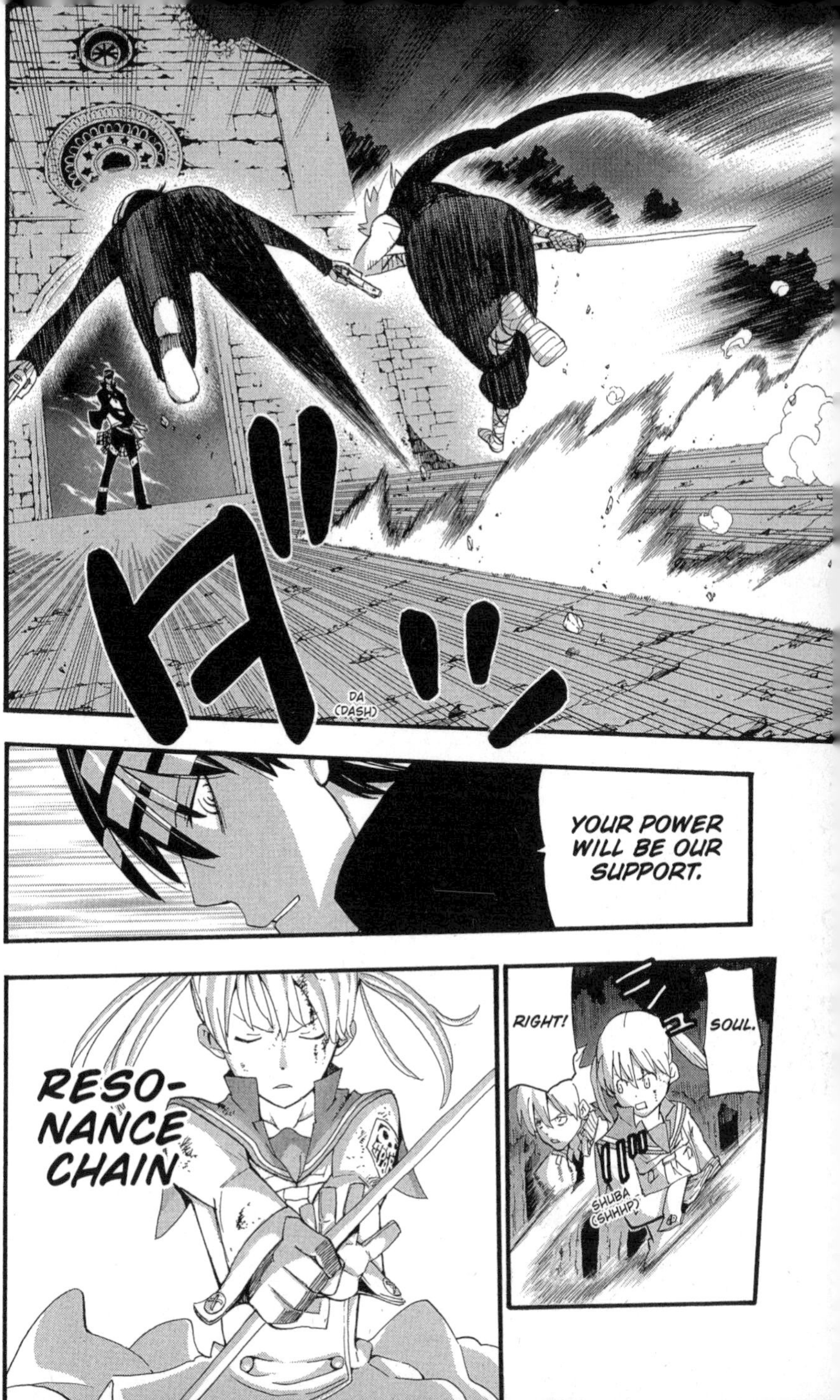
DA
(DASH)
YOUR POWER WILL BE OUR SUPPORT.
SOUL.
RIGHT!
SHUBA
(SHHHP)
RESO-NANCE CHAIN

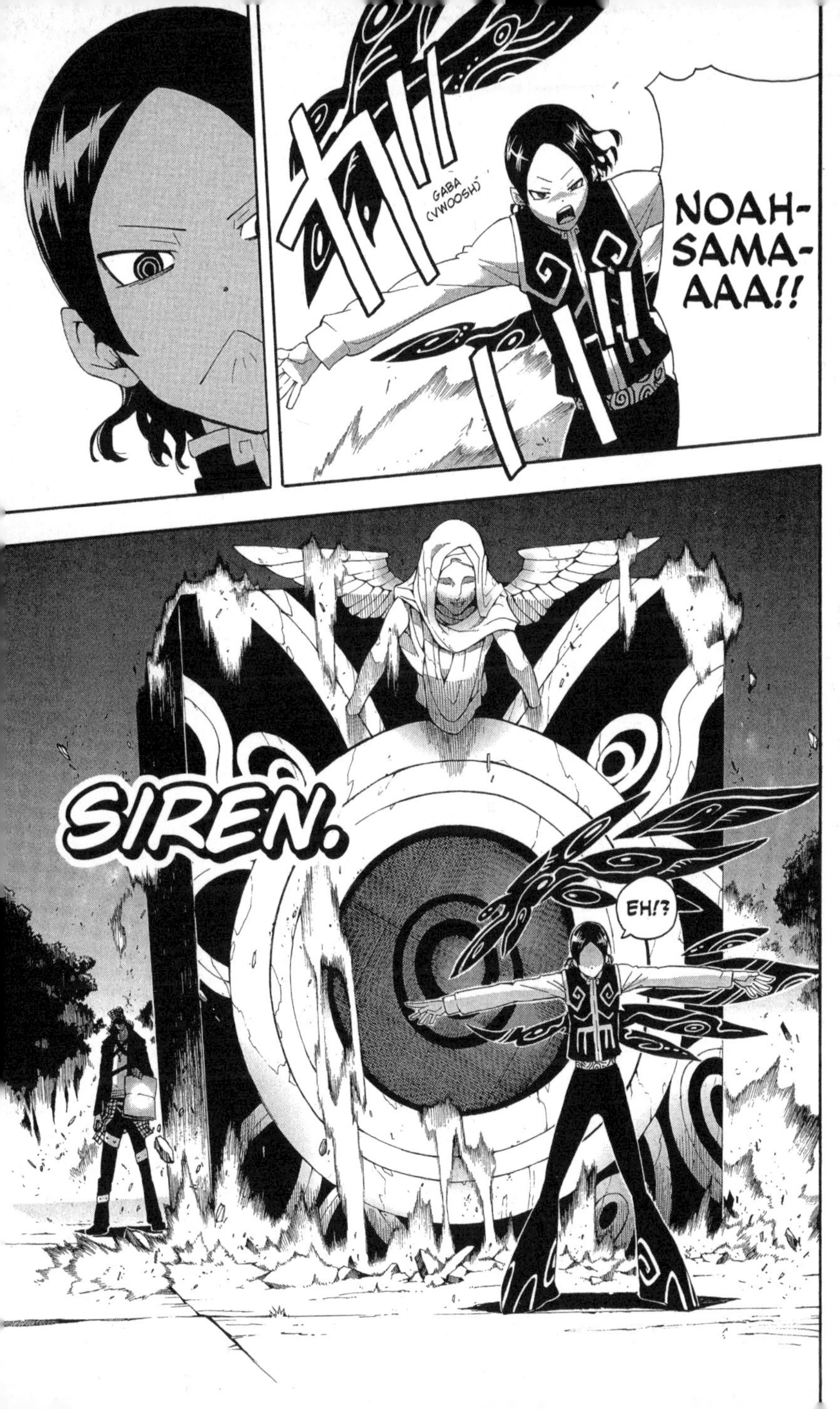
GABA (VWOOSH)
NOAH-SAMA-AAA!!
SIREN.
EH!?

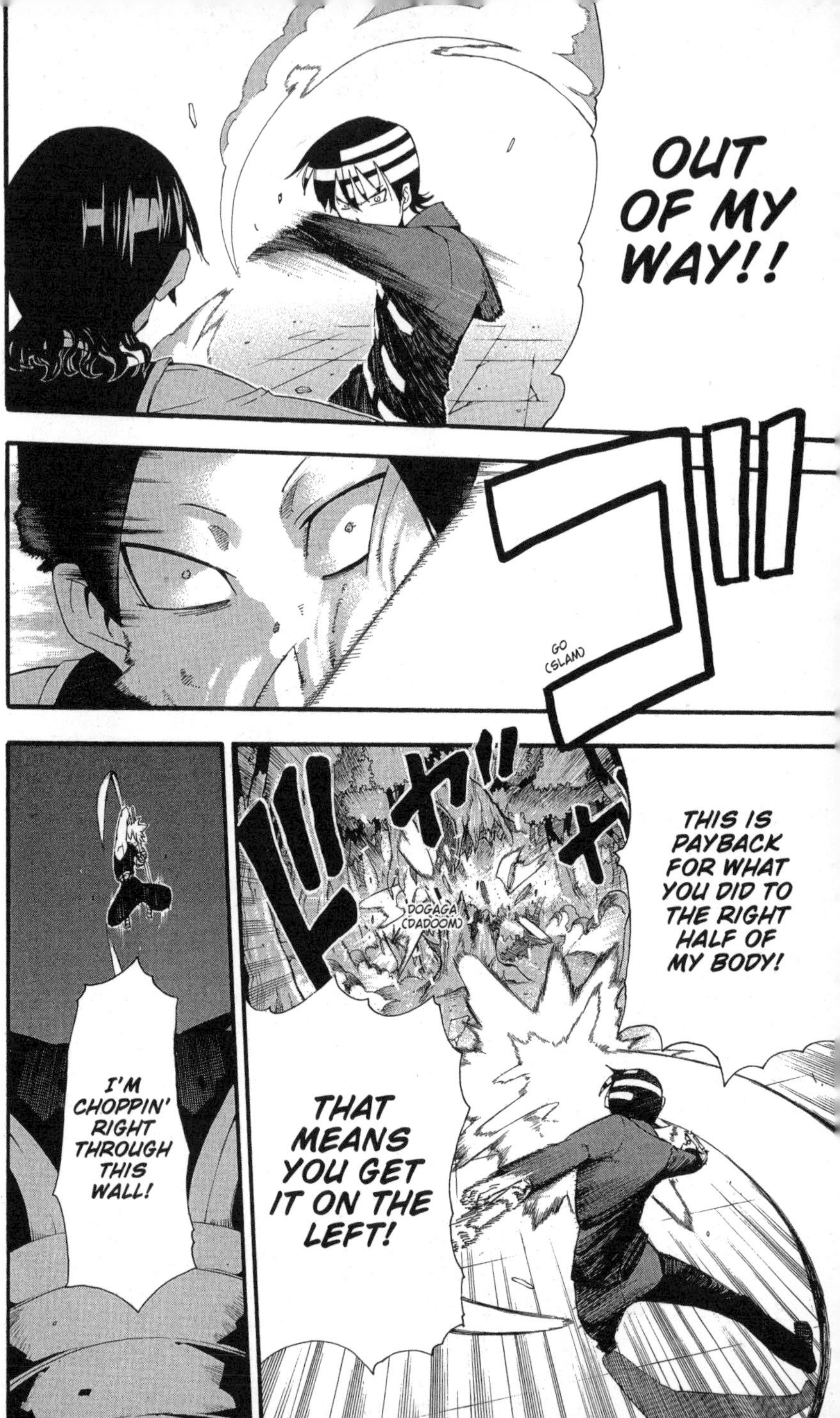
OUT OF MY WAY!!
GO (SLAM)
THIS IS PAYBACK FOR WHAT YOU DID TO THE RIGHT HALF OF MY BODY!
DOGAGA (DADOOM)
THAT MEANS YOU GET IT ON THE LEFT!
I'M CHOPPIN' RIGHT THROUGH THIS WALL!

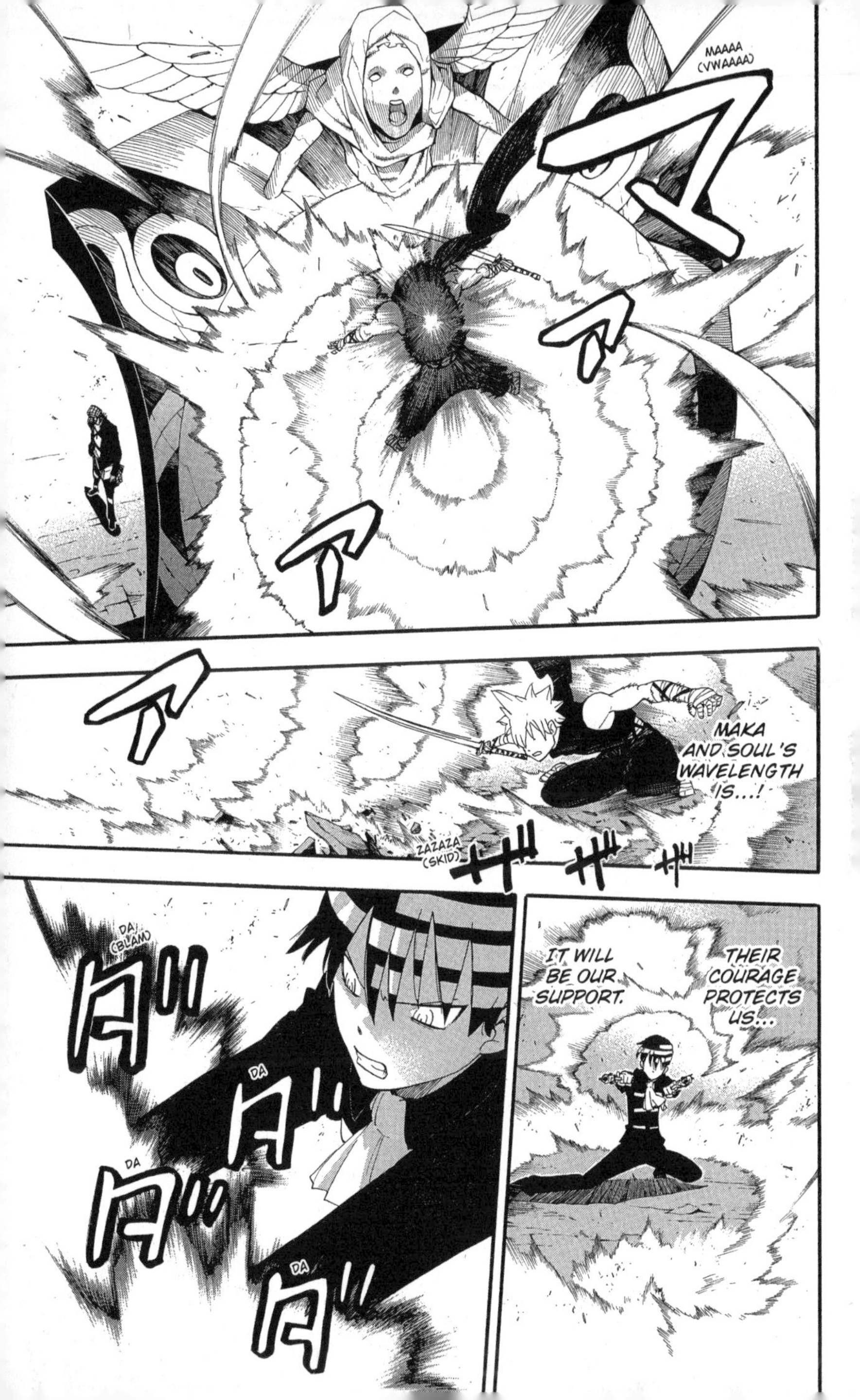
MAAAA (VWAAAA)
MAKA AND SOUL'S WAVELENGTH IS...!
ZAZAZA (SKID)
THEIR COURAGE PROTECTS US...
IT WILL BE OUR SUPPORT.
DA (BLAM)
DA
DA
DA

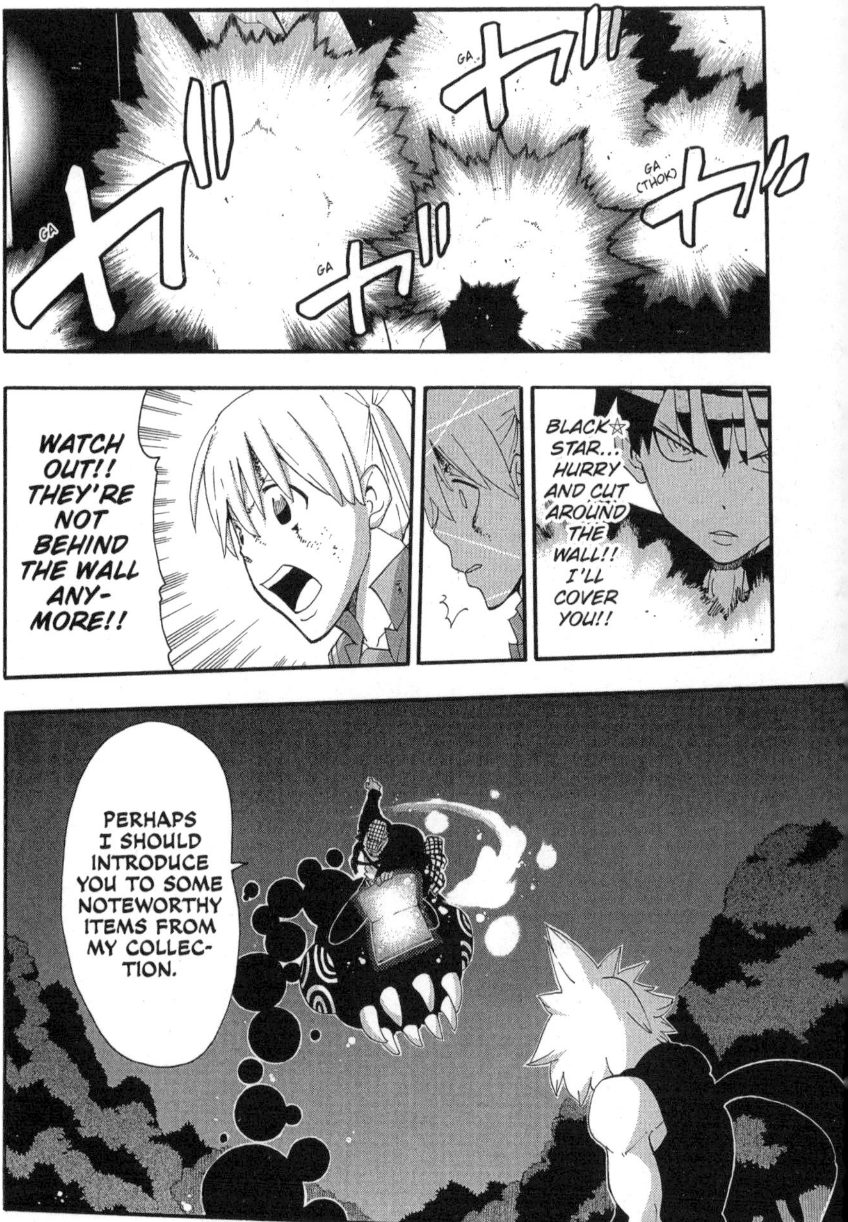
GA (THOK)
GA
GA
GA
BLACK☆STAR... HURRY AND CUT AROUND THE WALL!! I'LL COVER YOU!!
WATCH OUT!! THEY'RE NOT BEHIND THE WALL ANYMORE!!
PERHAPS I SHOULD INTRODUCE YOU TO SOME NOTEWORTHY ITEMS FROM MY COLLECTION.

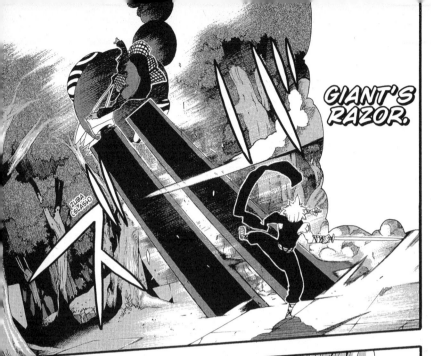

GIANT'S RAZOR.

ZUBA
(SLASH)

PERA
PERA
(FLIP)

SCREW YOU!!

WHA ....!?

FLY, MY SELECT GREMLINS!!

FLY!!

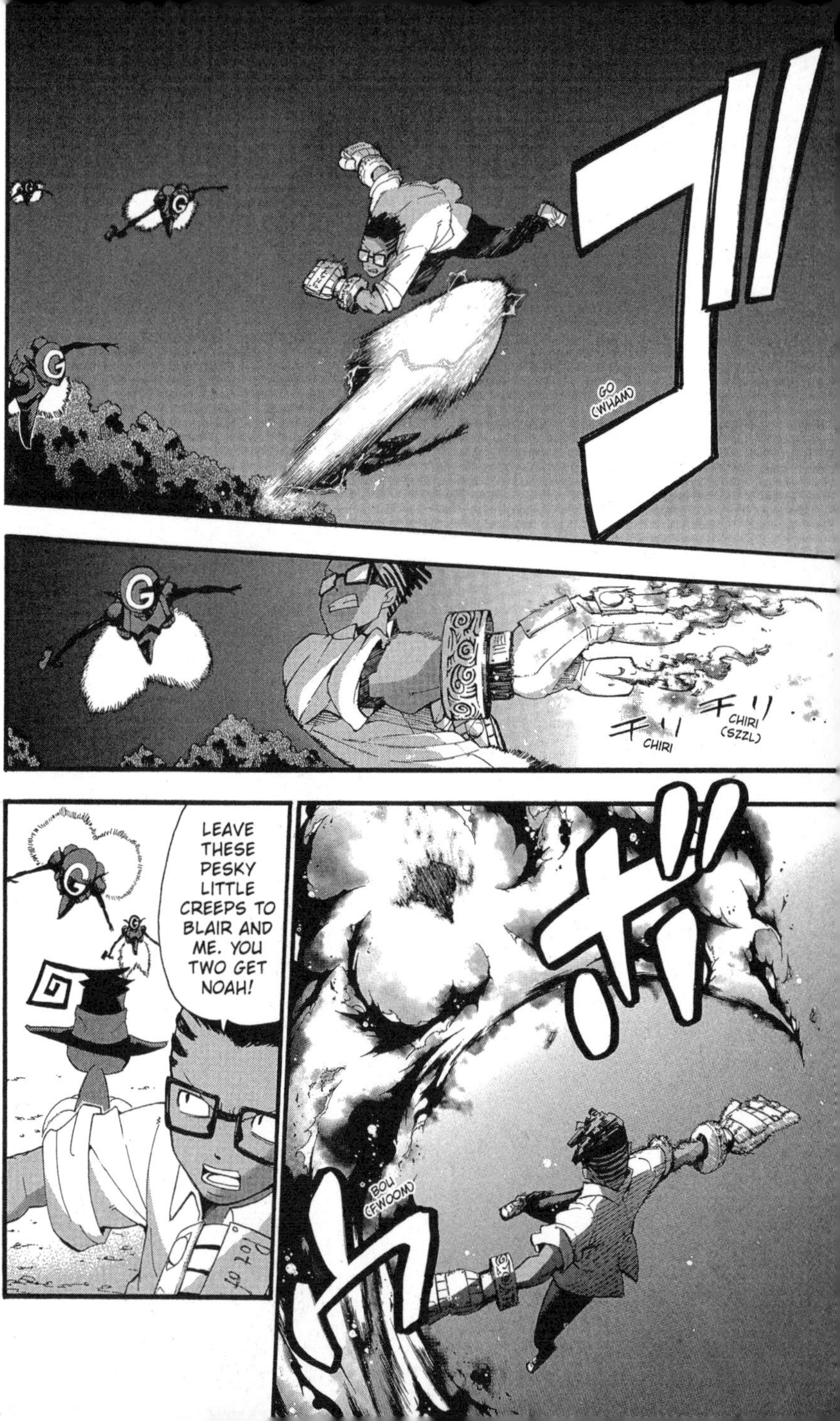
GO
(WHAM)
CHIRI
(SZZL)
CHIRI
BOU
(FWOOM)
LEAVE THESE PESKY LITTLE CREEPS TO BLAIR AND ME. YOU TWO GET NOAH!

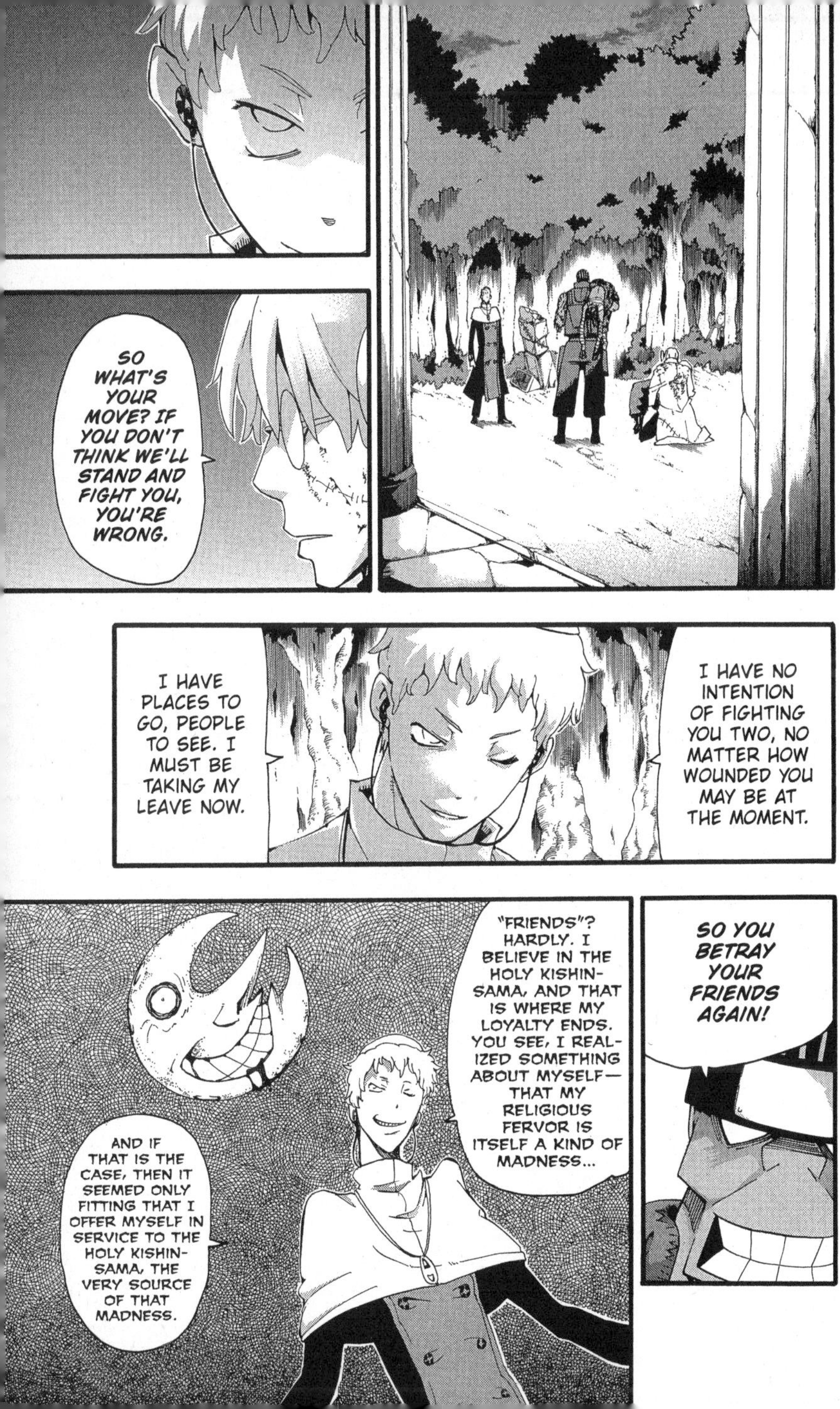
SO WHAT'S YOUR MOVE? IF YOU DON'T THINK WE'LL STAND AND FIGHT YOU, YOU'RE WRONG.
I HAVE NO INTENTION OF FIGHTING YOU TWO, NO MATTER HOW WOUNDED YOU MAY BE AT THE MOMENT.
I HAVE PLACES TO GO, PEOPLE TO SEE. I MUST BE TAKING MY LEAVE NOW.
SO YOU BETRAY YOUR FRIENDS AGAIN!
"FRIENDS"? HARDLY. I BELIEVE IN THE HOLY KISHIN-SAMA, AND THAT IS WHERE MY LOYALTY ENDS. YOU SEE, I REAL-IZED SOMETHING ABOUT MYSELF—THAT MY RELIGIOUS FERVOR IS ITSELF A KIND OF MADNESS...
AND IF THAT IS THE CASE, THEN IT SEEMED ONLY FITTING THAT I OFFER MYSELF IN SERVICE TO THE HOLY KISHIN-SAMA, THE VERY SOURCE OF THAT MADNESS.

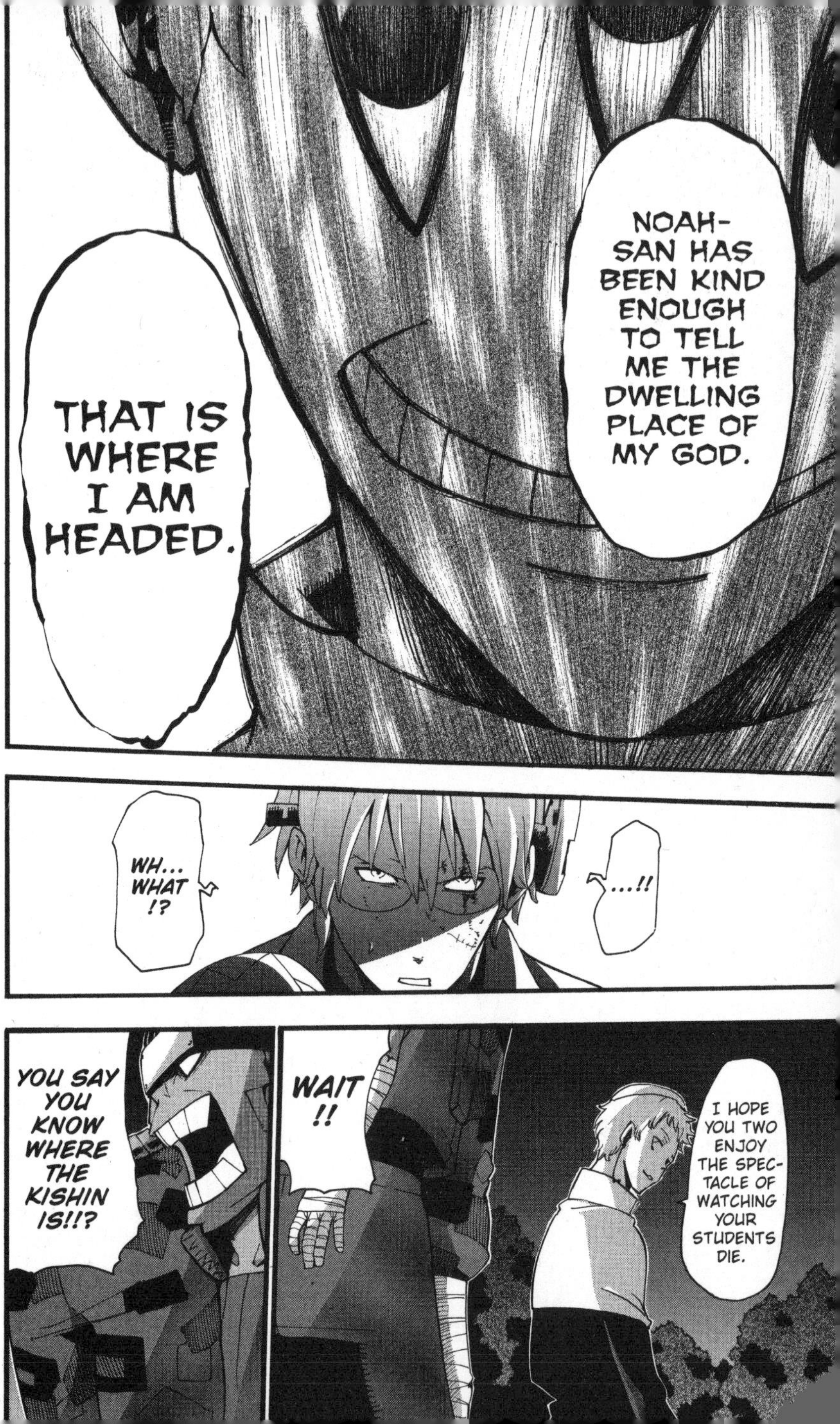
NOAH-SAN HAS BEEN KIND ENOUGH TO TELL ME THE DWELLING PLACE OF MY GOD.
THAT IS WHERE I AM HEADED.
...!!
WH... WHAT!?
I HOPE YOU TWO ENJOY THE SPECTACLE OF WATCHING YOUR STUDENTS DIE.
WAIT!!
YOU SAY YOU KNOW WHERE THE KISHIN IS!!?

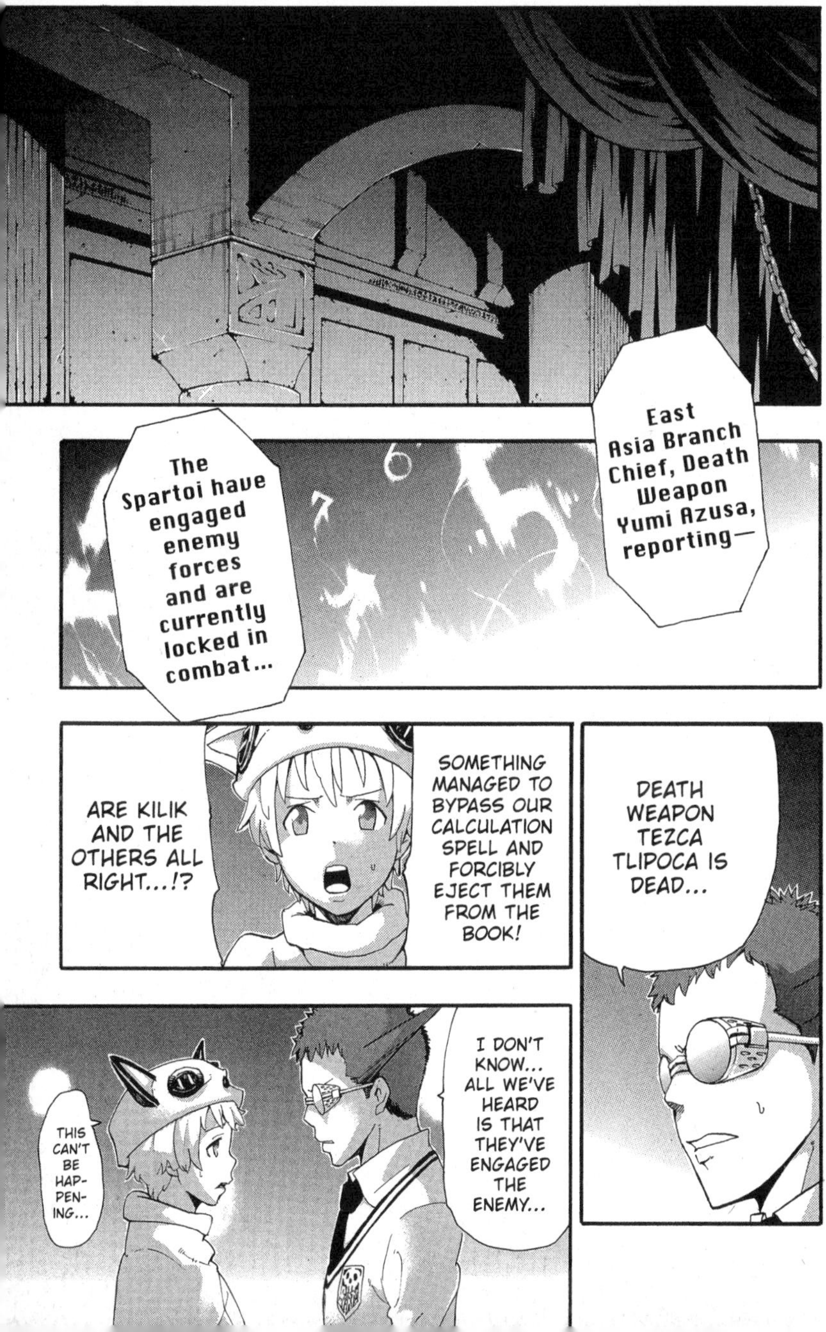
East Asia Branch Chief, Death Weapon Yumi Azusa, reporting—
The Spartoi have engaged enemy forces and are currently locked in combat...
DEATH WEAPON TEZCA TLIPOCA IS DEAD...
SOMETHING MANAGED TO BYPASS OUR CALCULATION SPELL AND FORCIBLY EJECT THEM FROM THE BOOK!
ARE KILIK AND THE OTHERS ALL RIGHT...!?
I DON'T KNOW... ALL WE'VE HEARD IS THAT THEY'VE ENGAGED THE ENEMY...
THIS CAN'T BE HAP-PEN-ING...

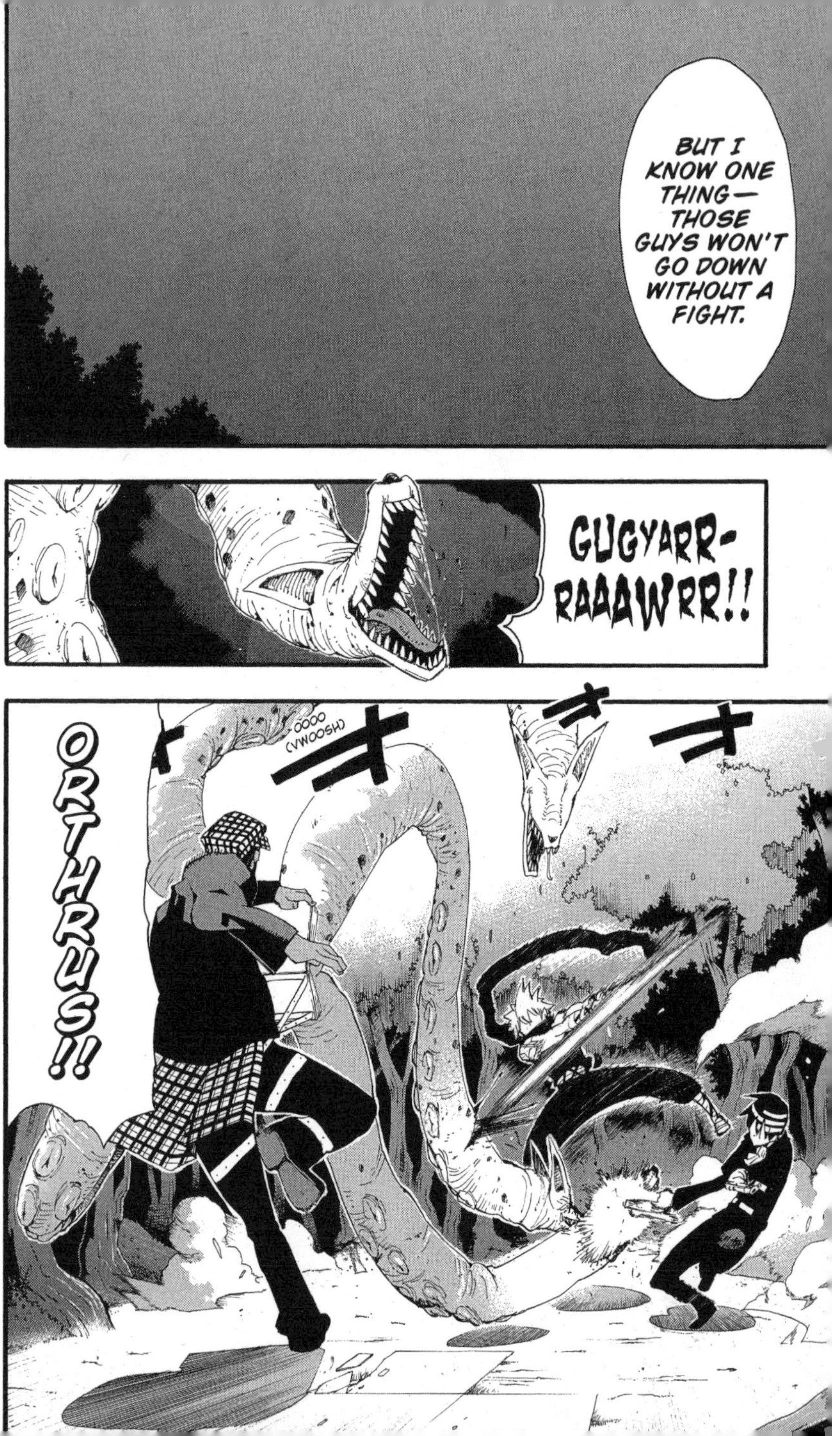
BUT I KNOW ONE THING—THOSE GUYS WON'T GO DOWN WITHOUT A FIGHT.
GUGYARR-RAAAWRR!!
ORTHRUS!!
OOOO (VWOOSH)

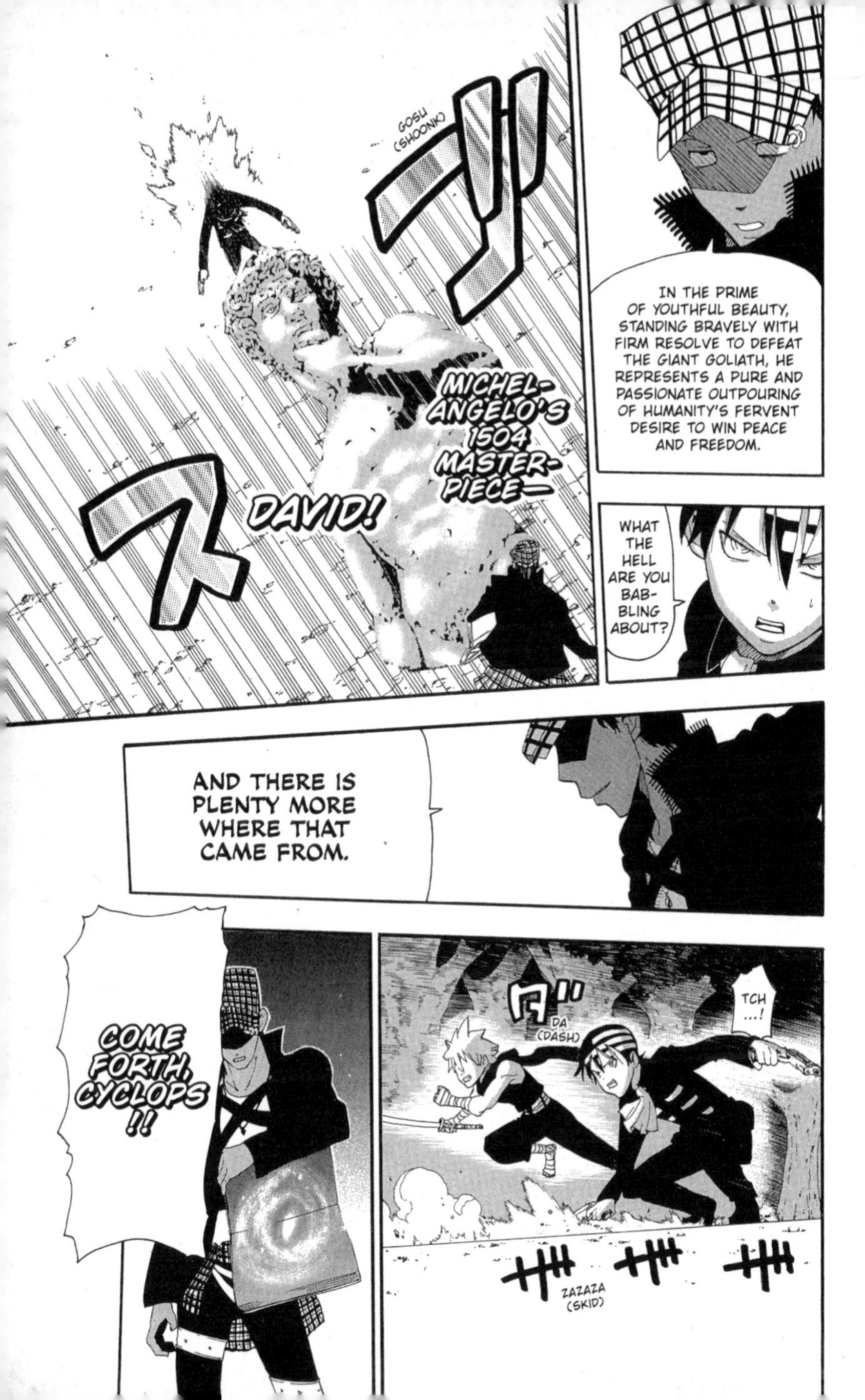
IN THE PRIME OF YOUTHFUL BEAUTY, STANDING BRAVELY WITH FIRM RESOLVE TO DEFEAT THE GIANT GOLIATH, HE REPRESENTS A PURE AND PASSIONATE OUTPOURING OF HUMANITY'S FERVENT DESIRE TO WIN PEACE AND FREEDOM.
WHAT THE HELL ARE YOU BAB-BLING ABOUT?
GOSU (SHOONK)
MICHEL-ANGELO'S 1504 MASTER-PIECE—
DAVID!
AND THERE IS PLENTY MORE WHERE THAT CAME FROM.
TCH ...!
DA (DASH)
ZAZAZA (SKID)
COME FORTH, CYCLOPS!!

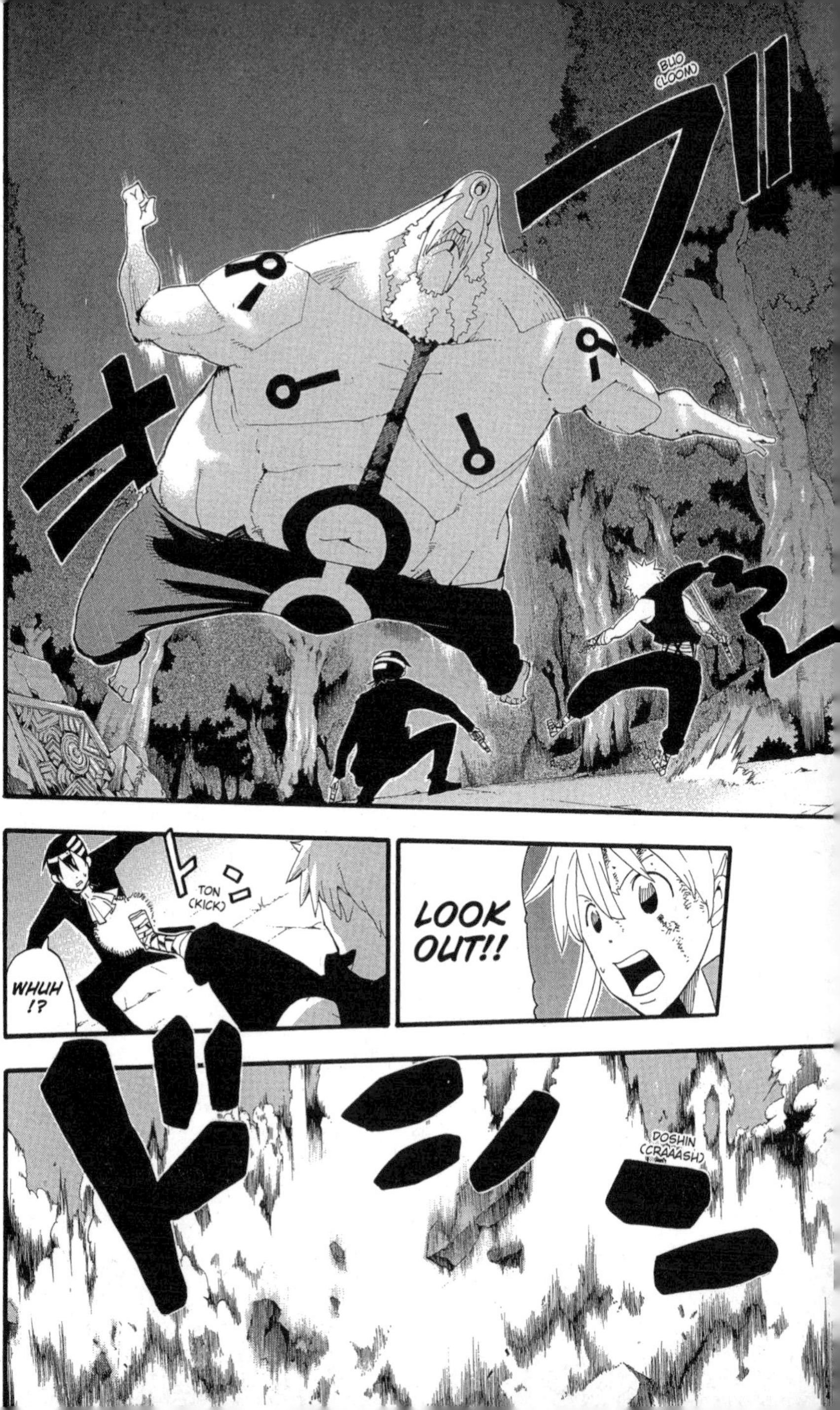
BUO (LOOM)
LOOK OUT!!
TON (KICK)
WHUH !?
DOSHIN (CRAAASH)

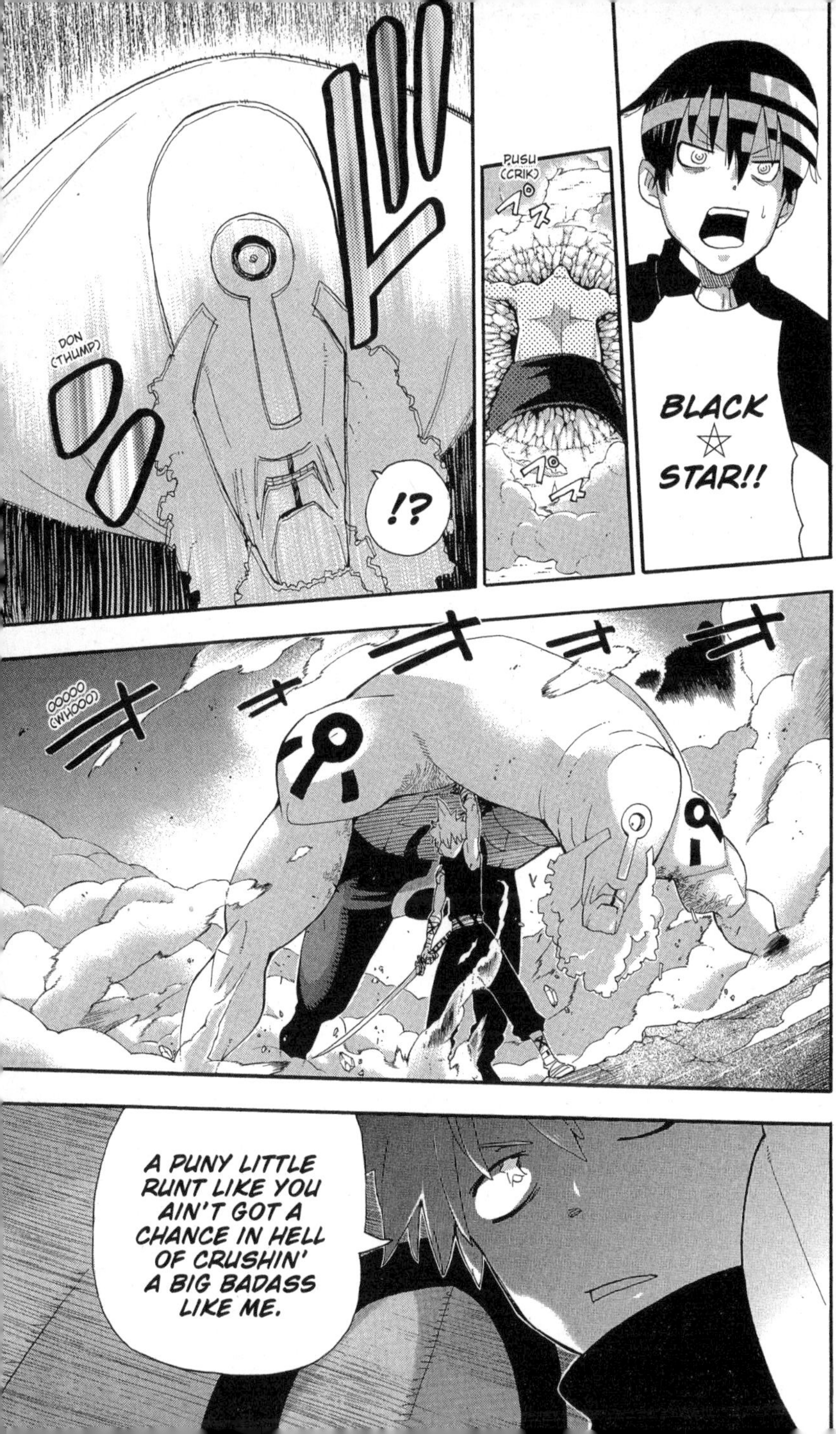
BLACK☆STAR!!
PUSU (CRIK)
DON (THUMP)
!?
OOOOO (WHOOO)
A PUNY LITTLE RUNT LIKE YOU AIN'T GOT A CHANCE IN HELL OF CRUSHIN' A BIG BADASS LIKE ME.

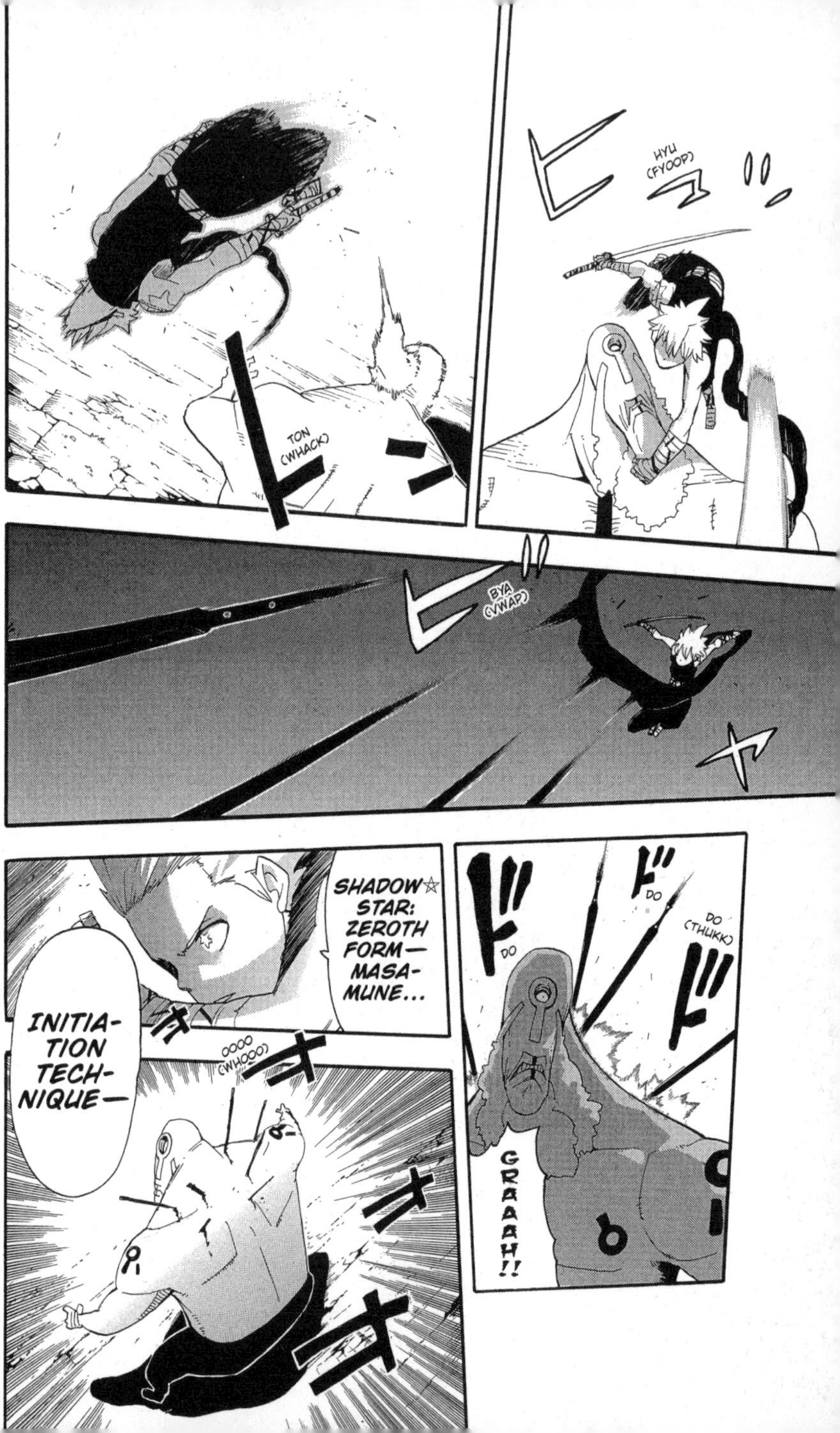
HYU (FYOOP)
TON (WHACK)
BYA (VWAP)
DO
DO (THUKK)
DO
GRAAAH!!
SHADOW☆STAR: ZEROTH FORM—MASAMUNE...
INITIATION-TION TECH-NIQUE—
OOOO (WHOOOO)

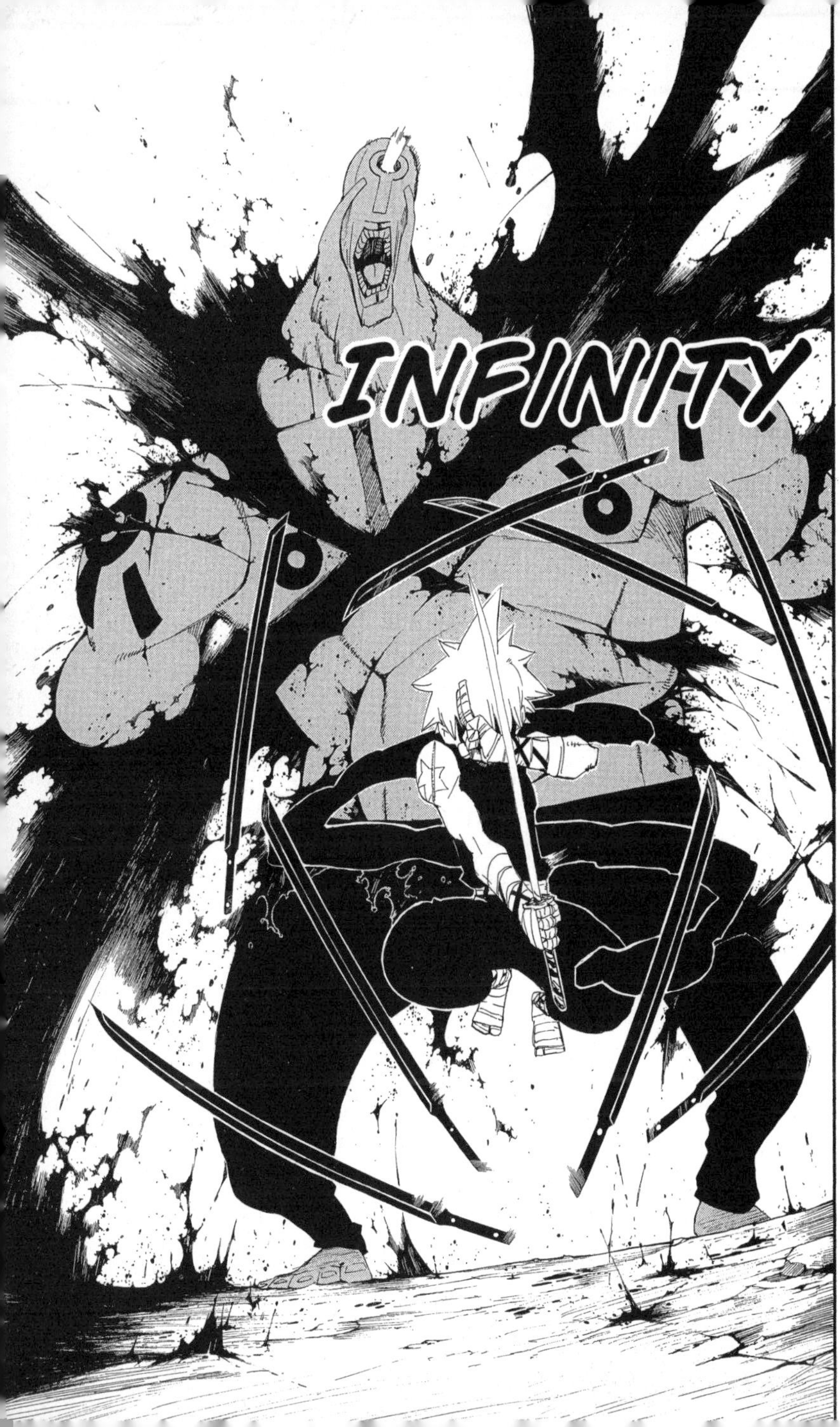
INFINITY

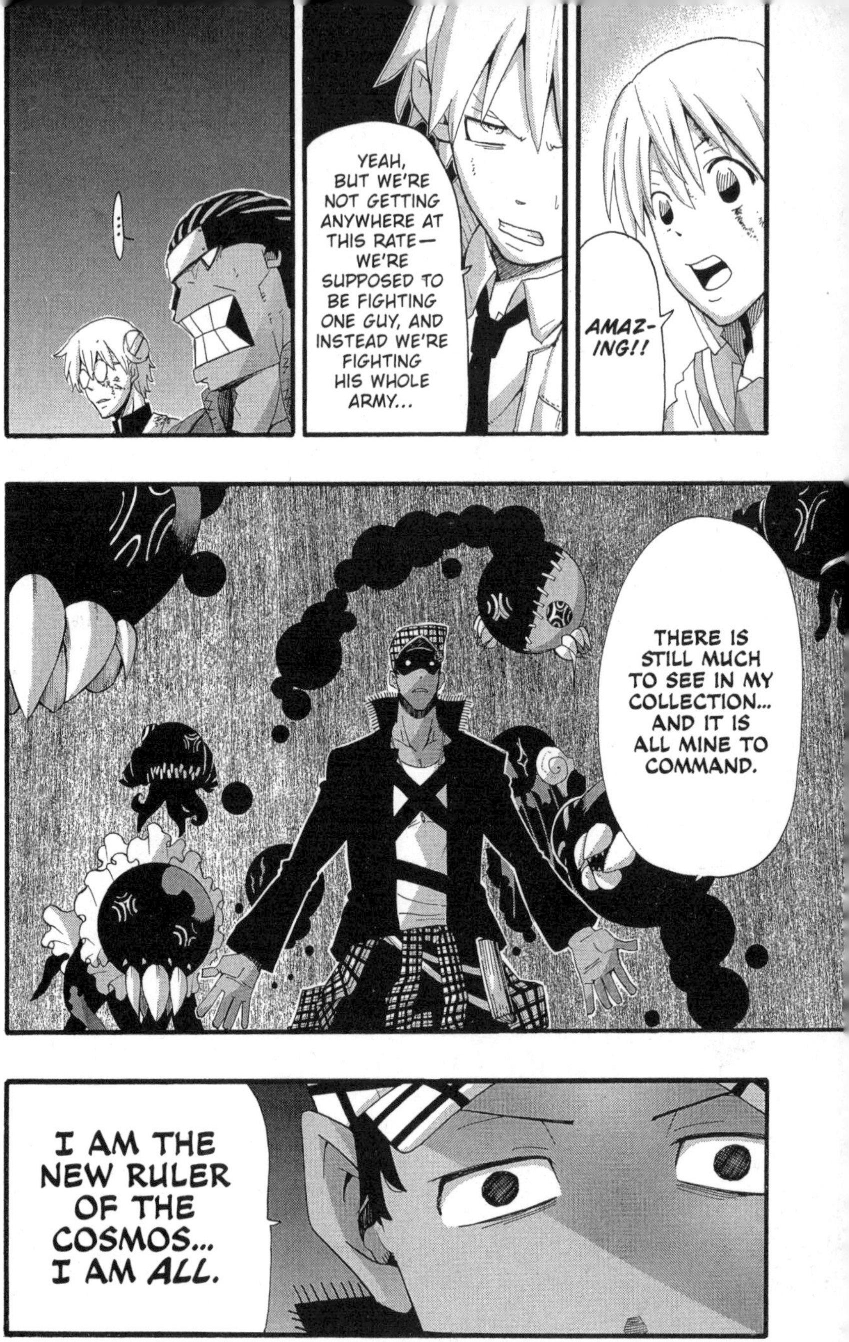
AMAZ-ING!!
YEAH, BUT WE'RE NOT GETTING ANYWHERE AT THIS RATE— WE'RE SUPPOSED TO BE FIGHTING ONE GUY, AND INSTEAD WE'RE FIGHTING HIS WHOLE ARMY...
...
THERE IS STILL MUCH TO SEE IN MY COLLECTION... AND IT IS ALL MINE TO COMMAND.
I AM THE NEW RULER OF THE COSMOS... I AM *ALL*.

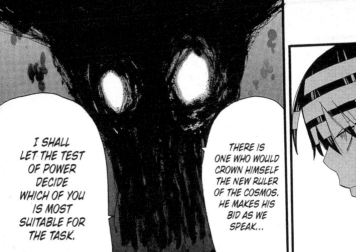

THERE IS ONE WHO WOULD CROWN HIMSELF THE NEW RULER OF THE COSMOS. HE MAKES HIS BID AS WE SPEAK...
I SHALL LET THE TEST OF POWER DECIDE WHICH OF YOU IS MOST SUITABLE FOR THE TASK.
FATHER...
YOU WILL BE THE SHINIGAMI OF THE NEXT GENERATION.

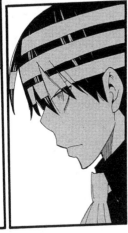

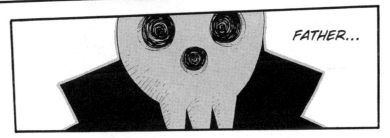

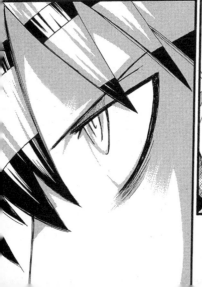

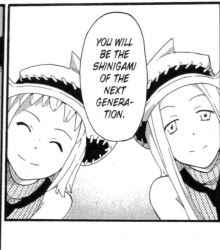

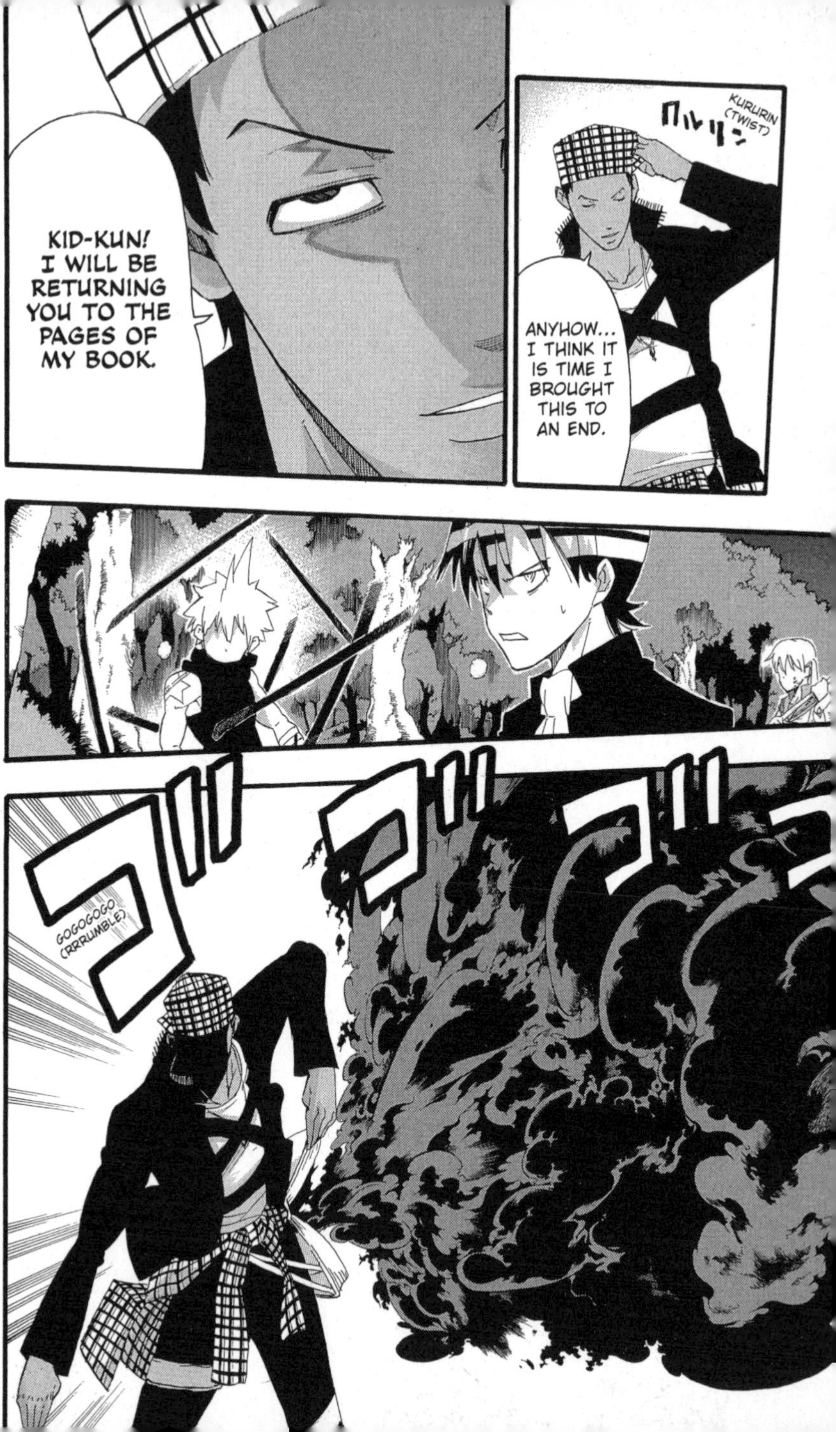
KURURIN (TWIST)
ANYHOW... I THINK IT IS TIME I BROUGHT THIS TO AN END.
KID-KUN! I WILL BE RETURNING YOU TO THE PAGES OF MY BOOK.
GOGOGOGO (RRRUMBLE)

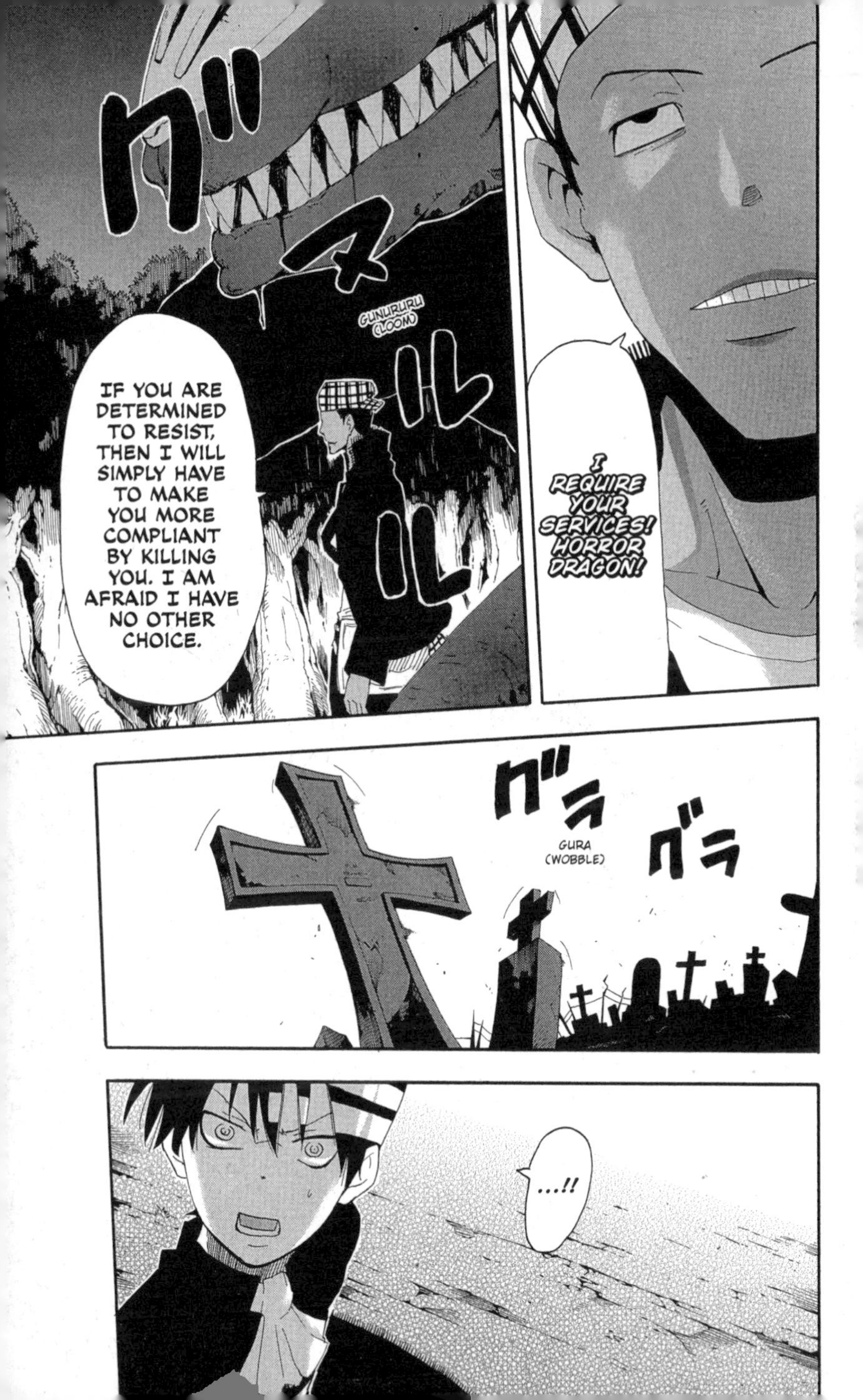
I REQUIRE YOUR SERVICES! HORROR DRAGON!
グヌルル
GUNURURU (LOOM)
IF YOU ARE DETERMINED TO RESIST, THEN I WILL SIMPLY HAVE TO MAKE YOU MORE COMPLIANT BY KILLING YOU. I AM AFRAID I HAVE NO OTHER CHOICE.
グラ グラ
GURA (WOBBLE)
...!!

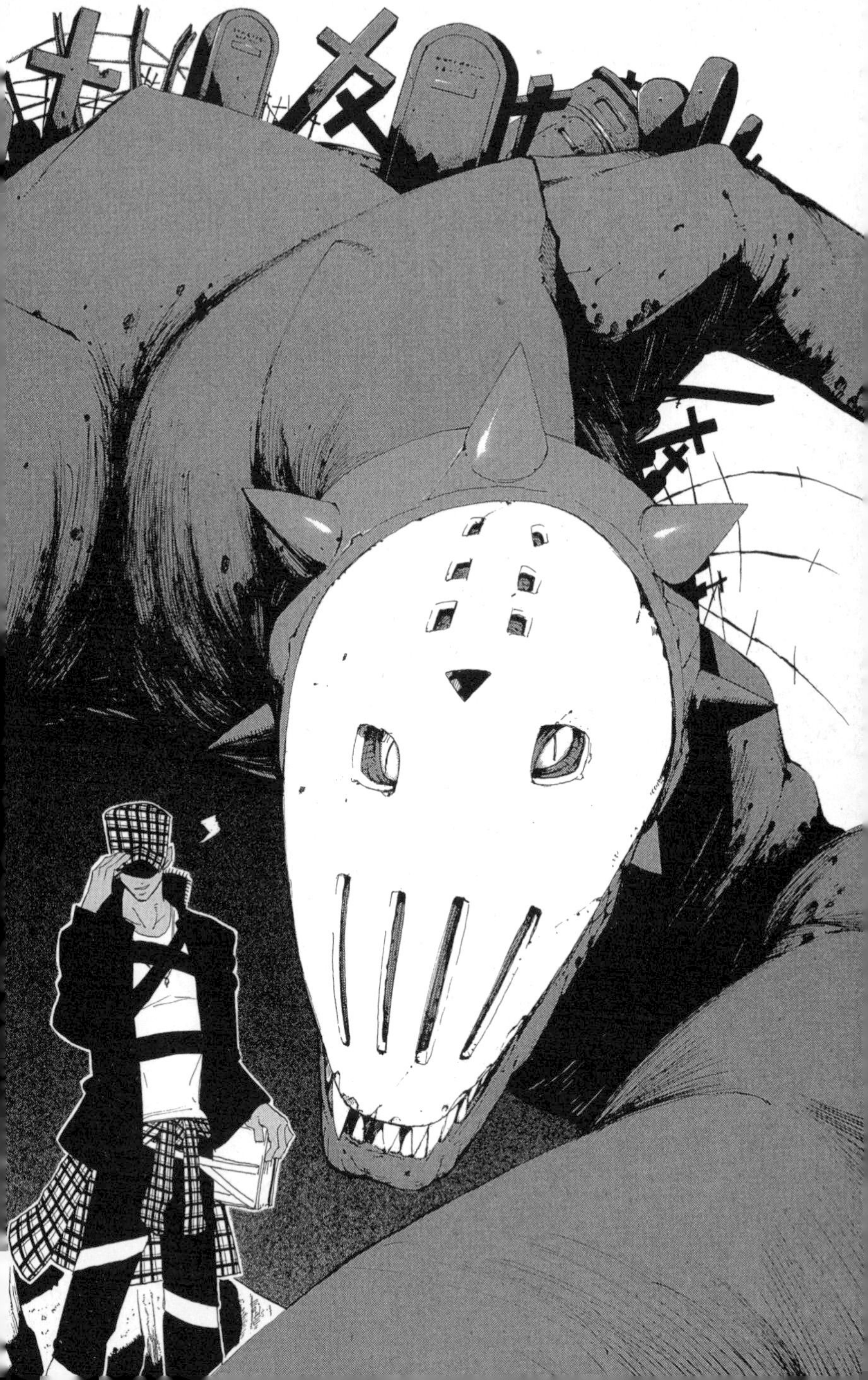

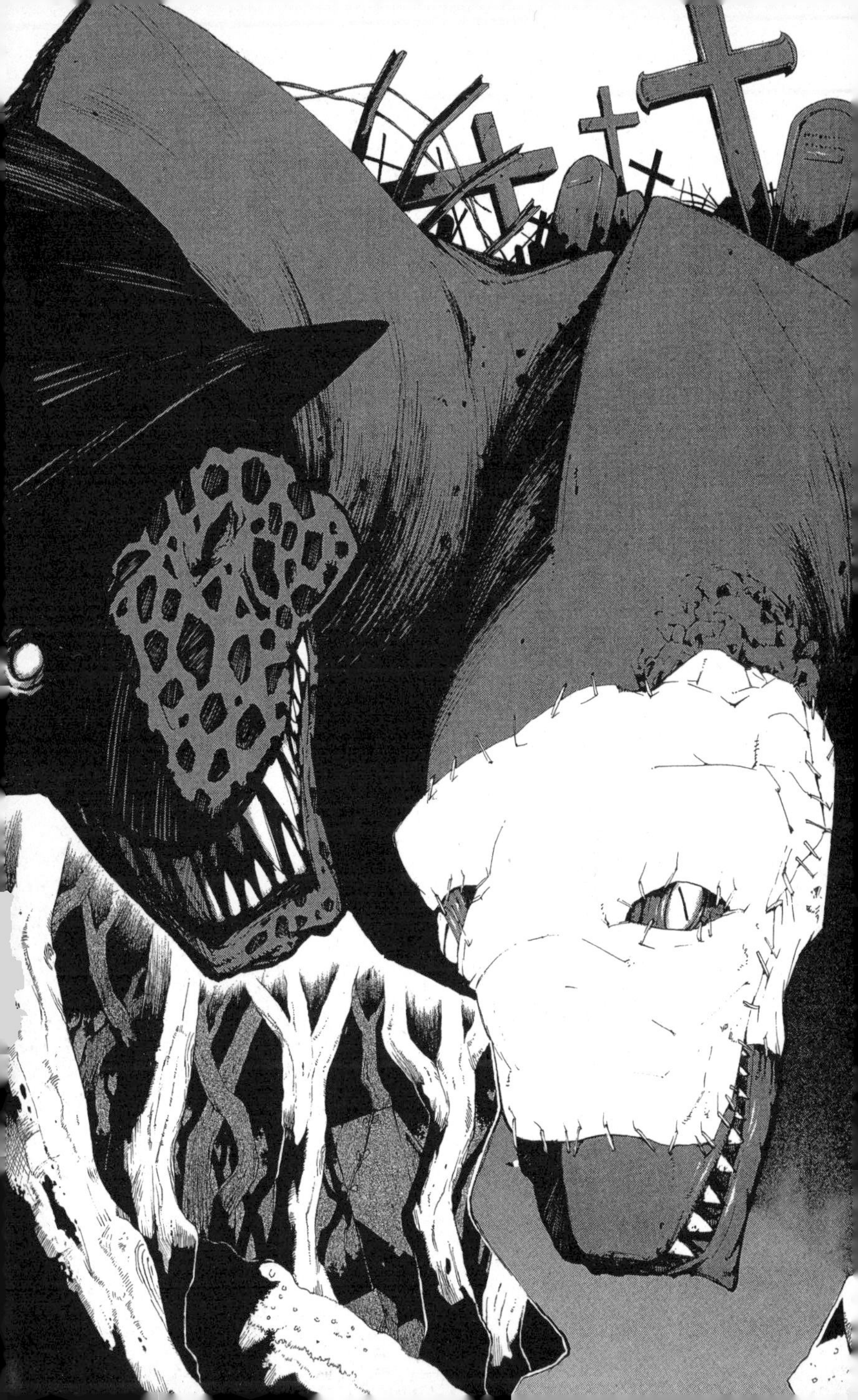

SOUL EATER

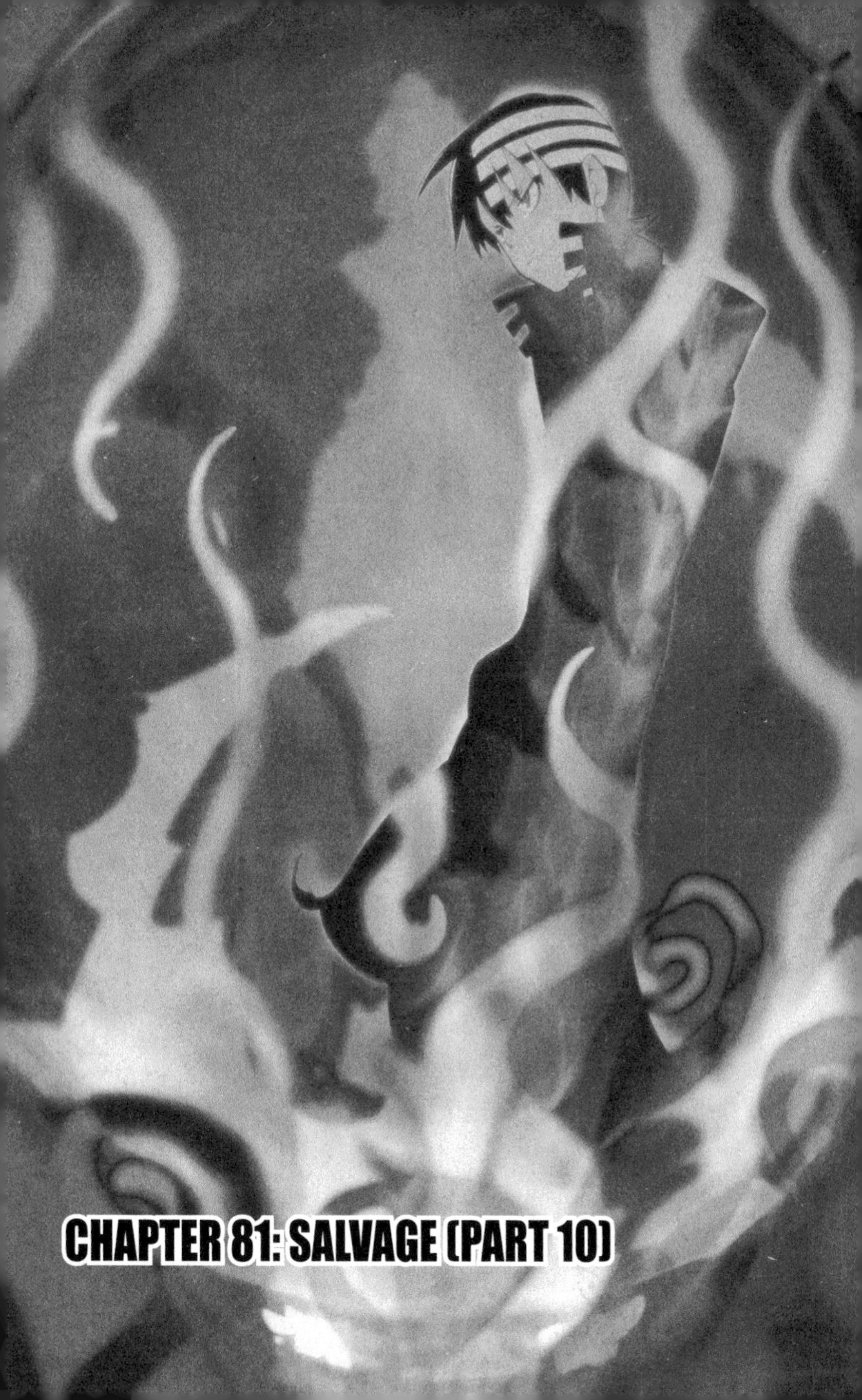

CHAPTER 81: SALVAGE (PART 10)

SOUL EATER

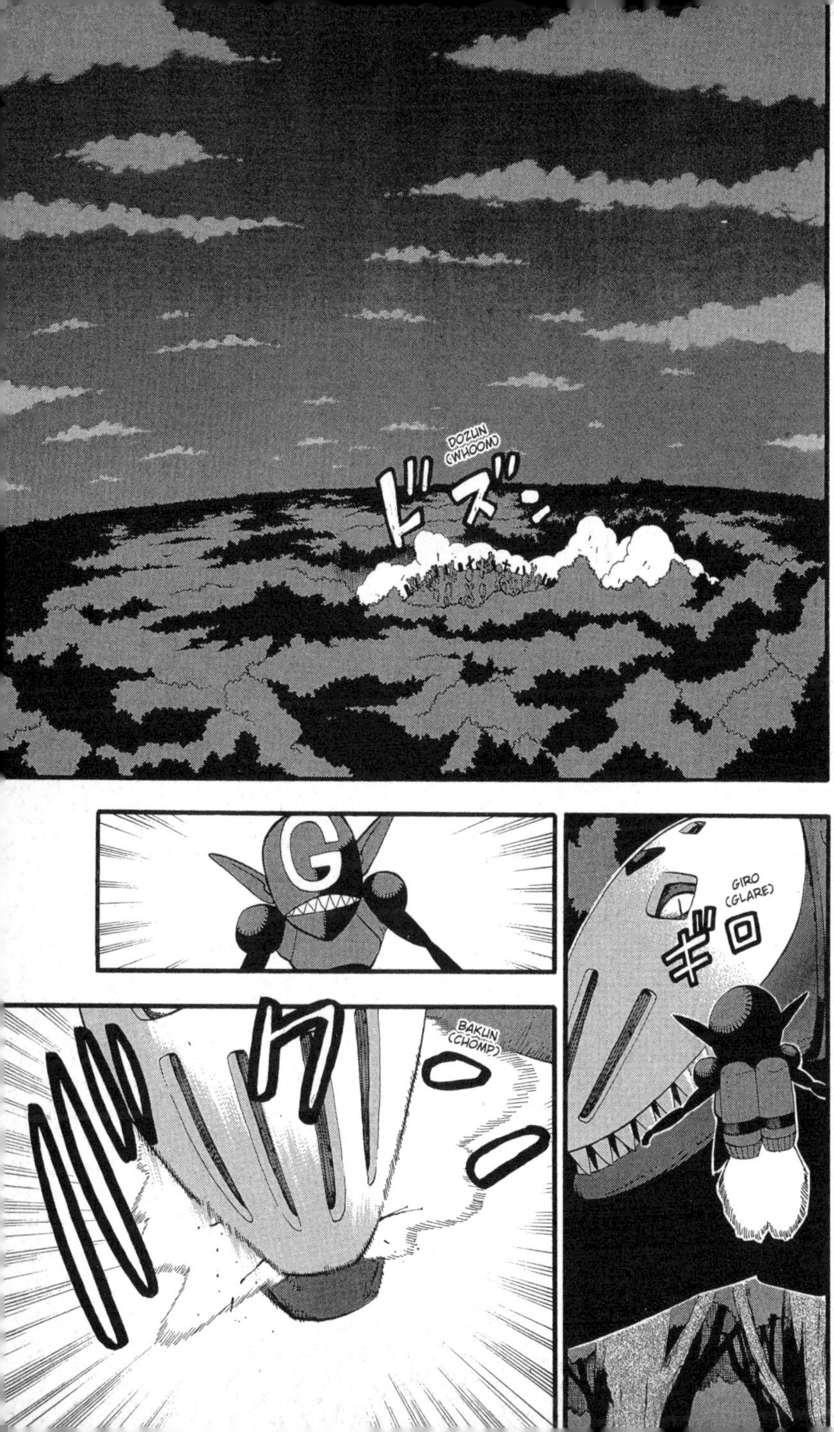
DOZUN (WHOOM)
ドズン
GIRO (GLARE)
ギロ
BAKUN (CHOMP)
バクン

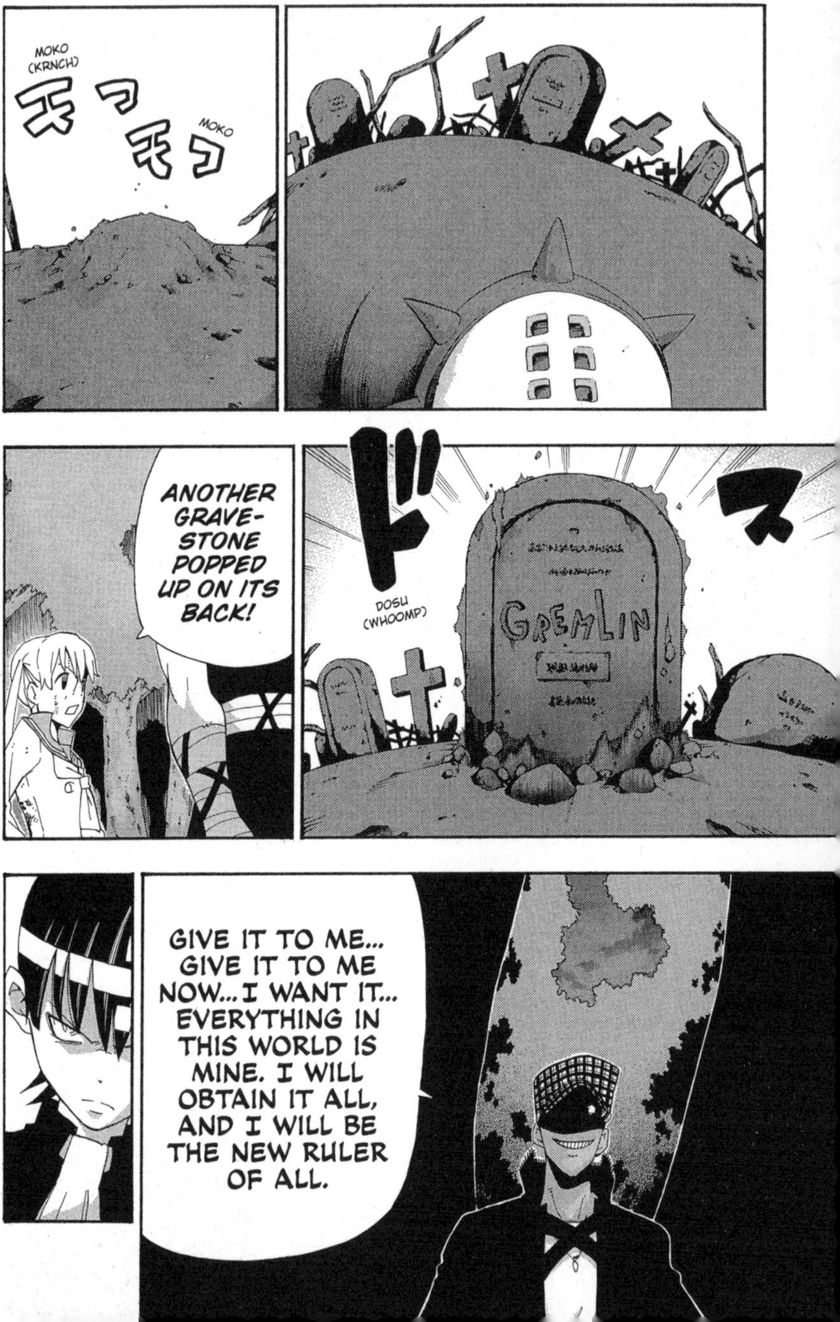
MOKO (KRNCH)
MOKO
ドス
DOSU (WHOOMP)
GREMLIN
ANOTHER GRAVESTONE POPPED UP ON ITS BACK!
GIVE IT TO ME... GIVE IT TO ME NOW...I WANT IT... EVERYTHING IN THIS WORLD IS MINE. I WILL OBTAIN IT ALL, AND I WILL BE THE NEW RULER OF ALL.

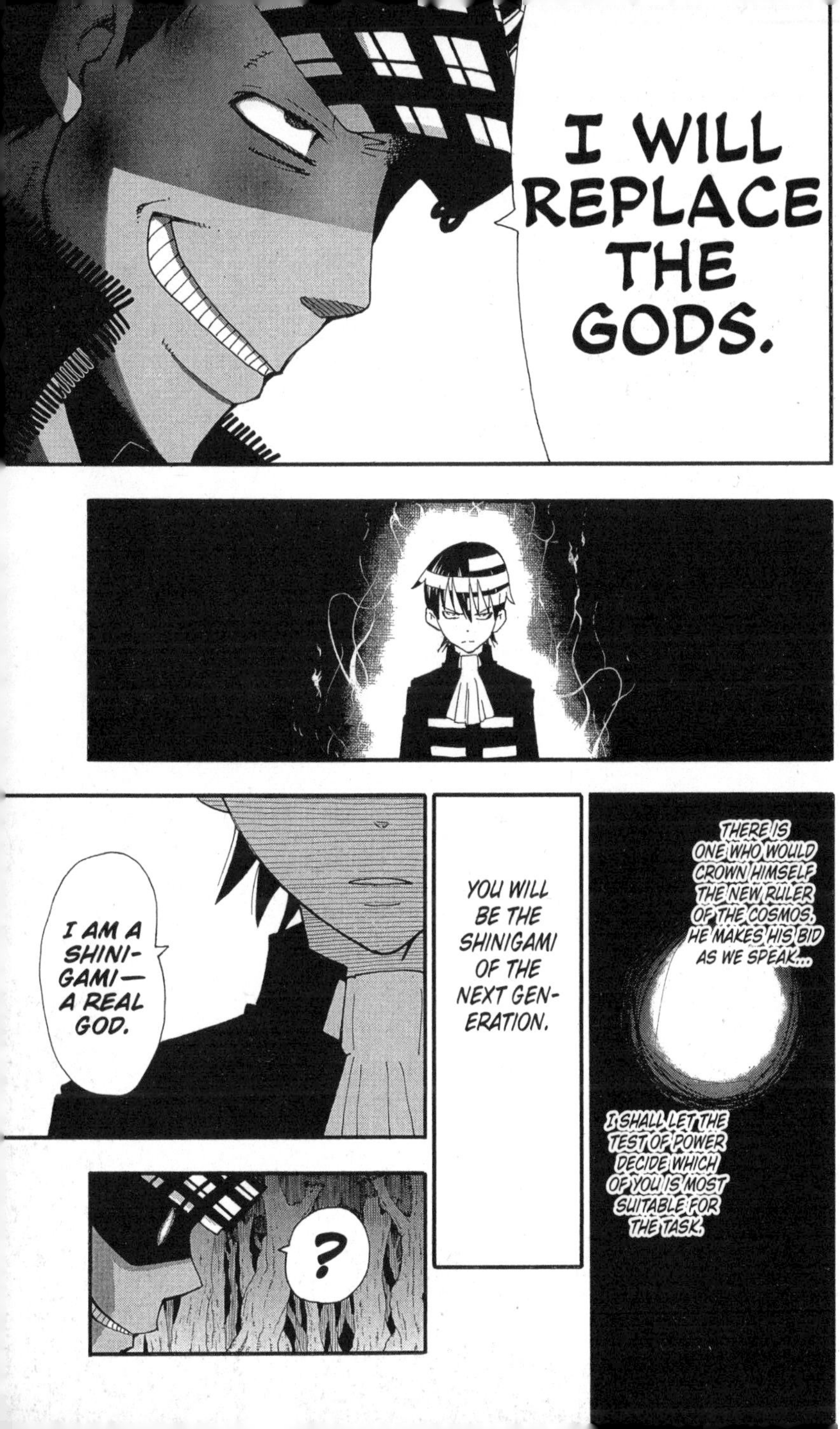
I WILL REPLACE THE GODS.
THERE IS ONE WHO WOULD CROWN HIMSELF THE NEW RULER OF THE COSMOS. HE MAKES HIS BID AS WE SPEAK...
I SHALL LET THE TEST OF POWER DECIDE WHICH OF YOU IS MOST SUITABLE FOR THE TASK.
YOU WILL BE THE SHINIGAMI OF THE NEXT GEN-ERATION.
I AM A SHINI-GAMI— A REAL GOD.
?

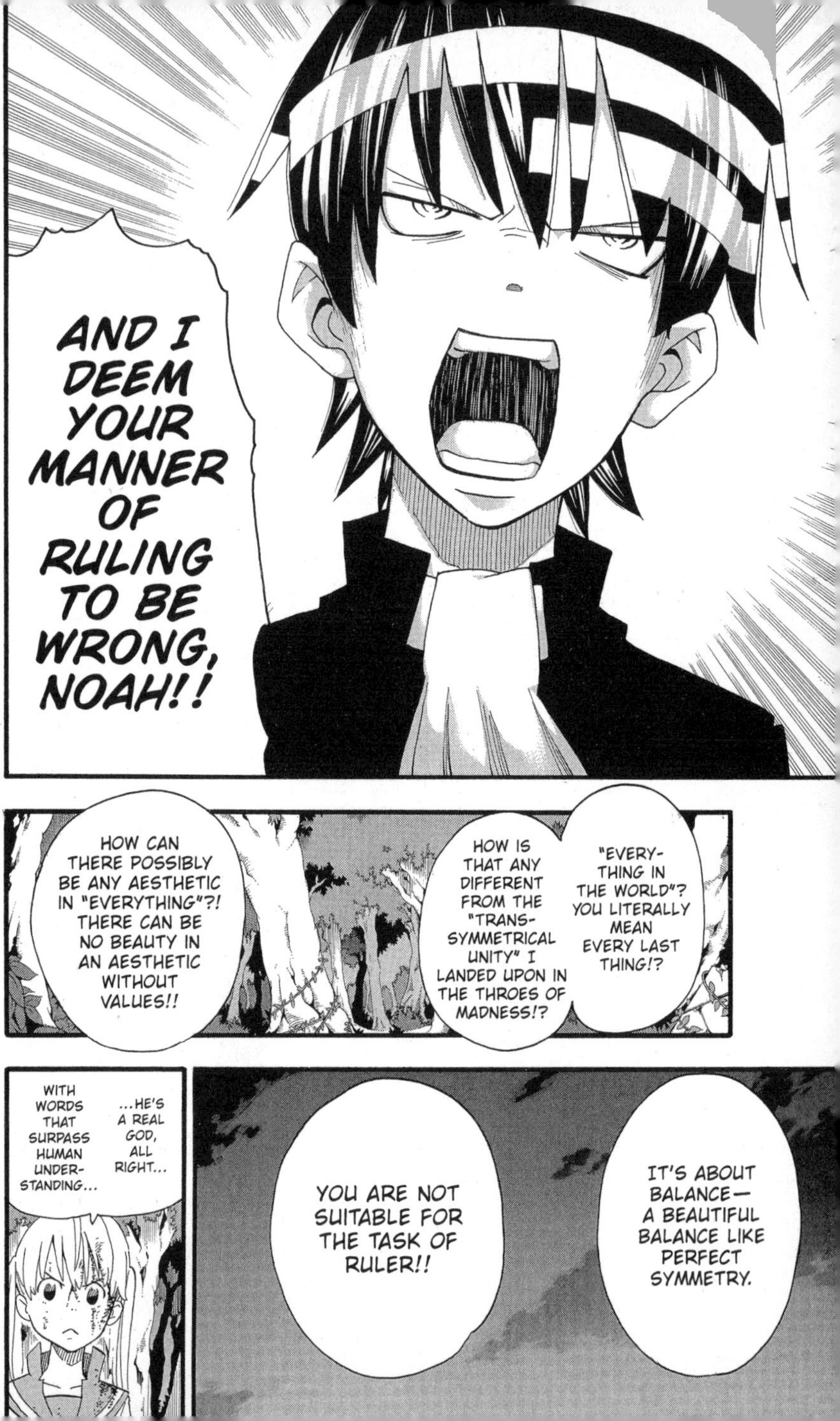
AND I DEEM YOUR MANNER OF RULING TO BE WRONG, NOAH!!
"EVERY-THING IN THE WORLD"? YOU LITERALLY MEAN EVERY LAST THING!?
HOW IS THAT ANY DIFFERENT FROM THE "TRANS-SYMMETRICAL UNITY" I LANDED UPON IN THE THROES OF MADNESS!?
HOW CAN THERE POSSIBLY BE ANY AESTHETIC IN "EVERYTHING"?! THERE CAN BE NO BEAUTY IN AN AESTHETIC WITHOUT VALUES!!
IT'S ABOUT BALANCE— A BEAUTIFUL BALANCE LIKE PERFECT SYMMETRY.
YOU ARE NOT SUITABLE FOR THE TASK OF RULER!!
...HE'S A REAL GOD, ALL RIGHT...
WITH WORDS THAT SURPASS HUMAN UNDER-STANDING...

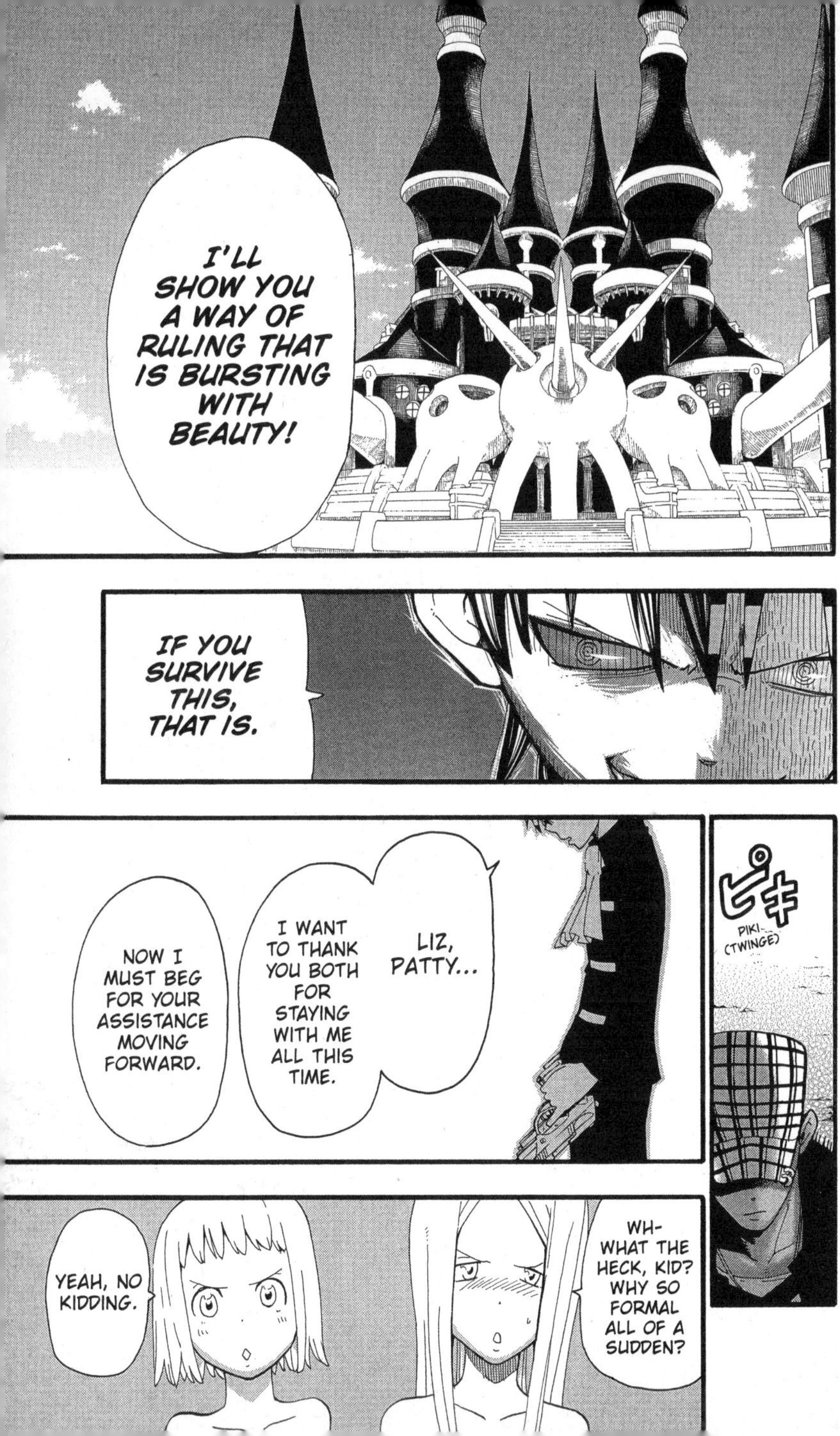
I'LL SHOW YOU A WAY OF RULING THAT IS BURSTING WITH BEAUTY!
IF YOU SURVIVE THIS, THAT IS.
ピキ
PIKI (TWINGE)
LIZ, PATTY...
I WANT TO THANK YOU BOTH FOR STAYING WITH ME ALL THIS TIME.
NOW I MUST BEG FOR YOUR ASSISTANCE MOVING FORWARD.
WH- WHAT THE HECK, KID? WHY SO FORMAL ALL OF A SUDDEN?
YEAH, NO KIDDING.

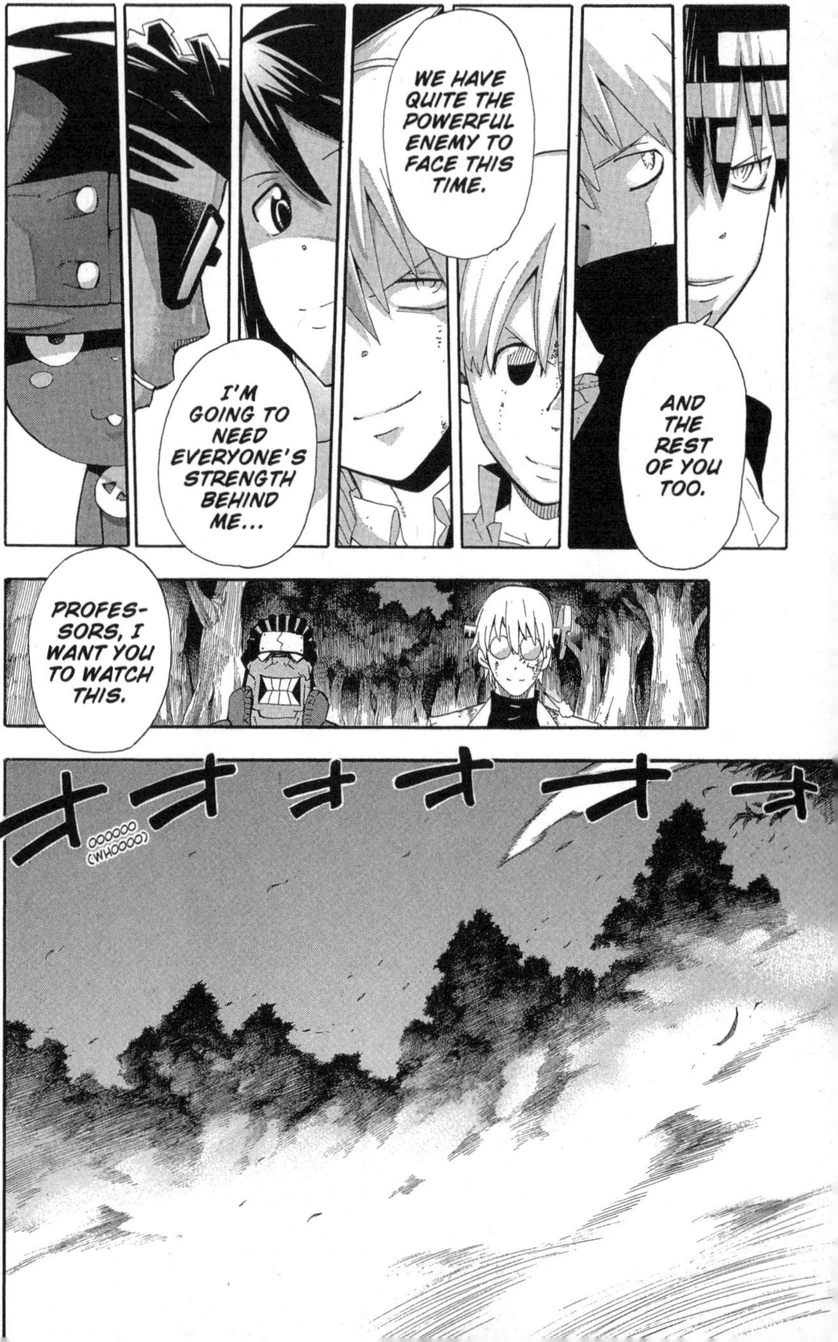
WE HAVE QUITE THE POWERFUL ENEMY TO FACE THIS TIME.
I'M GOING TO NEED EVERYONE'S STRENGTH BEHIND ME...
AND THE REST OF YOU TOO.
PROFES-SORS, I WANT YOU TO WATCH THIS.
OOOOOO (WHOOOOO)

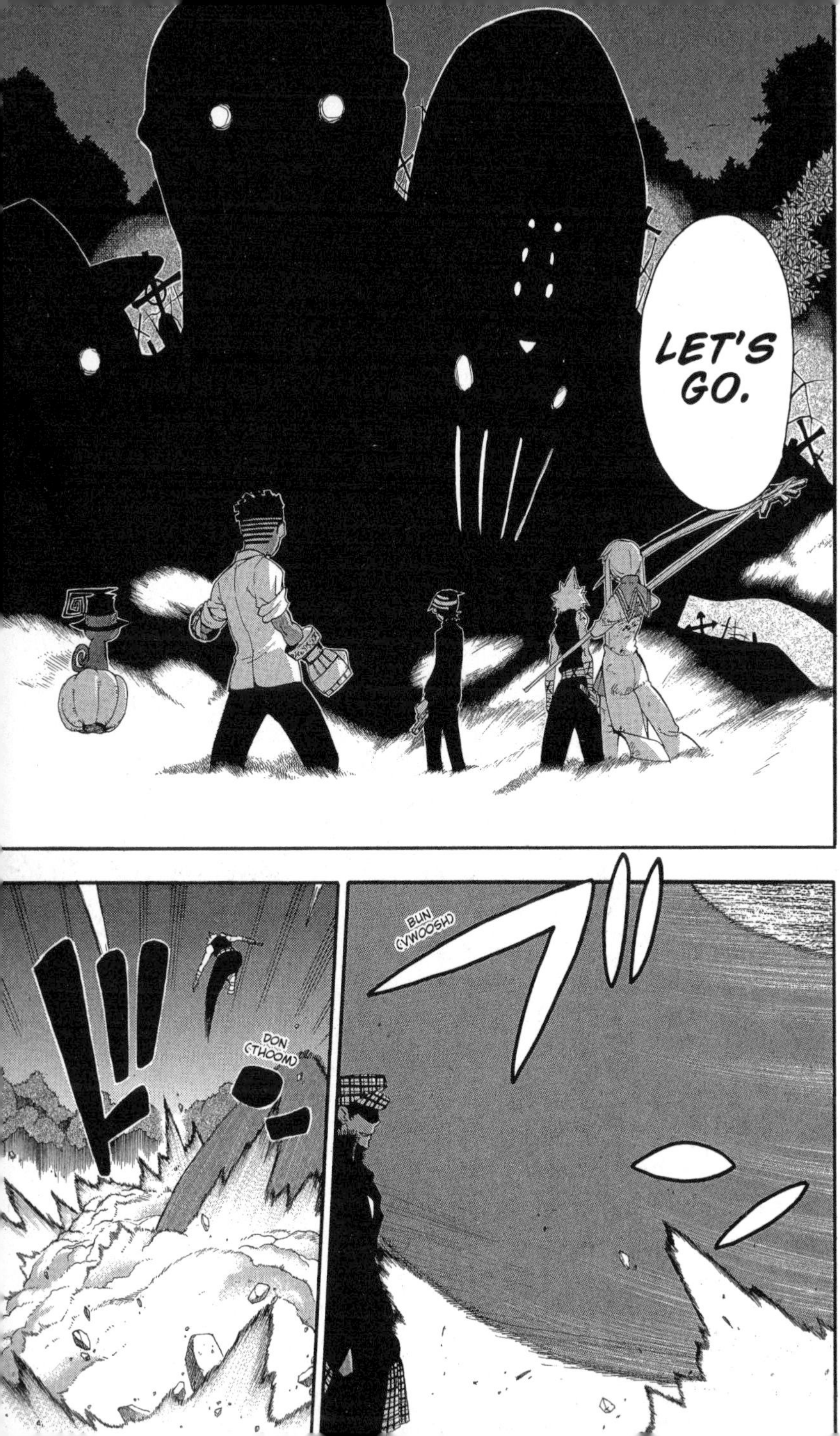
LET'S GO.
BUN (VWOOSH)
DON (THOOM)

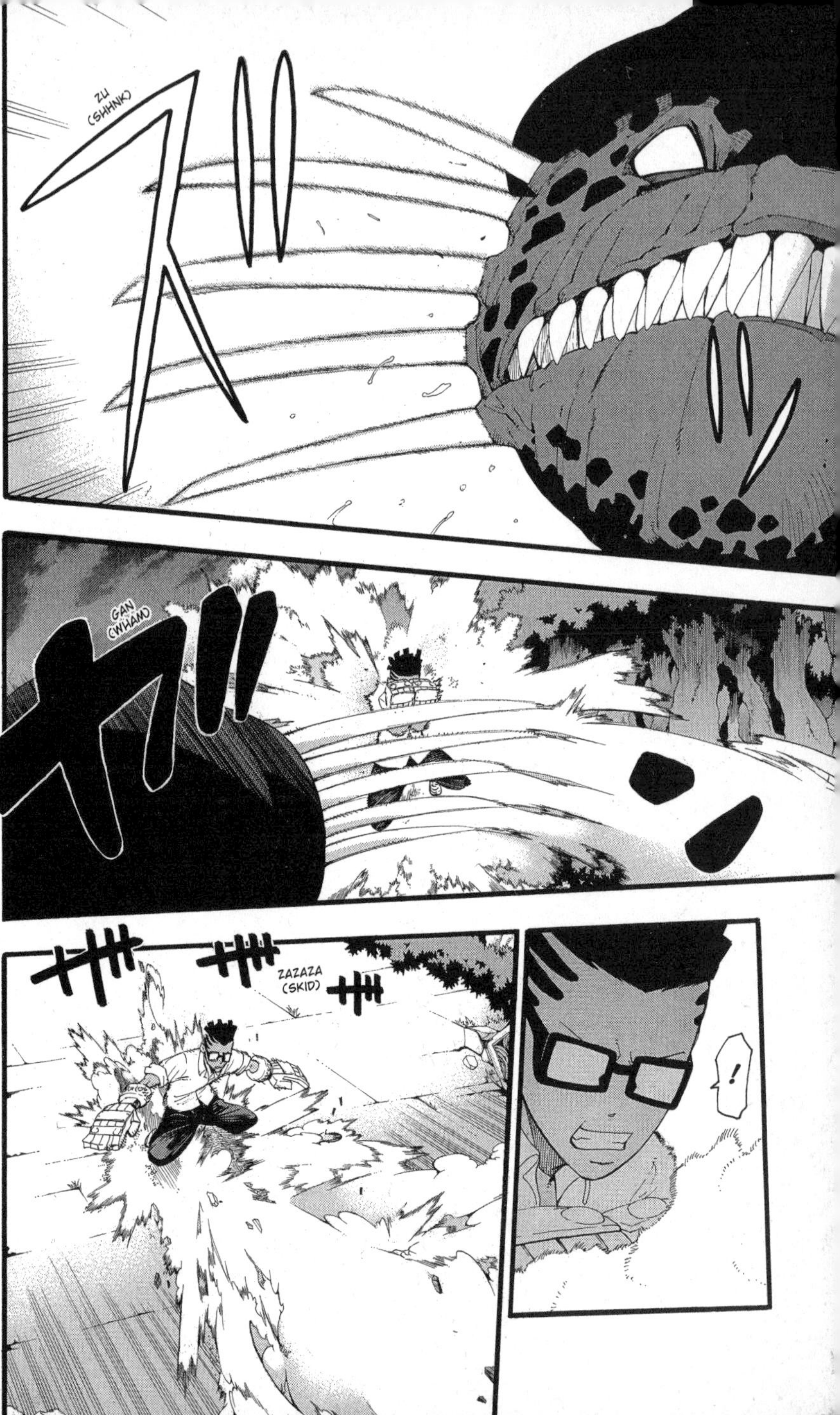
ZU (SHHNK)
GAN (WHAM)
!
ZAZAZA (SKID)

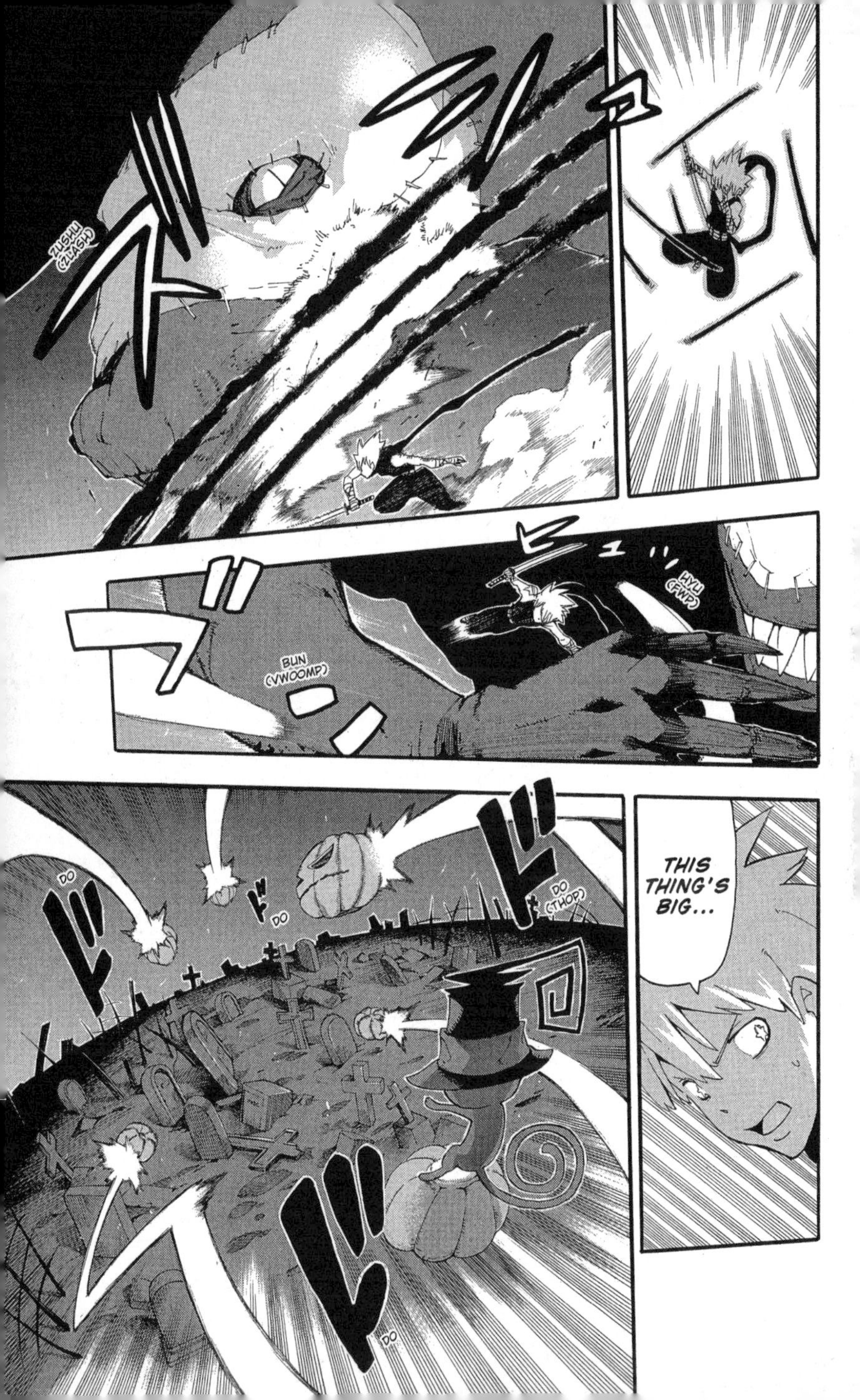
ZUSHU (ZLASH)
HYU (FWP)
BUN (VWOOMP)
THIS THING'S BIG...
DO (THOP)
DO
DO
DO

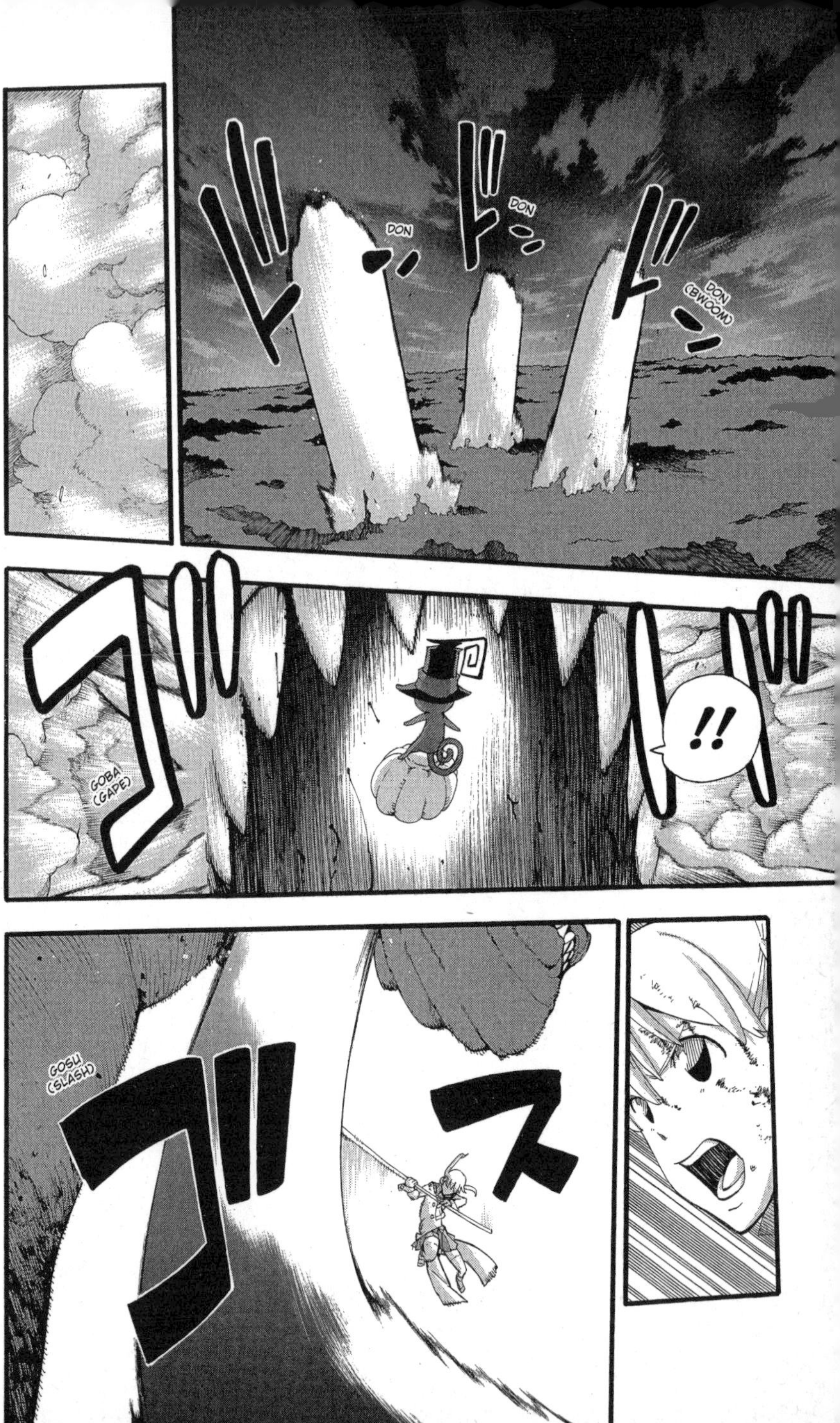
DON (BWOOM)
DON
DON
!!
GOBA (GAPE)
GOSU (SLASH)

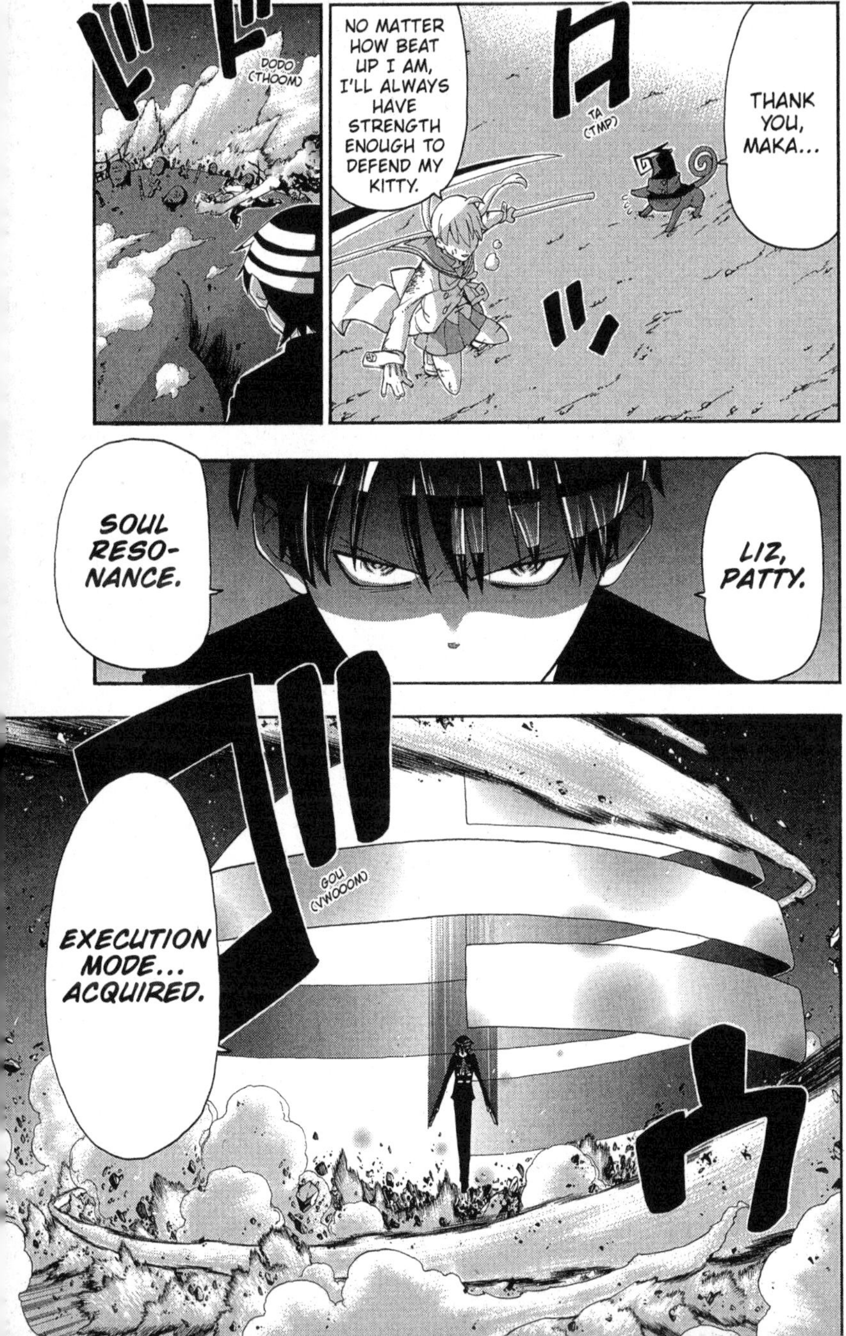
THANK YOU, MAKA...
TA (TMP)
NO MATTER HOW BEAT UP I AM, I'LL ALWAYS HAVE STRENGTH ENOUGH TO DEFEND MY KITTY.
DODO (THOOM)
LIZ, PATTY.
SOUL RESONANCE.
GOU (VWOOOM)
EXECUTION MODE... ACQUIRED.

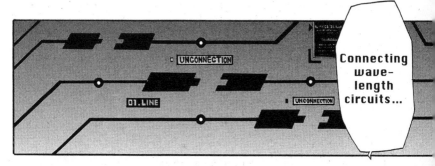

Connecting wave-length circuits...
UNCONNECTION
01.LINE
UNCONNECTION
CONNECTING
All clear.
Resonance rate, stable. Noise, 2.8%.
WHAT'S THIS WAVE-LENGTH...!?
SOME-THING I WON'T BE NEEDING FROM NOW ON.

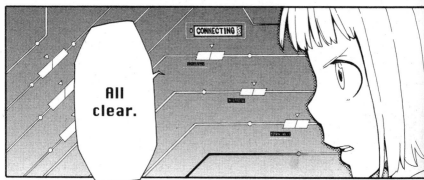

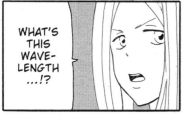

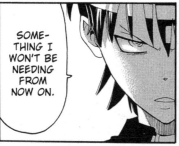

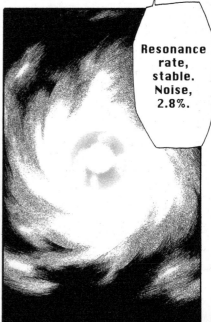

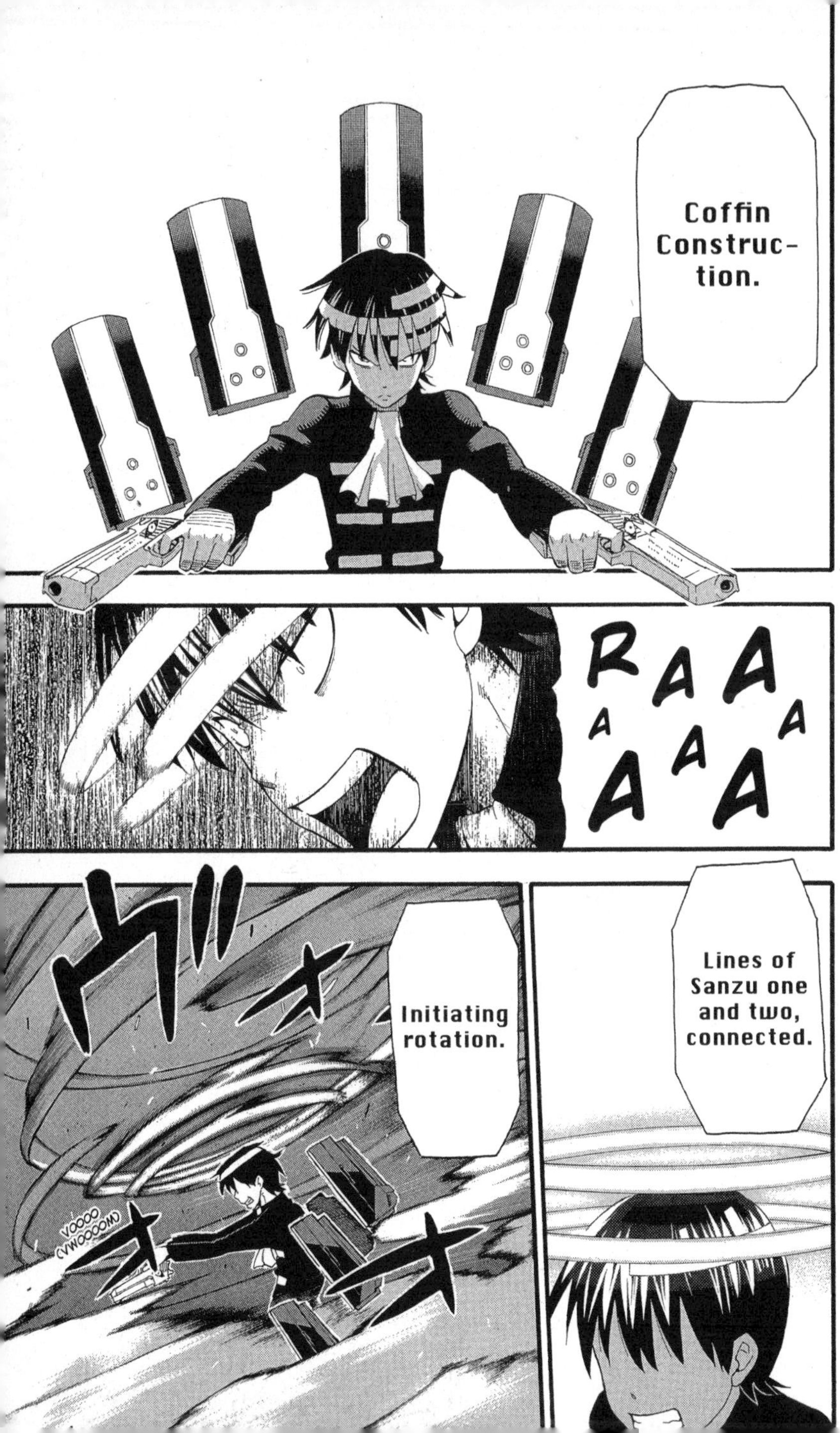

Coffin Construction.
RAAAAAAAA
Lines of Sanzu one and two, connected.
Initiating rotation.
ウヴォォ
VOOOO (VWOOOOM)

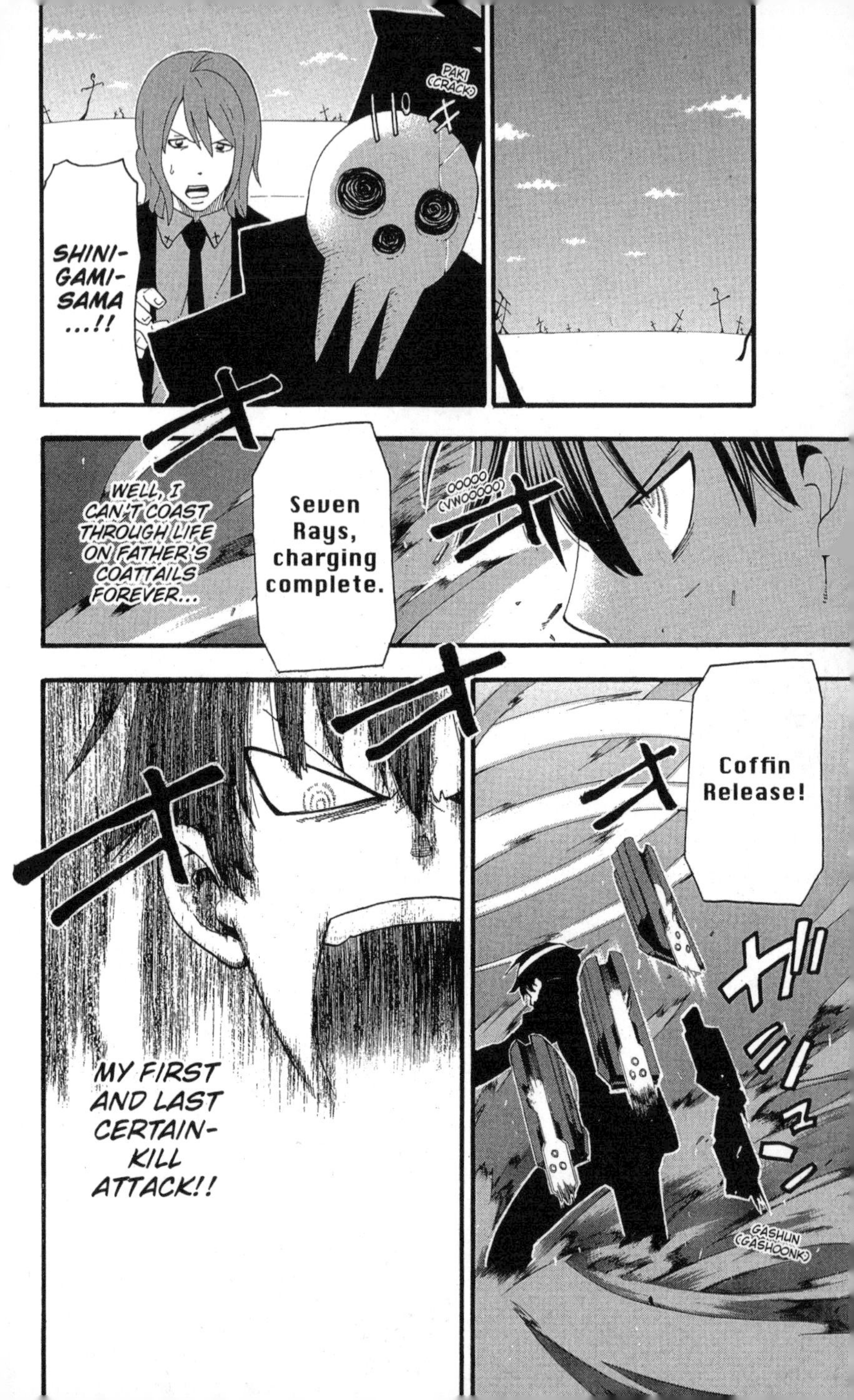
PAKI (CRACK)
SHINI-GAMI-SAMA...!!
OOOOO (VWOOOOO)
Seven Rays, charging complete.
WELL, I CAN'T COAST THROUGH LIFE ON FATHER'S COATTAILS FOREVER...
Coffin Release!
GASHUN (GASHOONK)
MY FIRST AND LAST CERTAIN-KILL ATTACK!!

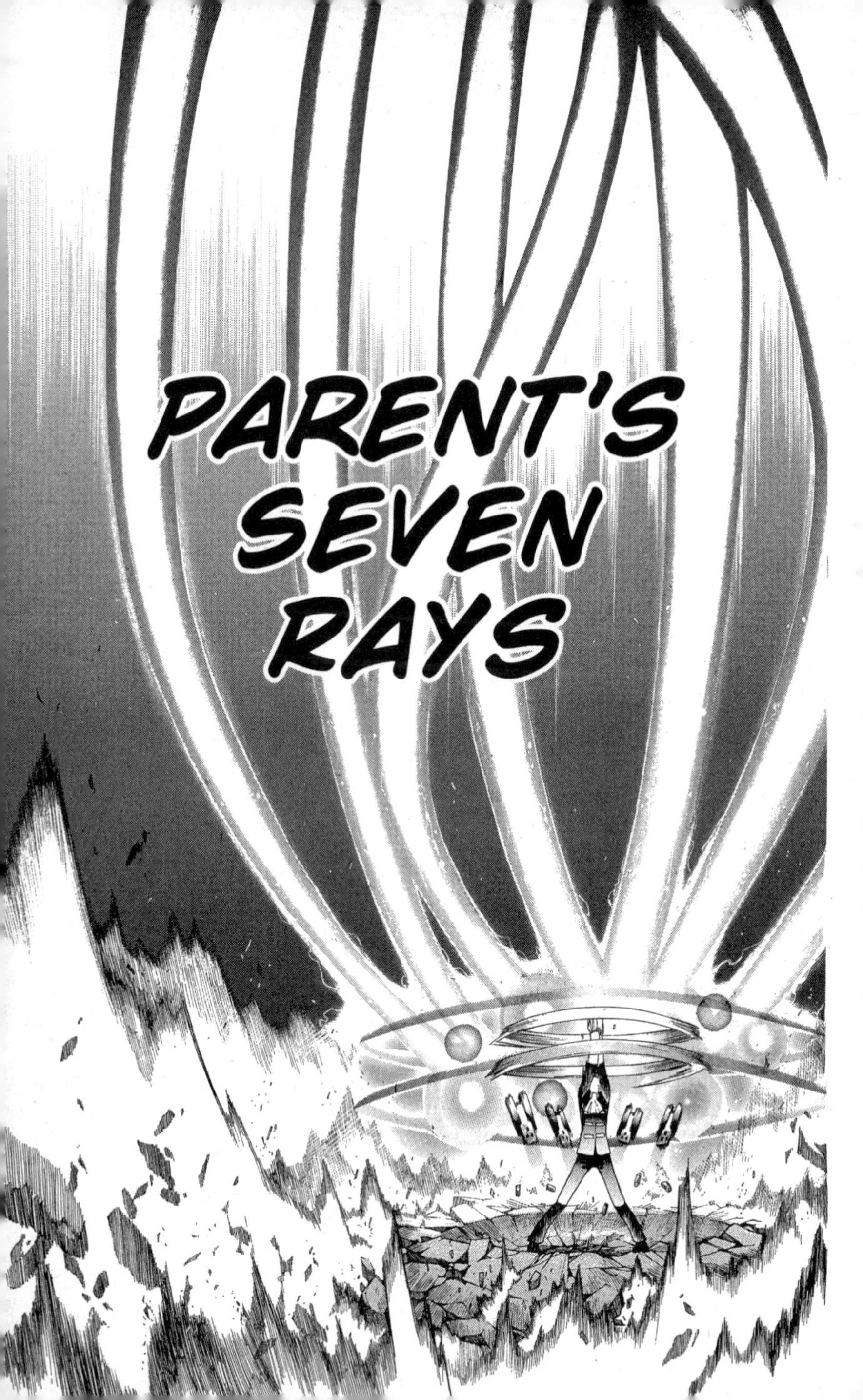
PARENT'S SEVEN RAYS

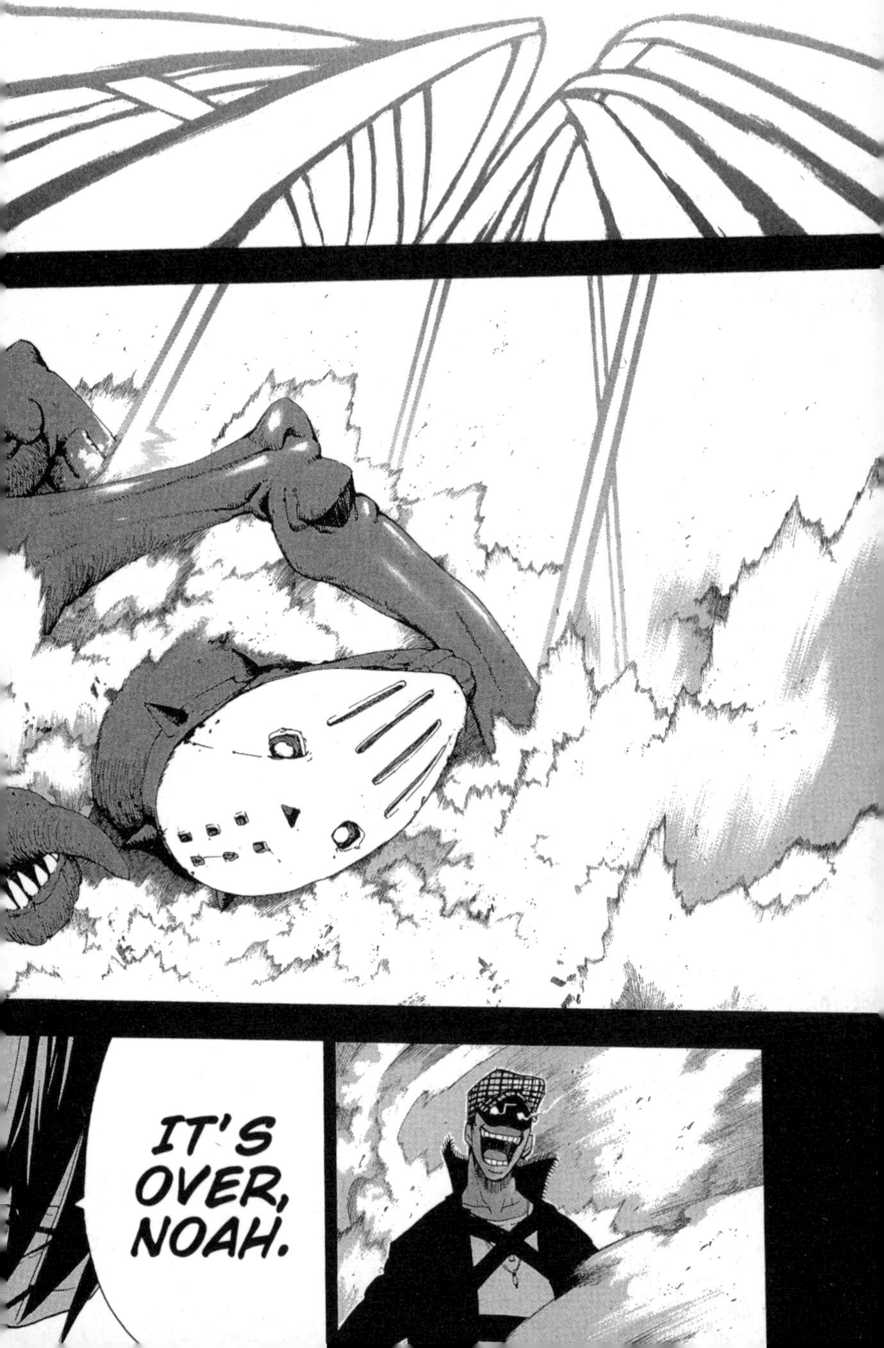
IT'S OVER, NOAH.

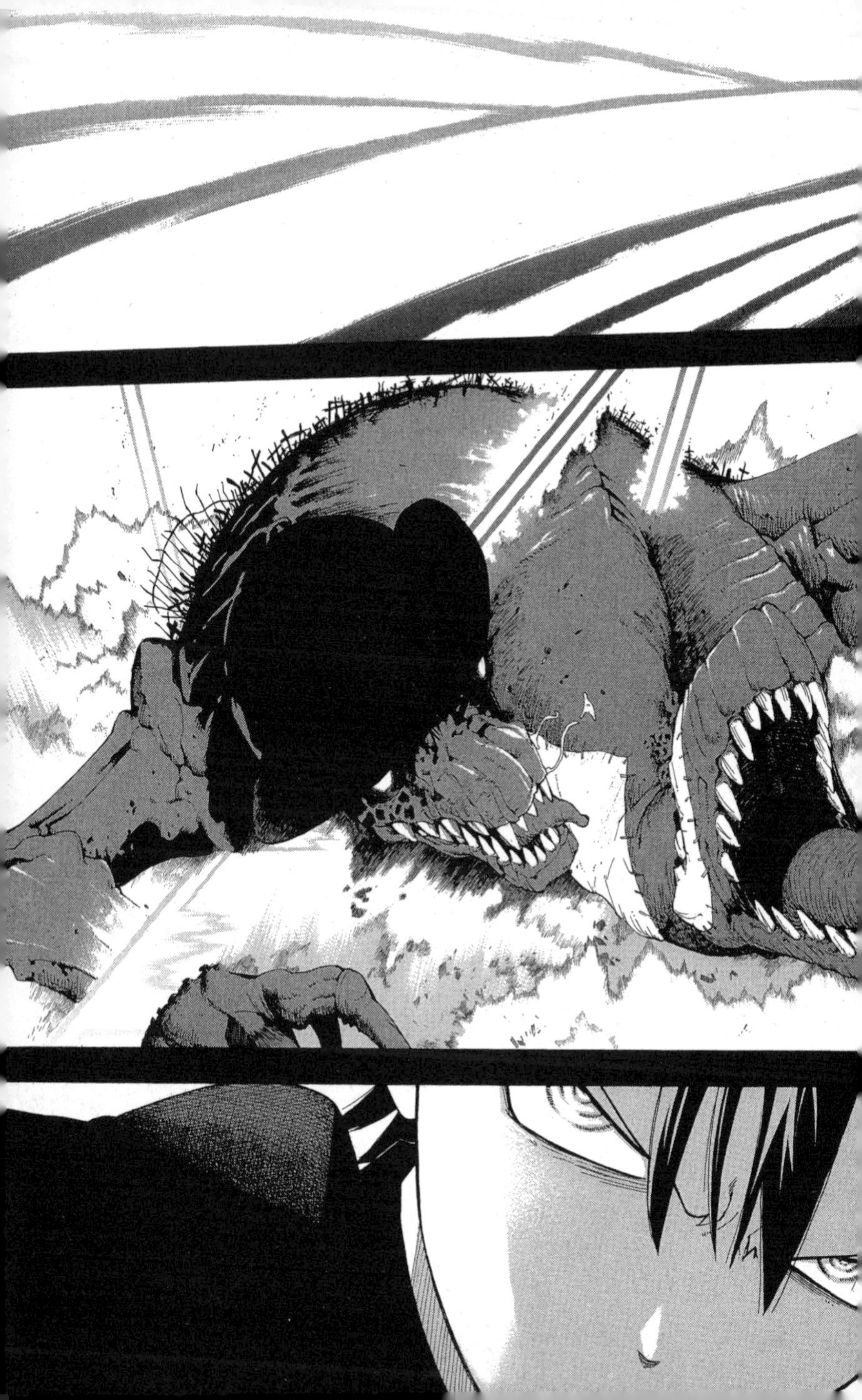

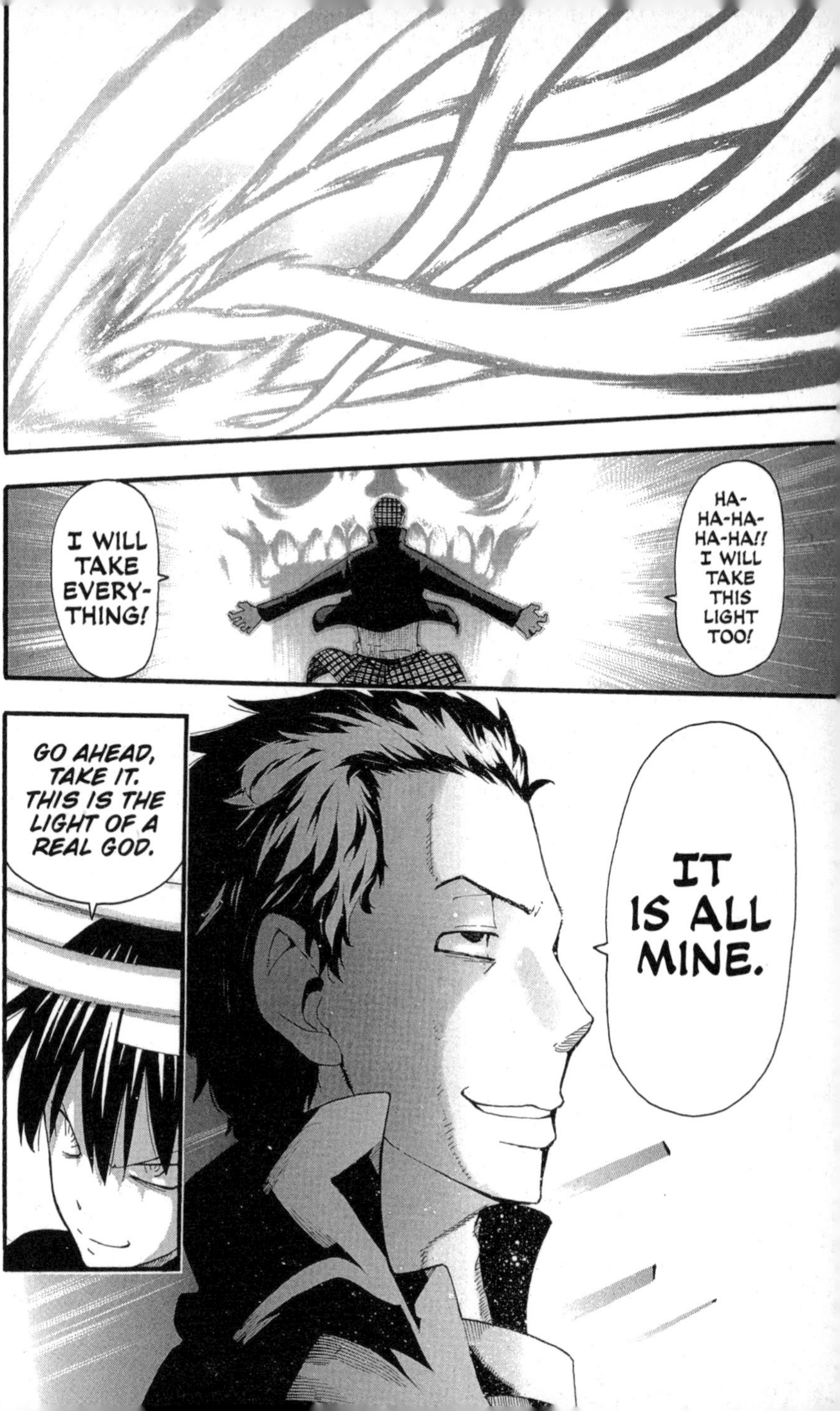
HA-HA-HA-HA-HA!! I WILL TAKE THIS LIGHT TOO!
I WILL TAKE EVERY-THING!
IT IS ALL MINE.
GO AHEAD, TAKE IT. THIS IS THE LIGHT OF A REAL GOD.

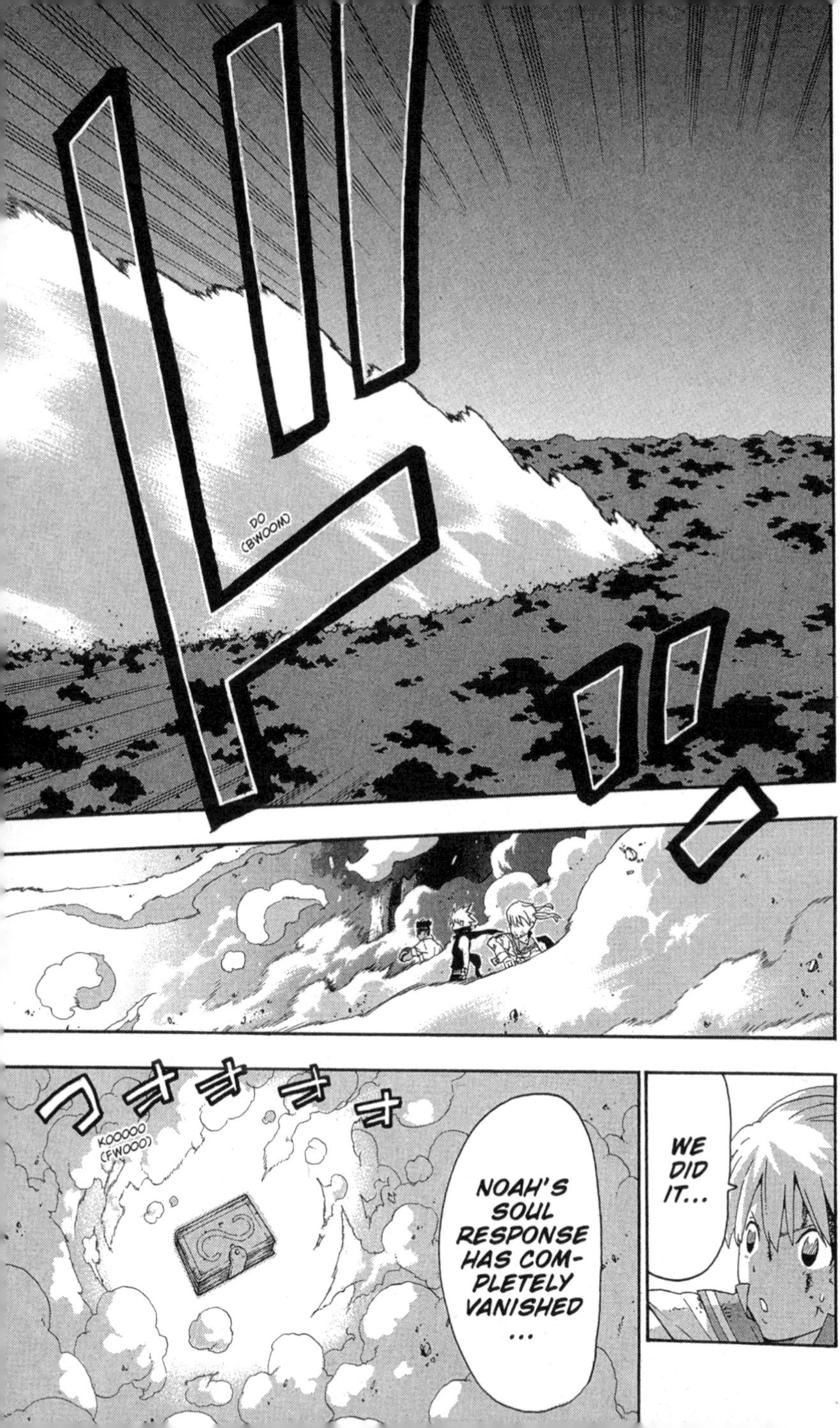
DO
(BWOOM)
WE DID IT...
KOOOOO
(FWOOO)
NOAH'S SOUL RESPONSE HAS COM-PLETELY VANISHED ...

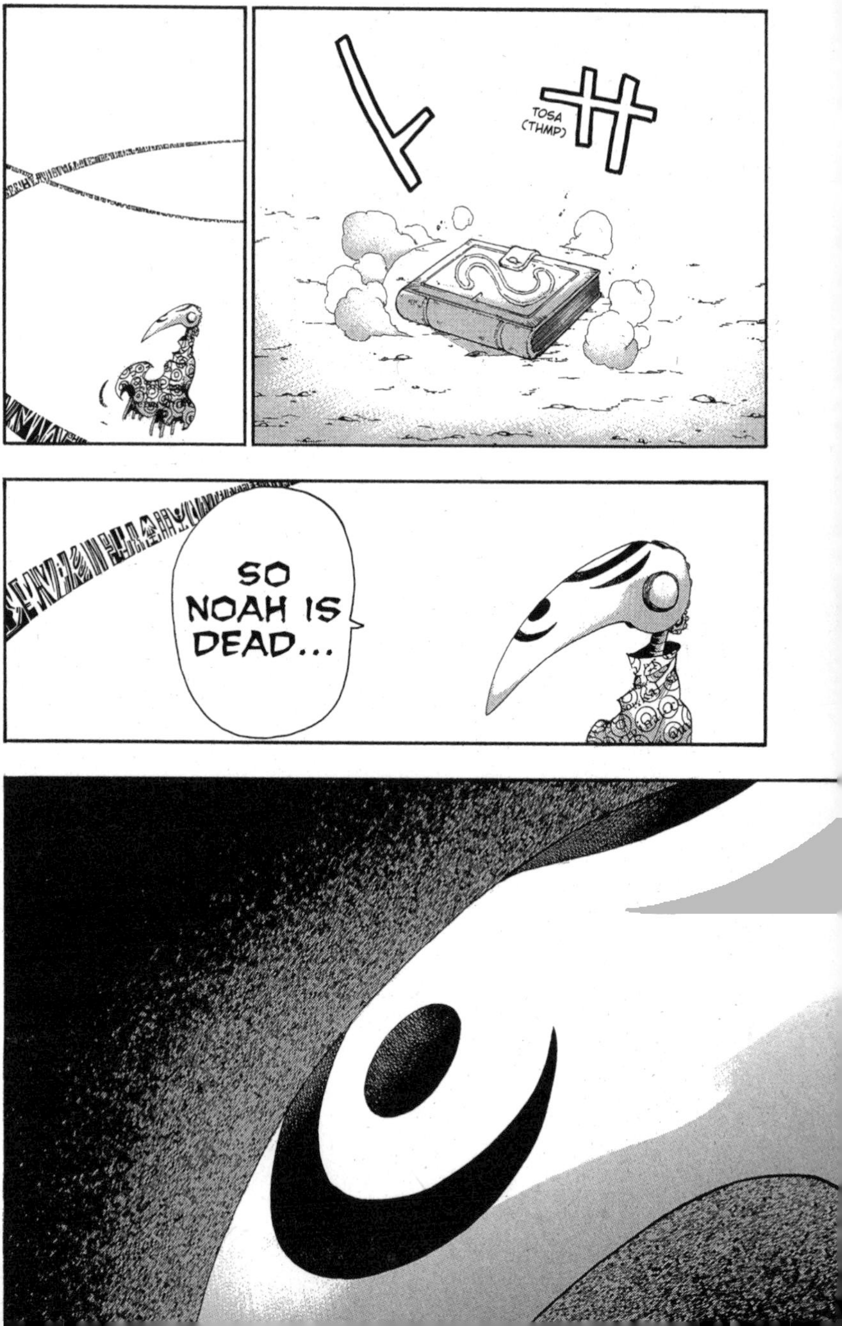
TOSA (THMP)
SO NOAH IS DEAD...

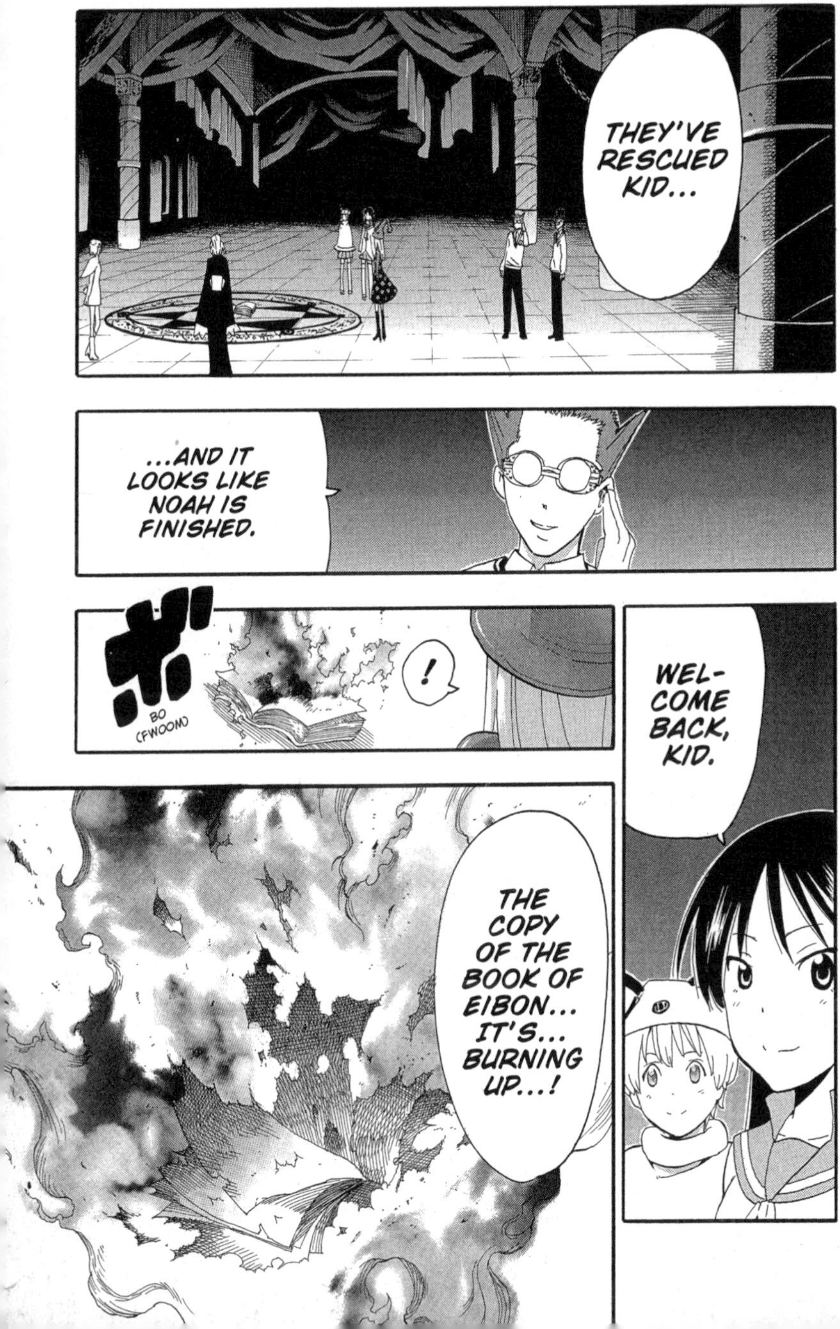
THEY'VE RESCUED KID...
...AND IT LOOKS LIKE NOAH IS FINISHED.
WEL-COME BACK, KID.
!
BO (FWOOM)
THE COPY OF THE BOOK OF EIBON... IT'S... BURNING UP...!

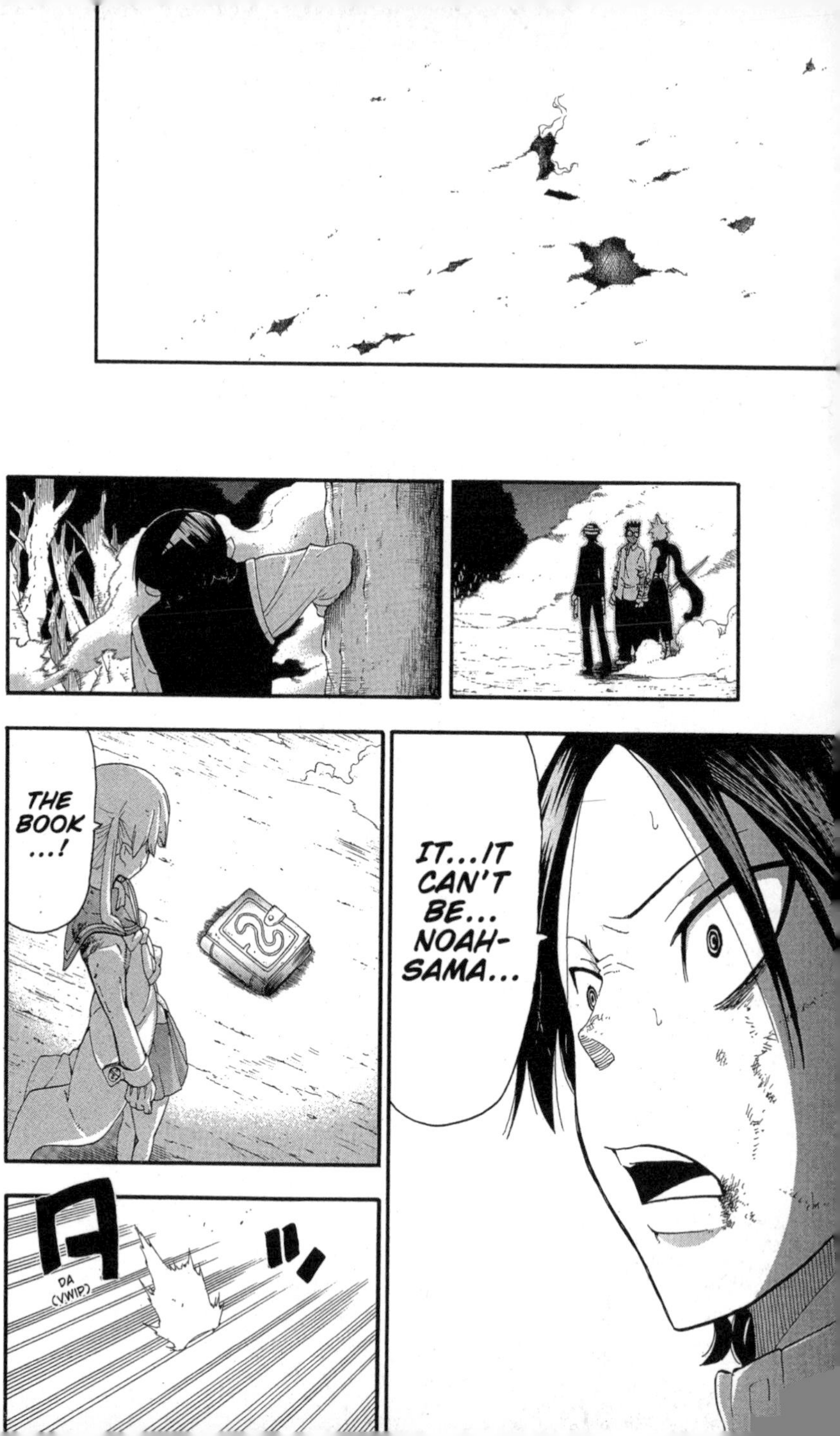
IT...IT CAN'T BE... NOAH-SAMA...
THE BOOK ...!
DA (VWIP)

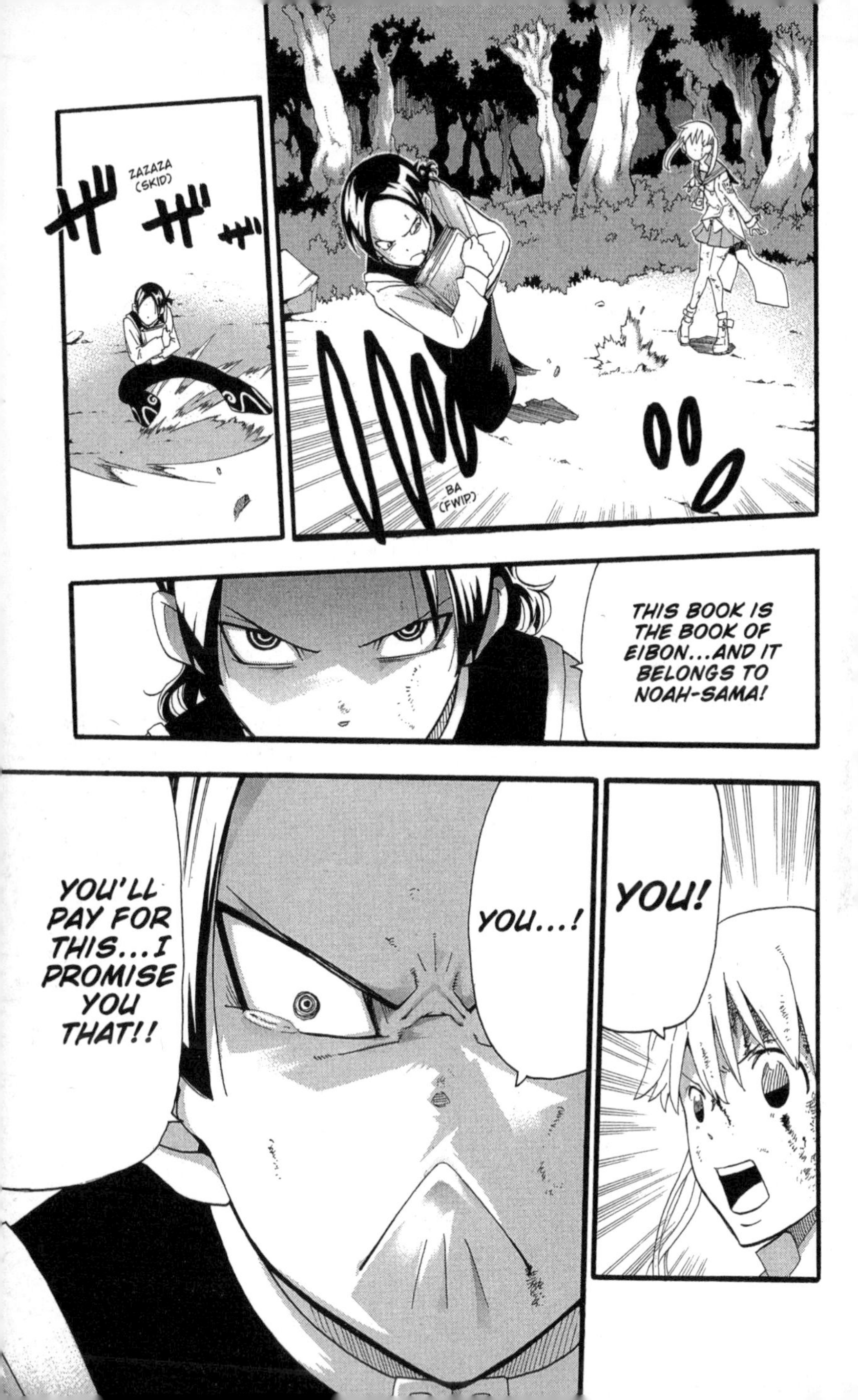
BA
(FWIP)
ZAZAZA
(SKID)
THIS BOOK IS THE BOOK OF EIBON...AND IT BELONGS TO NOAH-SAMA!
YOU!
YOU...!
YOU'LL PAY FOR THIS...I PROMISE YOU THAT!!

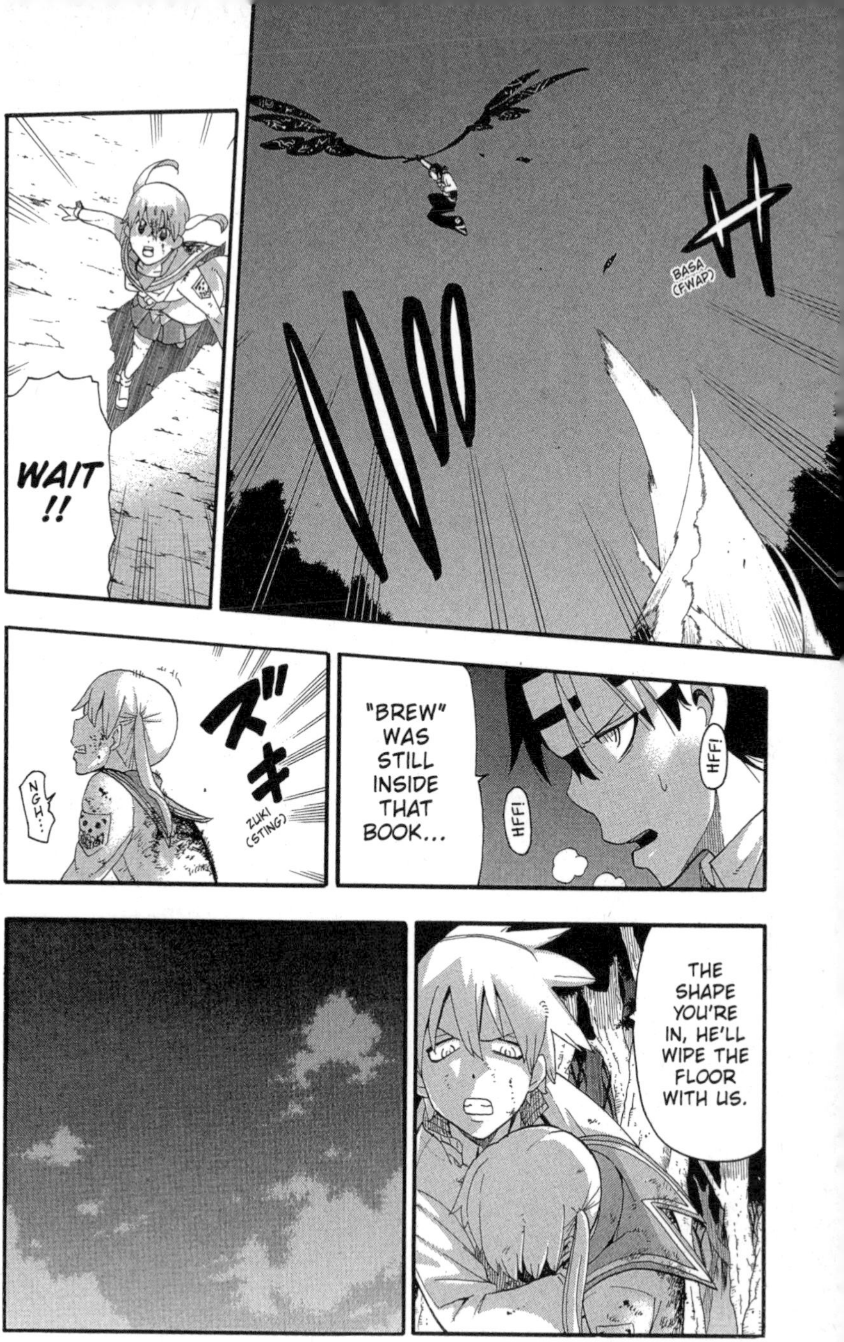
BASA (FWAP)
WAIT!!
"BREW" WAS STILL INSIDE THAT BOOK...
HFF!
HFF!
ズキ
ZUKI (STING)
NGH...
THE SHAPE YOU'RE IN, HE'LL WIPE THE FLOOR WITH US.

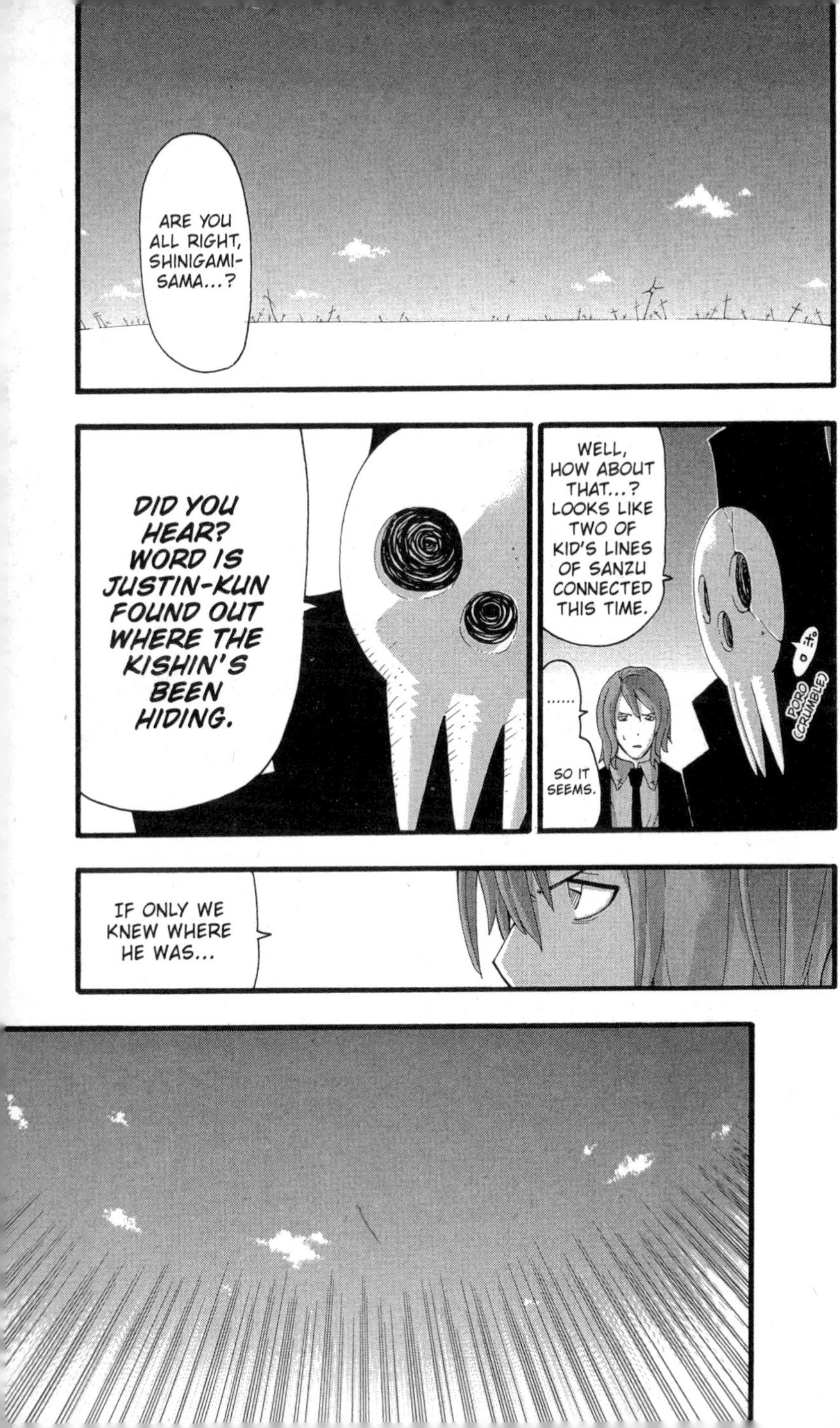

ARE YOU ALL RIGHT, SHINIGAMI-SAMA...?
WELL, HOW ABOUT THAT...? LOOKS LIKE TWO OF KID'S LINES OF SANZU CONNECTED THIS TIME.
PORO (CRUMBLE)
......
SO IT SEEMS.
DID YOU HEAR? WORD IS JUSTIN-KUN FOUND OUT WHERE THE KISHIN'S BEEN HIDING.
IF ONLY WE KNEW WHERE HE WAS...

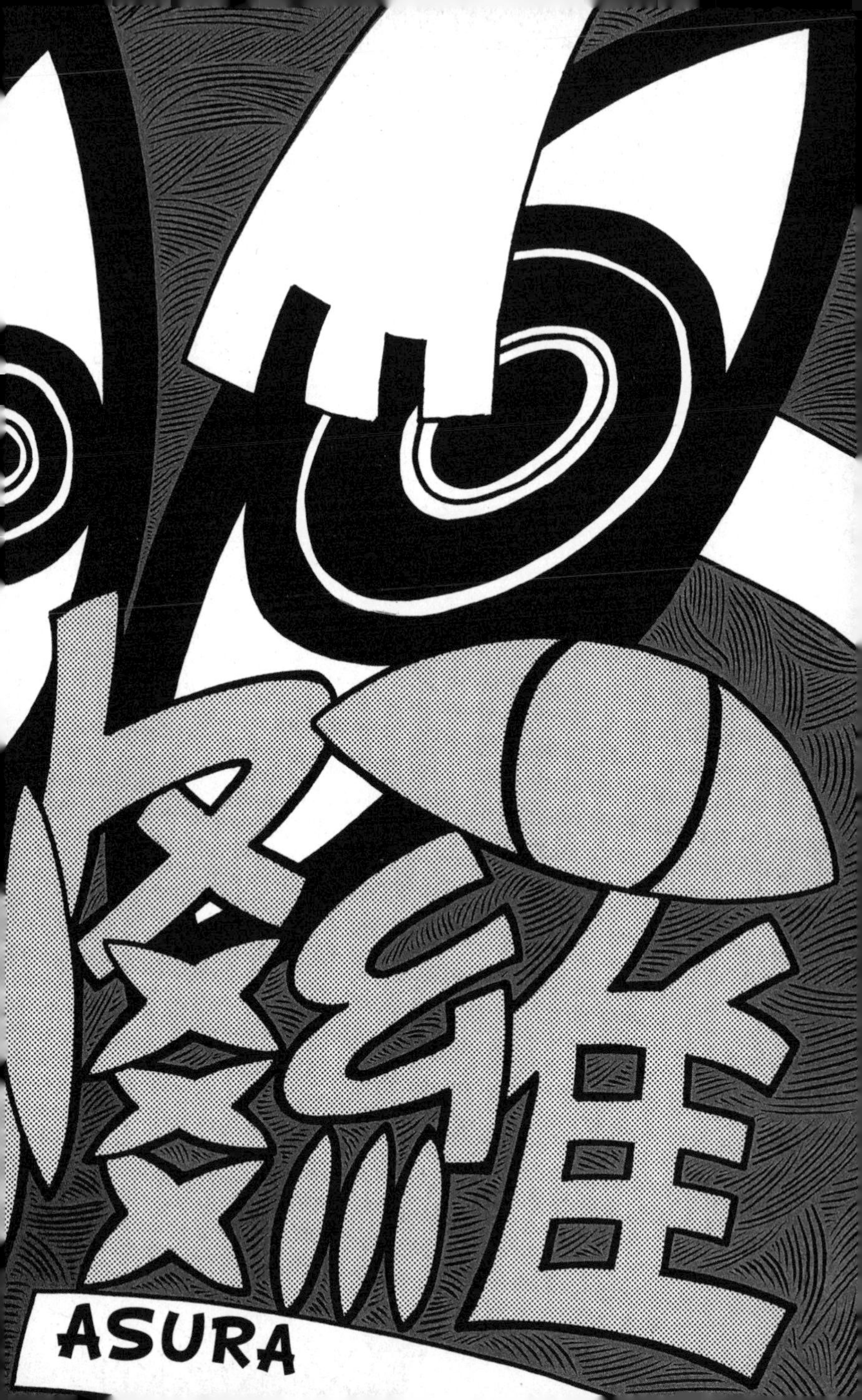
ASURA

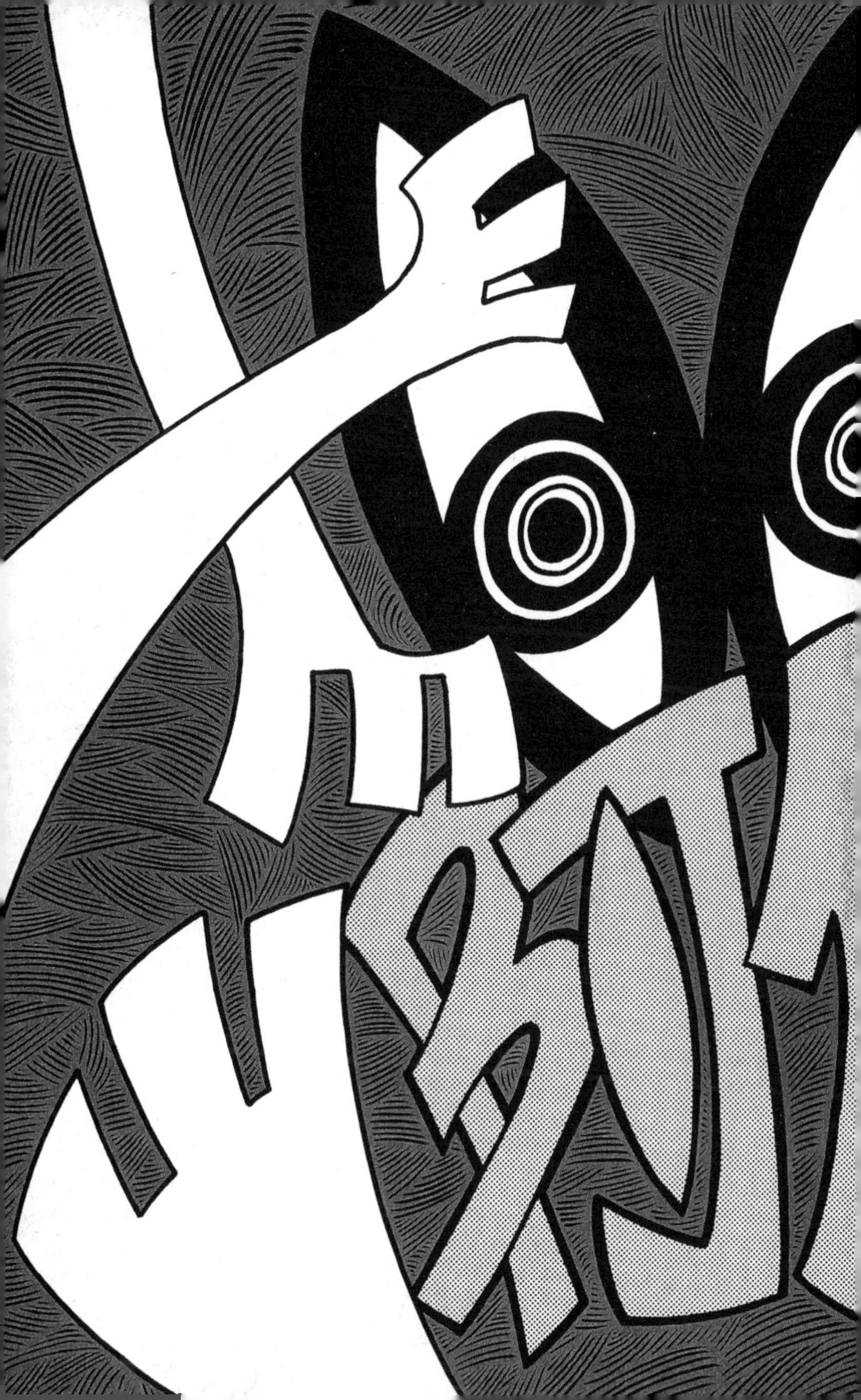

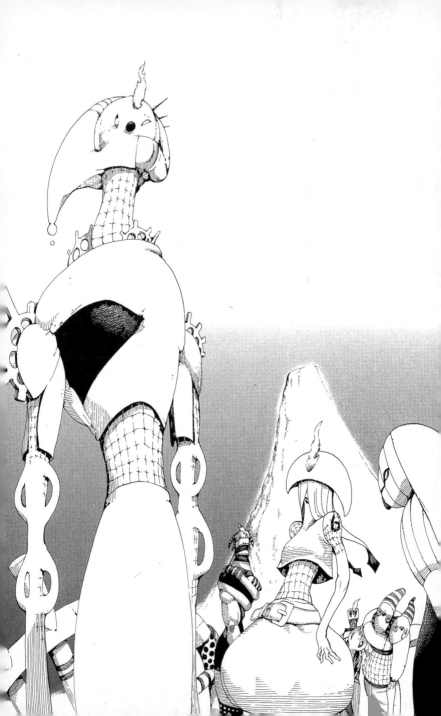

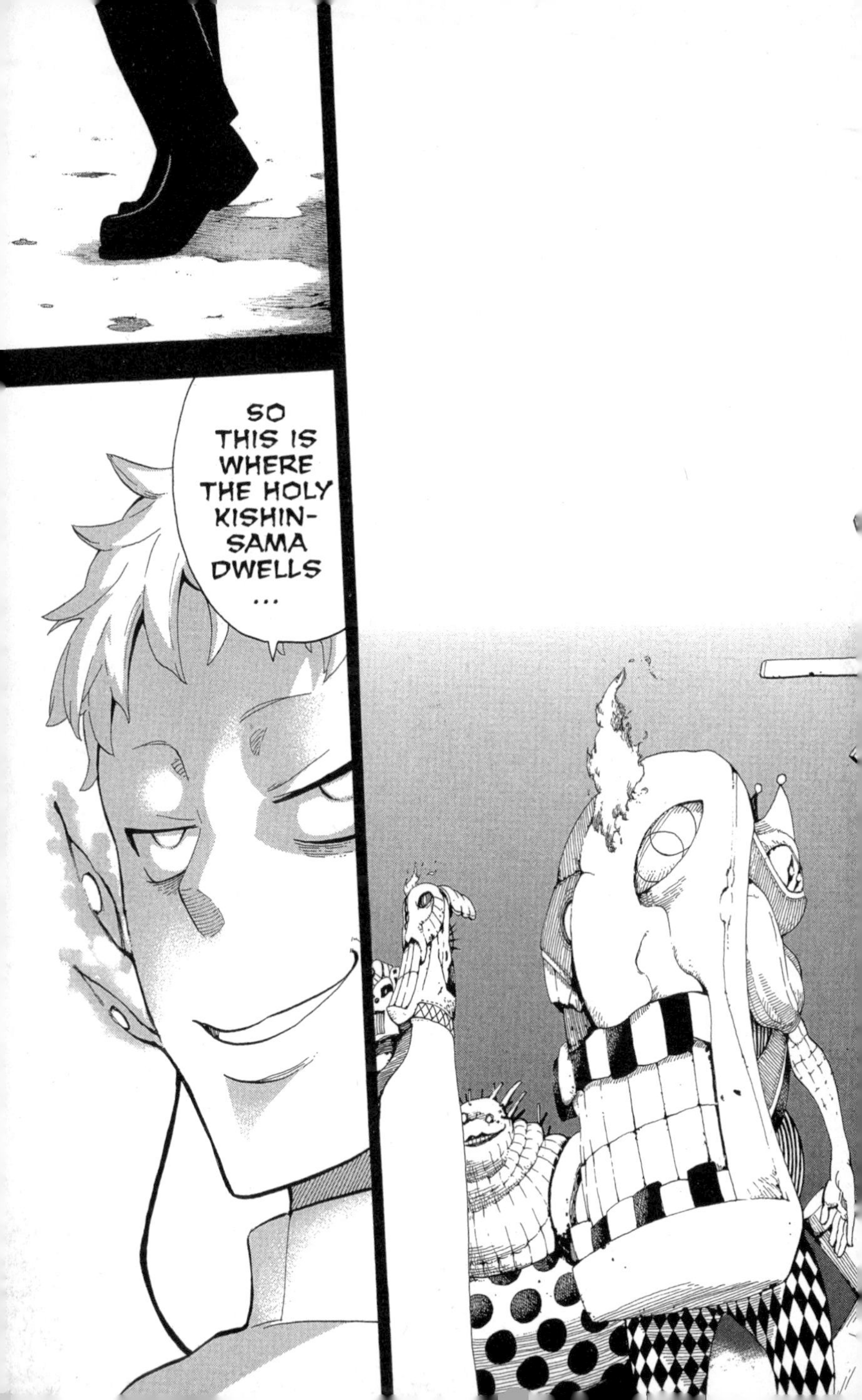
SO THIS IS WHERE THE HOLY KISHIN-SAMA DWELLS ...

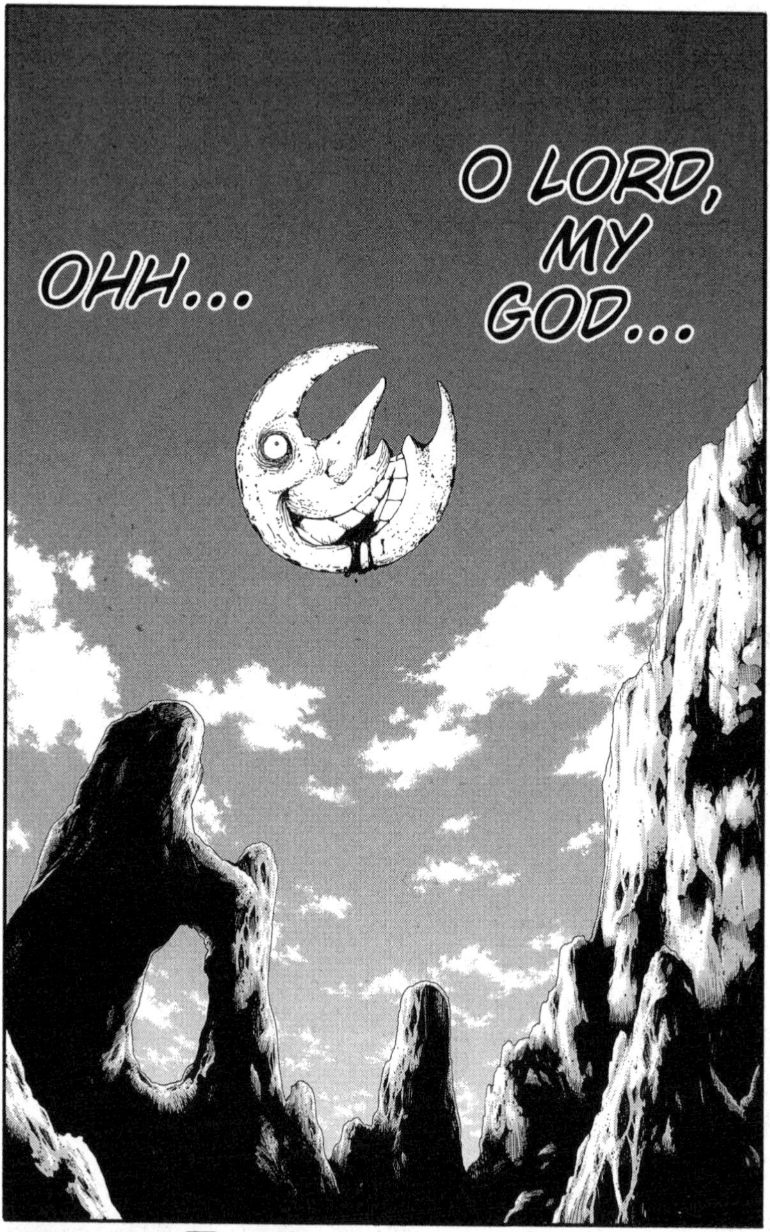
O LORD, MY GOD...
OHH...

SOUL EATER 19 END

SOUL EATER

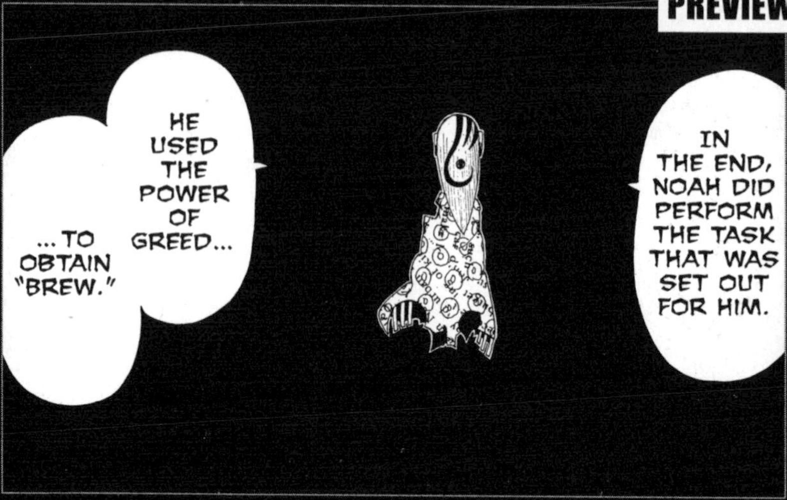
IN THE END, NOAH DID PERFORM THE TASK THAT WAS SET OUT FOR HIM.
HE USED THE POWER OF GREED...
...TO OBTAIN "BREW."

DWMA'S ELITE SPARTOI UNIT MAY HAVE DEFEATED THE SORCERER, NOAH...

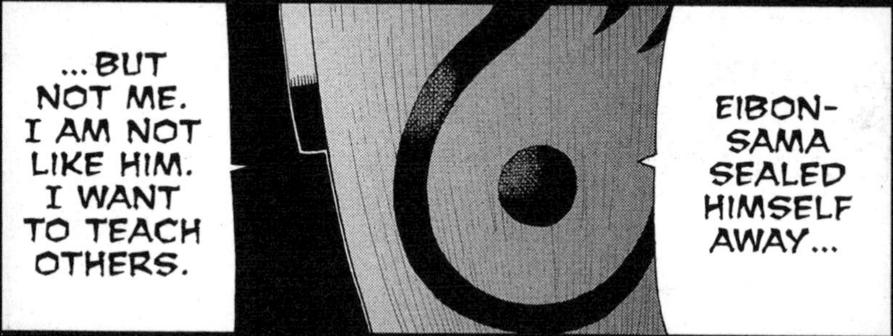
EIBON-SAMA SEALED HIMSELF AWAY...
...BUT NOT ME. I AM NOT LIKE HIM. I WANT TO TEACH OTHERS.

...BUT THE WORLD REMAINS ON THE BRINK OF BEING CONSUMED BY MADNESS

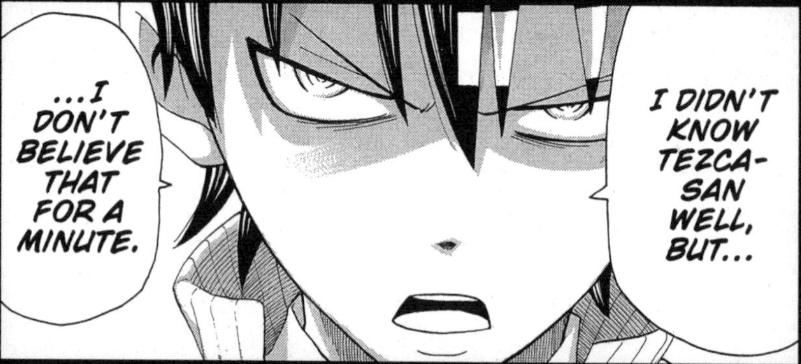
I DIDN'T KNOW TEZCA-SAN WELL, BUT...
...I DON'T BELIEVE THAT FOR A MINUTE.

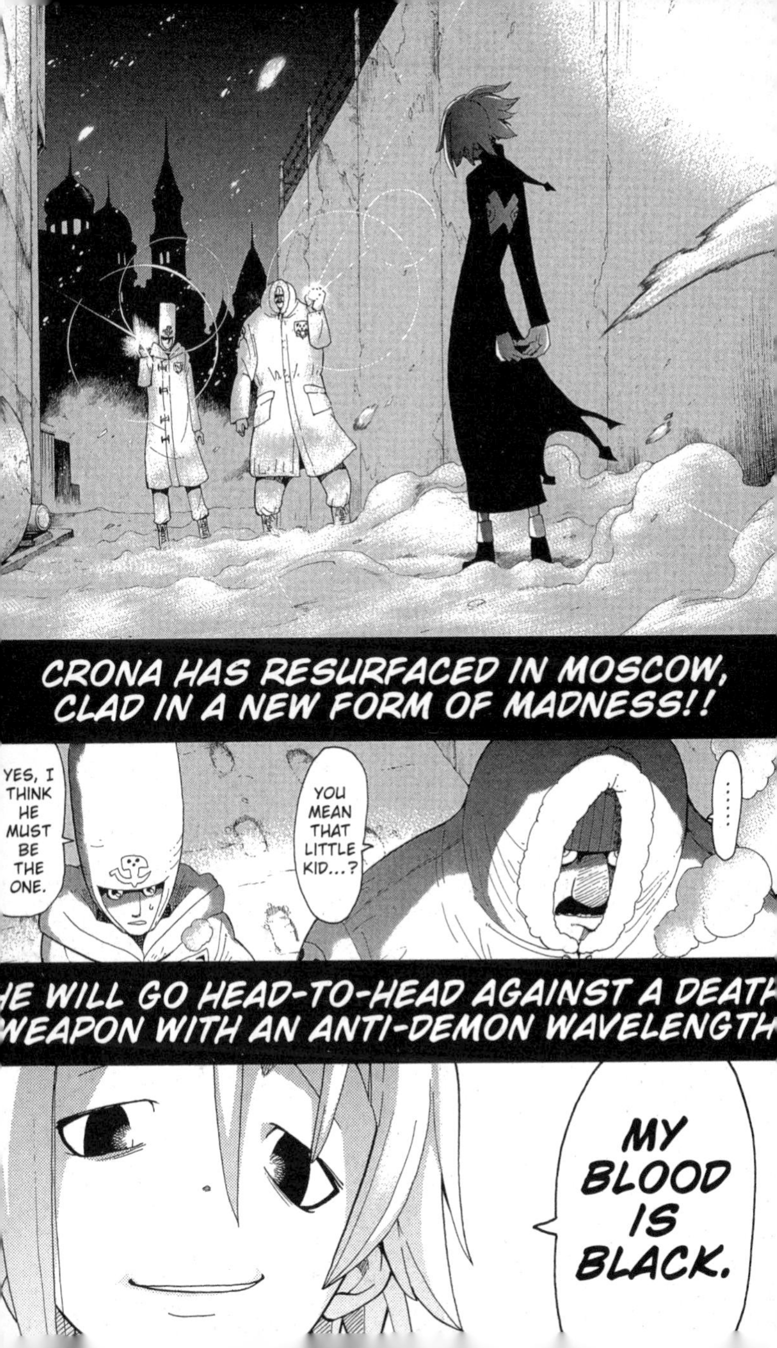
CRONA HAS RESURFACED IN MOSCOW, CLAD IN A NEW FORM OF MADNESS!!
......
YOU MEAN THAT LITTLE KID...?
YES, I THINK HE MUST BE THE ONE.
E WILL GO HEAD-TO-HEAD AGAINST A DEAT WEAPON WITH AN ANTI-DEMON WAVELENGTH
MY BLOOD IS BLACK.

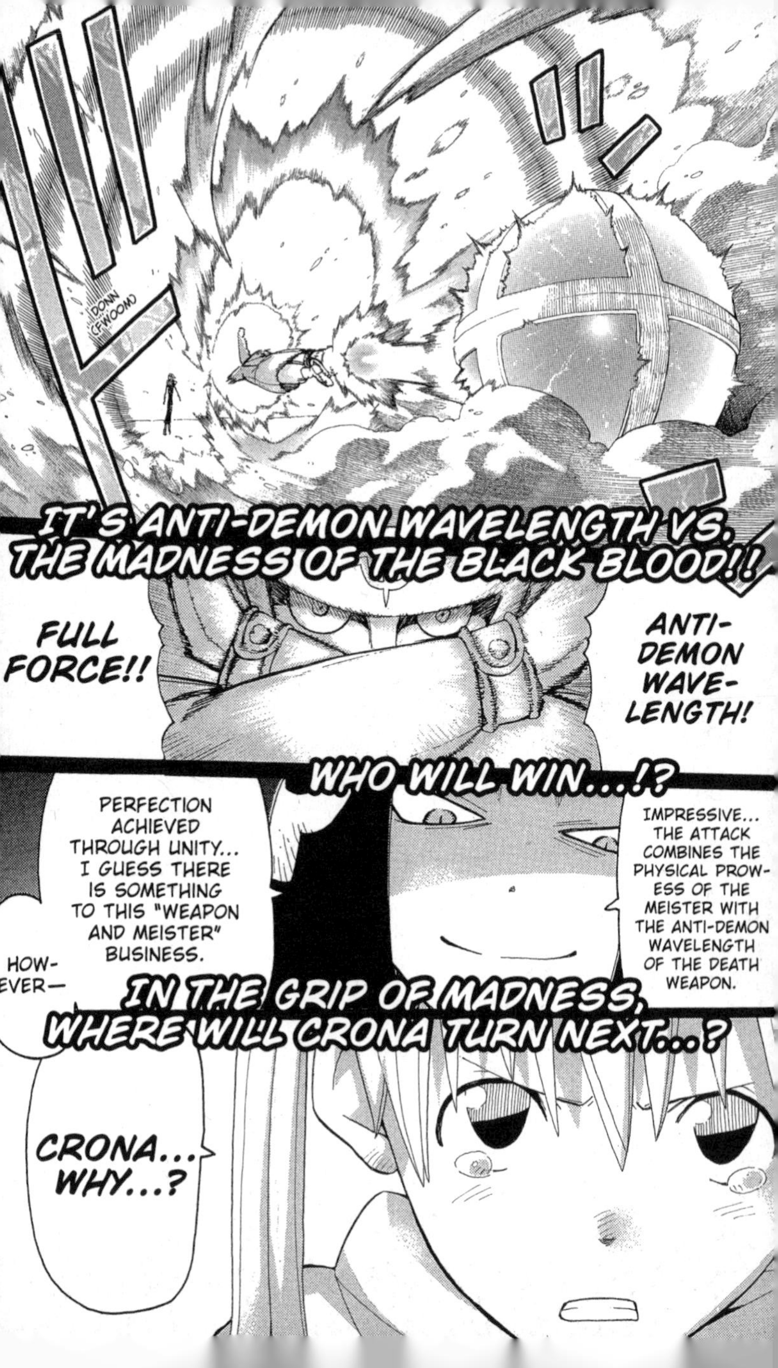
DONN (CFWOOM)
IT'S ANTI-DEMON WAVELENGTH VS. THE MADNESS OF THE BLACK BLOOD!!
ANTI-DEMON WAVE-LENGTH!
FULL FORCE!!
WHO WILL WIN...!?
IMPRESSIVE... THE ATTACK COMBINES THE PHYSICAL PROW-ESS OF THE MEISTER WITH THE ANTI-DEMON WAVELENGTH OF THE DEATH WEAPON.
PERFECTION ACHIEVED THROUGH UNITY... I GUESS THERE IS SOMETHING TO THIS "WEAPON AND MEISTER" BUSINESS.
HOW-EVER—
IN THE GRIP OF MADNESS, WHERE WILL CRONA TURN NEXT...?
CRONA... WHY...?

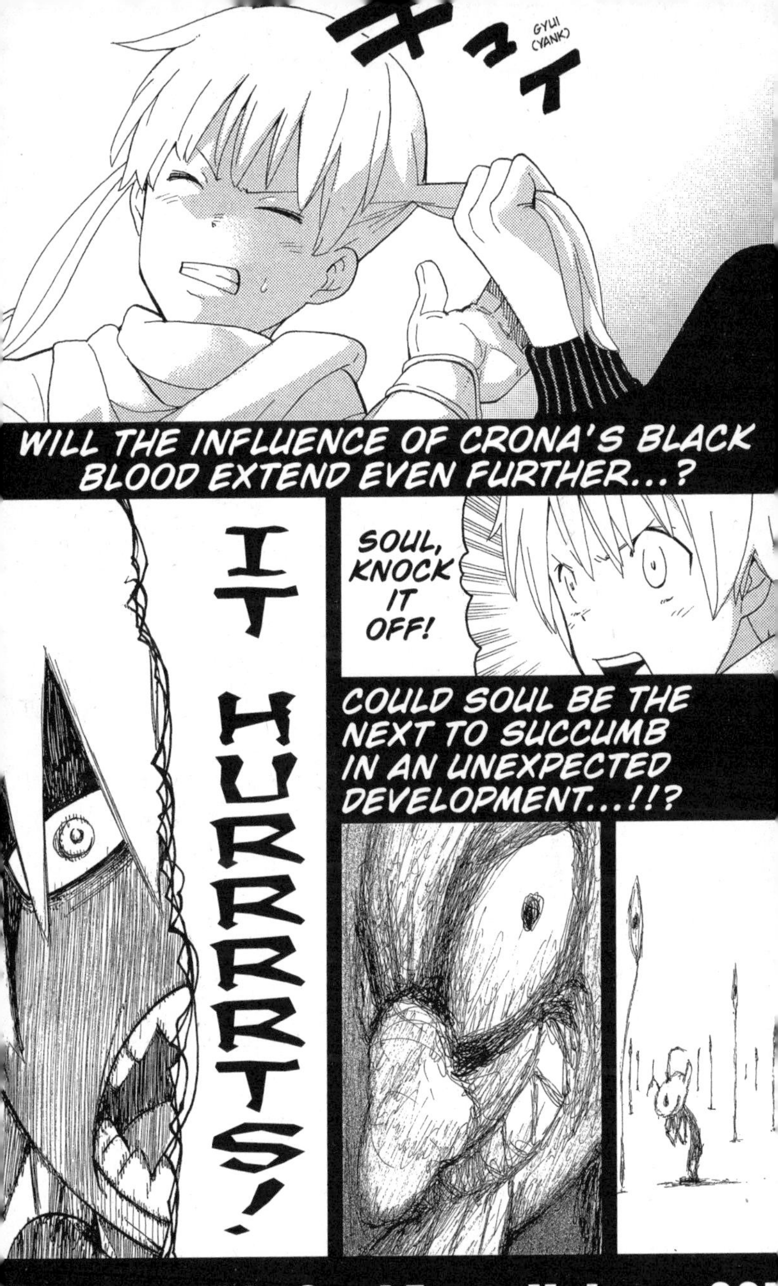
キュイ
GYUI (YANK)
WILL THE INFLUENCE OF CRONA'S BLACK BLOOD EXTEND EVEN FURTHER...?
SOUL, KNOCK IT OFF!
COULD SOUL BE THE NEXT TO SUCCUMB IN AN UNEXPECTED DEVELOPMENT...!!?
IT HURRRTS!

Continued in Soul Eater Volume 20!

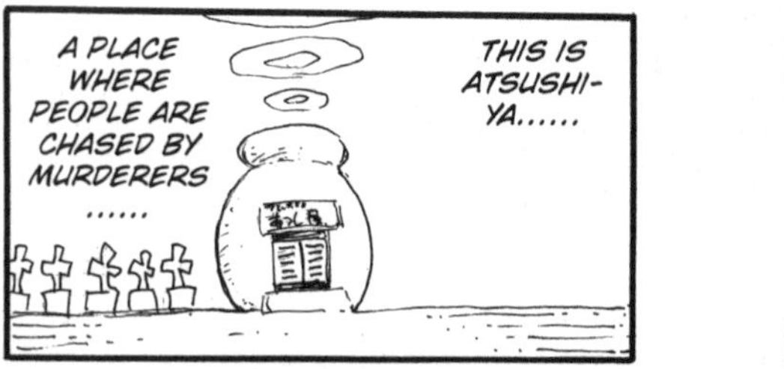
THIS IS ATSUSHI-YA......
A PLACE WHERE PEOPLE ARE CHASED BY MURDERERS ......

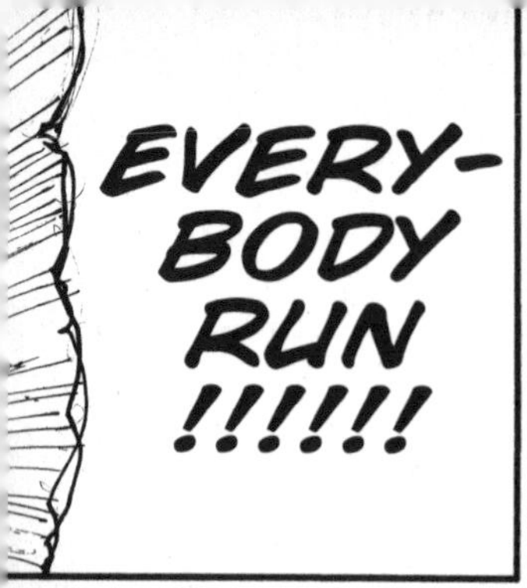
EVERY-BODY RUN !!!!!!

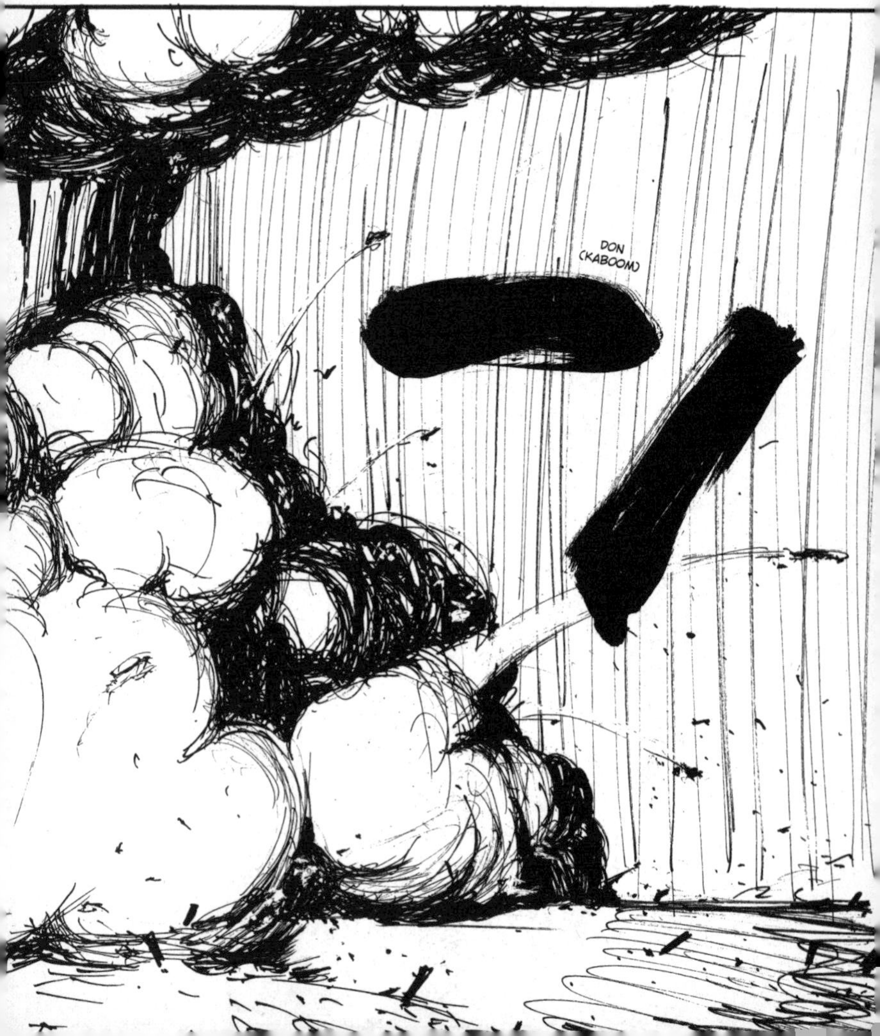
DON (KABOOM)

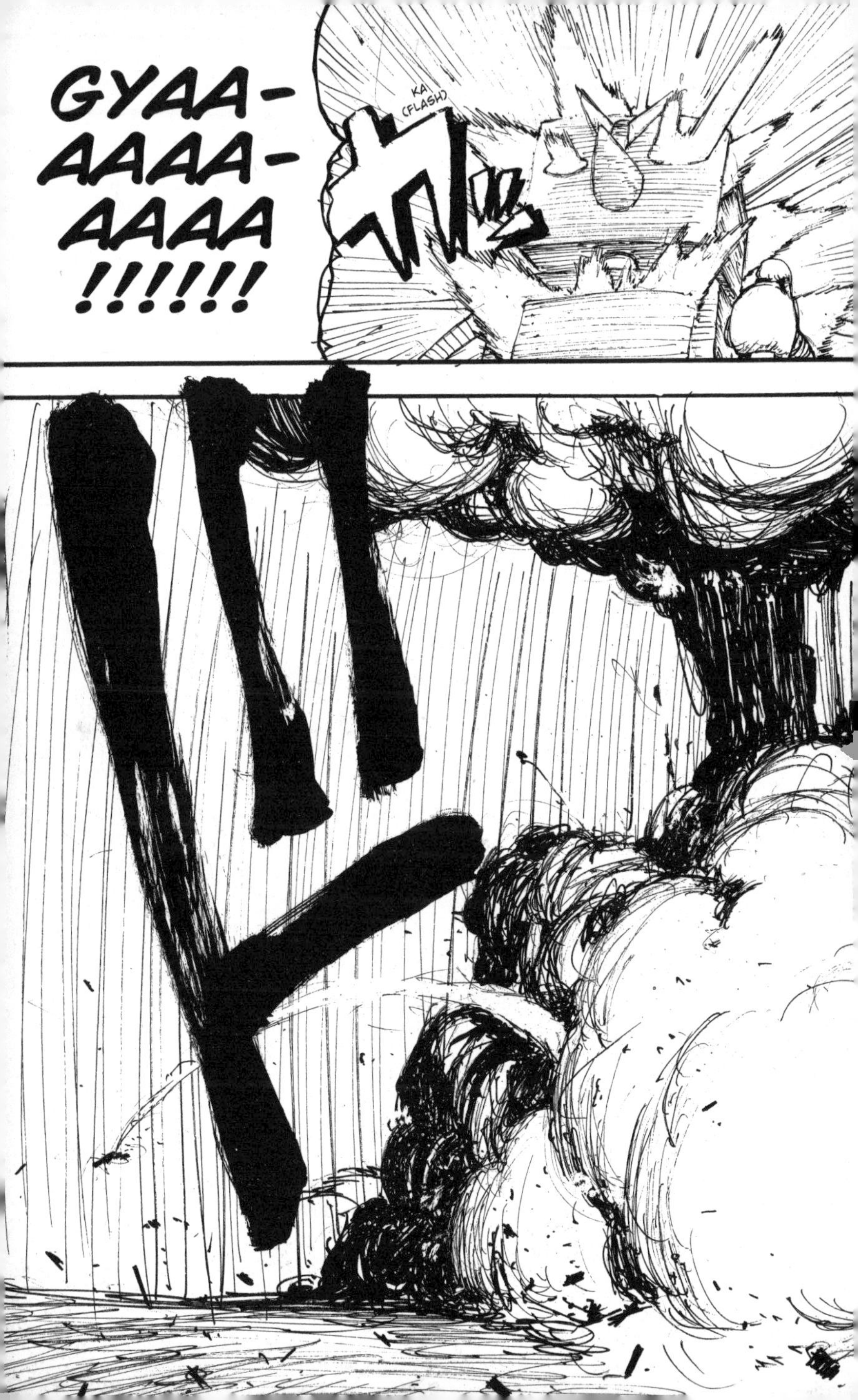
KA (FLASH)
GYAA-AAAA-AAAA!!!!!!

Translation Notes

Common Honorifics

no honorific: Indicates familiarity or closeness; if used without permission or reason, addressing someone in this manner would constitute an insult.

-san: The Japanese equivalent of Mr./Mrs./Miss. If a situation calls for politeness, this is the fail-safe honorific.

-sama: Conveys great respect; may also indicate that the social status of the speaker is lower than that of the addressee.

-kun: Used most often when referring to boys, this indicates affection or familiarity. Occasionally used by older men among their peers, but it may also be used by anyone referring to a person of lower standing.

-chan: An affectionate honorific indicating familiarity used mostly in reference to girls; also used in reference to cute persons or animals of either gender.

-senpai: A suffix used to address upperclassmen or more experienced coworkers.

-sensei: A respectful term for teachers, artists, or high-level professionals.

Page 66
Liz and Patty were known as the **Brooklyn Devils** during their time as petty criminals on the streets of New York, but the South Brooklyn Devils were an actual greaser gang from South Brooklyn in the 1950s. Their members were eventually incorporated into the infamous South Brooklyn Boys, a primarily Italian-American gang that is still active today.

Page 89
The Japanese idiom used here (translated **"might is right"**) is *kateba kangun, makereba zoku-gun* ("If you win, you're the government army; if you lose, you're the rebel army"). The meaning is very close to that of the English aphorism "might is right"—whoever has the most power exerts it to create the government they desire.

Page 105
"Pig in a cage on antibiotics" is taken from the Radiohead song "Fitter Happier" (*OK Computer*, 1997). The song mocks the sanitized lifestyles, sanctimonious corporatism, and ad-slogan-driven social values of modern consumerist society, bitingly summing up first-world middle-class existence as that of doped pigs in cages.

Page 107
A **manticore** is a mythical Persian beast somewhat akin to a sphinx. It is said to possess the head of a human, the body of a lion, and the tail of a scorpion.

"I choose you!!" This giggle-inducing line is a direct reference to the title of the very first episode of the very first season of the long-running TV anime and worldwide cultural phenomenon—Pokémon. In Japanese the episode title is "Pokémon, Kimi ni Kimeta!" (Pokémon, I Choose You!)

Page 129
The characters used to spell the name of the **Siren** literally mean "Reef of Temptation," a reference to the Sirens of classical Greek mythology who sang to passing ships in order to lure sailors to their deaths on the craggy reefs.

Page 138
The dog-beast **Orthrus** is another mythical Greek monster. The original legend describes a two-headed demon dog akin to Cerberus that was slain by Hercules as part of his tenth labor. (Orthrus was guarding the red cattle of Geryon, which Hercules needed, so Hercules clubbed it on the head and killed it.)

Page 139
The one-eyed giant **Cyclops** is yet another mythical Greek monster. The race of cyclopes was feared even by the gods for their sheer brute strength and pigheaded stubbornness.

Page 148
The **Horror Dragon** is so named because each of its three heads is themed with a famous horror-film villain (from left to right): Freddy Krueger (*A Nightmare on Elm Street*), Leatherface (*The Texas Chain Saw Massacre*), and Jason Vorhees (*Friday the 13th*).

Page 165
The origin of the name **"Line of Sanzu"** comes from Japanese Buddhist mythology. The Sanzu River (literally, "river of three crossings") is said to separate the land of the living from the land of the dead, playing a role similar to that of the River Styx in beliefs about the afterlife. According to the myth, a person's soul crosses in one of three ways depending on the weight of their sins (i.e., their karma): the good cross over a bridge, the neither good nor bad cross through the shallows, and the bad cross through deep waters where vicious snakes swim.

Pages 166–167
In Japanese there is a direct and obvious linguistic connection between the name of Kid's **Parent's Seven Rays** attack and this line about his **Father's coattails**. The phrase *chichiue no nanahikari* (literally, "Father's seven lights") means to enjoy undeserved privileges due to one's father's influence.

SOUL EATER ⑲

ATSUSHI OHKUBO

Translation: Jack Wiedrick

Lettering: Abigail Blackman

SOUL EATER Vol. 19 © 2011 Atsushi Ohkubo / SQUARE ENIX. First published in Japan in 2011 by SQUARE ENIX CO., LTD. English translation rights arranged with SQUARE ENIX CO., LTD. and Hachette Book Group through Tuttle-Mori Agency, Inc.

Translation © 2014 by SQUARE ENIX CO., LTD.

Yen Press
Hachette Book Group
237 Park Avenue, New York, NY 10017

HachetteBookGroup.com
YenPress.com

Yen Press is an imprint of Hachette Book Group, Inc. The Yen Press name and logo are trademarks of Hachette Book Group, Inc.

First Yen Press Edition: March 2014

ISBN: 978-0-316-40694-9

10 9 8 7 6 5 4 3 2

BVG

Printed in the United States of America